Arata
THE LEGEND

5

WE ARE MAN, BORN OF HEAVEN AND EARTH,
MOON AND SUN AND EVERYTHING UNDER THEM.

EYES, EARS, NOSE, TONGUE, BODY, MIND...

PURITY WILL PIERCE EVIL AND
OPEN UP THE WORLD OF DARKNESS.

ALL LIFE WILL BE REBORN AND INVIGORATED.

APPEAR NOW.

W9-DFI-734

STORY & ART BY
YUU WATASE

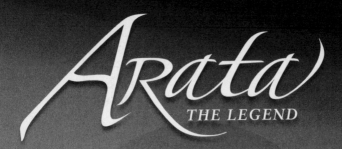

Arata THE LEGEND

CHARACTERS

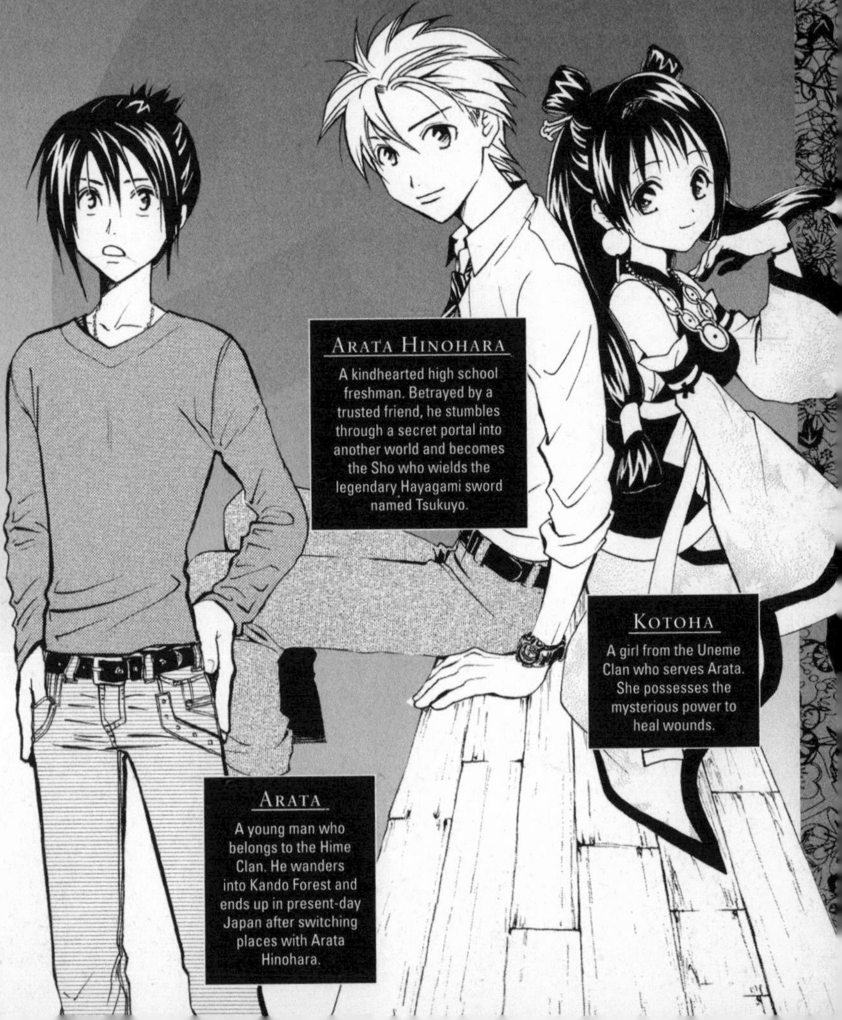
ARATA HINOHARA
A kindhearted high school freshman. Betrayed by a trusted friend, he stumbles through a secret portal into another world and becomes the Sho who wields the legendary Hayagami sword named Tsukuyo.
KOTOHA
A girl from the Uneme Clan who serves Arata. She possesses the mysterious power to heal wounds.
ARATA
A young man who belongs to the Hime Clan. He wanders into Kando Forest and ends up in present-day Japan after switching places with Arata Hinohara.

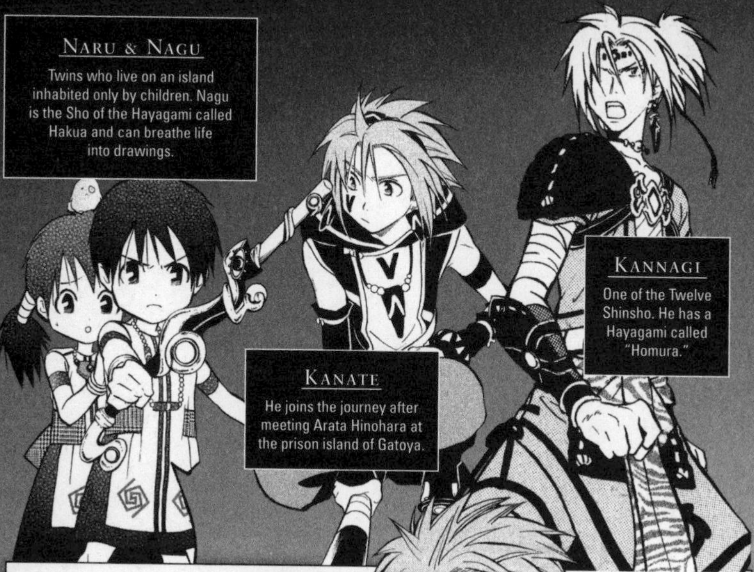
NARU & NAGU
Twins who live on an island inhabited only by children. Nagu is the Sho of the Hayagami called Hakua and can breathe life into drawings.
KANNAGI
One of the Twelve Shinsho. He has a Hayagami called "Homura."
KANATE
He joins the journey after meeting Arata Hinohara at the prison island of Gatoya.

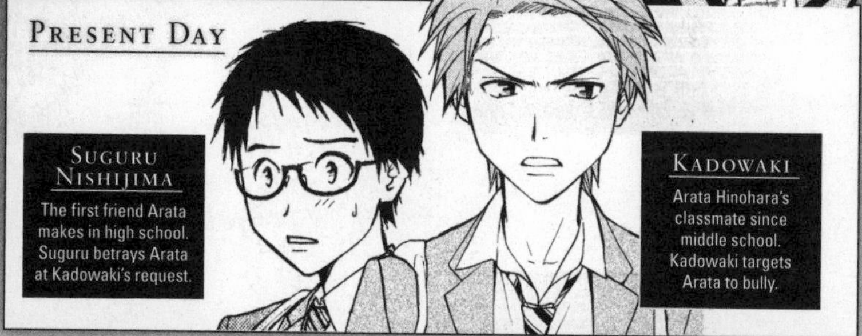
PRESENT DAY
SUGURU NISHIJIMA
The first friend Arata makes in high school. Suguru betrays Arata at Kadowaki's request.
KADOWAKI
Arata Hinohara's classmate since middle school. Kadowaki targets Arata to bully.

The Story Thus Far

Betrayed by his best friend, Arata Hinohara—a high school student in present-day Japan—wanders through a portal into another world where he and his companions journey onward to deliver his Hayagami sword to Princess Kikuri.

Akachi, one of the Twelve Shinsho, engages in a battle for the throne and kills countless people. Arata sees this slaughter and resolves to change the world—not through force but by changing the hearts of the Sho he encounters. He and his companions then arrive on an island inhabited only by children, where they encounter the twins Nagu and Naru. After a number of strange events, they discover that Nagu is a Sho and that all the other children are only drawings that were given life by Hakua.

5
Arata
THE LEGEND

CONTENTS

CHAPTER 38

THANK YOU

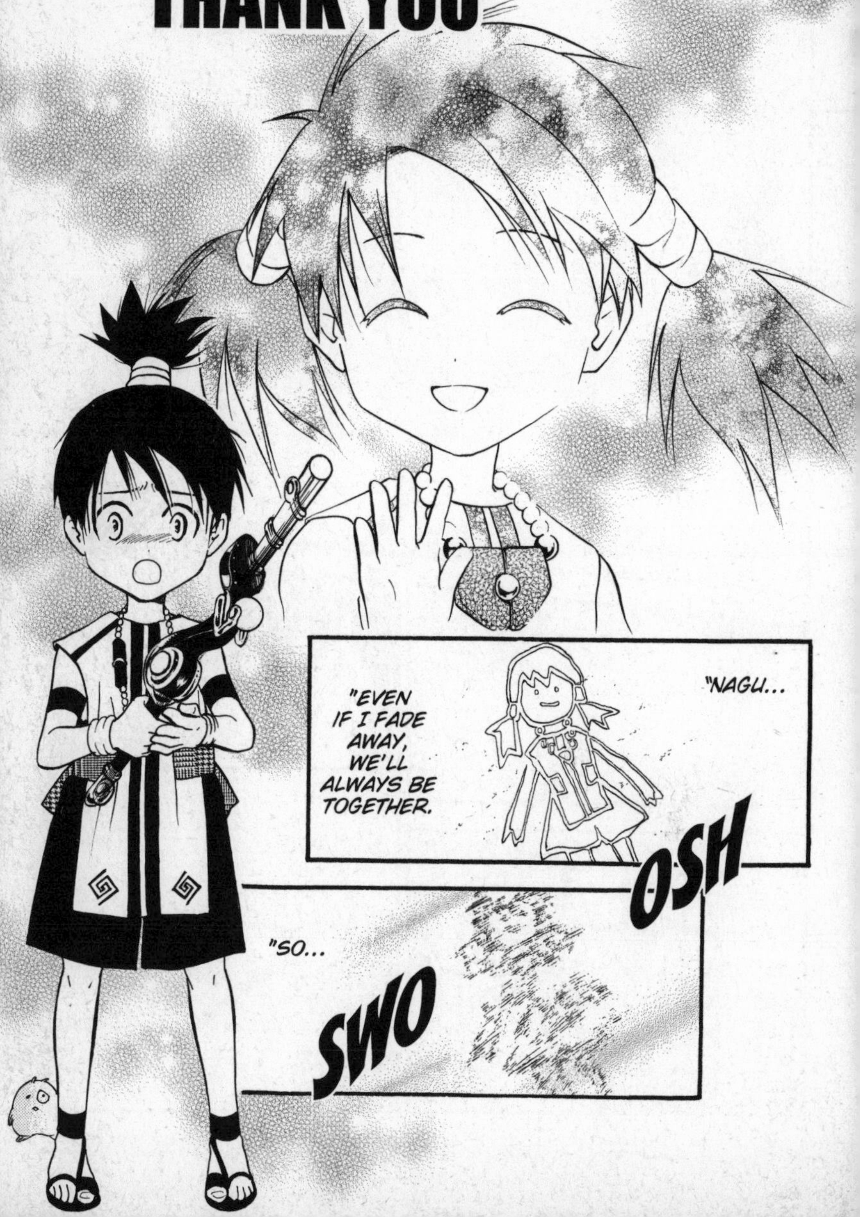
"NAGU...
"EVEN IF I FADE AWAY, WE'LL ALWAYS BE TOGETHER.
"SO...
SWO
OSH

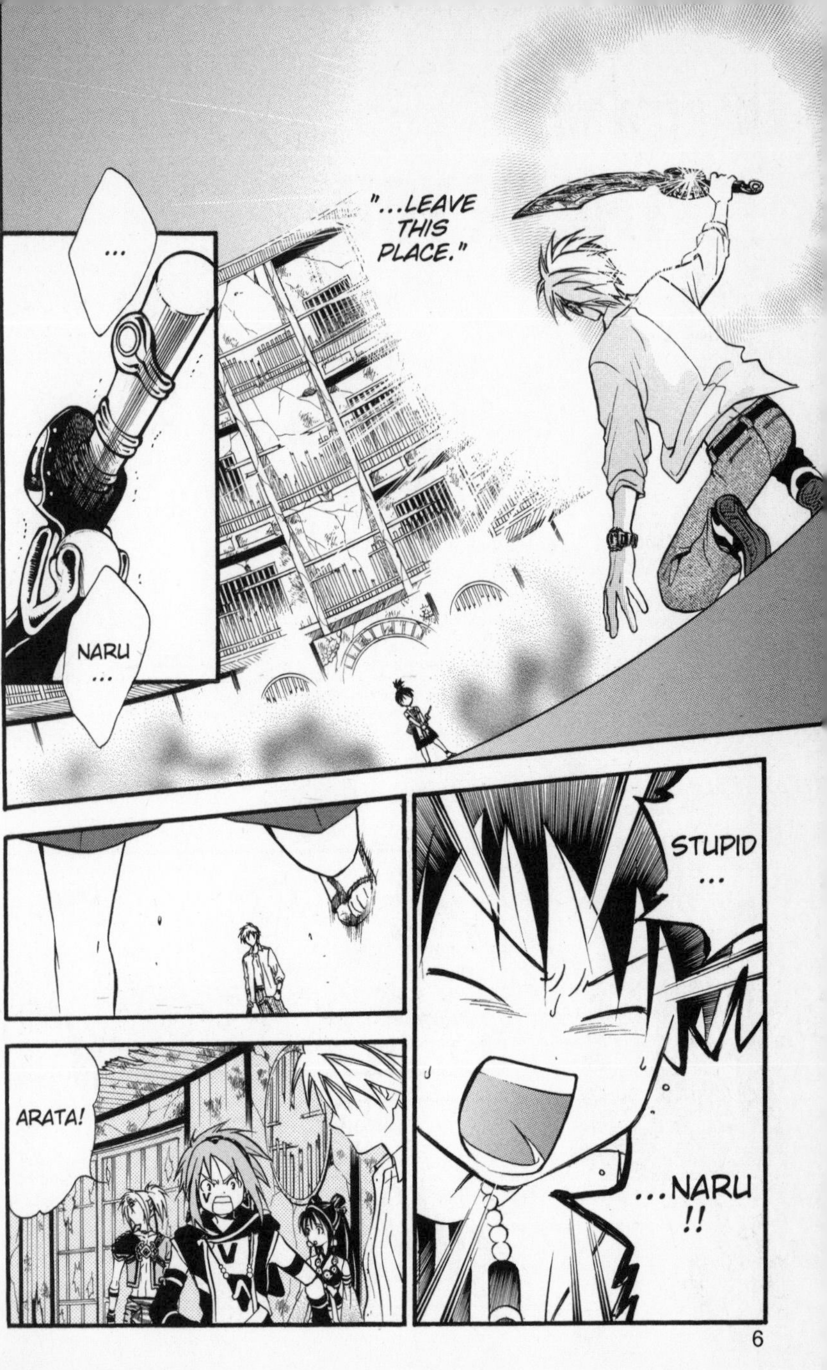
"...LEAVE THIS PLACE."
...
NARU ...
STUPID ...
...NARU !!
ARATA!

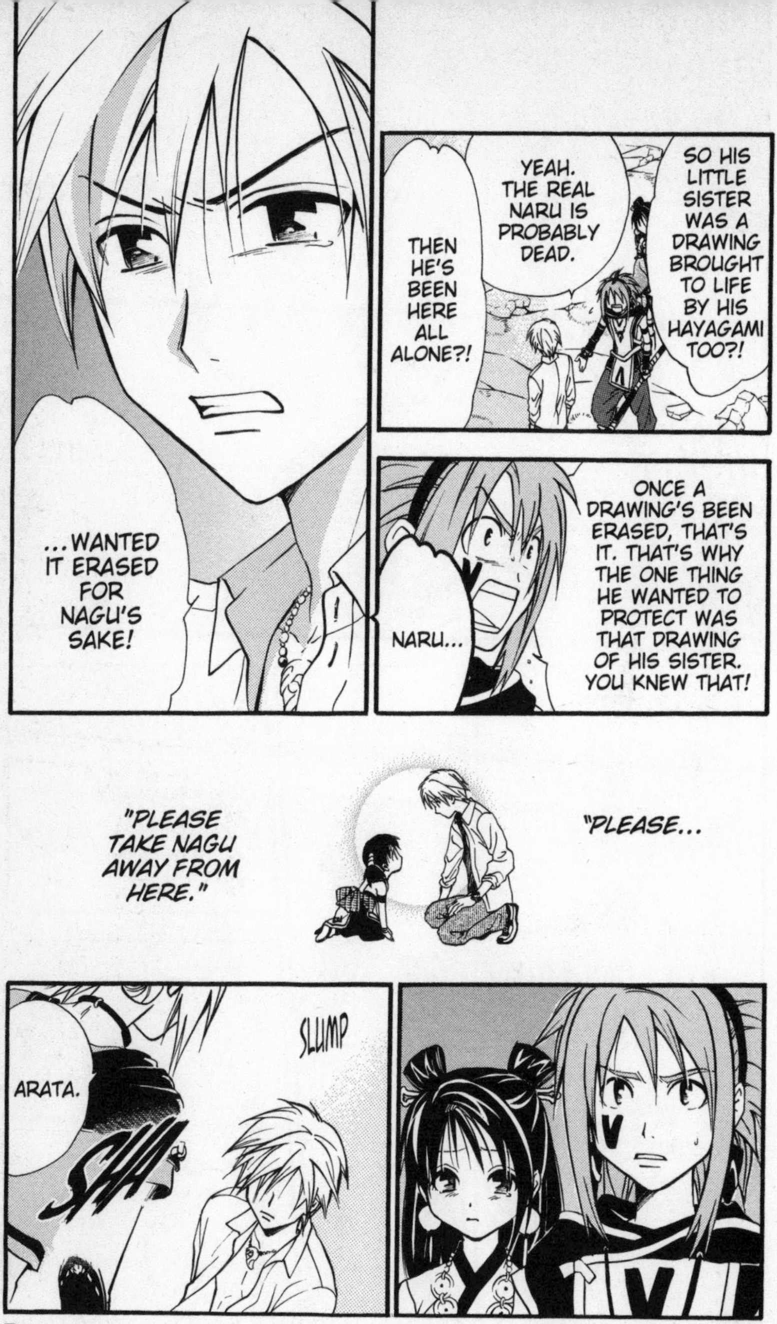
SO HIS LITTLE SISTER WAS A DRAWING BROUGHT TO LIFE BY HIS HAYAGAMI TOO?!
YEAH. THE REAL NARU IS PROBABLY DEAD.
THEN HE'S BEEN HERE ALL ALONE?!
ONCE A DRAWING'S BEEN ERASED, THAT'S IT. THAT'S WHY THE ONE THING HE WANTED TO PROTECT WAS THAT DRAWING OF HIS SISTER. YOU KNEW THAT!
NARU...
...WANTED IT ERASED FOR NAGU'S SAKE!
"PLEASE...
"PLEASE TAKE NAGU AWAY FROM HERE."
SLUMP
ARATA.

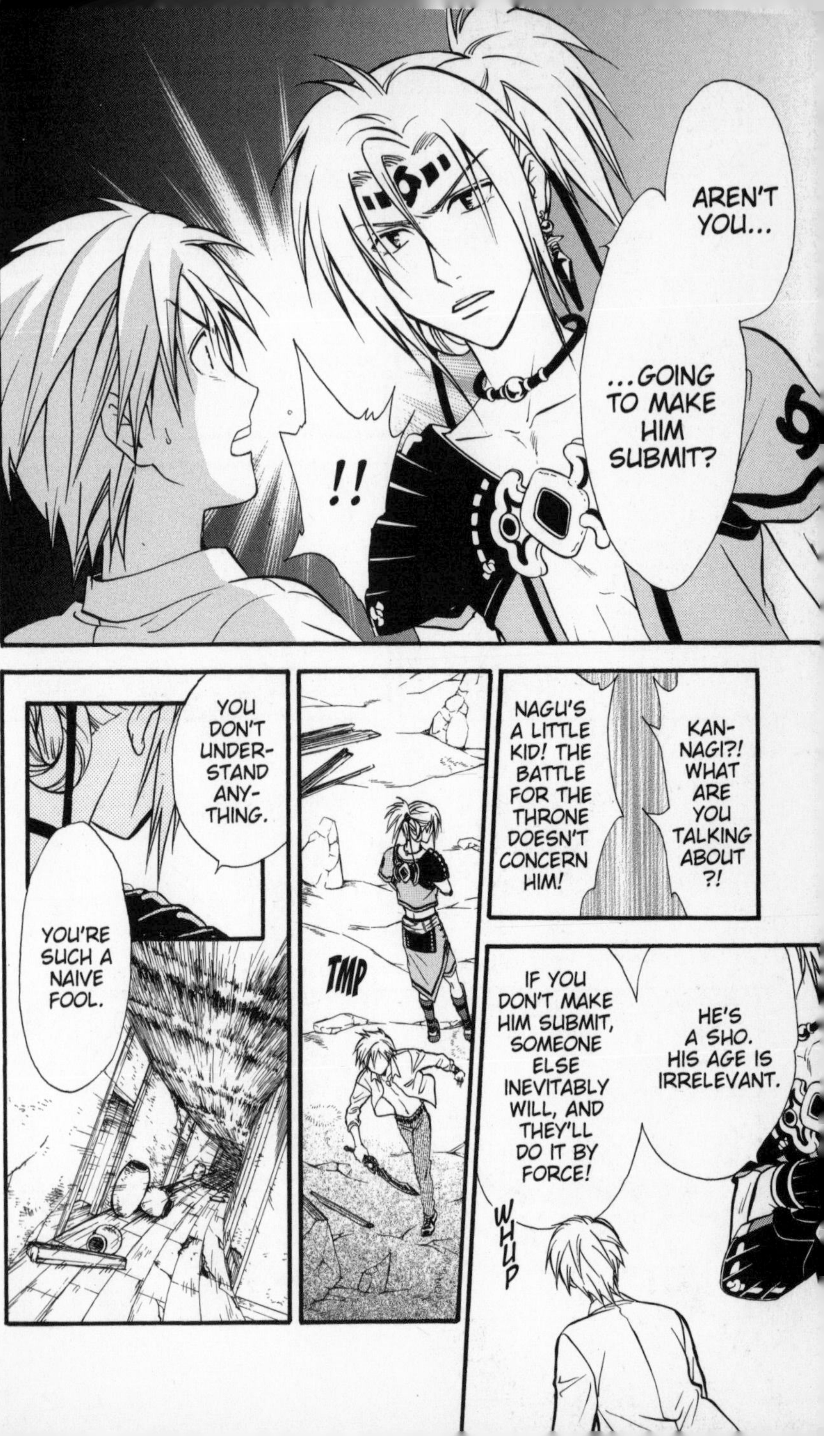
AREN'T YOU...
...GOING TO MAKE HIM SUBMIT?
!!
KAN-NAGI?! WHAT ARE YOU TALKING ABOUT?!
NAGU'S A LITTLE KID! THE BATTLE FOR THE THRONE DOESN'T CONCERN HIM!
HE'S A SHO. HIS AGE IS IRRELEVANT.
IF YOU DON'T MAKE HIM SUBMIT, SOMEONE ELSE INEVITABLY WILL, AND THEY'LL DO IT BY FORCE!
WHUP
TMP
YOU DON'T UNDER-STAND ANY-THING.
YOU'RE SUCH A NAIVE FOOL.

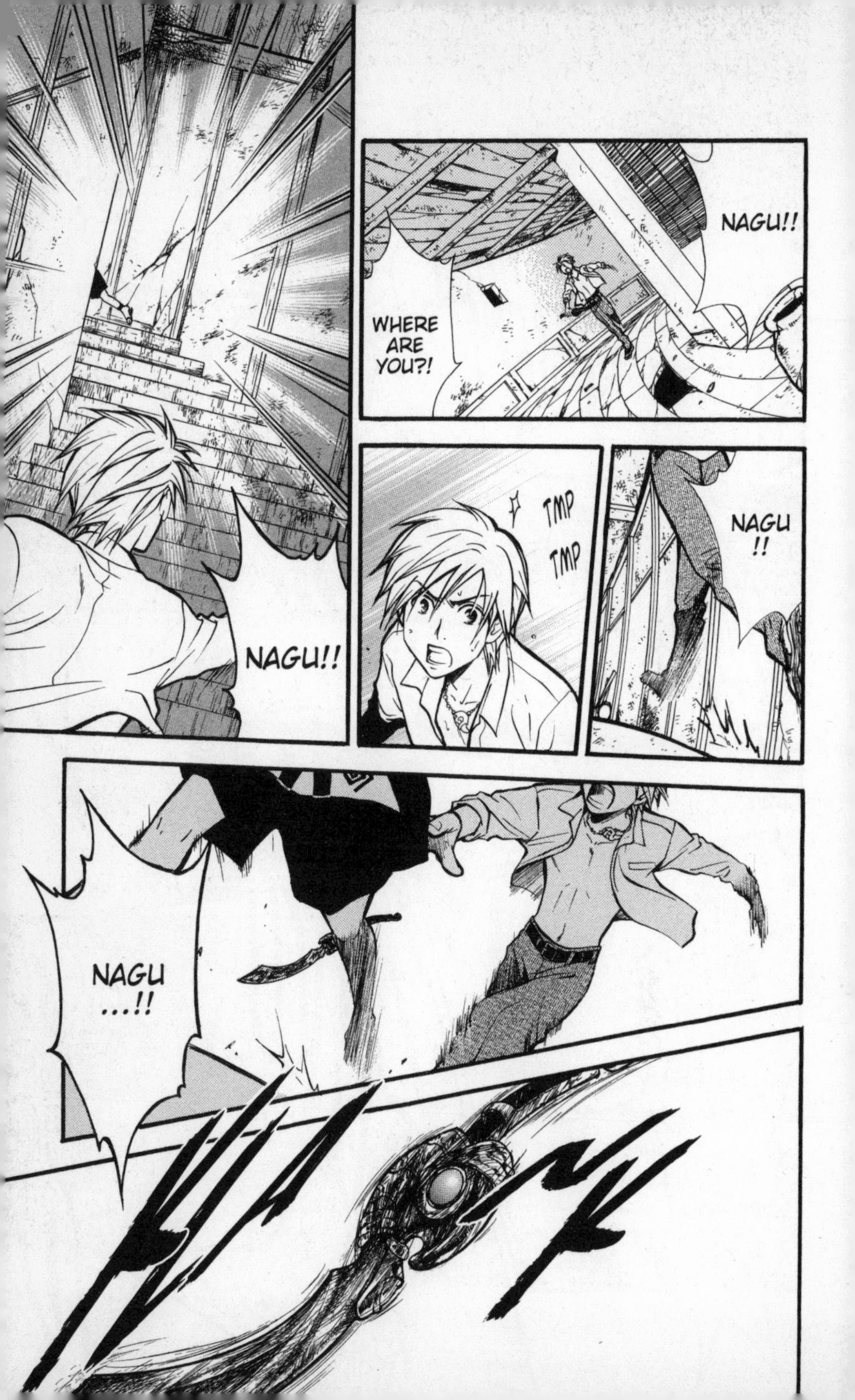
NAGU!!
WHERE ARE YOU?!
NAGU !!
TMP TMP
NAGU!!
NAGU ...!!

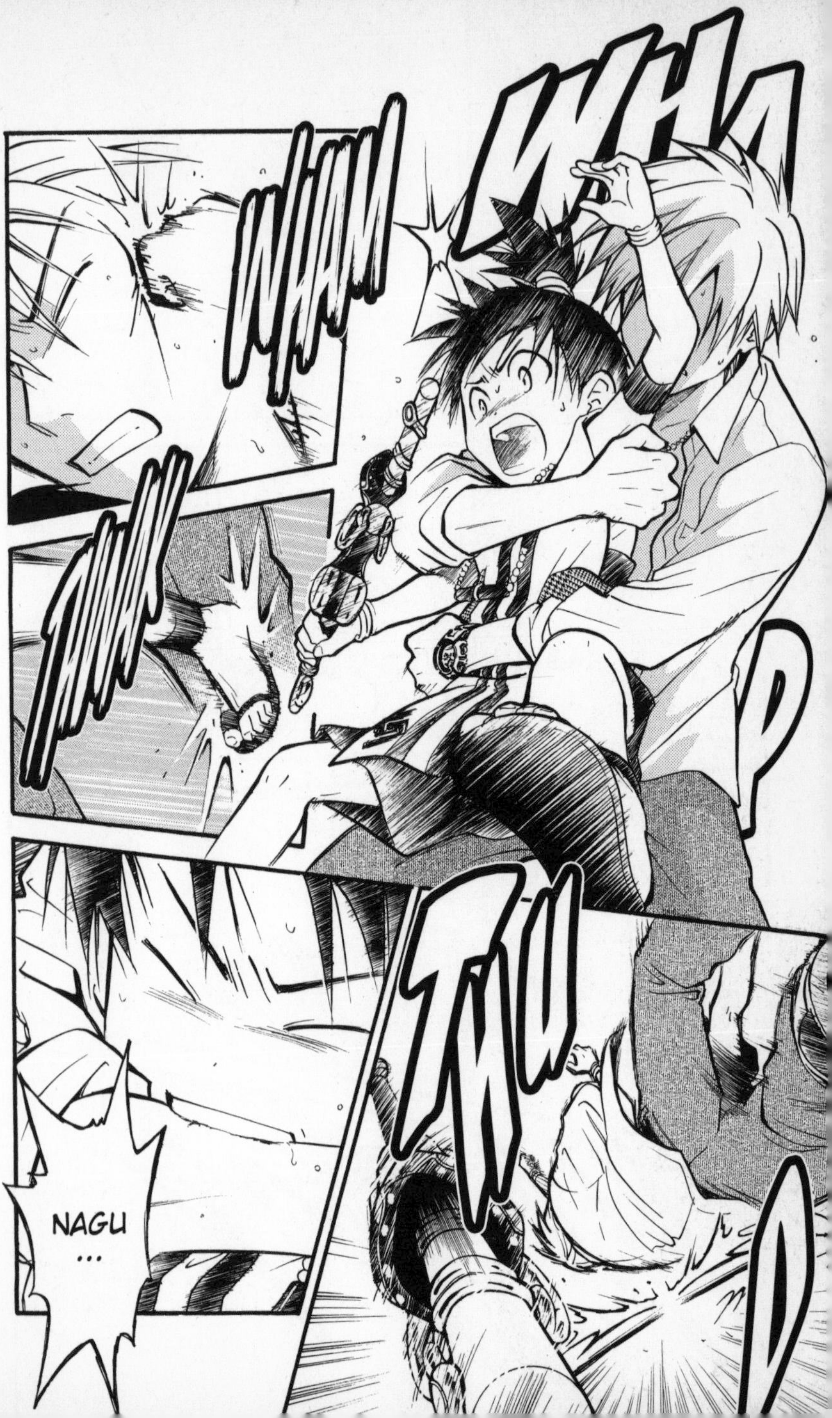

WHAP
WHAM
THUD
NAGU
...

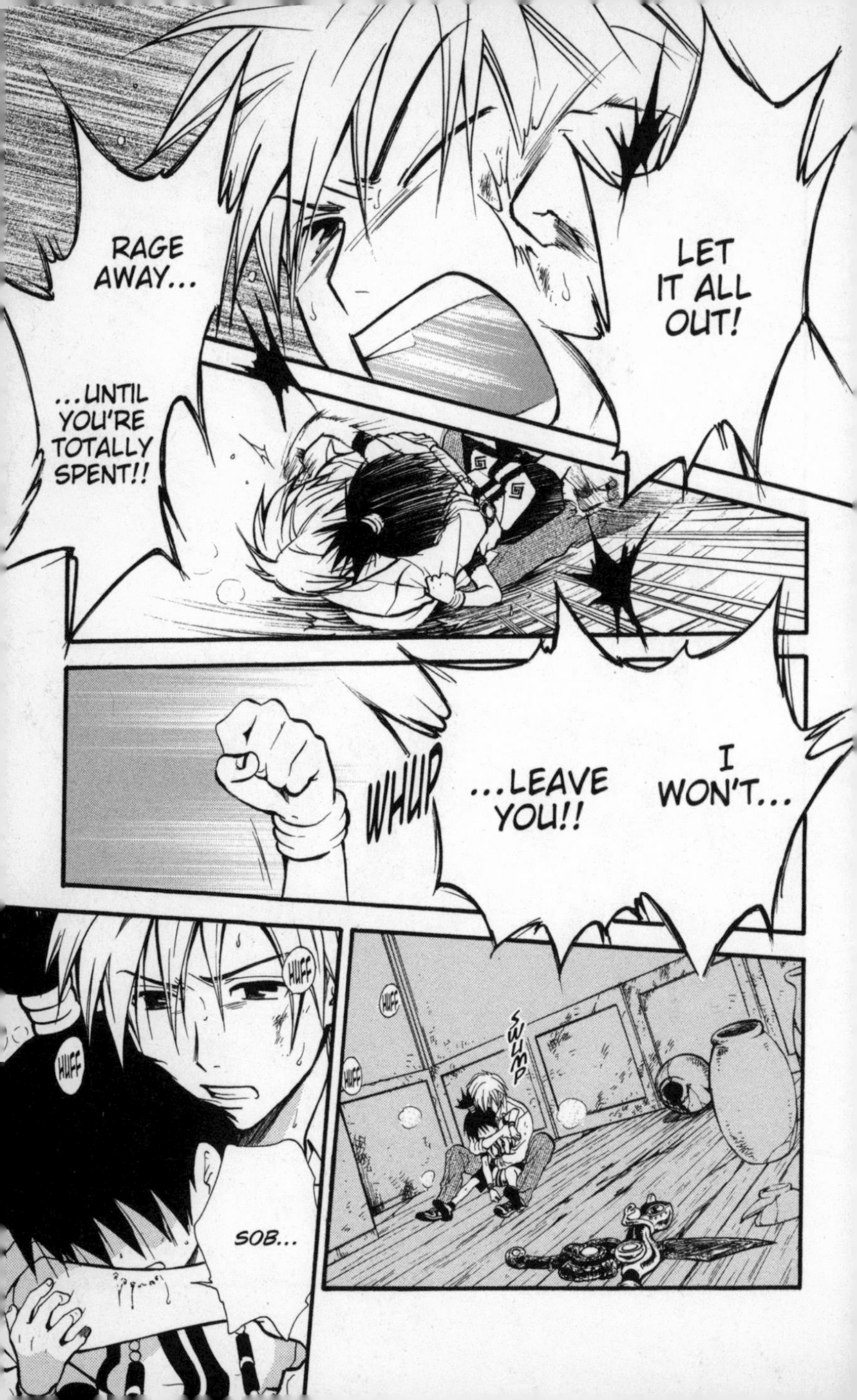
LET IT ALL OUT!
RAGE AWAY...
...UNTIL YOU'RE TOTALLY SPENT!!
I WON'T...
...LEAVE YOU!!
WHUP
HUFF
HUFF
SWUMP
HUFF
HUFF
SOB...

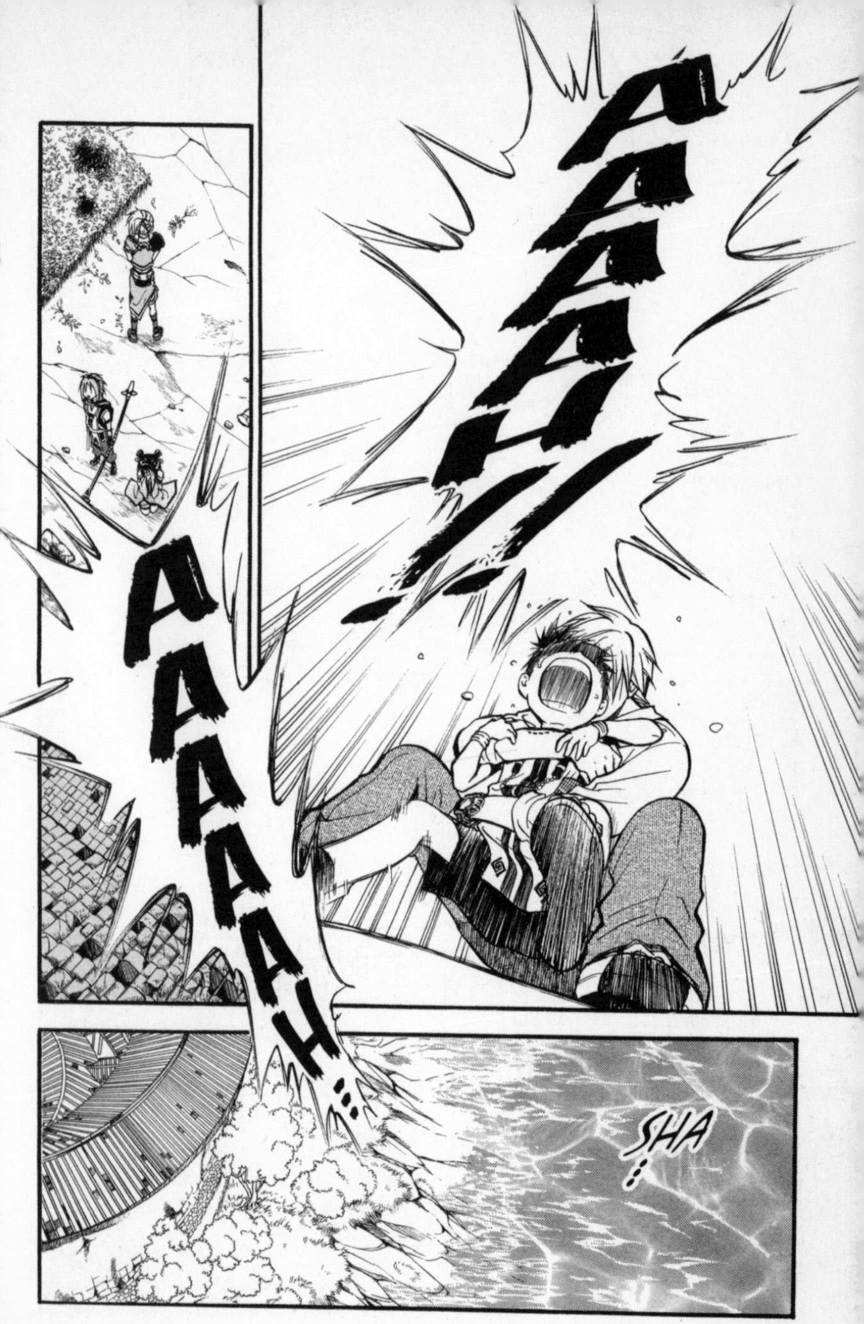
AAAAH—!!
AAAAAAH...
SHA...

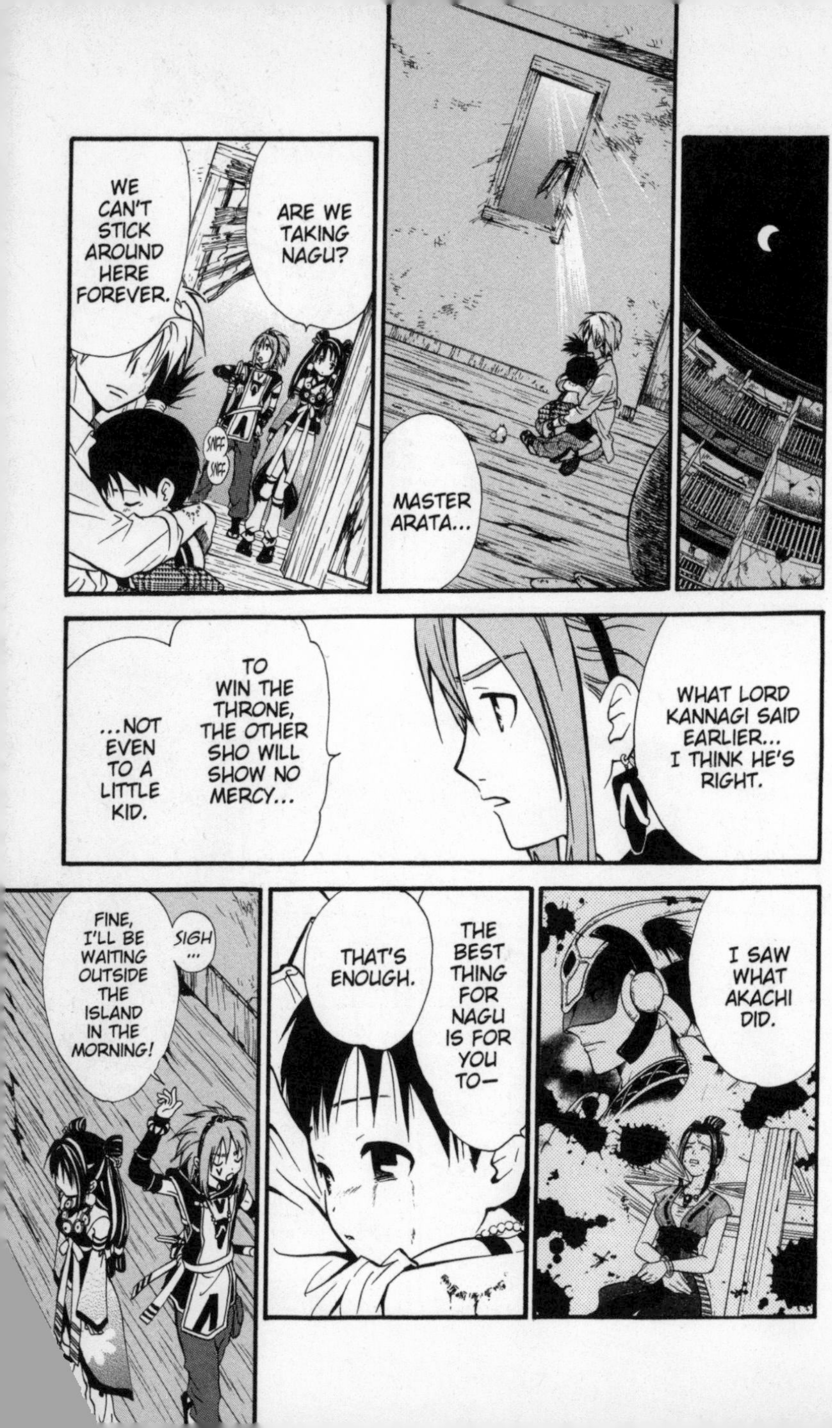
MASTER ARATA...
ARE WE TAKING NAGU?
WE CAN'T STICK AROUND HERE FOREVER.
SNIFF SNIFF
WHAT LORD KANNAGI SAID EARLIER... I THINK HE'S RIGHT.
TO WIN THE THRONE, THE OTHER SHO WILL SHOW NO MERCY...
...NOT EVEN TO A LITTLE KID.
I SAW WHAT AKACHI DID.
THE BEST THING FOR NAGU IS FOR YOU TO—
THAT'S ENOUGH.
SIGH...
FINE, I'LL BE WAITING OUTSIDE THE ISLAND IN THE MORNING!

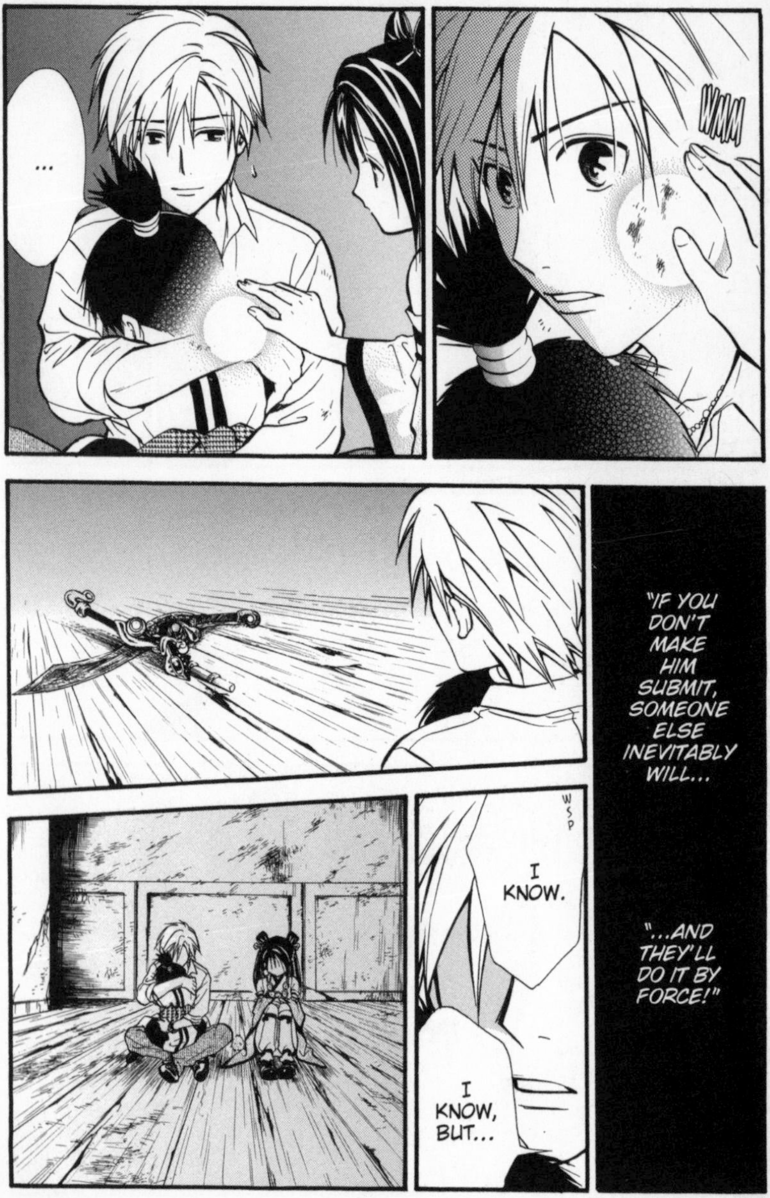
WMM
...
"IF YOU DON'T MAKE HIM SUBMIT, SOMEONE ELSE INEVITABLY WILL...
"...AND THEY'LL DO IT BY FORCE!"
WSP
I KNOW.
I KNOW, BUT...

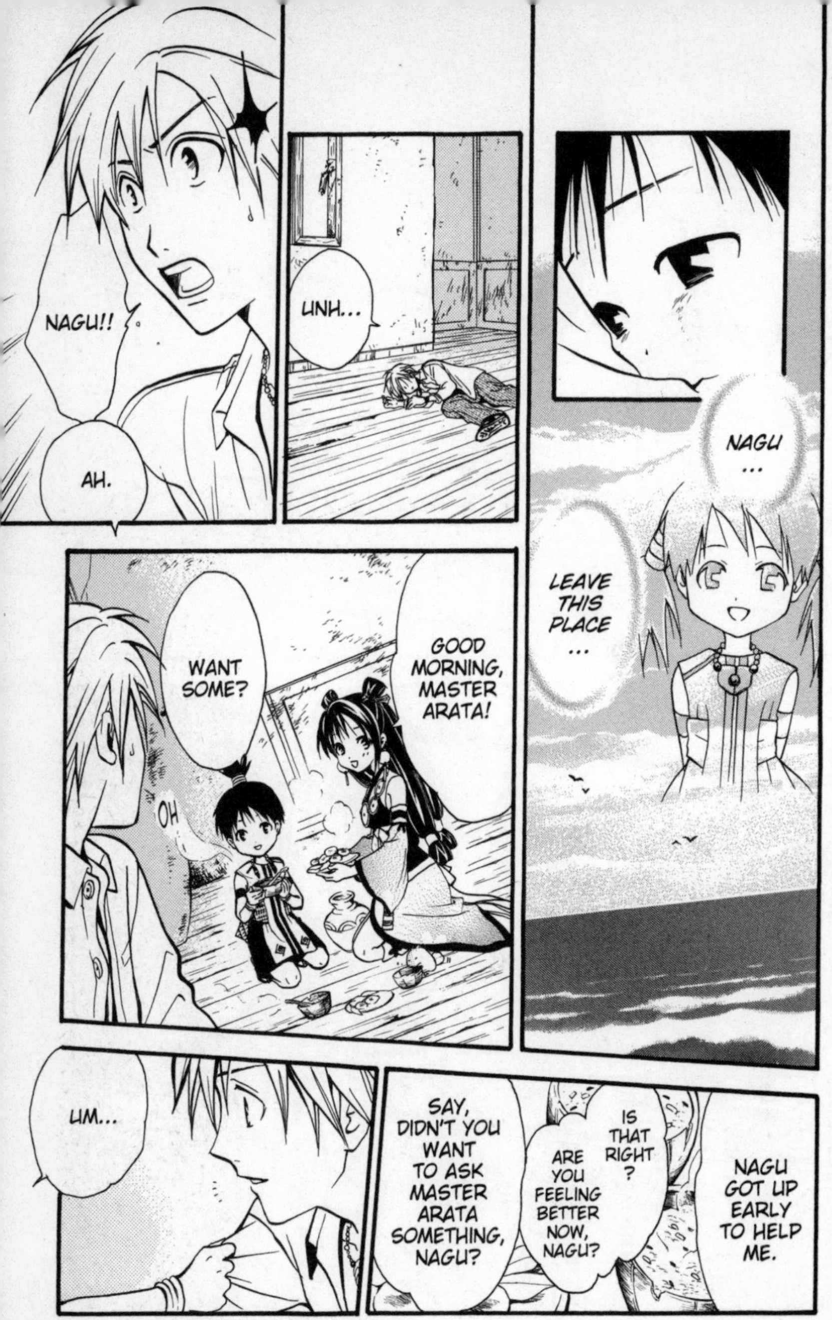
NAGU ...
LEAVE THIS PLACE ...
UNH...
NAGU!!
AH.
GOOD MORNING, MASTER ARATA!
WANT SOME?
OH
NAGU GOT UP EARLY TO HELP ME.
IS THAT RIGHT?
ARE YOU FEELING BETTER NOW, NAGU?
SAY, DIDN'T YOU WANT TO ASK MASTER ARATA SOMETHING, NAGU?
UM...

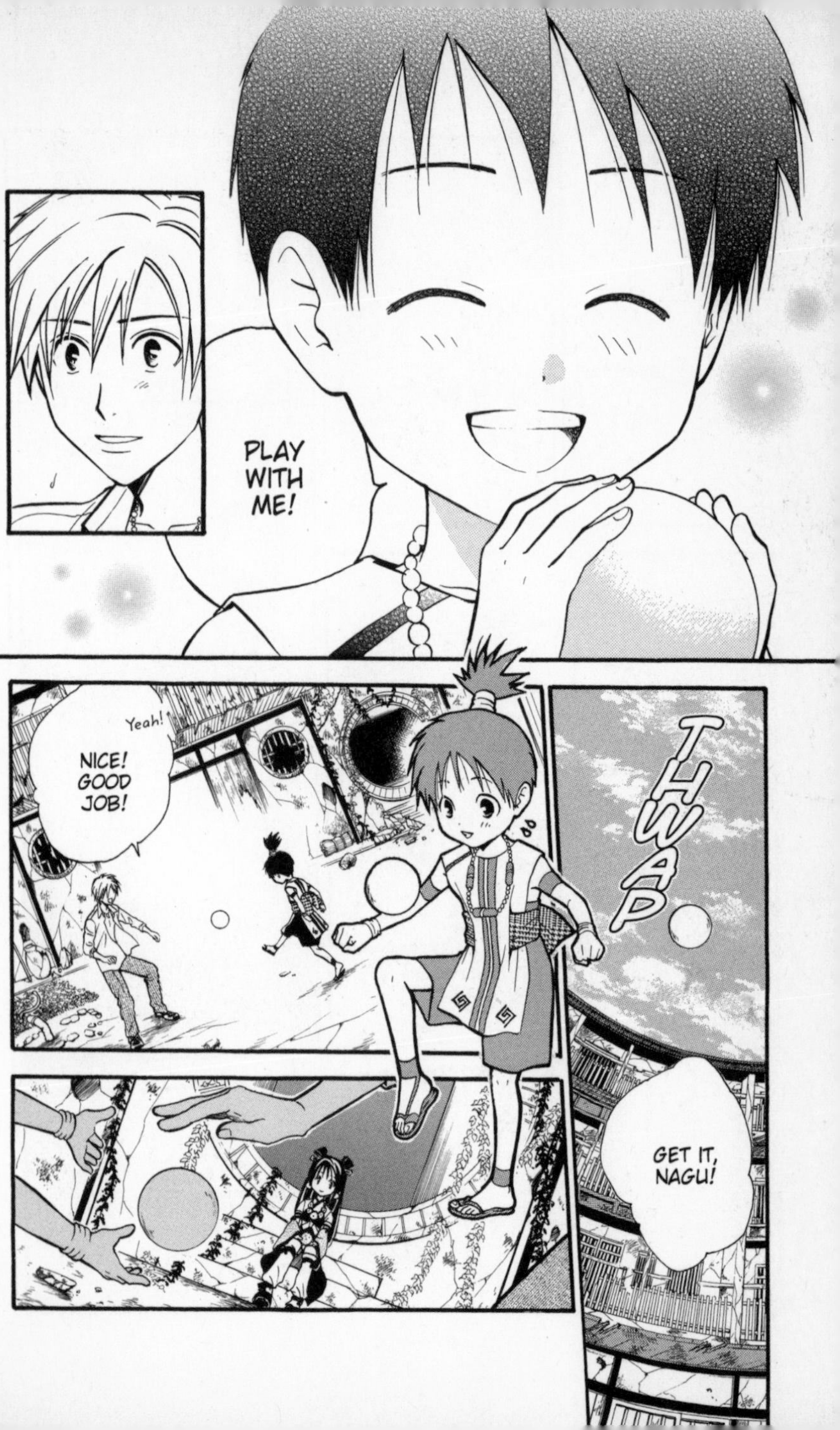
PLAY WITH ME!
THWAP
GET IT, NAGU!
Yeah!
NICE! GOOD JOB!

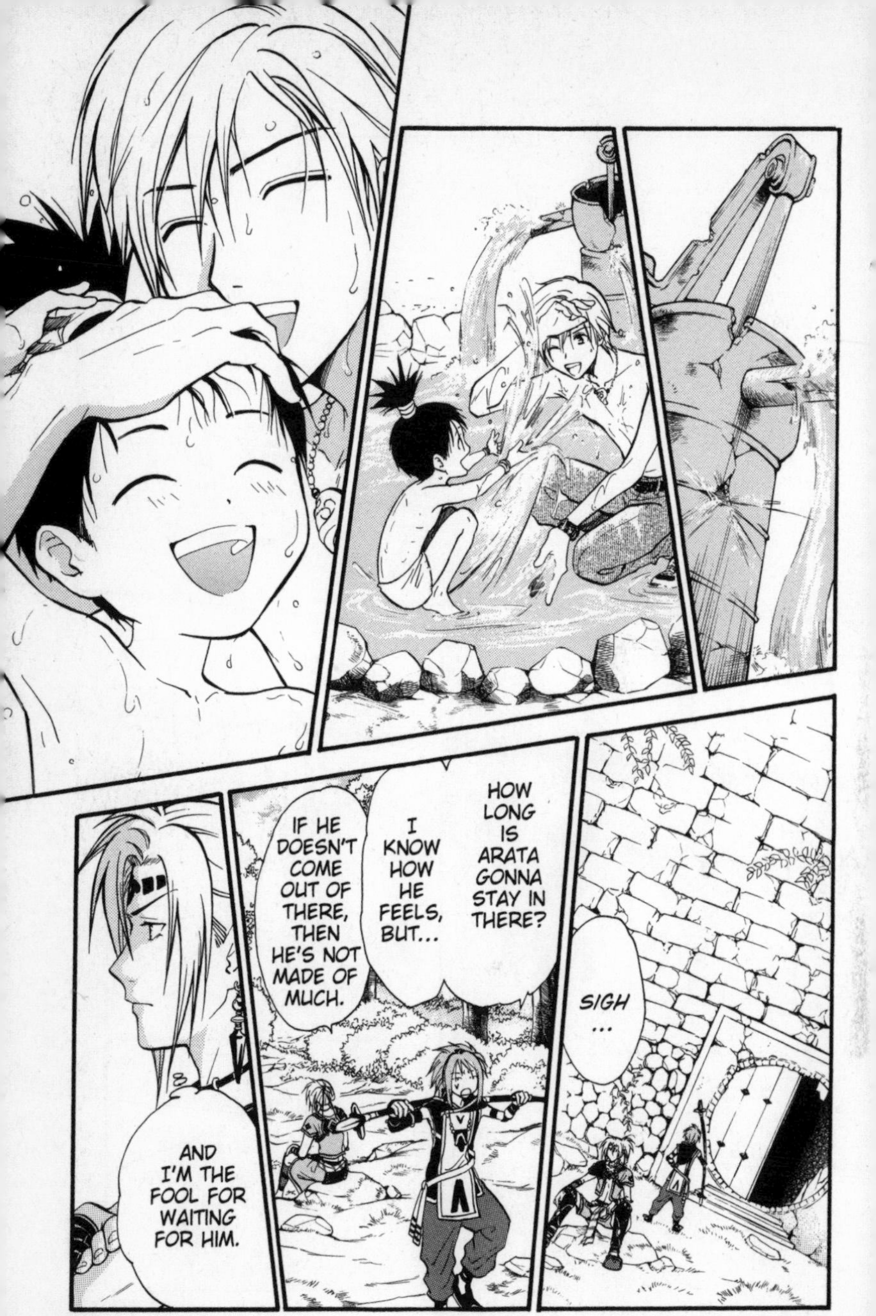
SIGH...
HOW LONG IS ARATA GONNA STAY IN THERE?
I KNOW HOW HE FEELS, BUT...
IF HE DOESN'T COME OUT OF THERE, THEN HE'S NOT MADE OF MUCH.
AND I'M THE FOOL FOR WAITING FOR HIM.

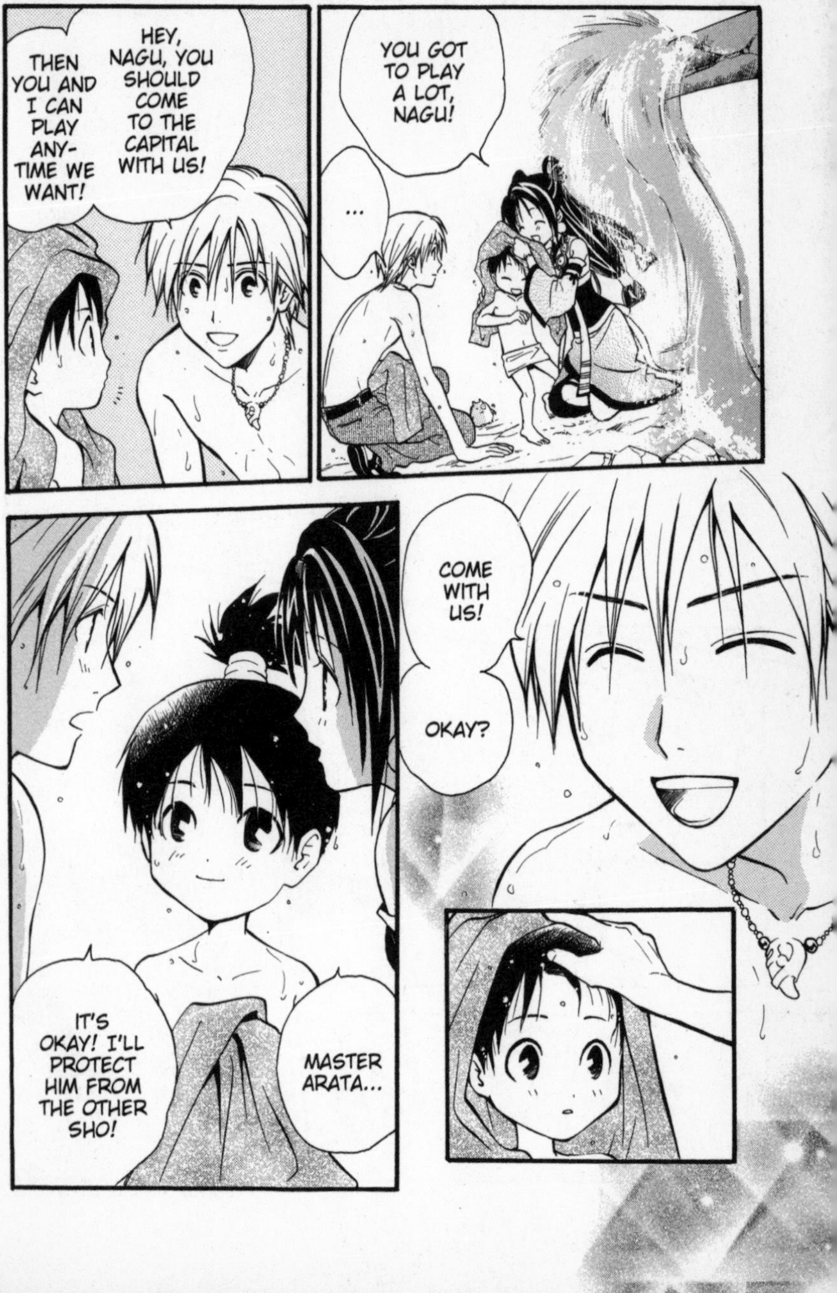
YOU GOT TO PLAY A LOT, NAGU!
...
HEY, NAGU, YOU SHOULD COME TO THE CAPITAL WITH US!
THEN YOU AND I CAN PLAY ANY-TIME WE WANT!
COME WITH US!
OKAY?
MASTER ARATA...
IT'S OKAY! I'LL PROTECT HIM FROM THE OTHER SHO!

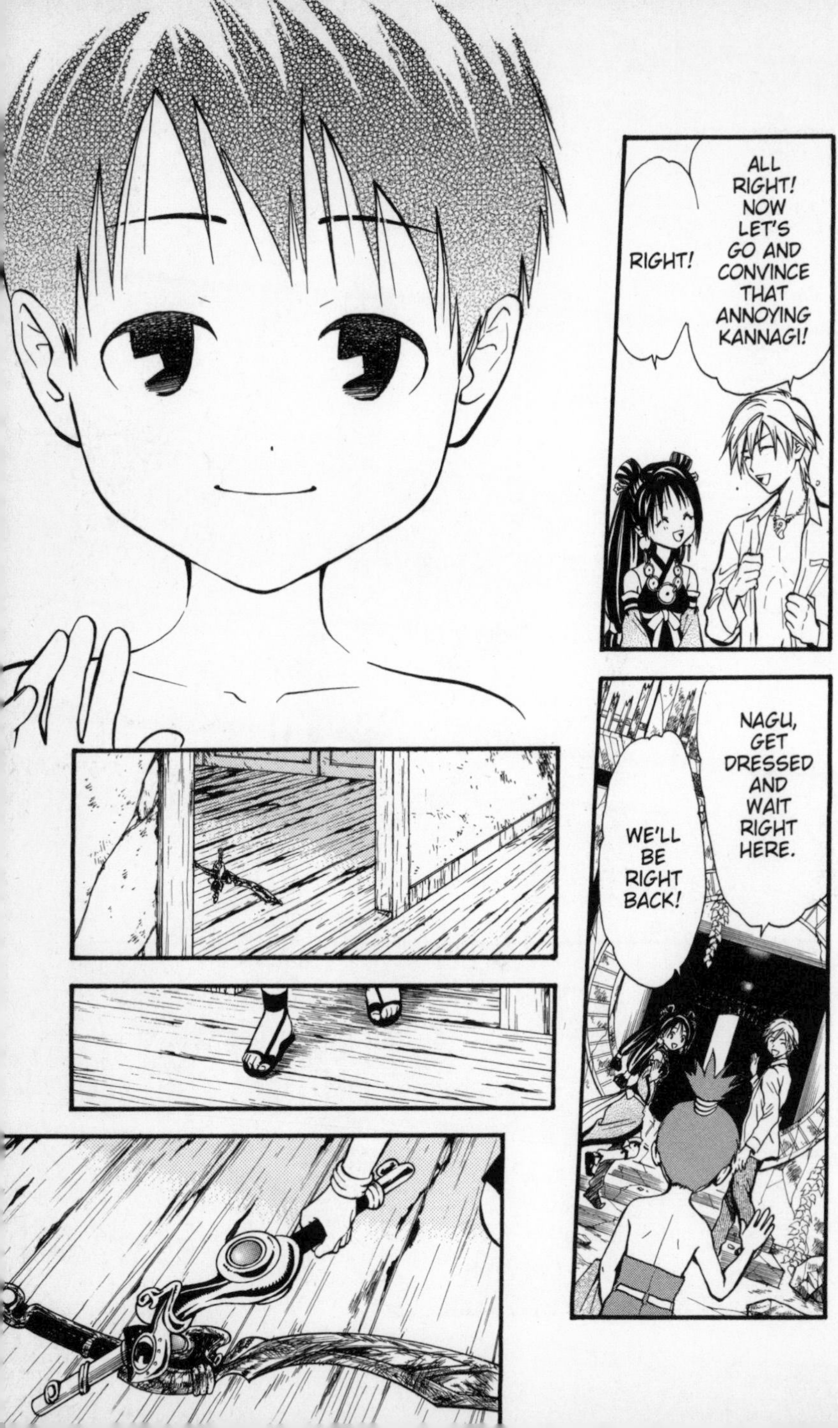
ALL RIGHT! NOW LET'S GO AND CONVINCE THAT ANNOYING KANNAGI!
RIGHT!
NAGU, GET DRESSED AND WAIT RIGHT HERE.
WE'LL BE RIGHT BACK!

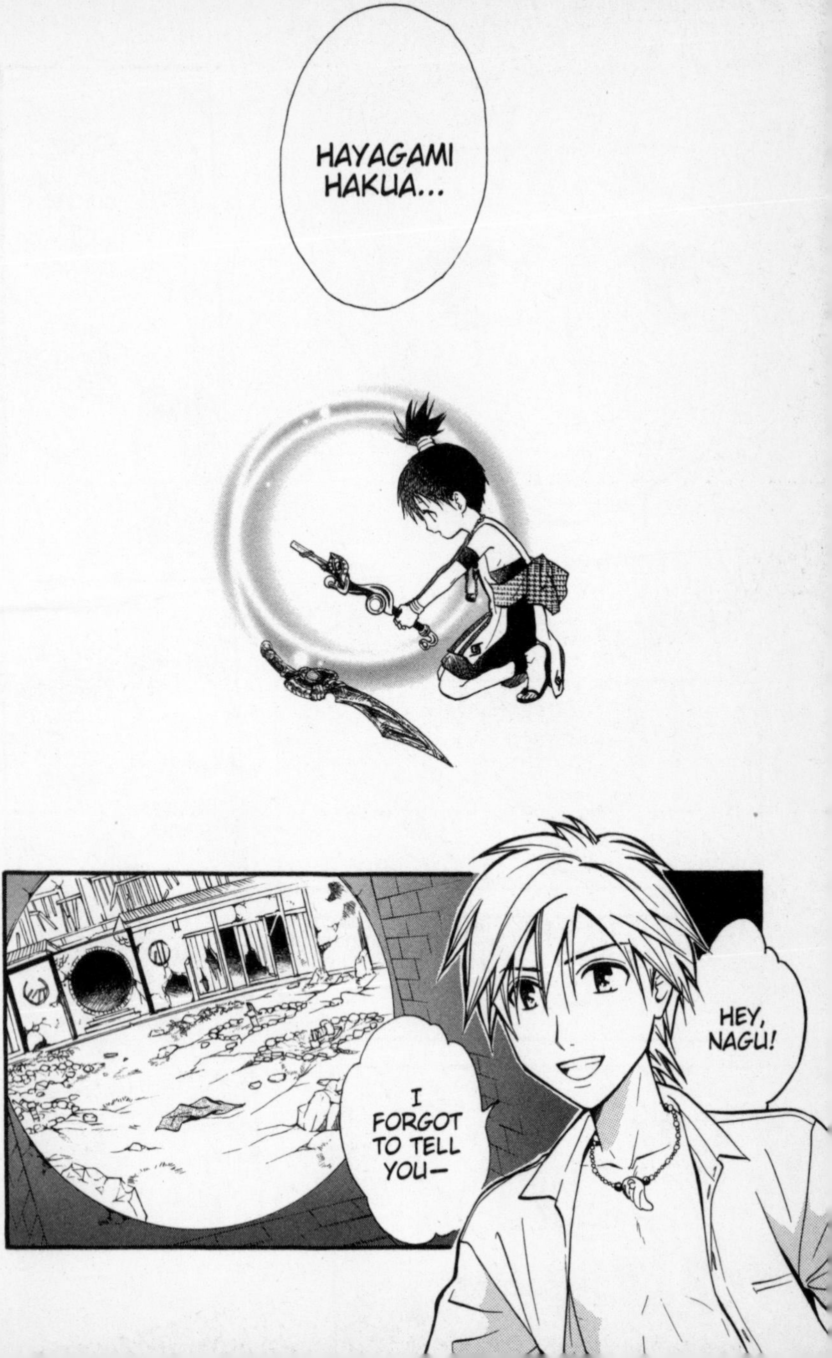
HAYAGAMI HAKUA...
HEY, NAGU!
I FORGOT TO TELL YOU—

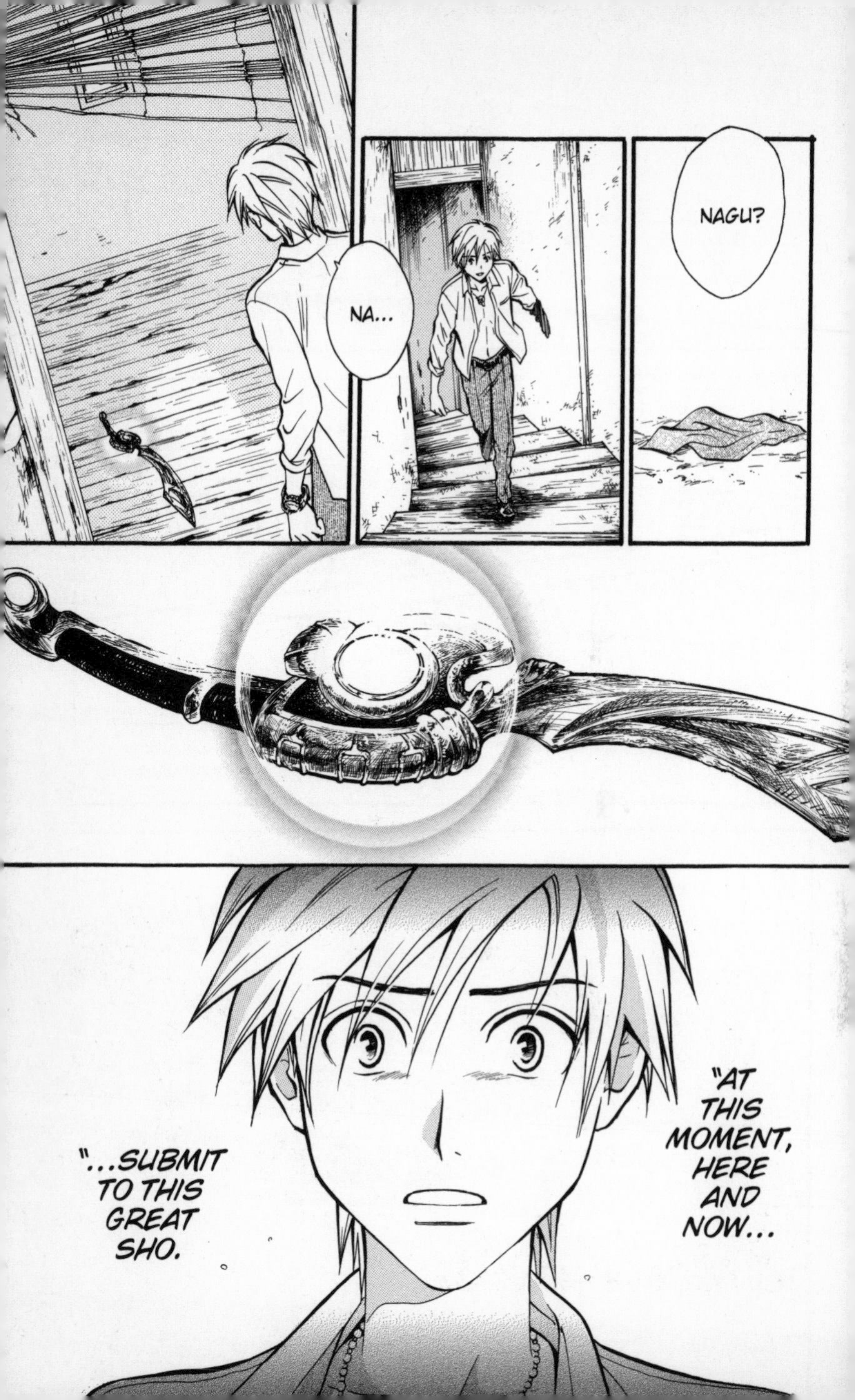
NAGU?
NA...
"AT THIS MOMENT, HERE AND NOW...
"...SUBMIT TO THIS GREAT SHO.

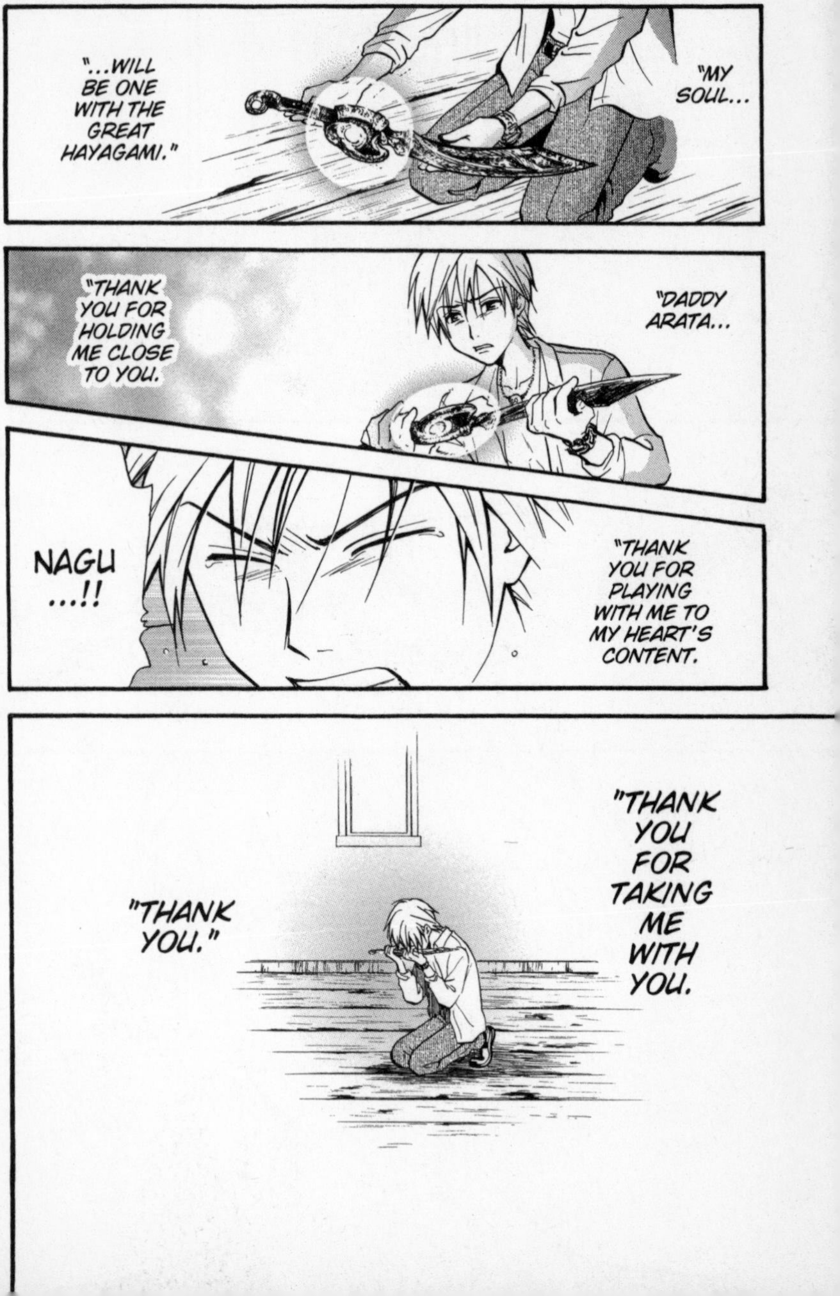
"MY SOUL...
"...WILL BE ONE WITH THE GREAT HAYAGAMI."
"DADDY ARATA...
"THANK YOU FOR HOLDING ME CLOSE TO YOU.
"THANK YOU FOR PLAYING WITH ME TO MY HEART'S CONTENT.
NAGU ...!!
"THANK YOU FOR TAKING ME WITH YOU.
"THANK YOU."

CHAPTER 39
OMEN

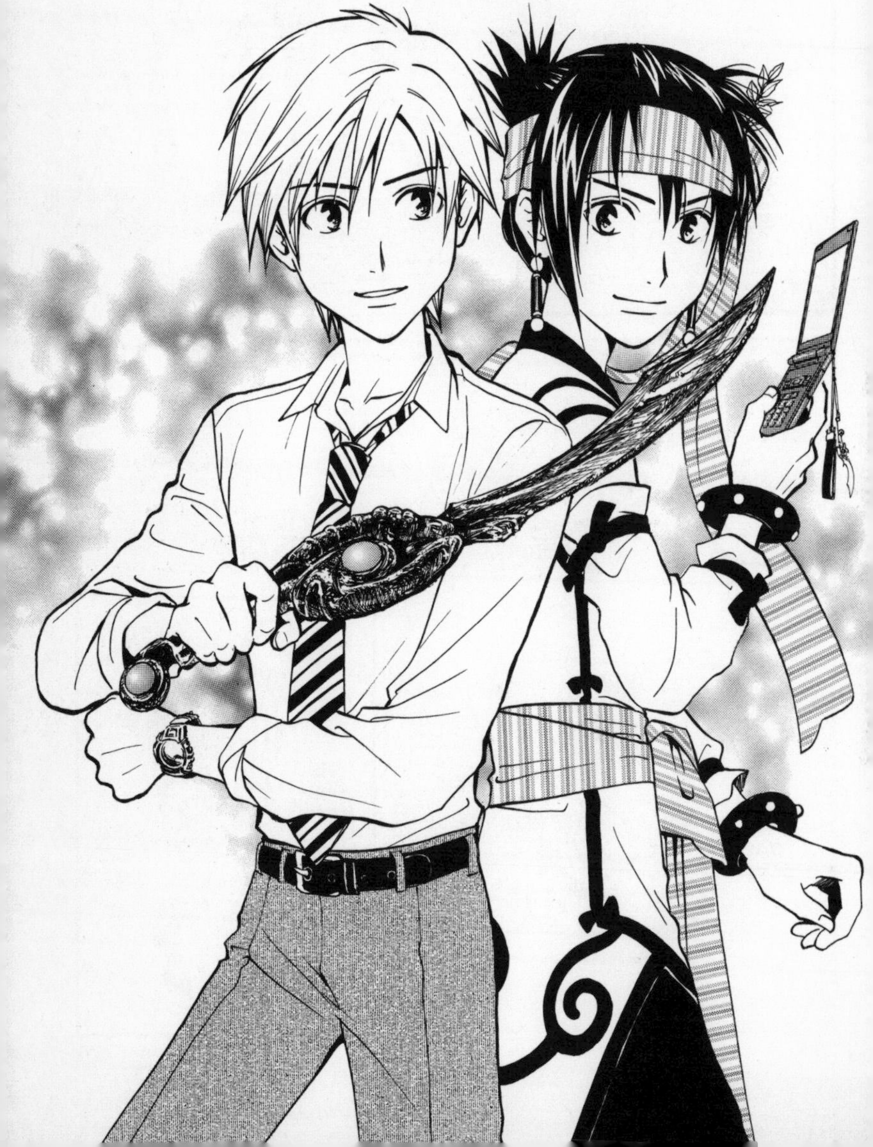

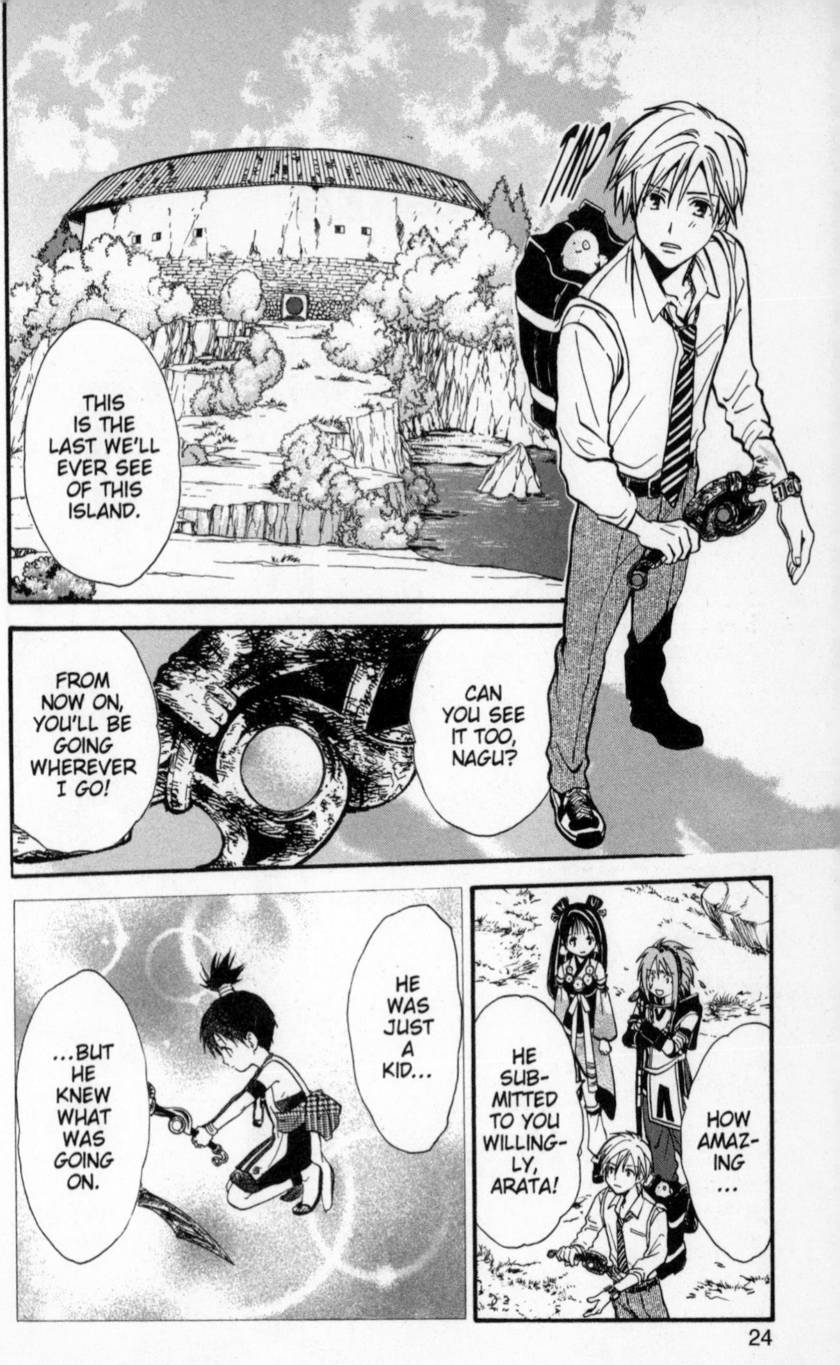
TMP
THIS IS THE LAST WE'LL EVER SEE OF THIS ISLAND.
CAN YOU SEE IT TOO, NAGU?
FROM NOW ON, YOU'LL BE GOING WHEREVER I GO!
HOW AMAZ-ING...
HE SUB-MITTED TO YOU WILLING-LY, ARATA!
HE WAS JUST A KID...
...BUT HE KNEW WHAT WAS GOING ON.

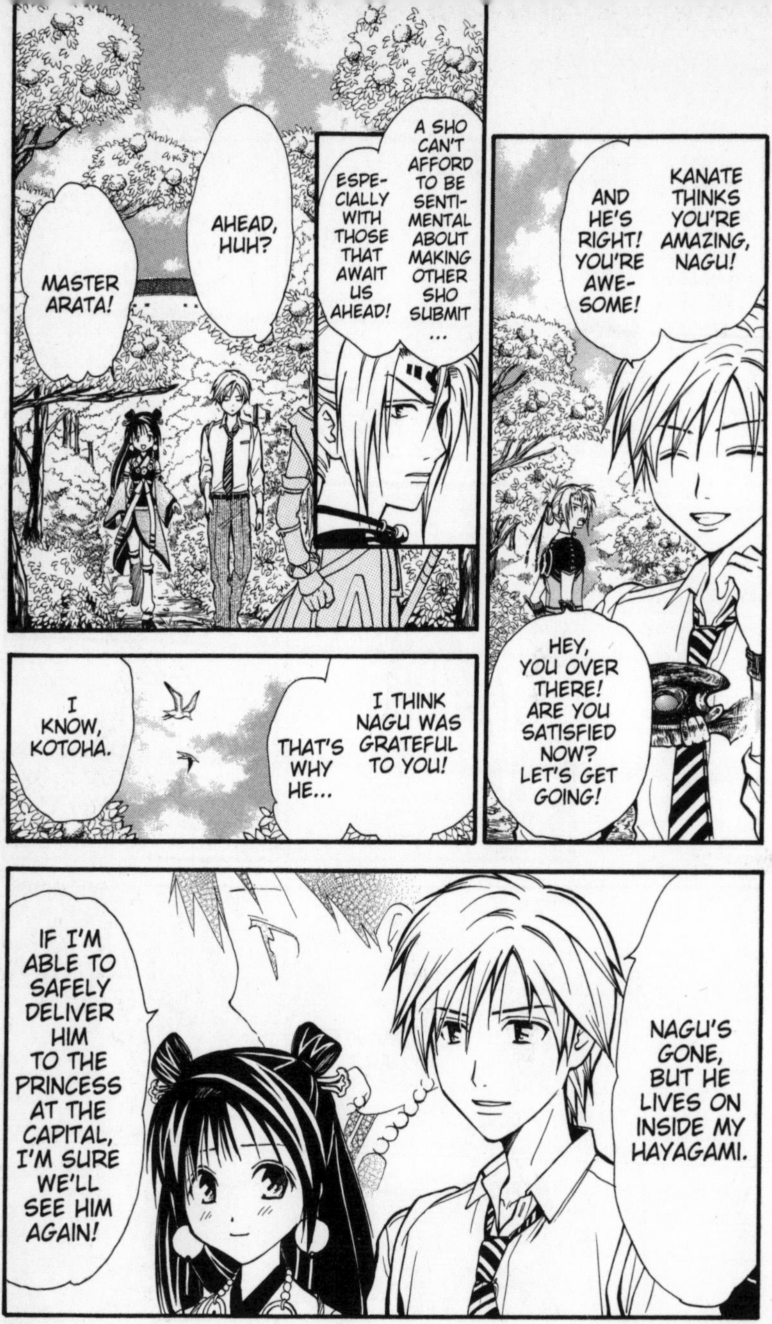
KANATE THINKS YOU'RE AMAZING, NAGU!
AND HE'S RIGHT! YOU'RE AWE-SOME!
HEY, YOU OVER THERE! ARE YOU SATISFIED NOW? LET'S GET GOING!
A SHO CAN'T AFFORD TO BE SENTI-MENTAL ABOUT MAKING OTHER SHO SUBMIT...
ESPE-CIALLY WITH THOSE THAT AWAIT US AHEAD!
AHEAD, HUH?
MASTER ARATA!
I THINK NAGU WAS GRATEFUL TO YOU!
THAT'S WHY HE...
I KNOW, KOTOHA.
NAGU'S GONE, BUT HE LIVES ON INSIDE MY HAYAGAMI.
IF I'M ABLE TO SAFELY DELIVER HIM TO THE PRINCESS AT THE CAPITAL, I'M SURE WE'LL SEE HIM AGAIN!

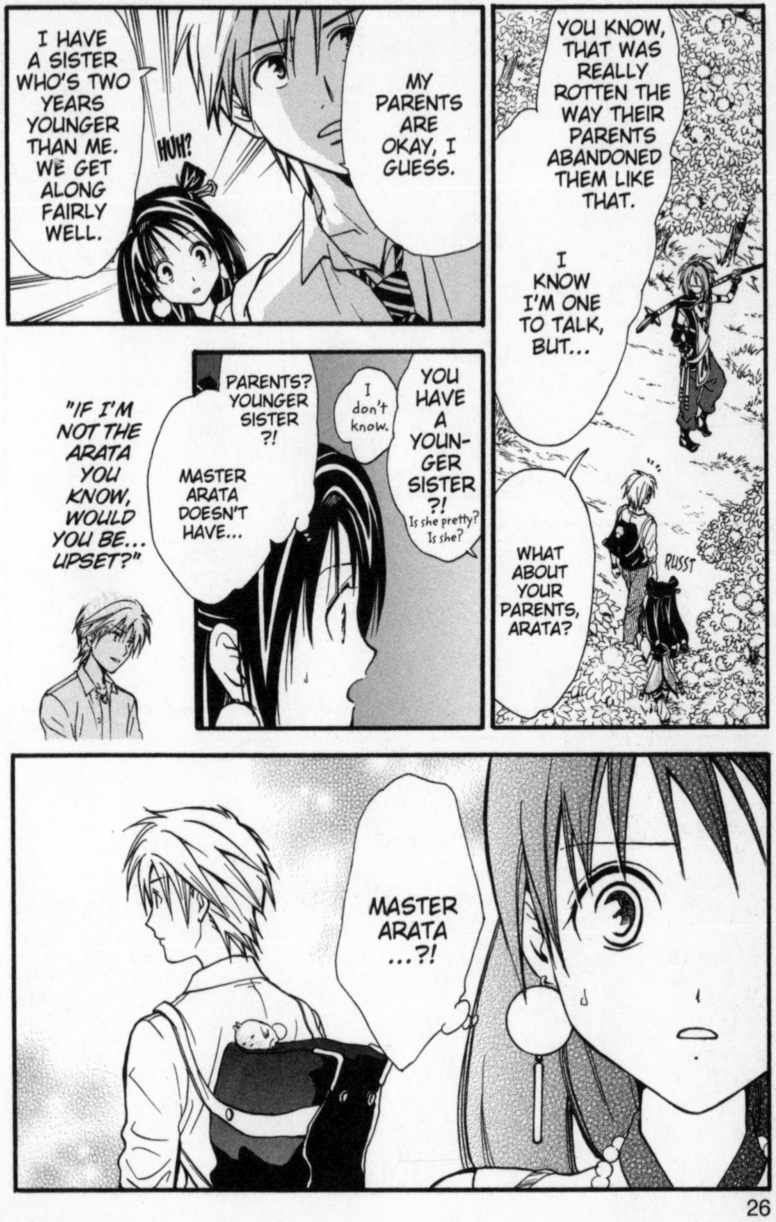
YOU KNOW, THAT WAS REALLY ROTTEN THE WAY THEIR PARENTS ABANDONED THEM LIKE THAT.
I KNOW I'M ONE TO TALK, BUT...
WHAT ABOUT YOUR PARENTS, ARATA?
RUSST
MY PARENTS ARE OKAY, I GUESS.
I HAVE A SISTER WHO'S TWO YEARS YOUNGER THAN ME. WE GET ALONG FAIRLY WELL.
HUH?
YOU HAVE A YOUNGER SISTER?!
Is she pretty? Is she?
I don't know.
PARENTS? YOUNGER SISTER?!
MASTER ARATA DOESN'T HAVE...
"IF I'M NOT THE ARATA YOU KNOW, WOULD YOU BE... UPSET?"
MASTER ARATA...?!

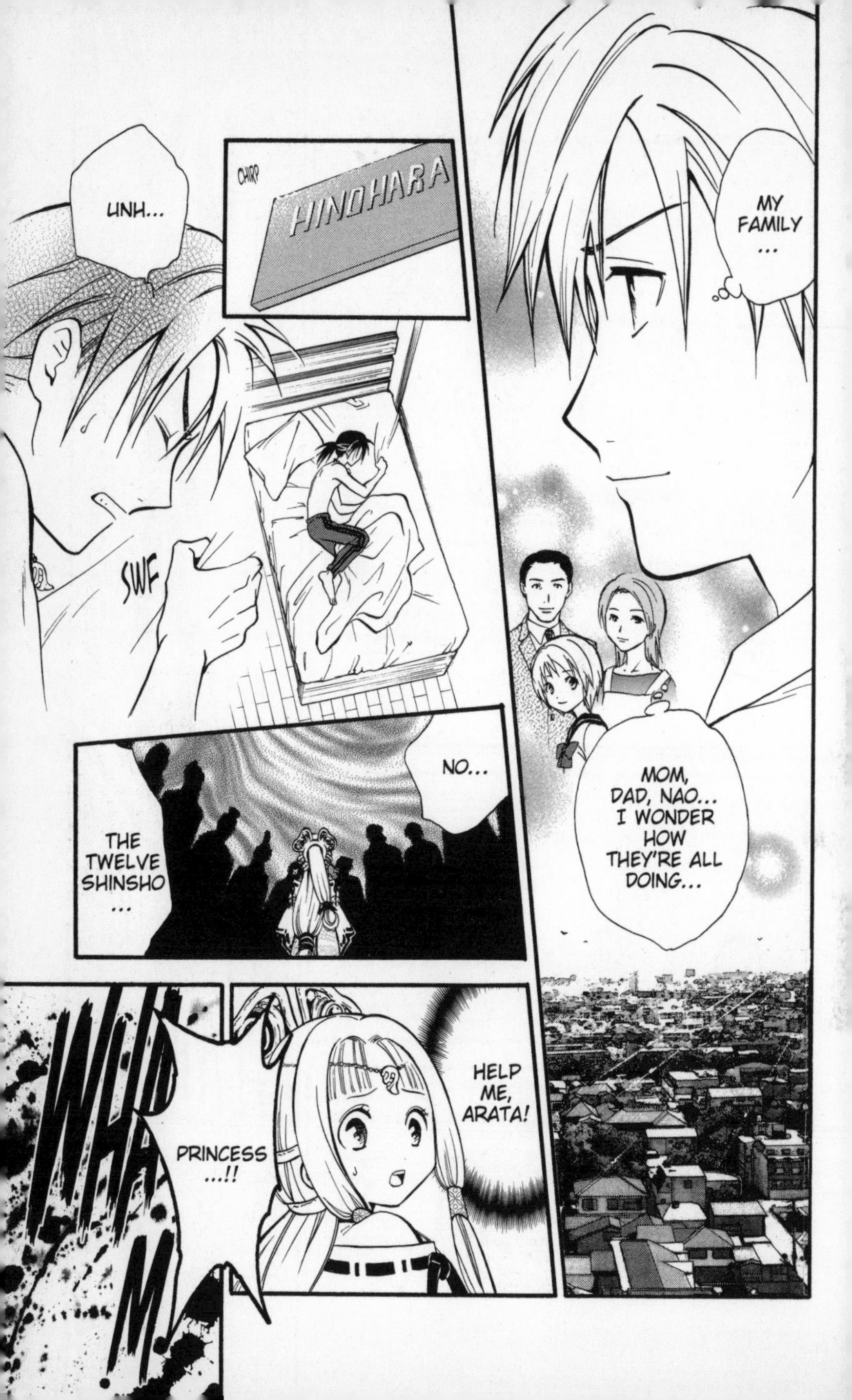
MY FAMILY...
MOM, DAD, NAO... I WONDER HOW THEY'RE ALL DOING...
CHIRP
HINOHARA
UNH...
SWF
NO...
THE TWELVE SHINSHO...
HELP ME, ARATA!
PRINCESS...!!

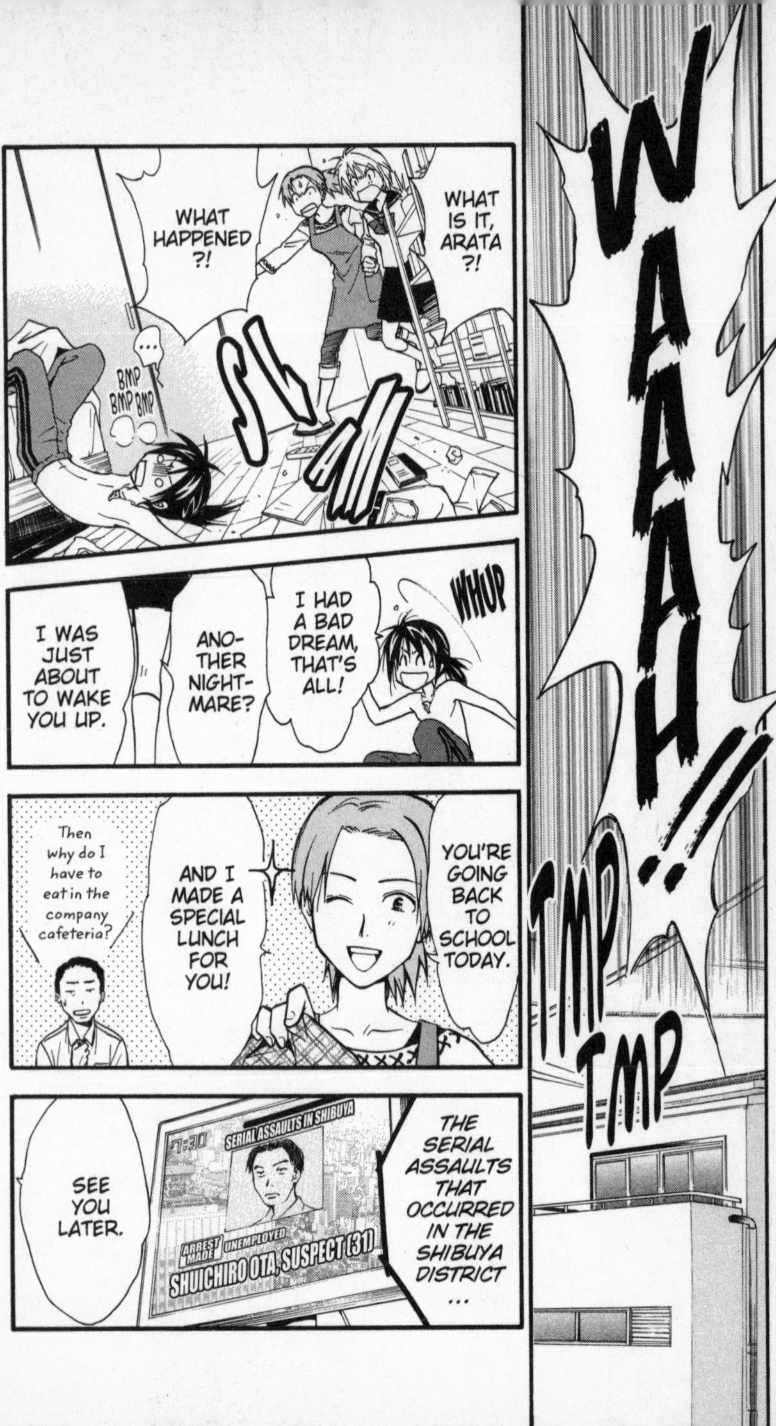
WAAAH!!
TMP TMP
WHAT IS IT, ARATA?!
WHAT HAPPENED?!
SLAM
...
BMP BMP BMP
WHUP
I HAD A BAD DREAM, THAT'S ALL!
ANOTHER NIGHTMARE?
I WAS JUST ABOUT TO WAKE YOU UP.
YOU'RE GOING BACK TO SCHOOL TODAY.
AND I MADE A SPECIAL LUNCH FOR YOU!
Then why do I have to eat in the company cafeteria?
THE SERIAL ASSAULTS THAT OCCURRED IN THE SHIBUYA DISTRICT...
SERIAL ASSAULTS IN SHIBUYA
7:30
ARREST MADE
UNEMPLOYED
SHUICHIRO OTA, SUSPECT (31)
SEE YOU LATER.

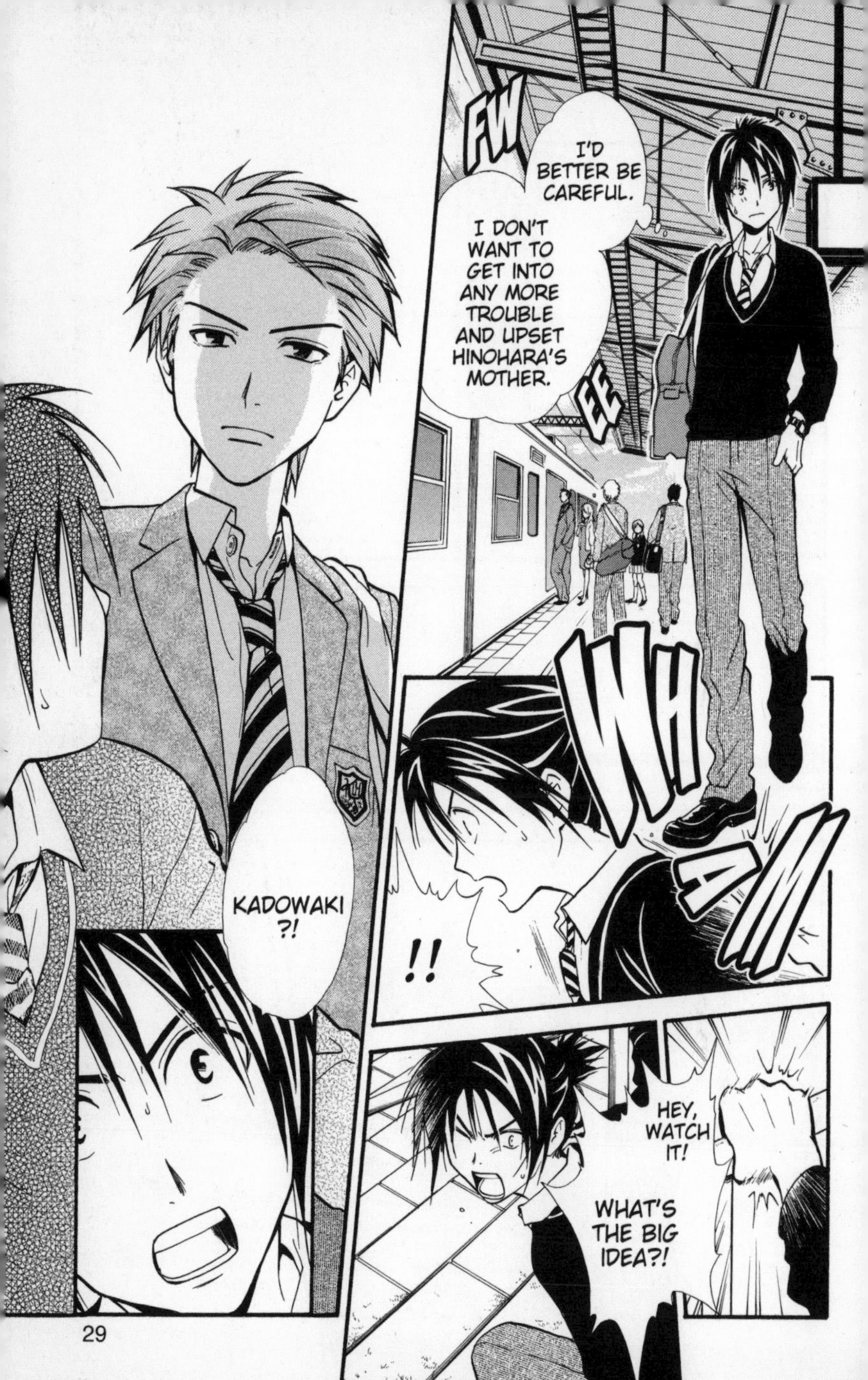
FW
I'D BETTER BE CAREFUL.
I DON'T WANT TO GET INTO ANY MORE TROUBLE AND UPSET HINOHARA'S MOTHER.
EE
WHAM
!!
HEY, WATCH IT!
WHAT'S THE BIG IDEA?!
KADOWAKI ?!

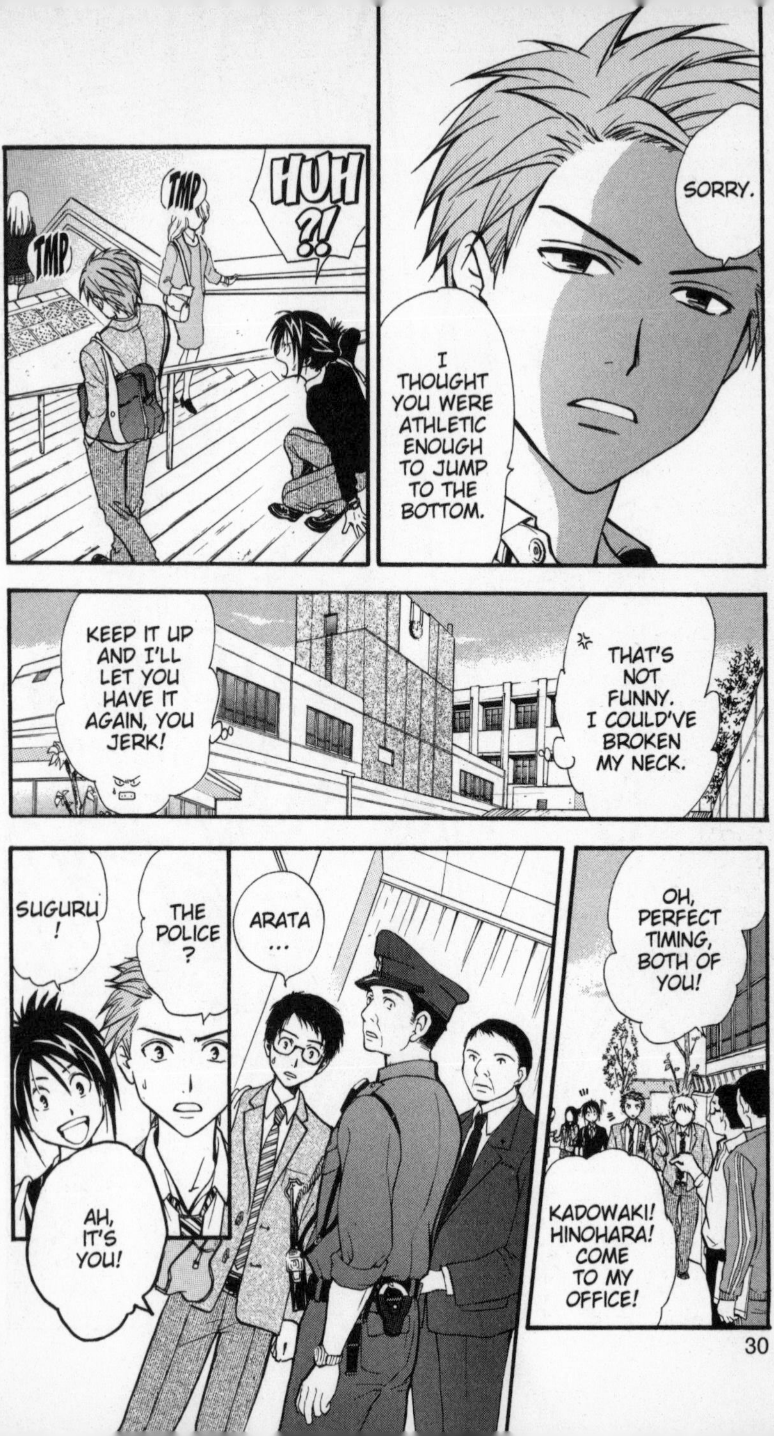
SORRY.
I THOUGHT YOU WERE ATHLETIC ENOUGH TO JUMP TO THE BOTTOM.
HUH ?!
TMP
TMP
THAT'S NOT FUNNY. I COULD'VE BROKEN MY NECK.
KEEP IT UP AND I'LL LET YOU HAVE IT AGAIN, YOU JERK!
OH, PERFECT TIMING, BOTH OF YOU!
KADOWAKI! HINOHARA! COME TO MY OFFICE!
ARATA...
THE POLICE?
SUGURU!
AH, IT'S YOU!

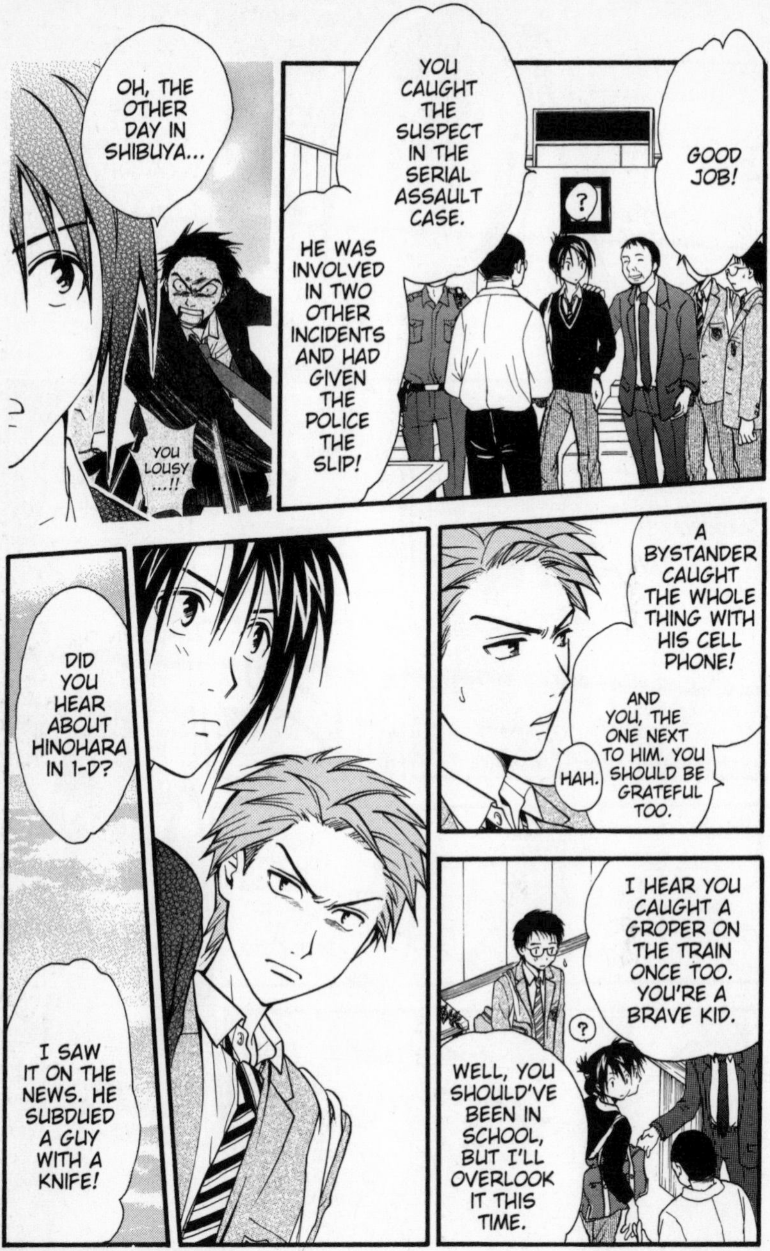
GOOD JOB!
YOU CAUGHT THE SUSPECT IN THE SERIAL ASSAULT CASE.
HE WAS INVOLVED IN TWO OTHER INCIDENTS AND HAD GIVEN THE POLICE THE SLIP!
?
OH, THE OTHER DAY IN SHIBUYA...
YOU LOUSY ...!!
A BYSTANDER CAUGHT THE WHOLE THING WITH HIS CELL PHONE!
AND YOU, THE ONE NEXT TO HIM. YOU SHOULD BE GRATEFUL TOO.
HAH.
I HEAR YOU CAUGHT A GROPER ON THE TRAIN ONCE TOO. YOU'RE A BRAVE KID.
?
WELL, YOU SHOULD'VE BEEN IN SCHOOL, BUT I'LL OVERLOOK IT THIS TIME.
DID YOU HEAR ABOUT HINOHARA IN 1-D?
I SAW IT ON THE NEWS. HE SUBDUED A GUY WITH A KNIFE!

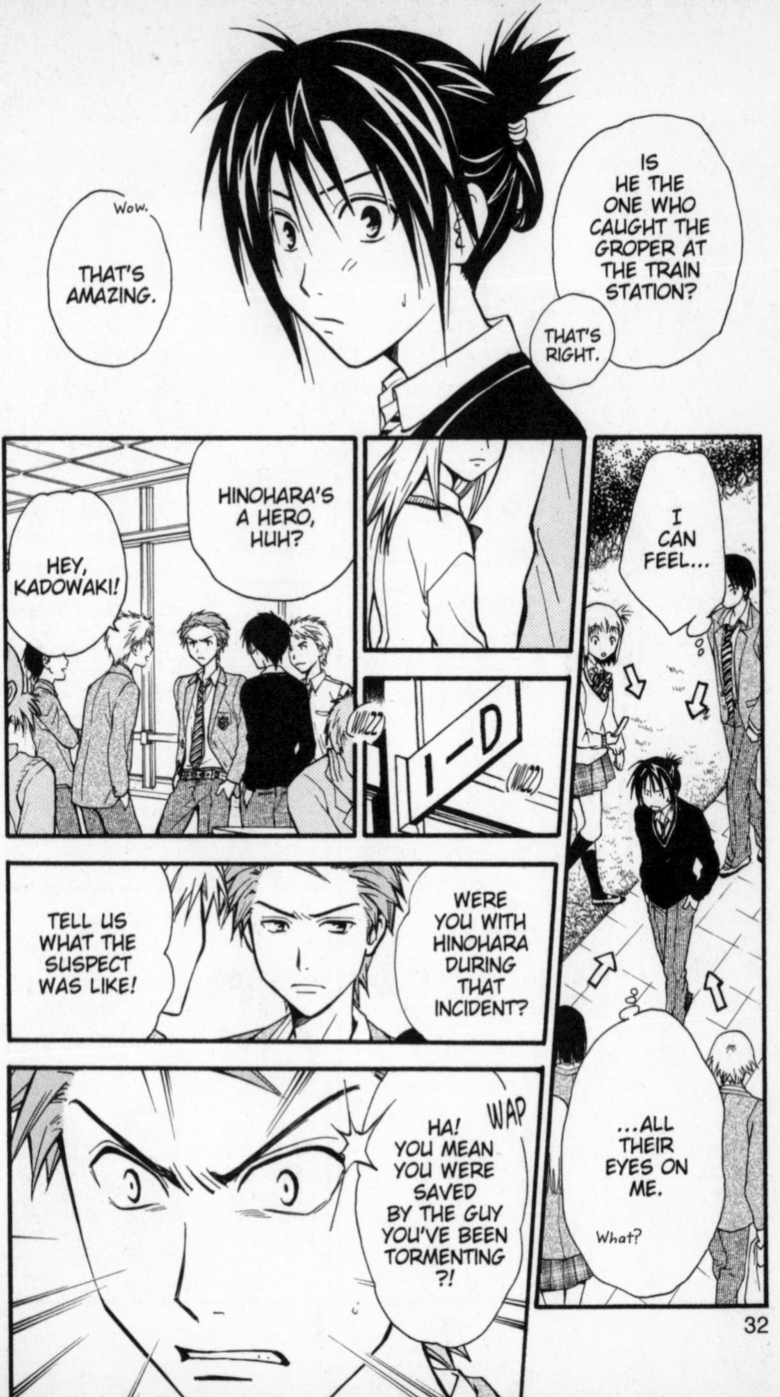
IS HE THE ONE WHO CAUGHT THE GROPER AT THE TRAIN STATION?
THAT'S RIGHT.
Wow.
THAT'S AMAZING.
I CAN FEEL...
...ALL THEIR EYES ON ME.
What?
(WHIZZ)
I-D
(WHIZZ)
HINOHARA'S A HERO, HUH?
HEY, KADOWAKI!
WERE YOU WITH HINOHARA DURING THAT INCIDENT?
TELL US WHAT THE SUSPECT WAS LIKE!
WAP
HA! YOU MEAN YOU WERE SAVED BY THE GUY YOU'VE BEEN TORMENTING ?!

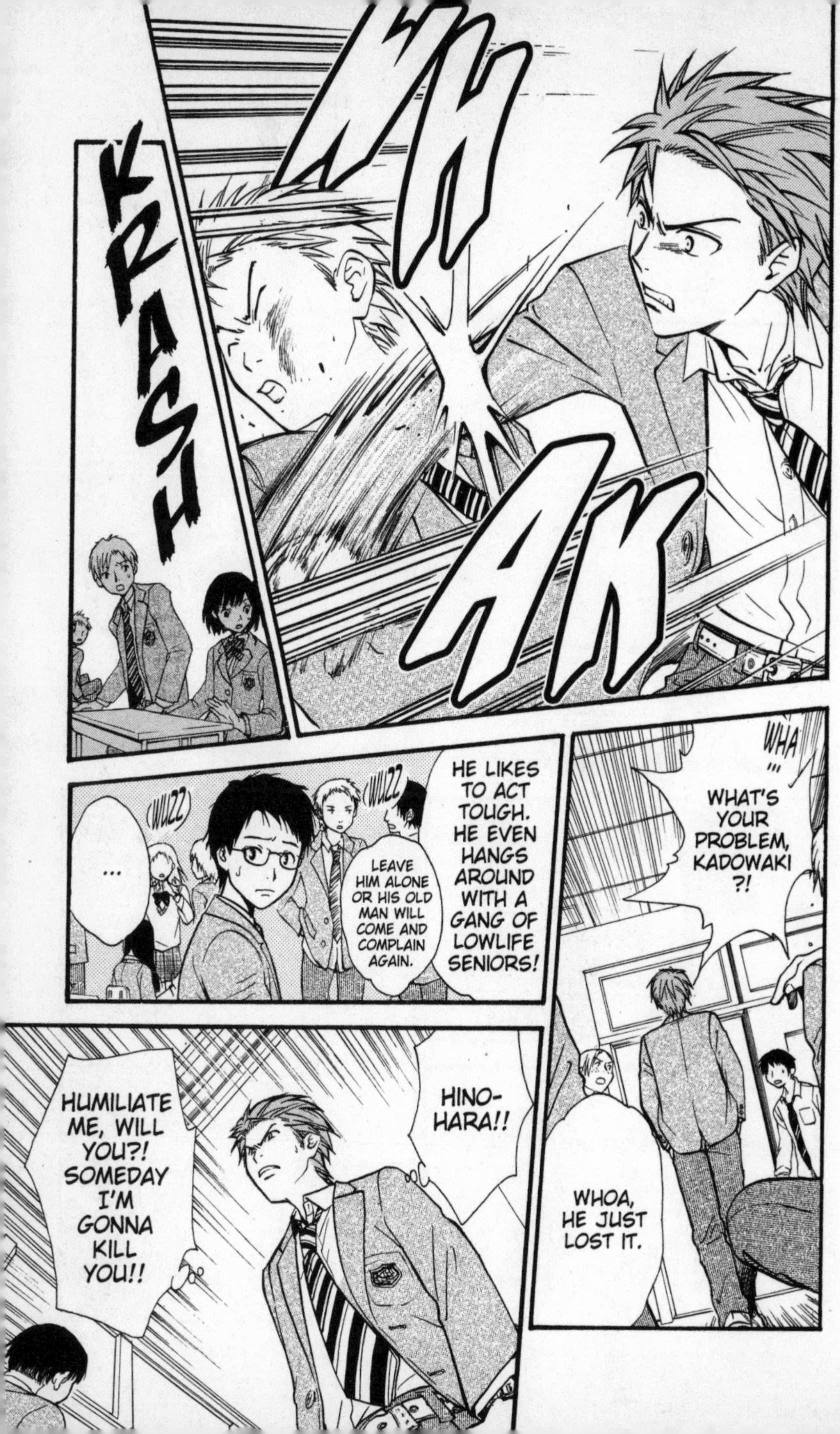
WHA
AK
KRASH
WHA ...
WHAT'S YOUR PROBLEM, KADOWAKI?!
WHOA, HE JUST LOST IT.
HE LIKES TO ACT TOUGH. HE EVEN HANGS AROUND WITH A GANG OF LOWLIFE SENIORS!
(WUZZ)
LEAVE HIM ALONE OR HIS OLD MAN WILL COME AND COMPLAIN AGAIN.
(WUZZ)
...
HINO-HARA!!
HUMILIATE ME, WILL YOU?! SOMEDAY I'M GONNA KILL YOU!!

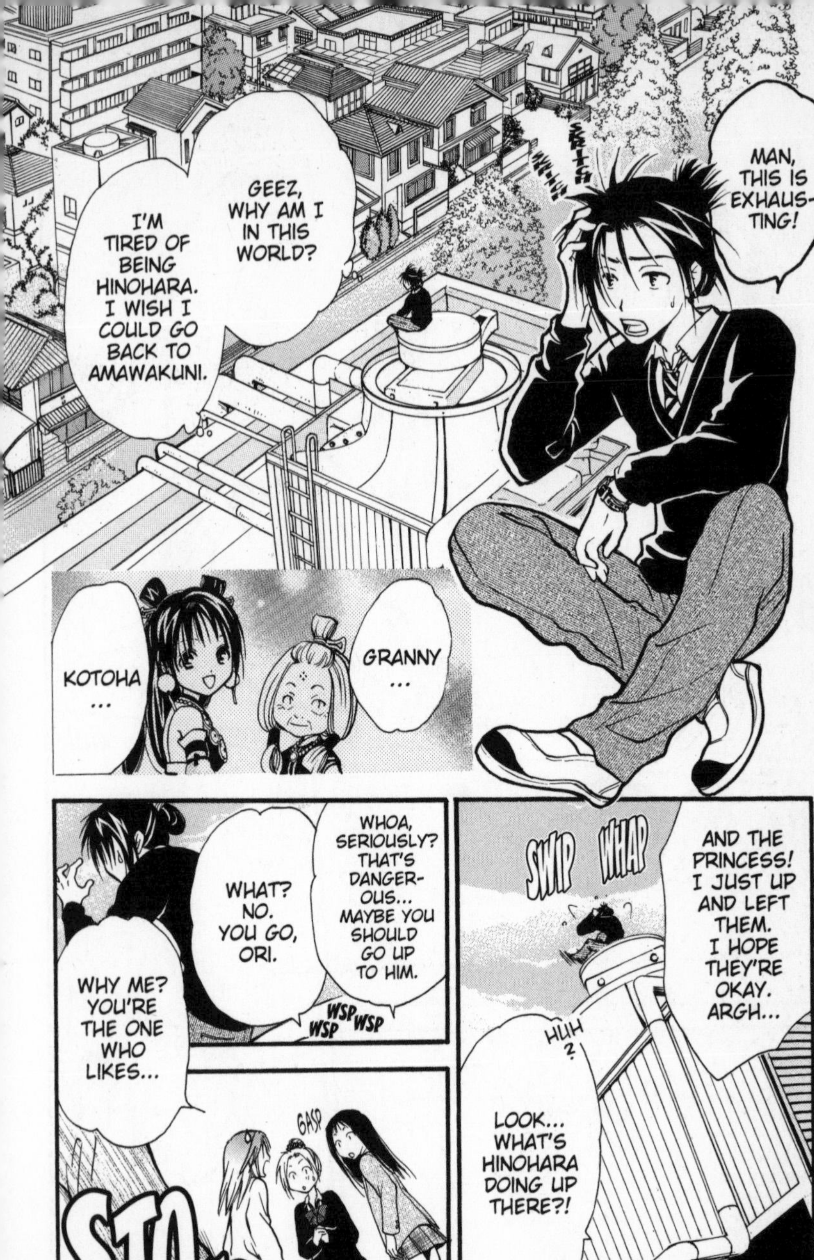
MAN, THIS IS EXHAUS-TING!
SKRITCH
GEEZ, WHY AM I IN THIS WORLD?
I'M TIRED OF BEING HINOHARA. I WISH I COULD GO BACK TO AMAWAKUNI.
GRANNY...
KOTOHA...
SWIP
WHAP
AND THE PRINCESS! I JUST UP AND LEFT THEM. I HOPE THEY'RE OKAY. ARGH...
HUH?
LOOK... WHAT'S HINOHARA DOING UP THERE?!
WHOA, SERIOUSLY? THAT'S DANGER-OUS... MAYBE YOU SHOULD GO UP TO HIM.
WHAT? NO. YOU GO, ORI.
WSP WSP WSP
WHY ME? YOU'RE THE ONE WHO LIKES...
GASP
STOMP

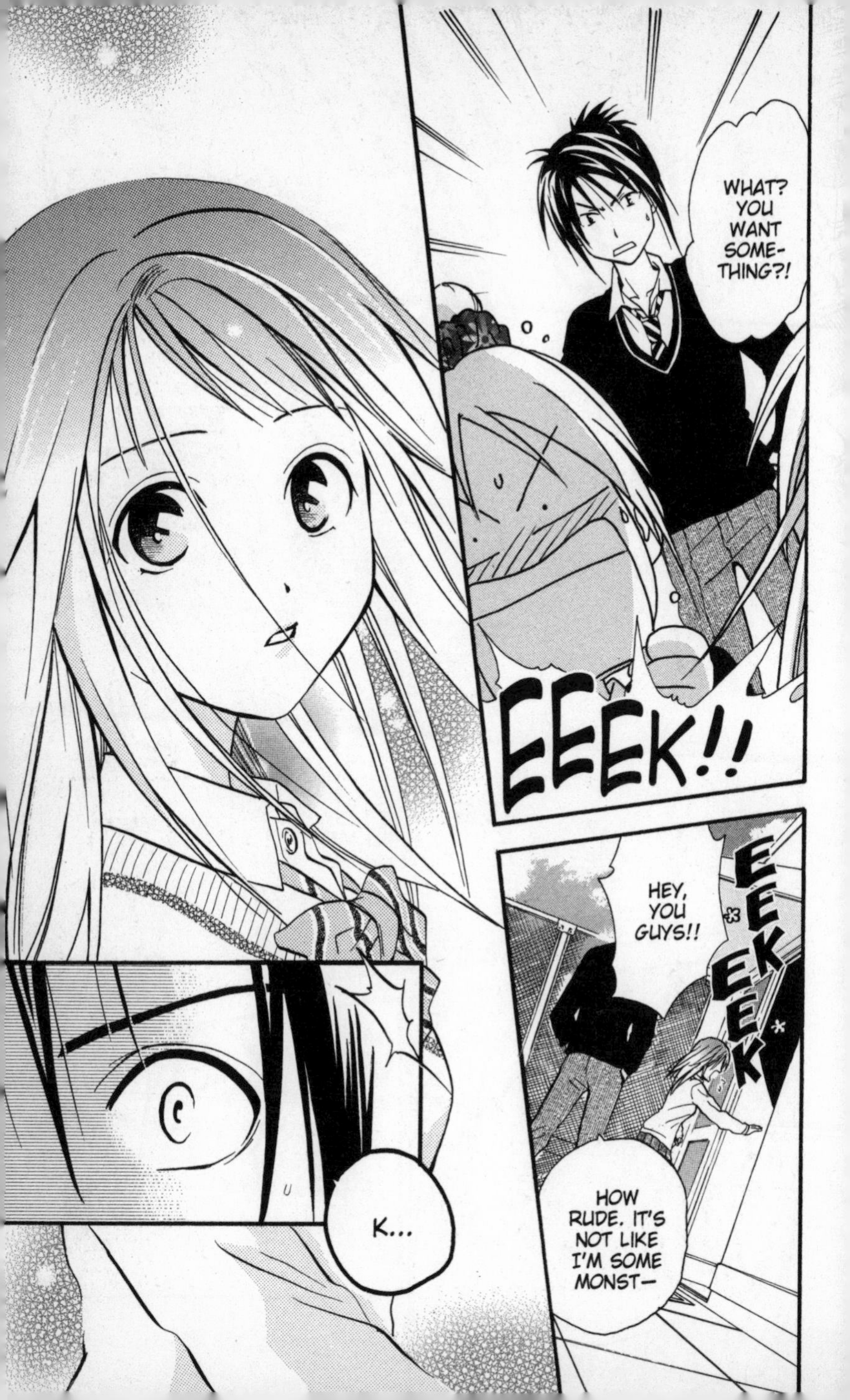
WHAT? YOU WANT SOMETHING?!
EEEK!!
HEY, YOU GUYS!!
EEK EEK EEK
HOW RUDE. IT'S NOT LIKE I'M SOME MONST—
K...

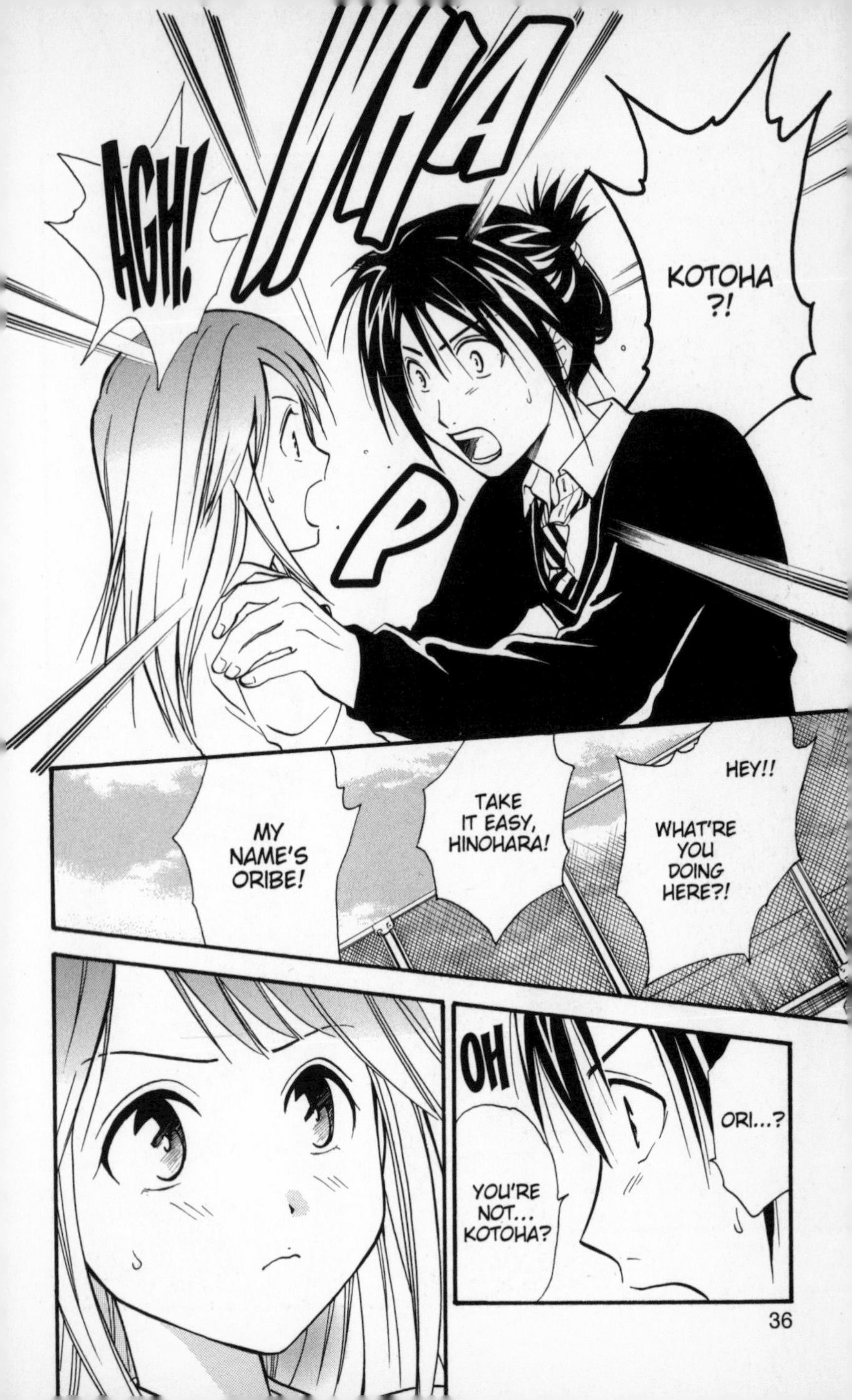
KOTOHA ?!
WHA
P
AGH!
HEY!!
WHAT'RE YOU DOING HERE?!
TAKE IT EASY, HINOHARA!
MY NAME'S ORIBE!
ORI...?
YOU'RE NOT... KOTOHA?
OH

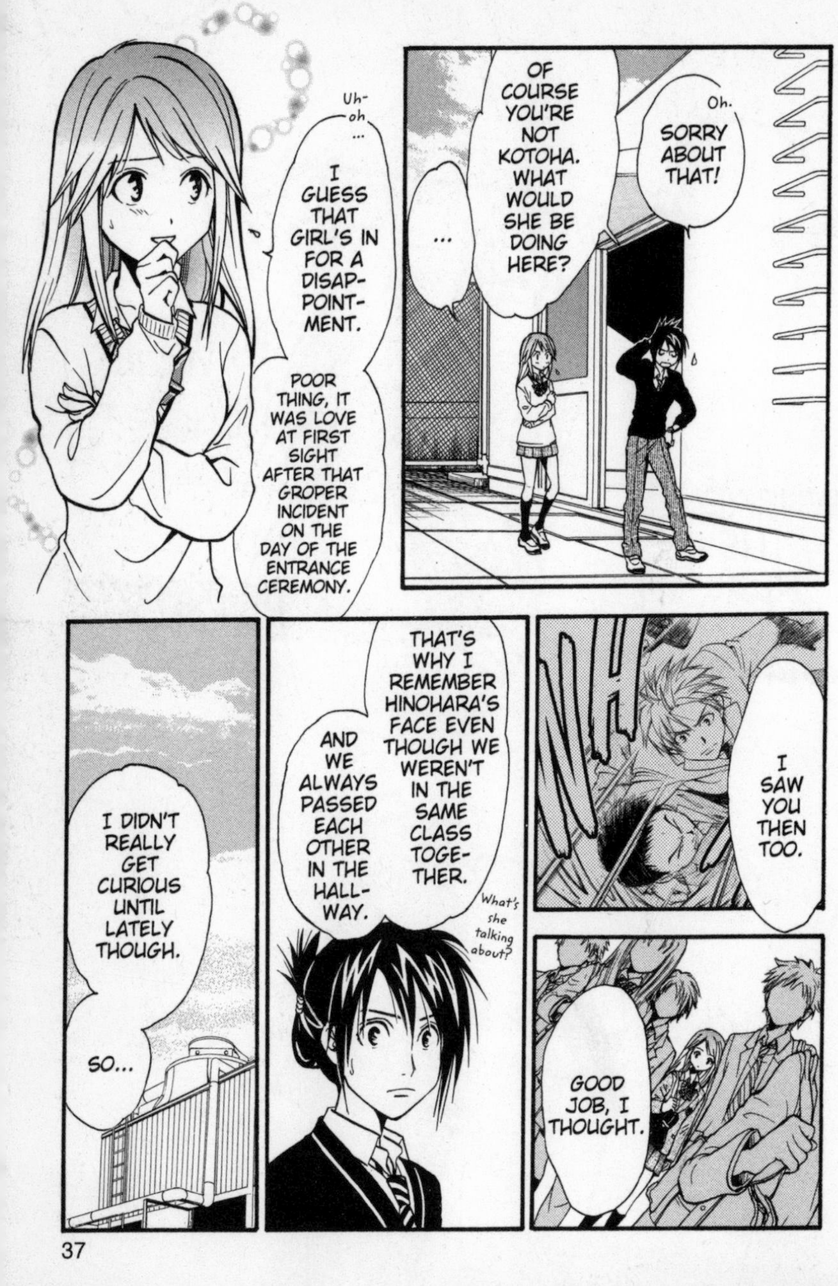
Oh.
SORRY ABOUT THAT!
OF COURSE YOU'RE NOT KOTOHA. WHAT WOULD SHE BE DOING HERE?
...
Uh-oh...
I GUESS THAT GIRL'S IN FOR A DISAPPOINTMENT.
POOR THING, IT WAS LOVE AT FIRST SIGHT AFTER THAT GROPER INCIDENT ON THE DAY OF THE ENTRANCE CEREMONY.
I SAW YOU THEN TOO.
GOOD JOB, I THOUGHT.
THAT'S WHY I REMEMBER HINOHARA'S FACE EVEN THOUGH WE WEREN'T IN THE SAME CLASS TOGETHER.
AND WE ALWAYS PASSED EACH OTHER IN THE HALLWAY.
What's she talking about?
I DIDN'T REALLY GET CURIOUS UNTIL LATELY THOUGH.
SO...

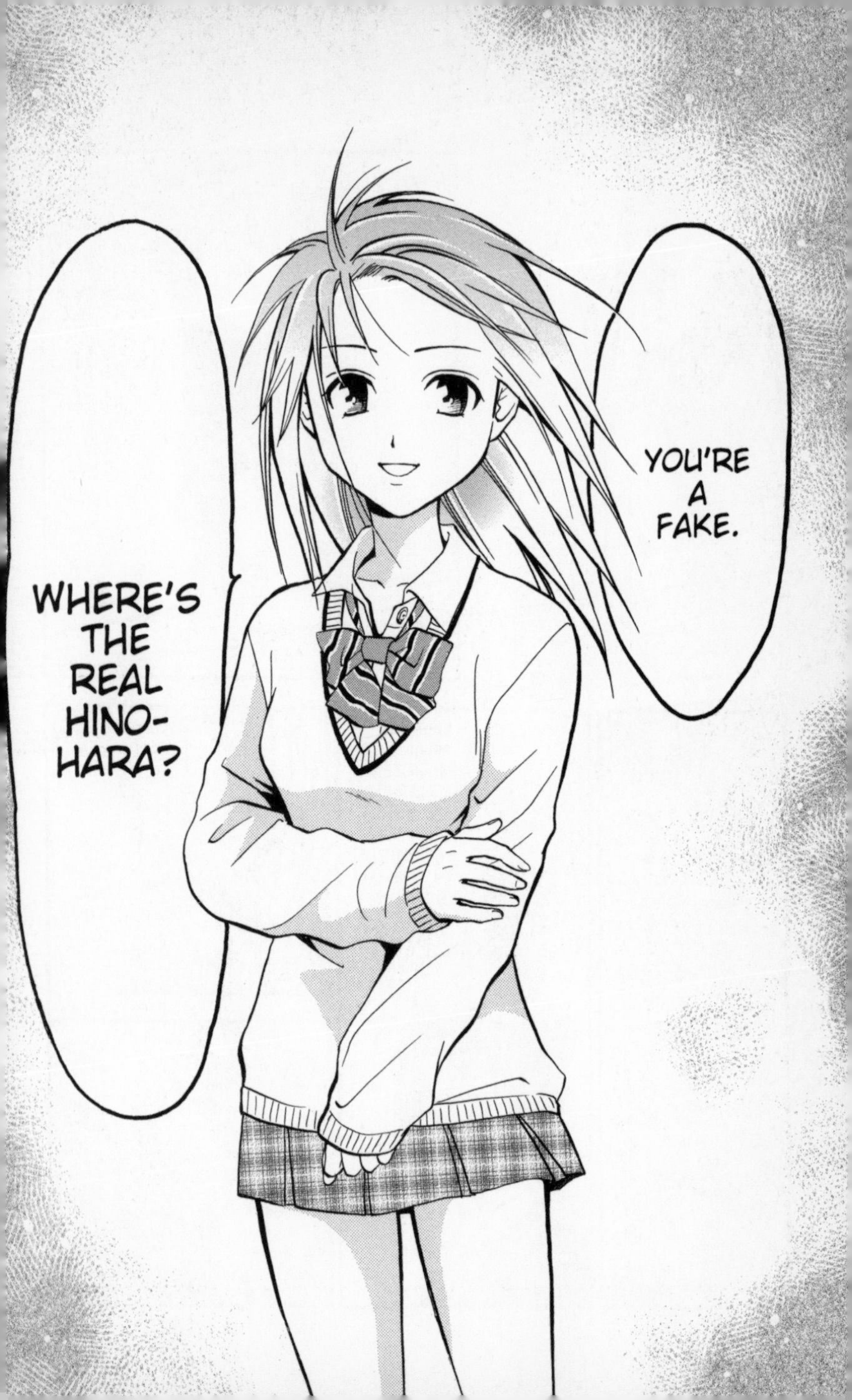
YOU'RE A FAKE.
WHERE'S THE REAL HINO-HARA?

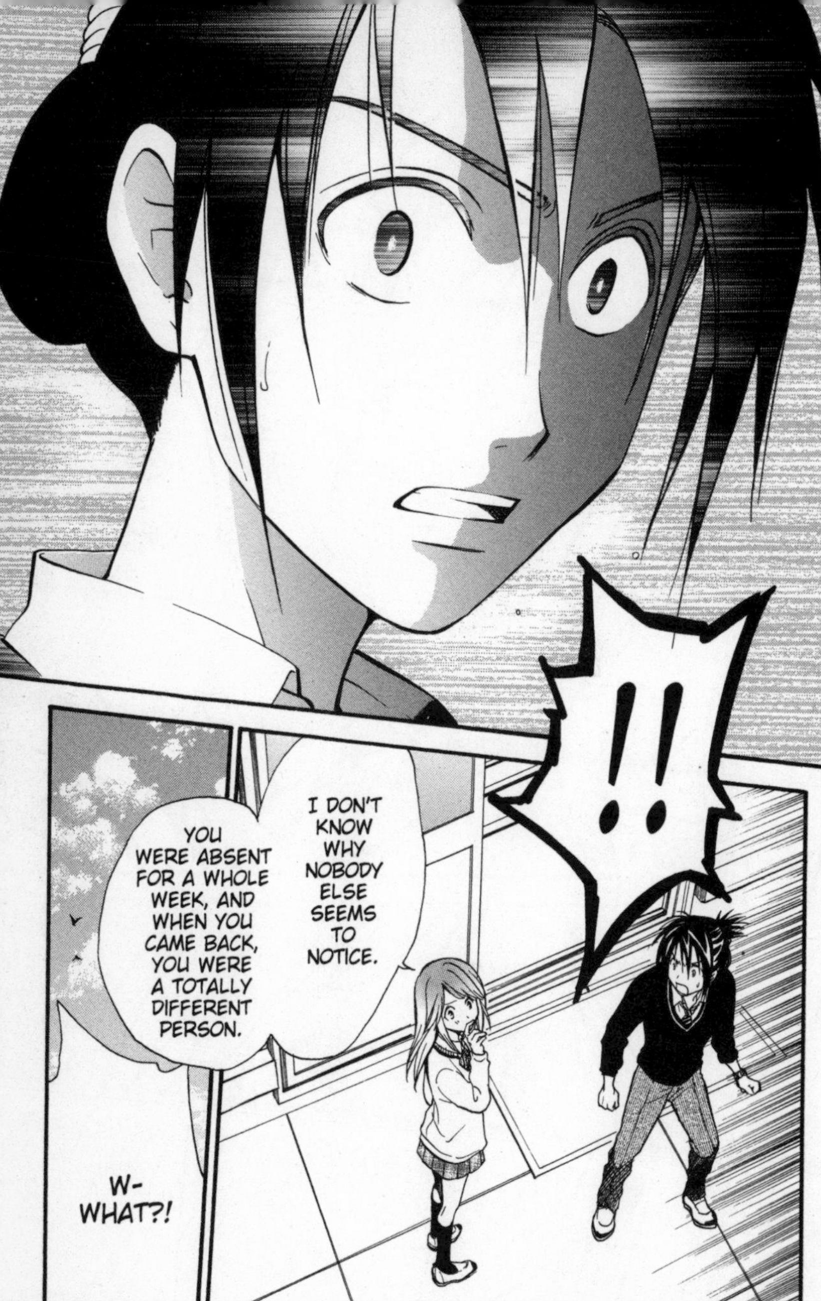
!!
I DON'T KNOW WHY NOBODY ELSE SEEMS TO NOTICE.
YOU WERE ABSENT FOR A WHOLE WEEK, AND WHEN YOU CAME BACK, YOU WERE A TOTALLY DIFFERENT PERSON.
W-WHAT?!

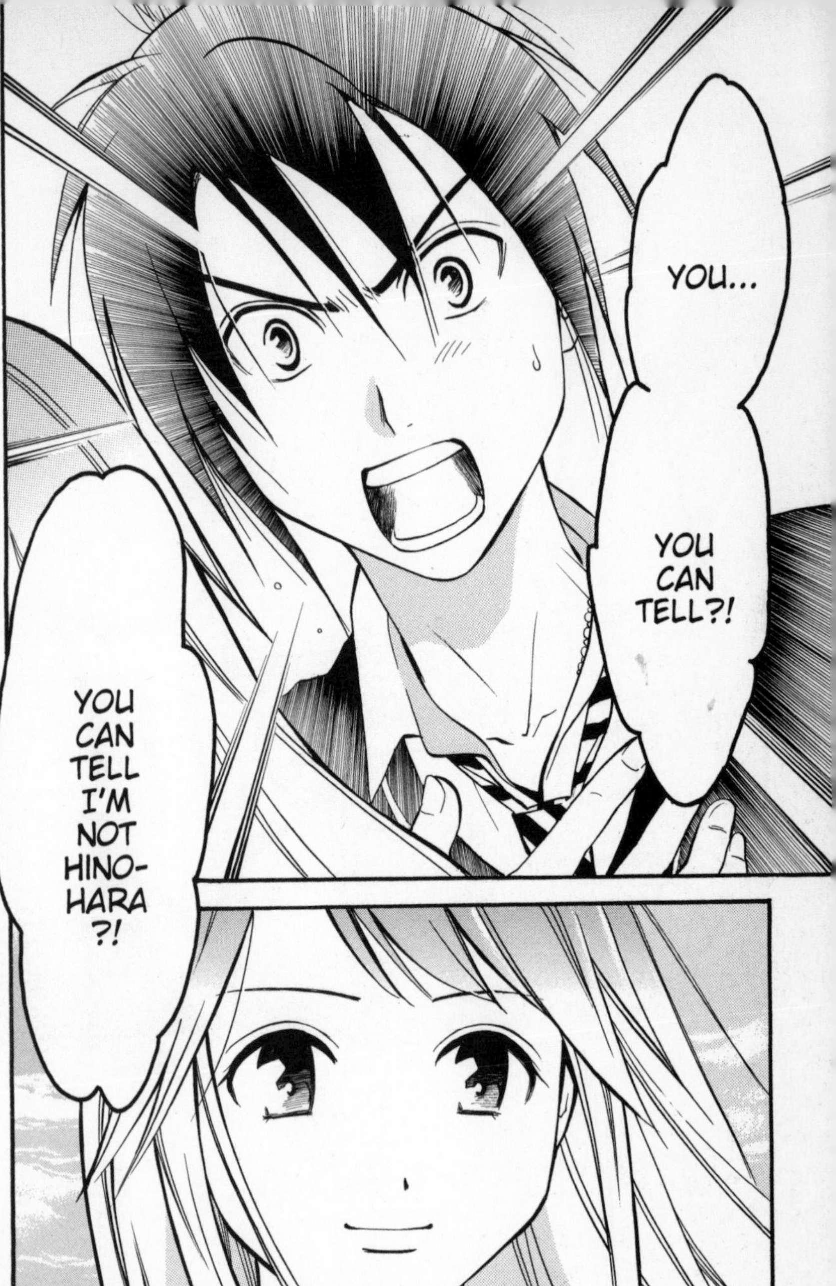
YOU...
YOU CAN TELL?!
YOU CAN TELL I'M NOT HINO-HARA?!

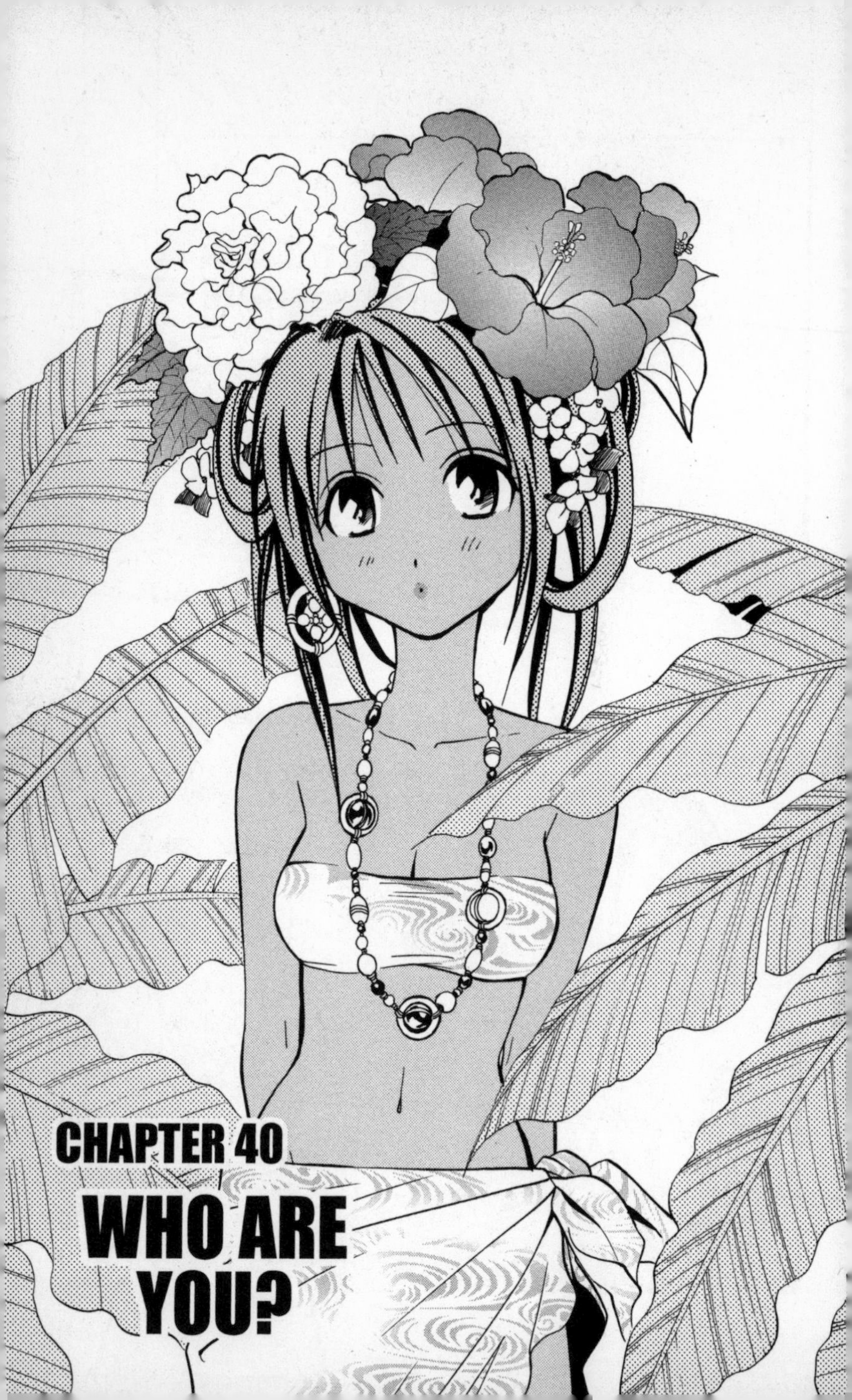
CHAPTER 40
WHO ARE YOU?

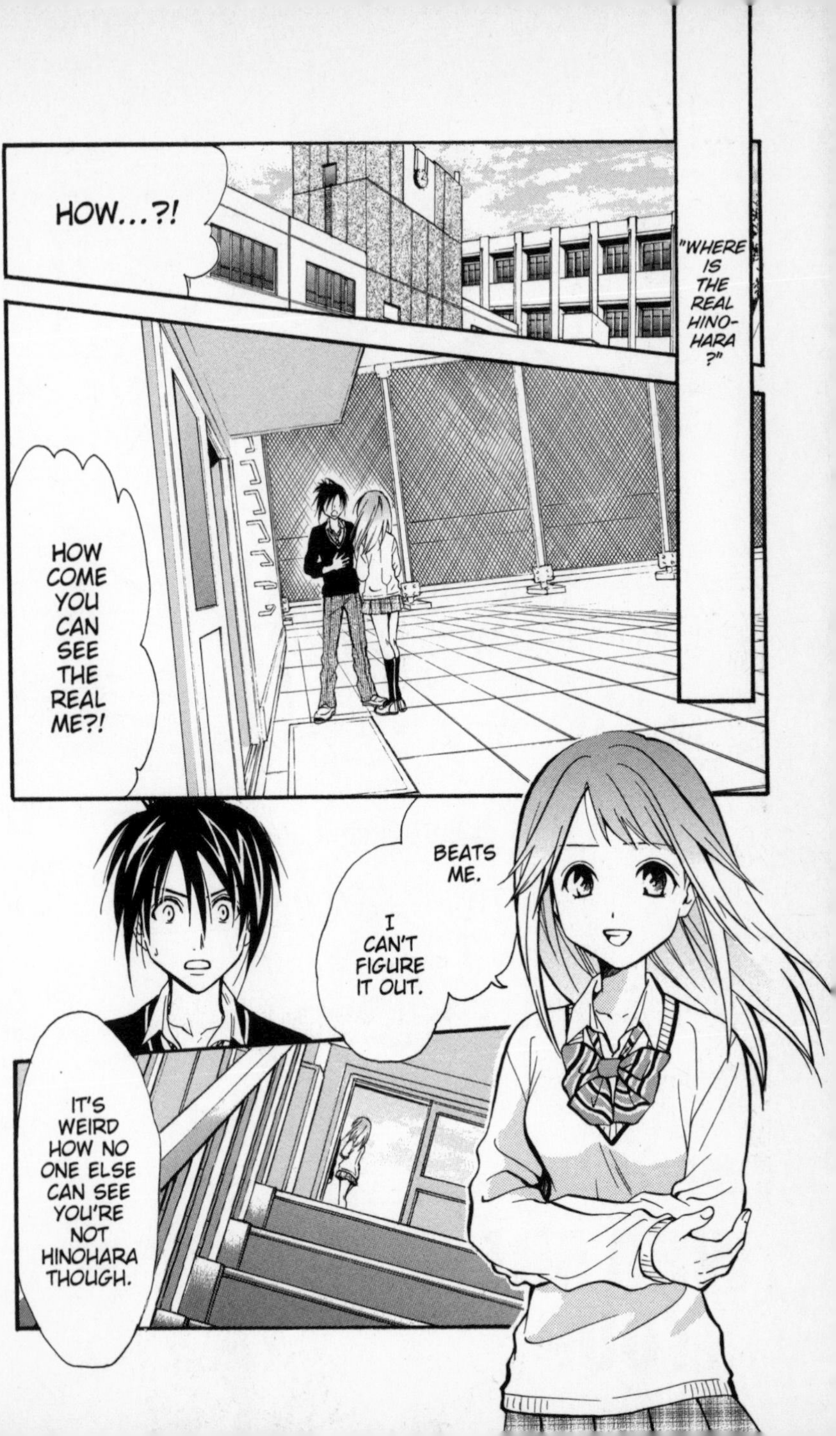
"WHERE IS THE REAL HINO-HARA?"
HOW...?!
HOW COME YOU CAN SEE THE REAL ME?!
BEATS ME.
I CAN'T FIGURE IT OUT.
IT'S WEIRD HOW NO ONE ELSE CAN SEE YOU'RE NOT HINOHARA THOUGH.

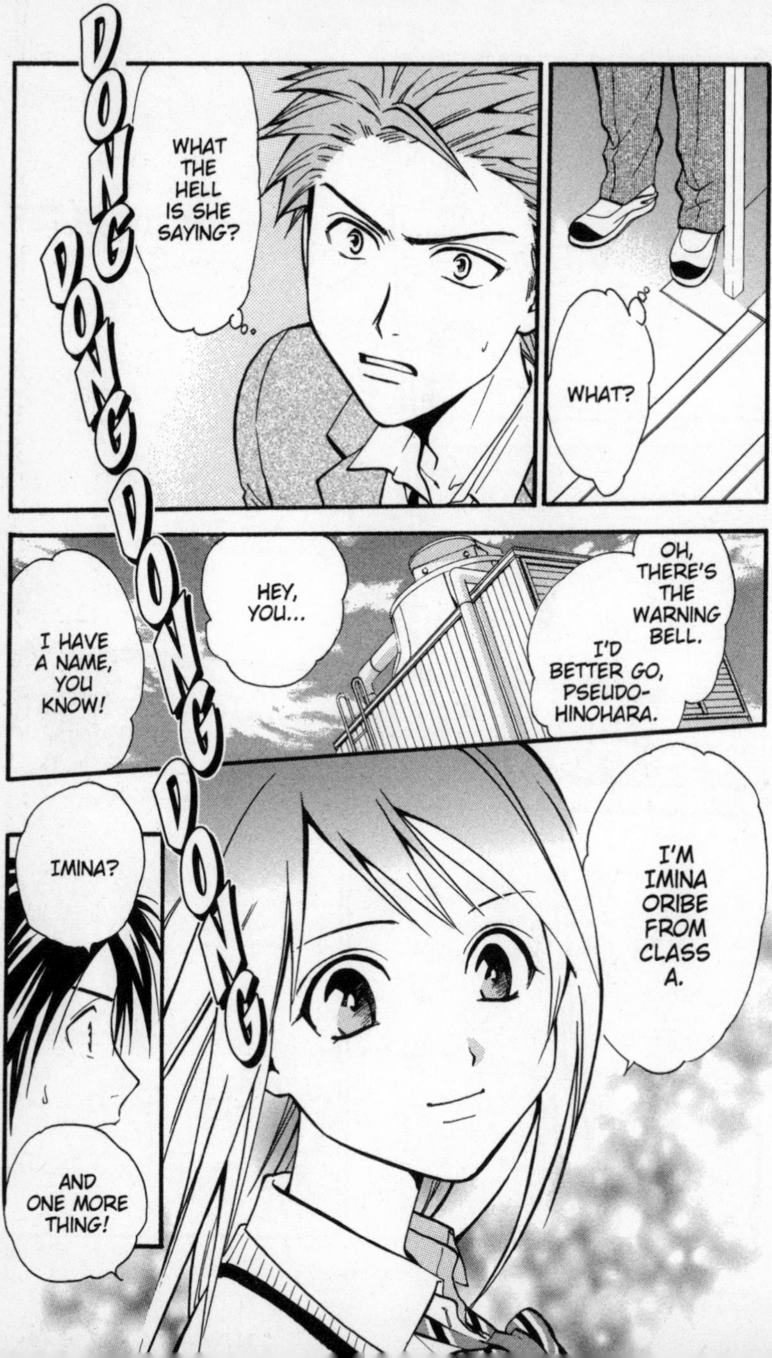
WHAT?
WHAT THE HELL IS SHE SAYING?
DONG DONG DONG DONG DONG
OH, THERE'S THE WARNING BELL.
I'D BETTER GO, PSEUDO-HINOHARA.
HEY, YOU...
I HAVE A NAME, YOU KNOW!
I'M IMINA ORIBE FROM CLASS A.
IMINA?
AND ONE MORE THING!

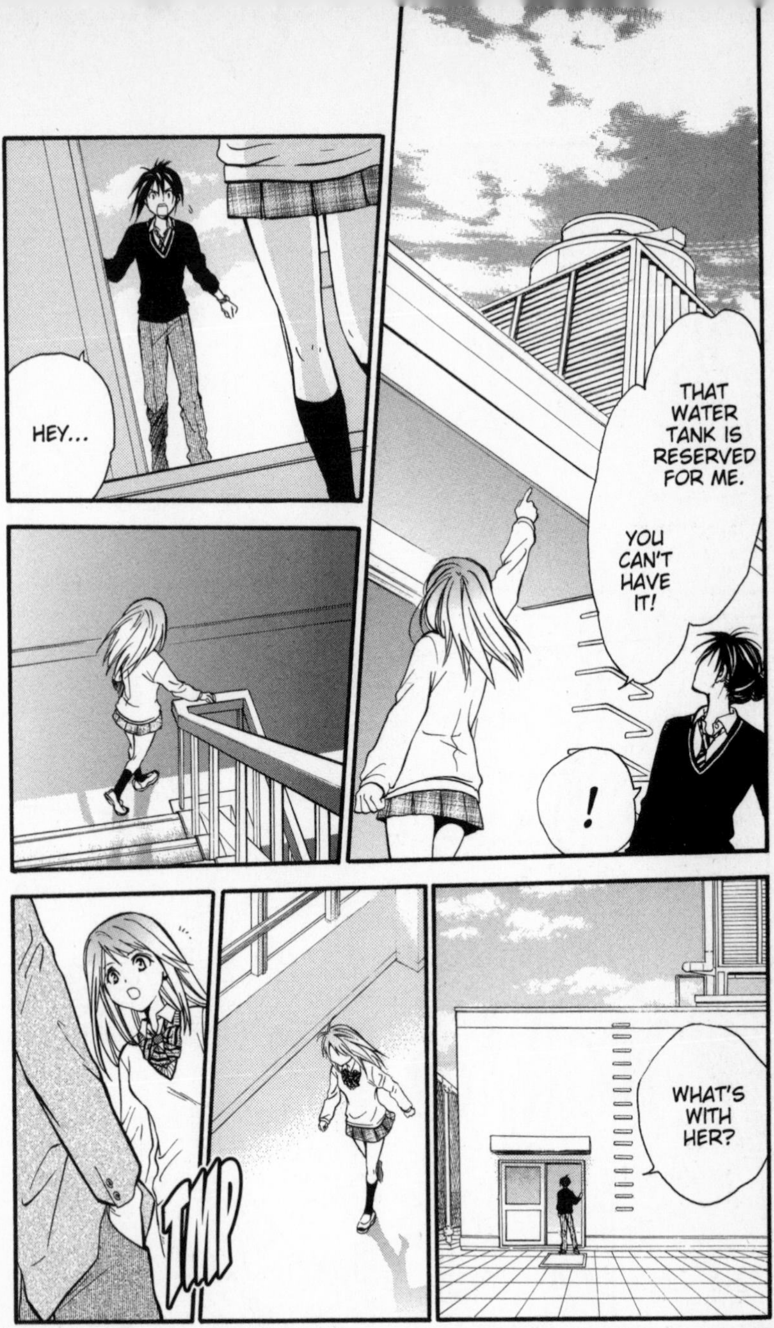
THAT WATER TANK IS RESERVED FOR ME.
YOU CAN'T HAVE IT!
!
HEY...
WHAT'S WITH HER?
TMP

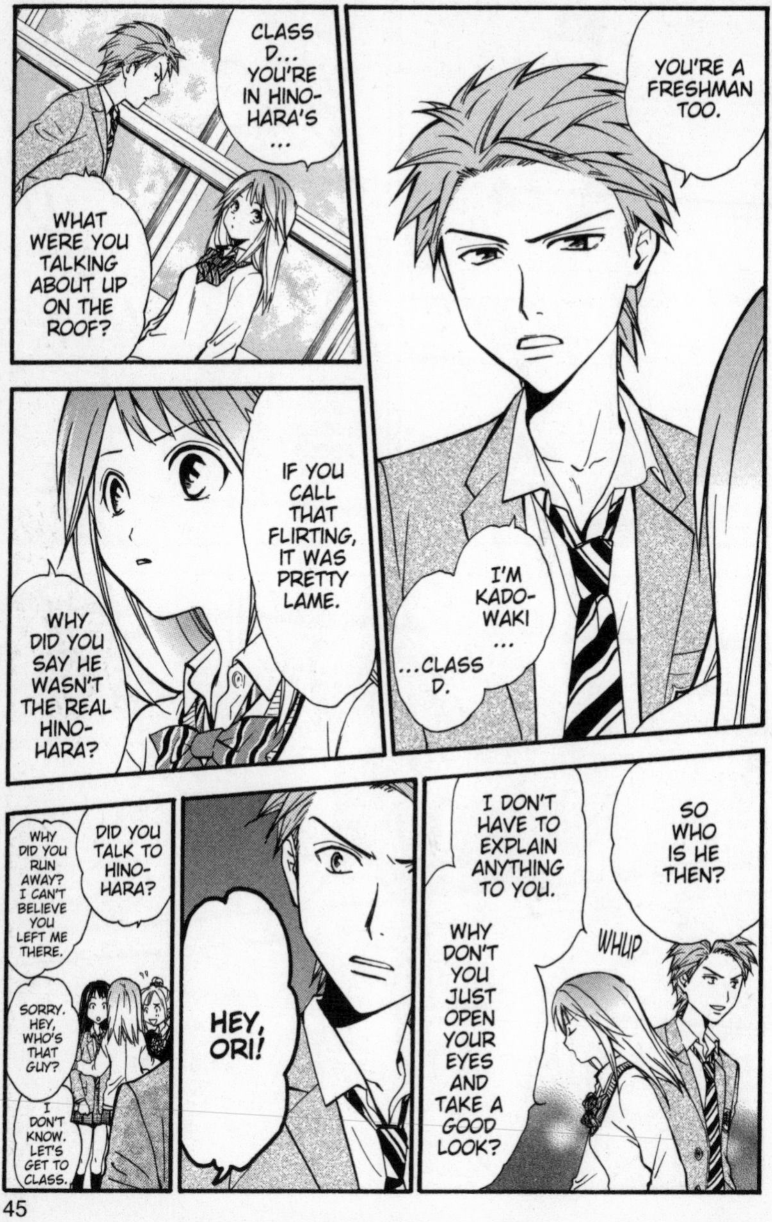

YOU'RE A FRESHMAN TOO.
I'M KADO-WAKI...
...CLASS D.
CLASS D... YOU'RE IN HINO-HARA'S...
WHAT WERE YOU TALKING ABOUT UP ON THE ROOF?
IF YOU CALL THAT FLIRTING, IT WAS PRETTY LAME.
WHY DID YOU SAY HE WASN'T THE REAL HINO-HARA?
SO WHO IS HE THEN?
WHUP
I DON'T HAVE TO EXPLAIN ANYTHING TO YOU.
WHY DON'T YOU JUST OPEN YOUR EYES AND TAKE A GOOD LOOK?
HEY, ORI!
DID YOU TALK TO HINO-HARA?
WHY DID YOU RUN AWAY? I CAN'T BELIEVE YOU LEFT ME THERE.
SORRY. HEY, WHO'S THAT GUY?
I DON'T KNOW. LET'S GET TO CLASS.

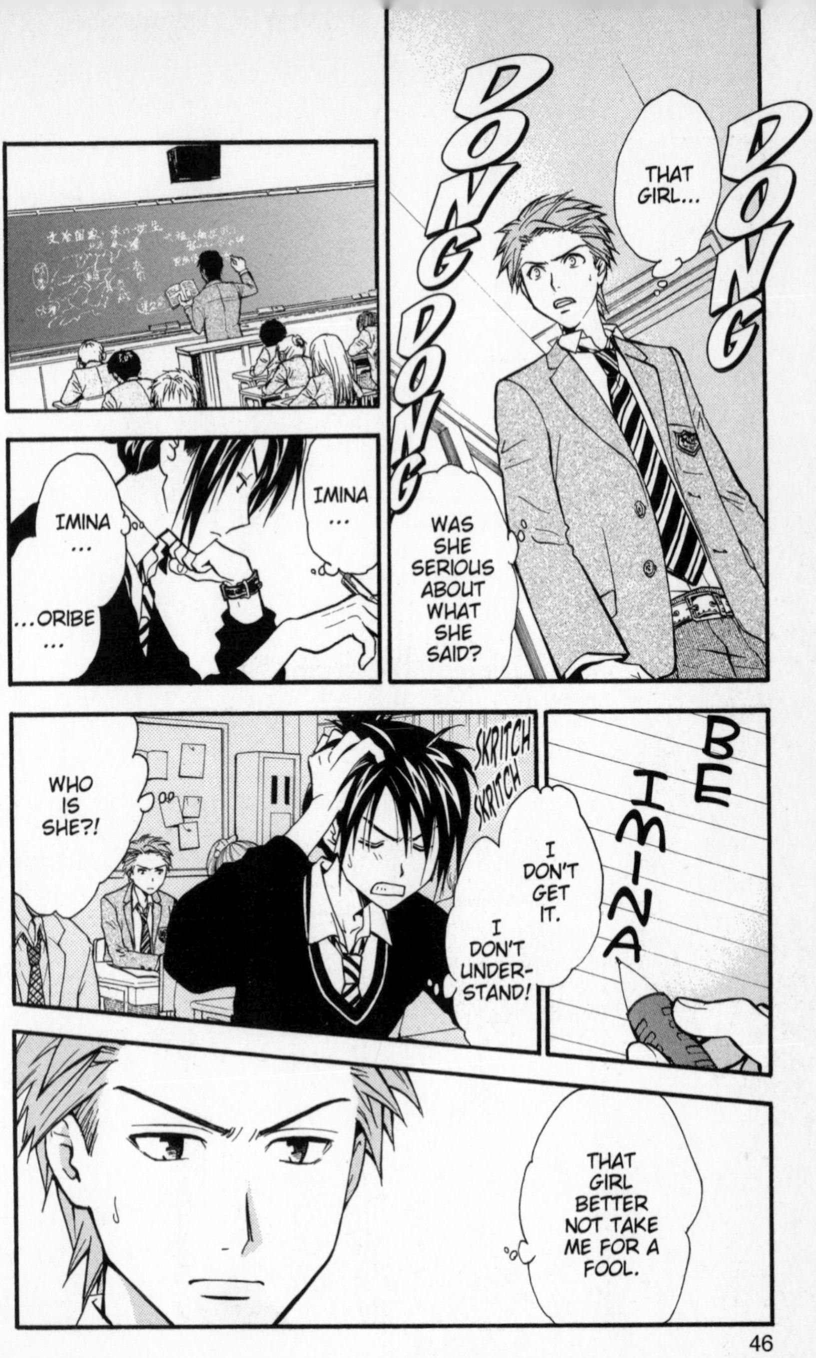
DONG
THAT GIRL...
DONG
DONG
DONG
WAS SHE SERIOUS ABOUT WHAT SHE SAID?
IMINA ...
IMINA ...
...ORIBE ...
BE IMINA
SKRITCH
SKRITCH
I DON'T GET IT.
I DON'T UNDERSTAND!
WHO IS SHE?!
THAT GIRL BETTER NOT TAKE ME FOR A FOOL.

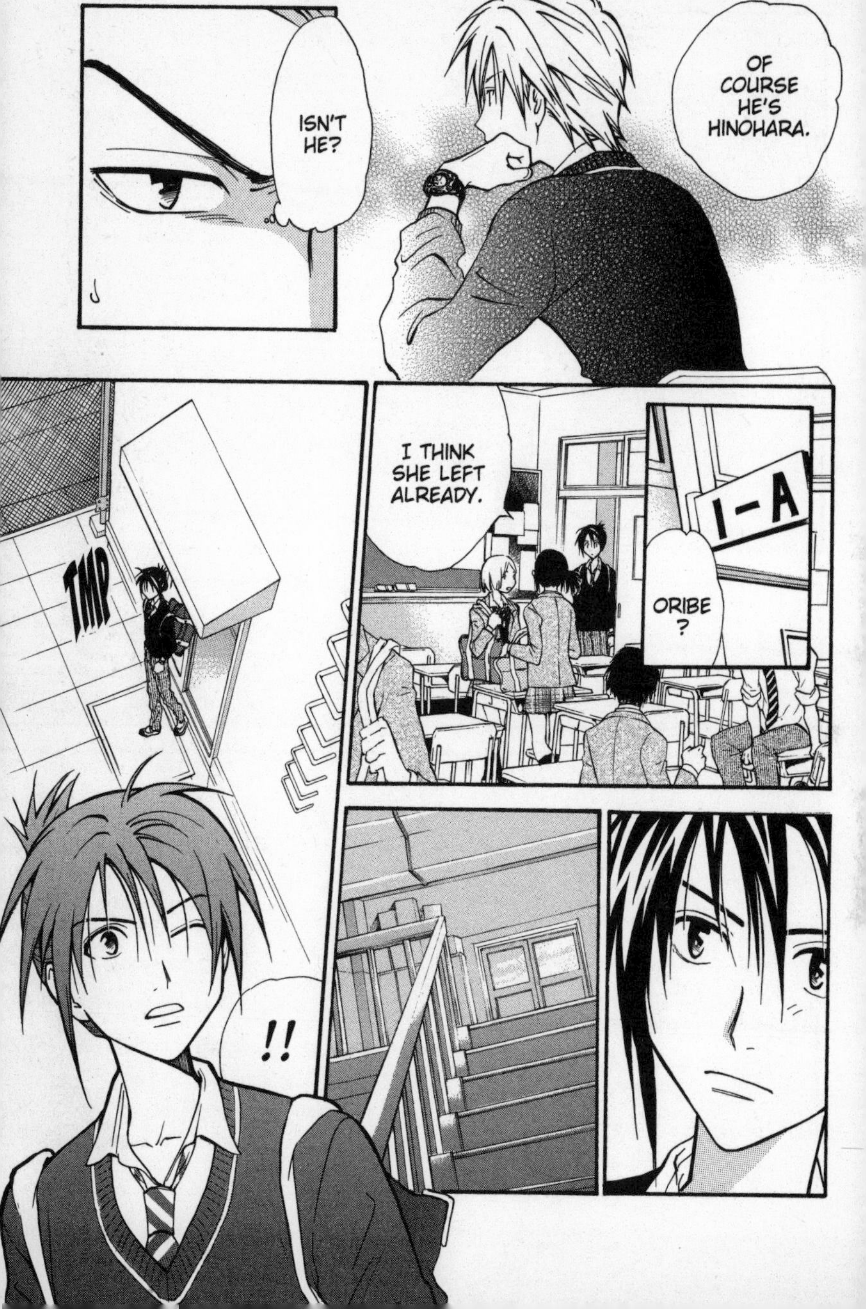
OF COURSE HE'S HINOHARA.
ISN'T HE?
ORIBE?
I THINK SHE LEFT ALREADY.
TMP
!!

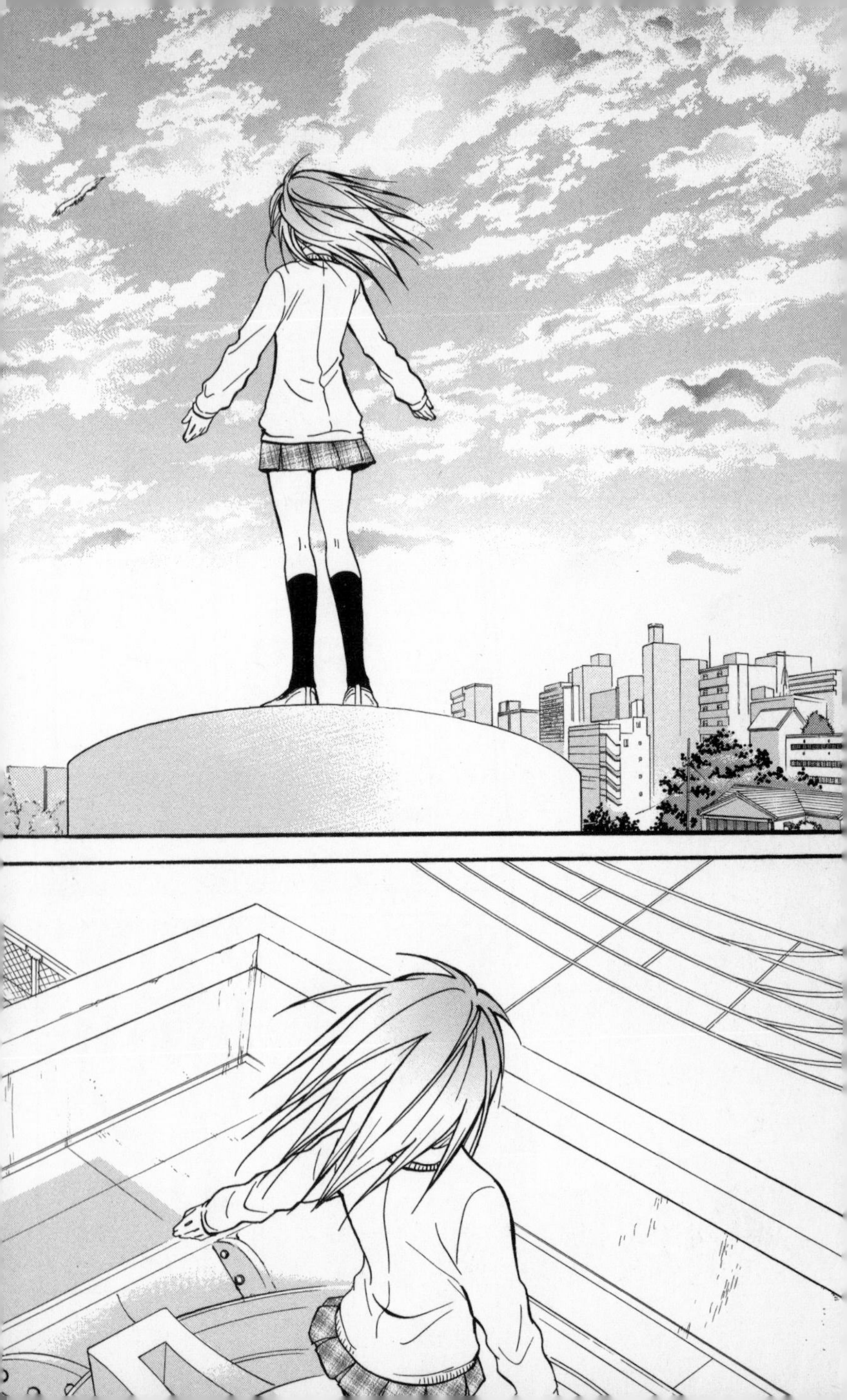

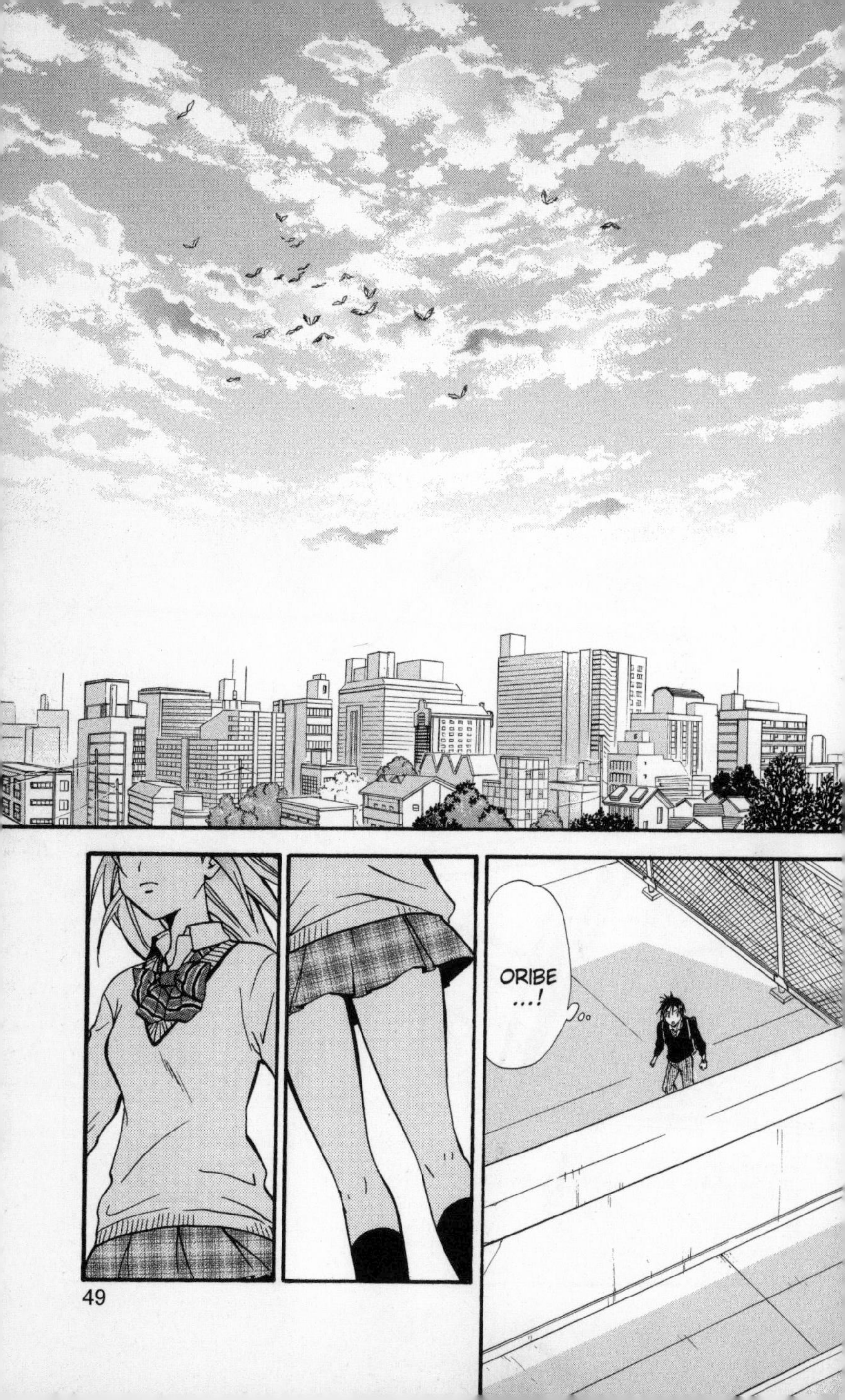
ORIBE ...!

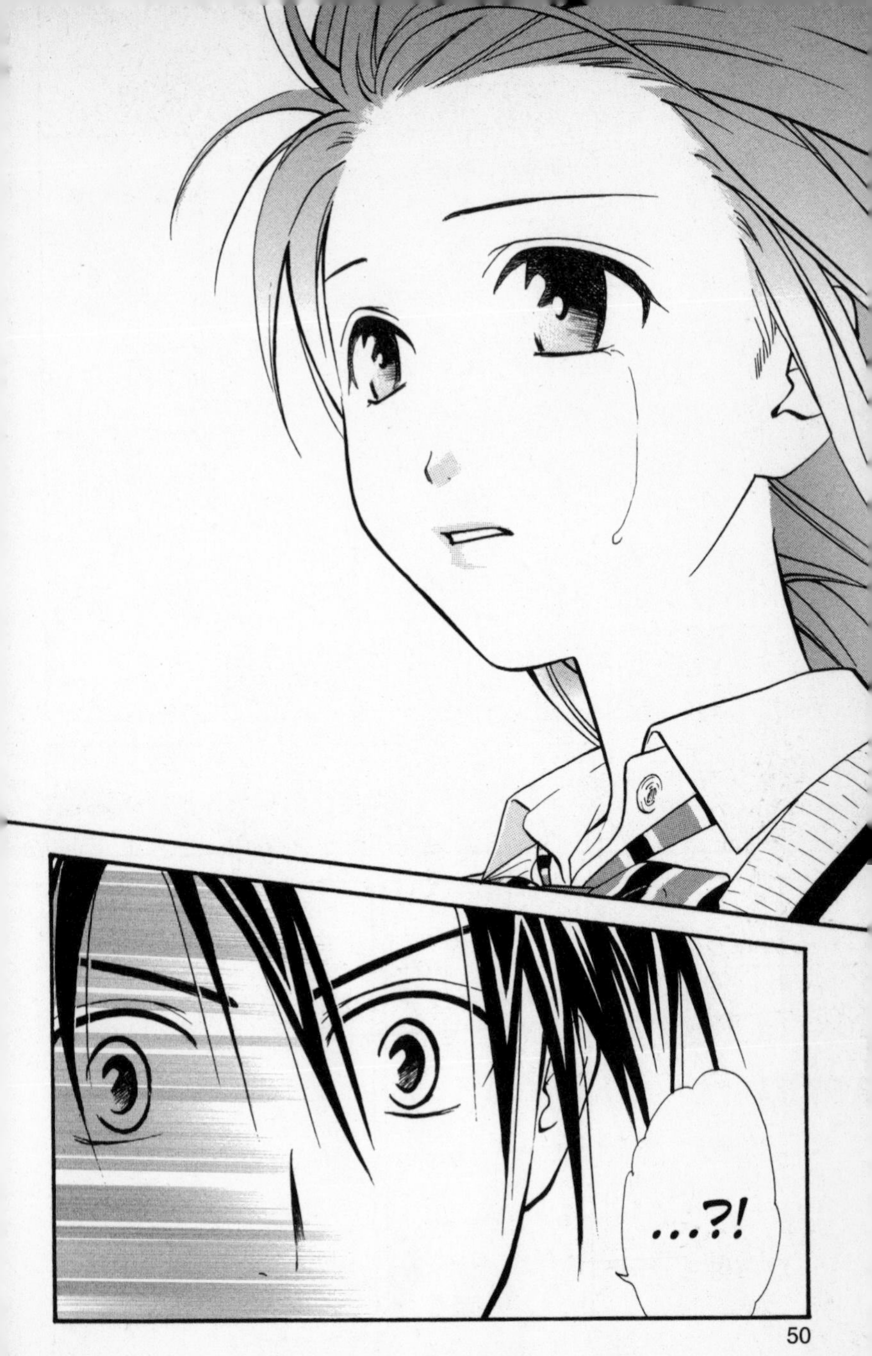
...?!

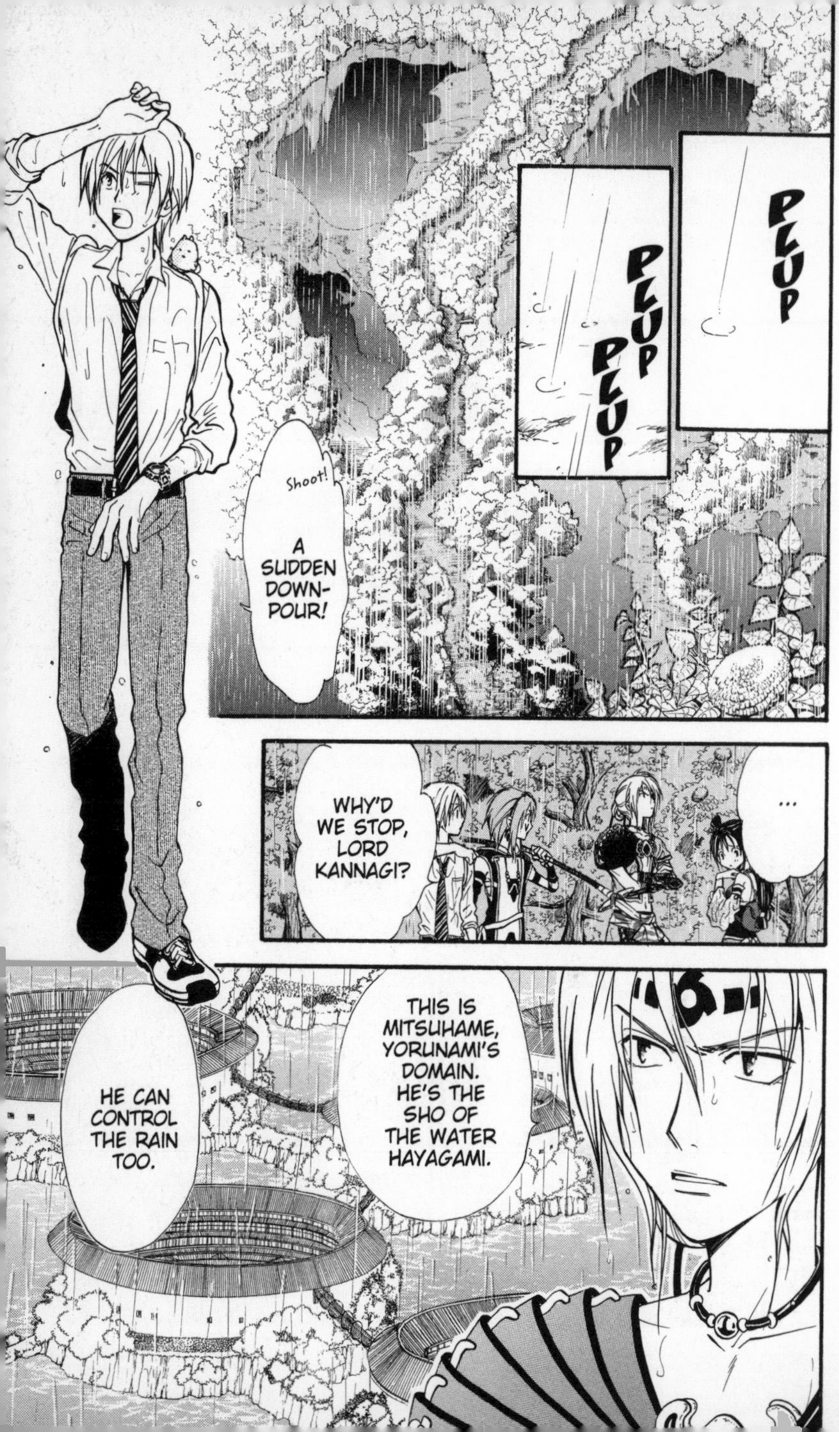
PLUP
PLUP PLUP
Shoot!
A SUDDEN DOWNPOUR!
...
WHY'D WE STOP, LORD KANNAGI?
THIS IS MITSUHAME, YORUNAMI'S DOMAIN. HE'S THE SHO OF THE WATER HAYAGAMI.
HE CAN CONTROL THE RAIN TOO.

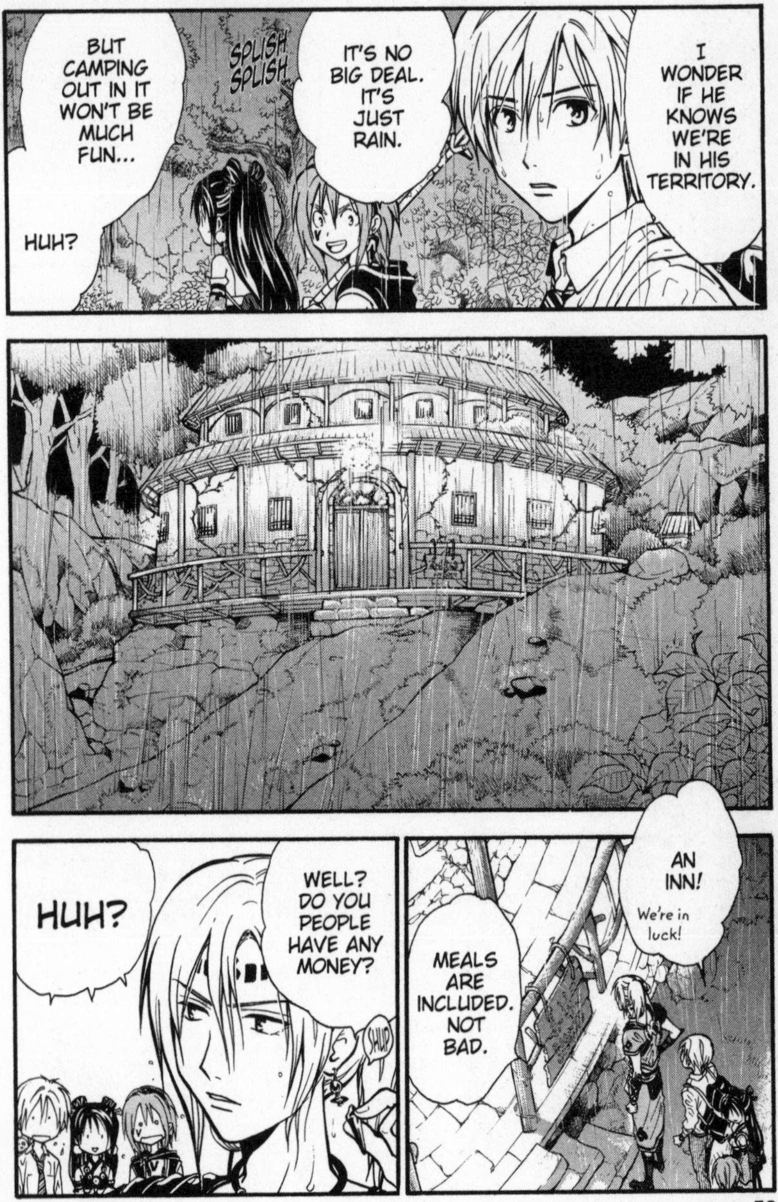
I WONDER IF HE KNOWS WE'RE IN HIS TERRITORY.
IT'S NO BIG DEAL. IT'S JUST RAIN.
SPLISH SPLISH
BUT CAMPING OUT IN IT WON'T BE MUCH FUN...
HUH?
AN INN!
We're in luck!
MEALS ARE INCLUDED. NOT BAD.
WELL? DO YOU PEOPLE HAVE ANY MONEY?
SHUP
HUH?

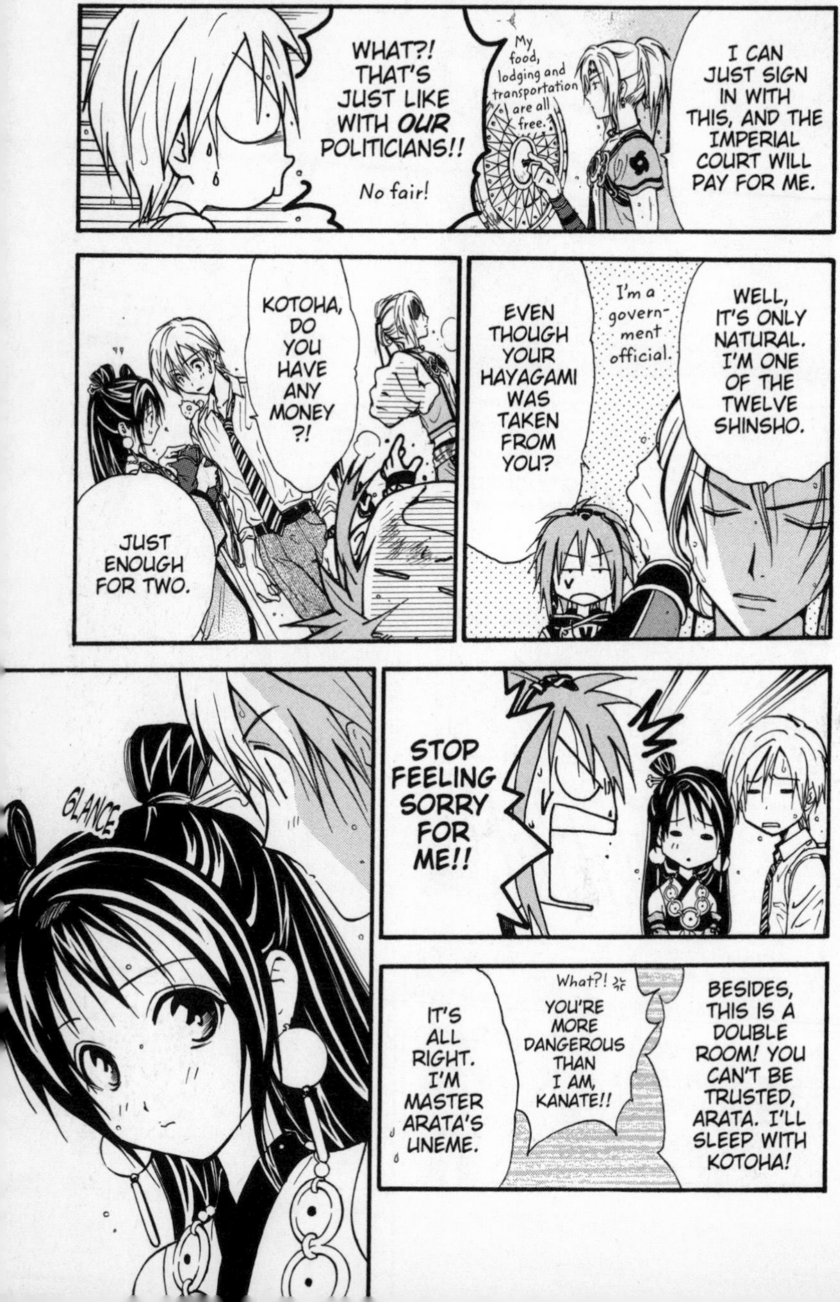
I CAN JUST SIGN IN WITH THIS, AND THE IMPERIAL COURT WILL PAY FOR ME.
My food, lodging and transportation are all free.
WHAT?! THAT'S JUST LIKE WITH ***OUR*** POLITICIANS!!
No fair!
WELL, IT'S ONLY NATURAL. I'M ONE OF THE TWELVE SHINSHO.
I'm a government official.
EVEN THOUGH YOUR HAYAGAMI WAS TAKEN FROM YOU?
KOTOHA, DO YOU HAVE ANY MONEY?!
JUST ENOUGH FOR TWO.
STOP FEELING SORRY FOR ME!!
BESIDES, THIS IS A DOUBLE ROOM! YOU CAN'T BE TRUSTED, ARATA. I'LL SLEEP WITH KOTOHA!
What?!
YOU'RE MORE DANGEROUS THAN I AM, KANATE!!
IT'S ALL RIGHT. I'M MASTER ARATA'S UNEME.
GLANCE

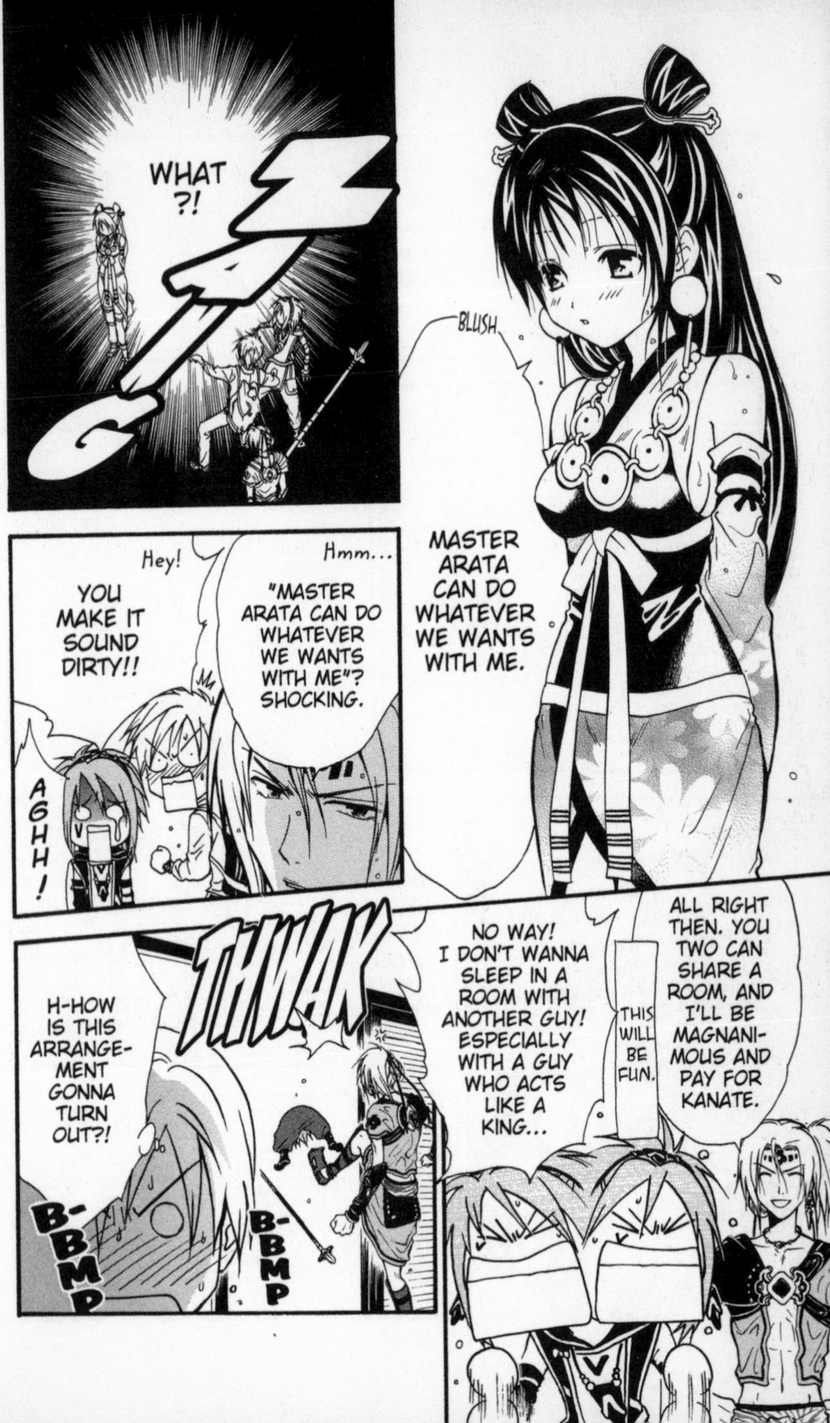
BLUSH
MASTER ARATA CAN DO WHATEVER WE WANTS WITH ME.
WHAT ?!
ZING
Hmm...
"MASTER ARATA CAN DO WHATEVER WE WANTS WITH ME"? SHOCKING.
Hey!
YOU MAKE IT SOUND DIRTY!!
AGHH!
ALL RIGHT THEN. YOU TWO CAN SHARE A ROOM, AND I'LL BE MAGNANIMOUS AND PAY FOR KANATE.
THIS WILL BE FUN.
NO WAY! I DON'T WANNA SLEEP IN A ROOM WITH ANOTHER GUY! ESPECIALLY WITH A GUY WHO ACTS LIKE A KING...
THWAK
H-HOW IS THIS ARRANGEMENT GONNA TURN OUT?!
B-BBMP
B-BBMP

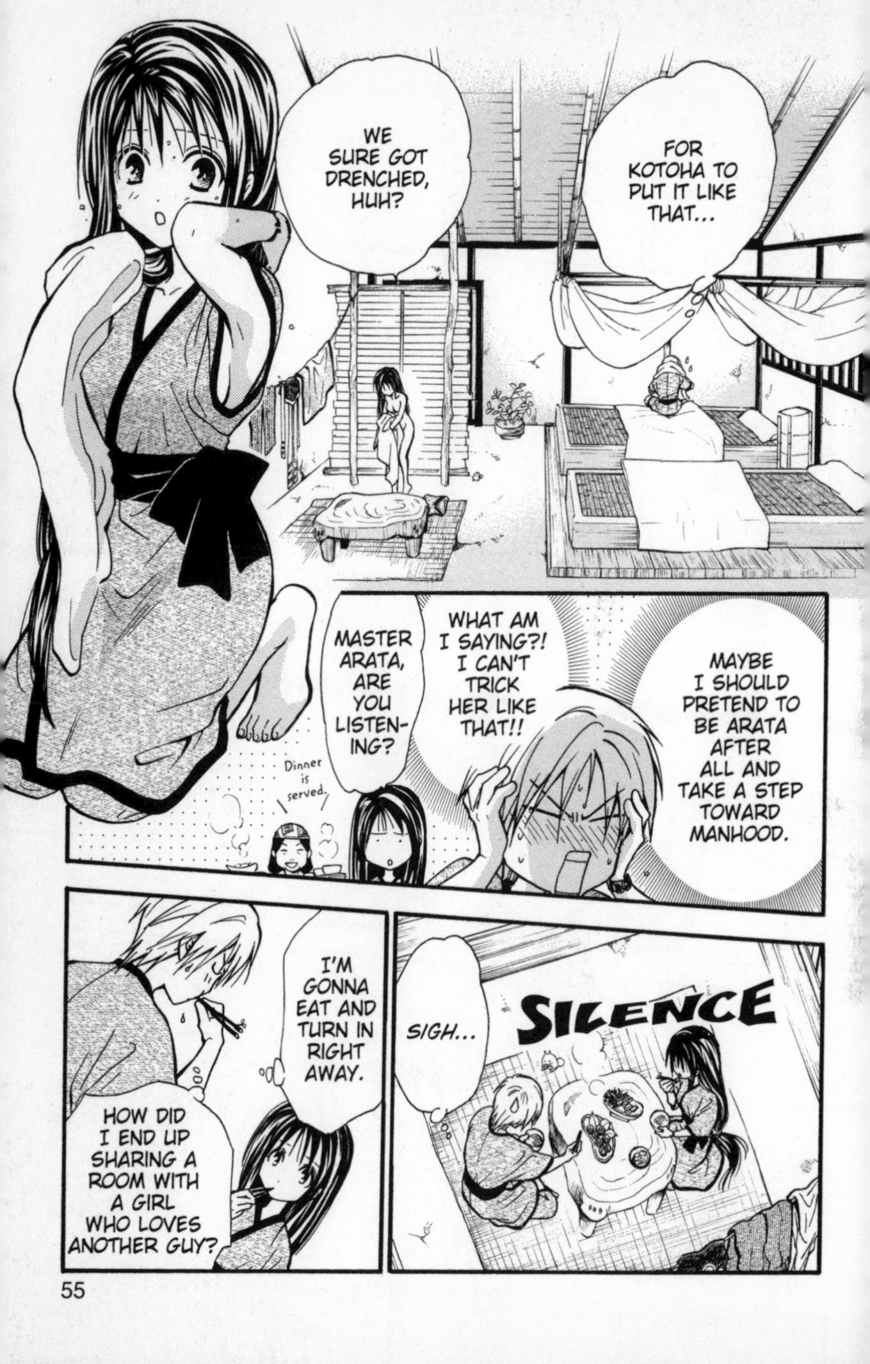
FOR KOTOHA TO PUT IT LIKE THAT...
WE SURE GOT DRENCHED, HUH?
MAYBE I SHOULD PRETEND TO BE ARATA AFTER ALL AND TAKE A STEP TOWARD MANHOOD.
WHAT AM I SAYING?! I CAN'T TRICK HER LIKE THAT!!
MASTER ARATA, ARE YOU LISTENING-ING?
Dinner is served.
SILENCE
SIGH...
I'M GONNA EAT AND TURN IN RIGHT AWAY.
HOW DID I END UP SHARING A ROOM WITH A GIRL WHO LOVES ANOTHER GUY?

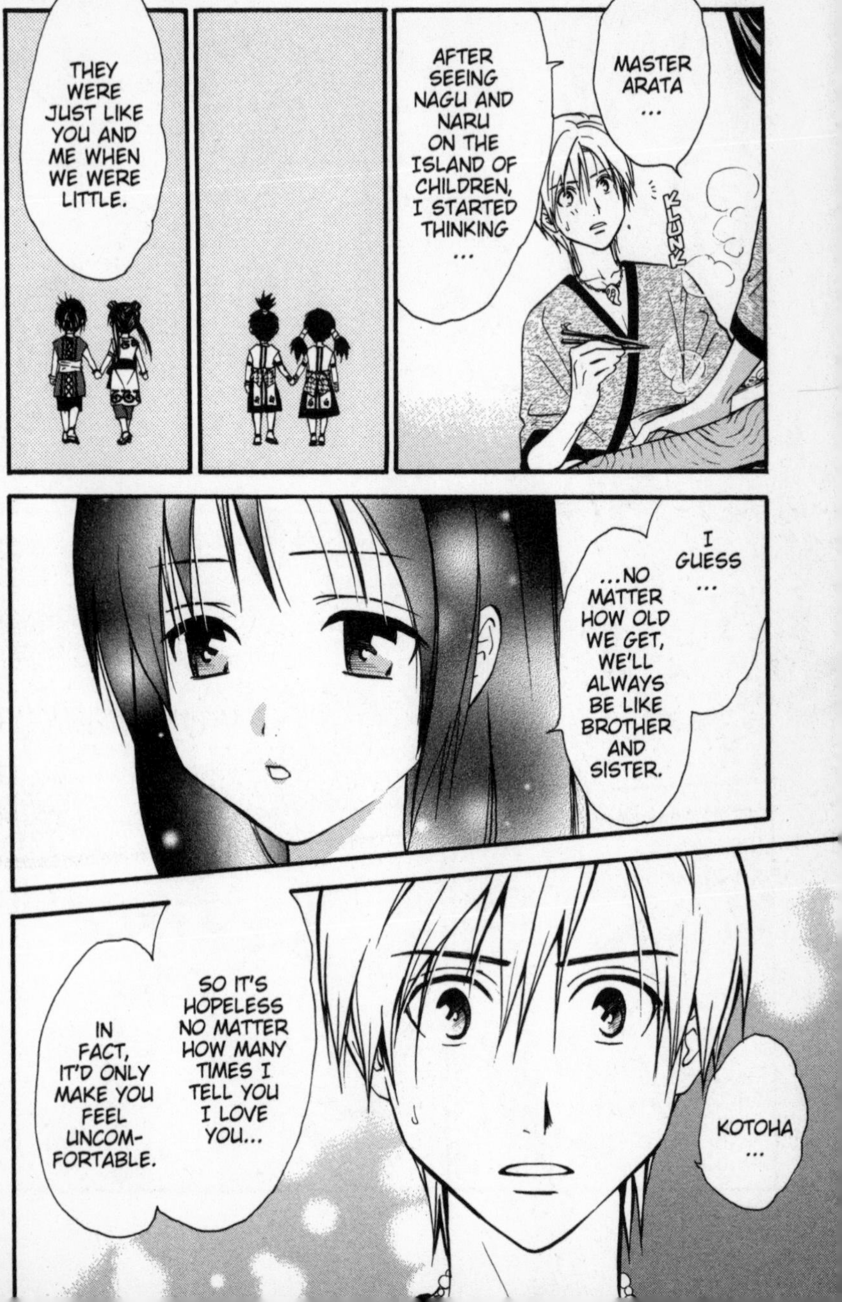
MASTER ARATA ...
AFTER SEEING NAGU AND NARU ON THE ISLAND OF CHILDREN, I STARTED THINKING ...
THEY WERE JUST LIKE YOU AND ME WHEN WE WERE LITTLE.
I GUESS ...
...NO MATTER HOW OLD WE GET, WE'LL ALWAYS BE LIKE BROTHER AND SISTER.
KOTOHA ...
SO IT'S HOPELESS NO MATTER HOW MANY TIMES I TELL YOU I LOVE YOU...
IN FACT, IT'D ONLY MAKE YOU FEEL UNCOM-FORTABLE.

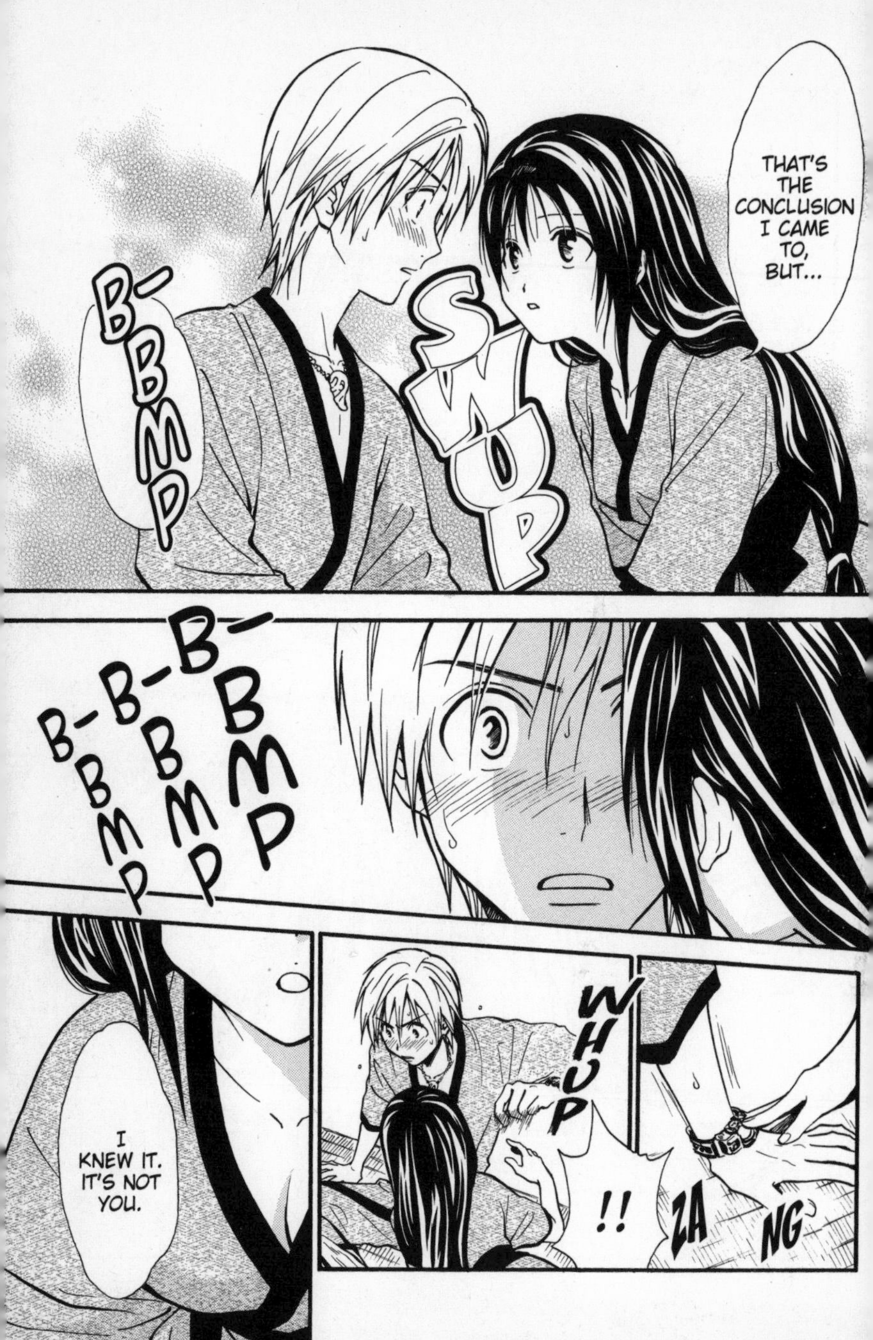
THAT'S THE CONCLUSION I CAME TO, BUT...
SWUP
B-BBMP
B-BBMP
B-BBMP
B-BBMP
ZA NG
WHUP
!!
I KNEW IT. IT'S NOT YOU.

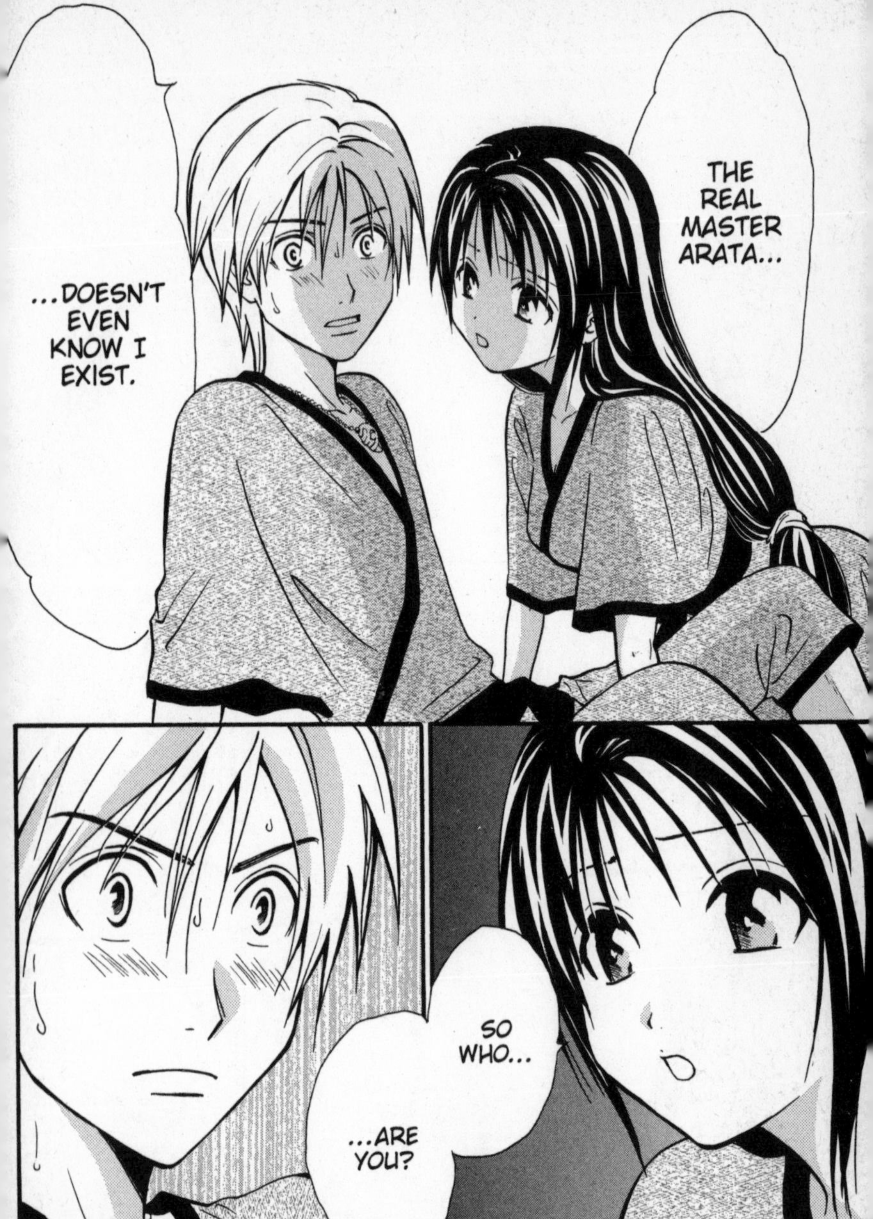
THE REAL MASTER ARATA...
...DOESN'T EVEN KNOW I EXIST.
SO WHO...
...ARE YOU?

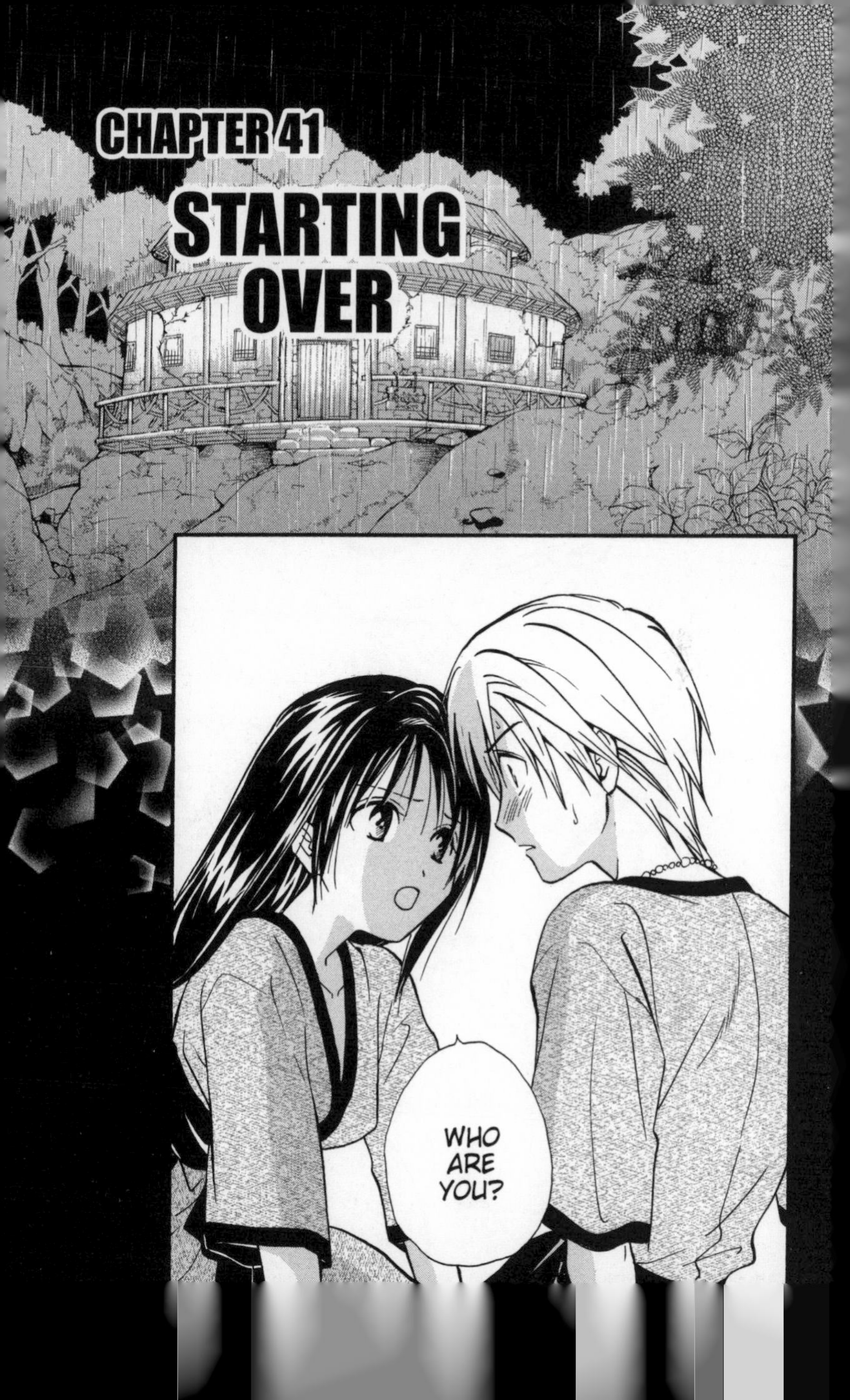
CHAPTER 41
STARTING OVER
WHO ARE YOU?

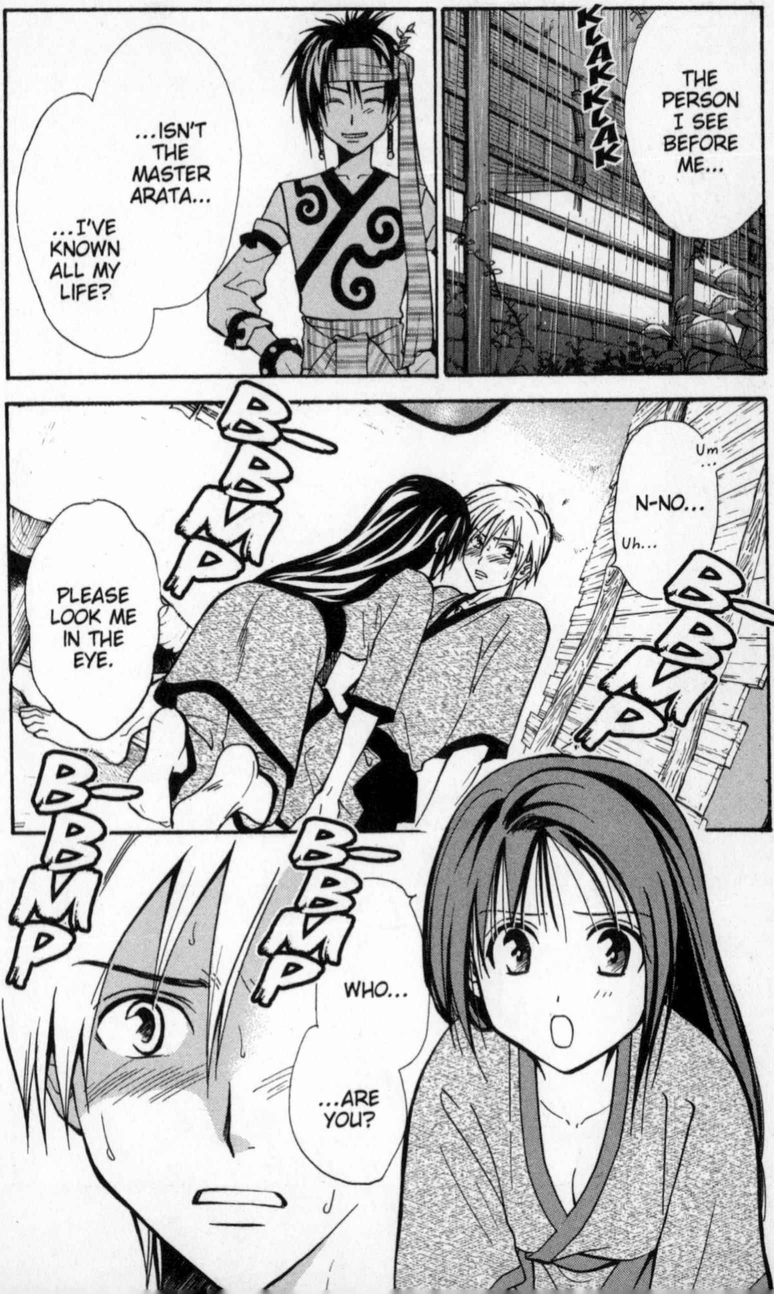
KLAKKLAK
THE PERSON I SEE BEFORE ME...
...ISN'T THE MASTER ARATA...
...I'VE KNOWN ALL MY LIFE?
Um...
N-NO...
Uh...
B-BMP
B-BMP
PLEASE LOOK ME IN THE EYE.
B-BMP
WHO...
...ARE YOU?
B-BMP

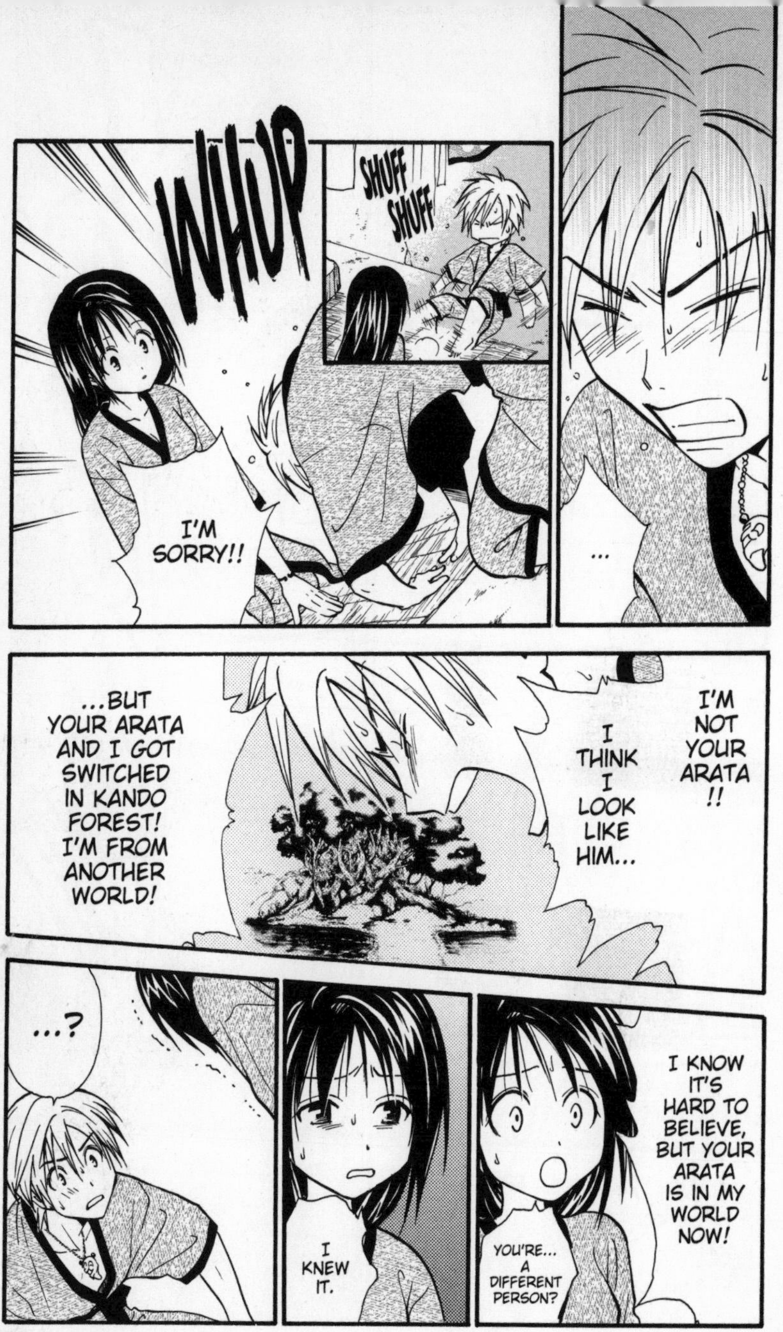
...
SHUFF SHUFF
WHUP
I'M SORRY!!
I'M NOT YOUR ARATA!!
I THINK I LOOK LIKE HIM...
...BUT YOUR ARATA AND I GOT SWITCHED IN KANDO FOREST! I'M FROM ANOTHER WORLD!
I KNOW IT'S HARD TO BELIEVE, BUT YOUR ARATA IS IN MY WORLD NOW!
YOU'RE... A DIFFERENT PERSON?
I KNEW IT.
...?

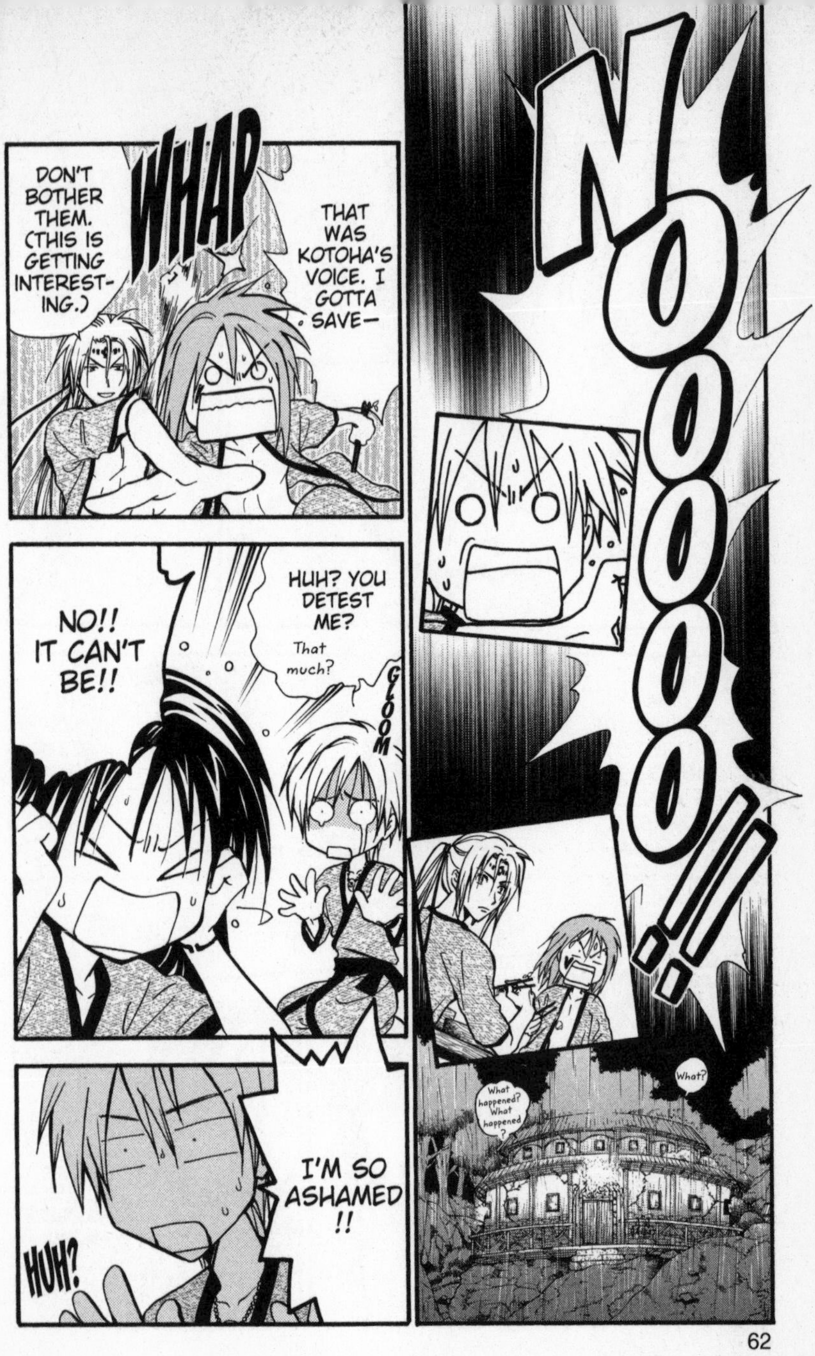
NOOOOOOO!!
What happened? What happened?
What?
THAT WAS KOTOHA'S VOICE. I GOTTA SAVE—
WHAP
DON'T BOTHER THEM. (THIS IS GETTING INTEREST-ING.)
HUH? YOU DETEST ME?
That much?
GLOOM
NO!! IT CAN'T BE!!
I'M SO ASHAMED!!
HUH?

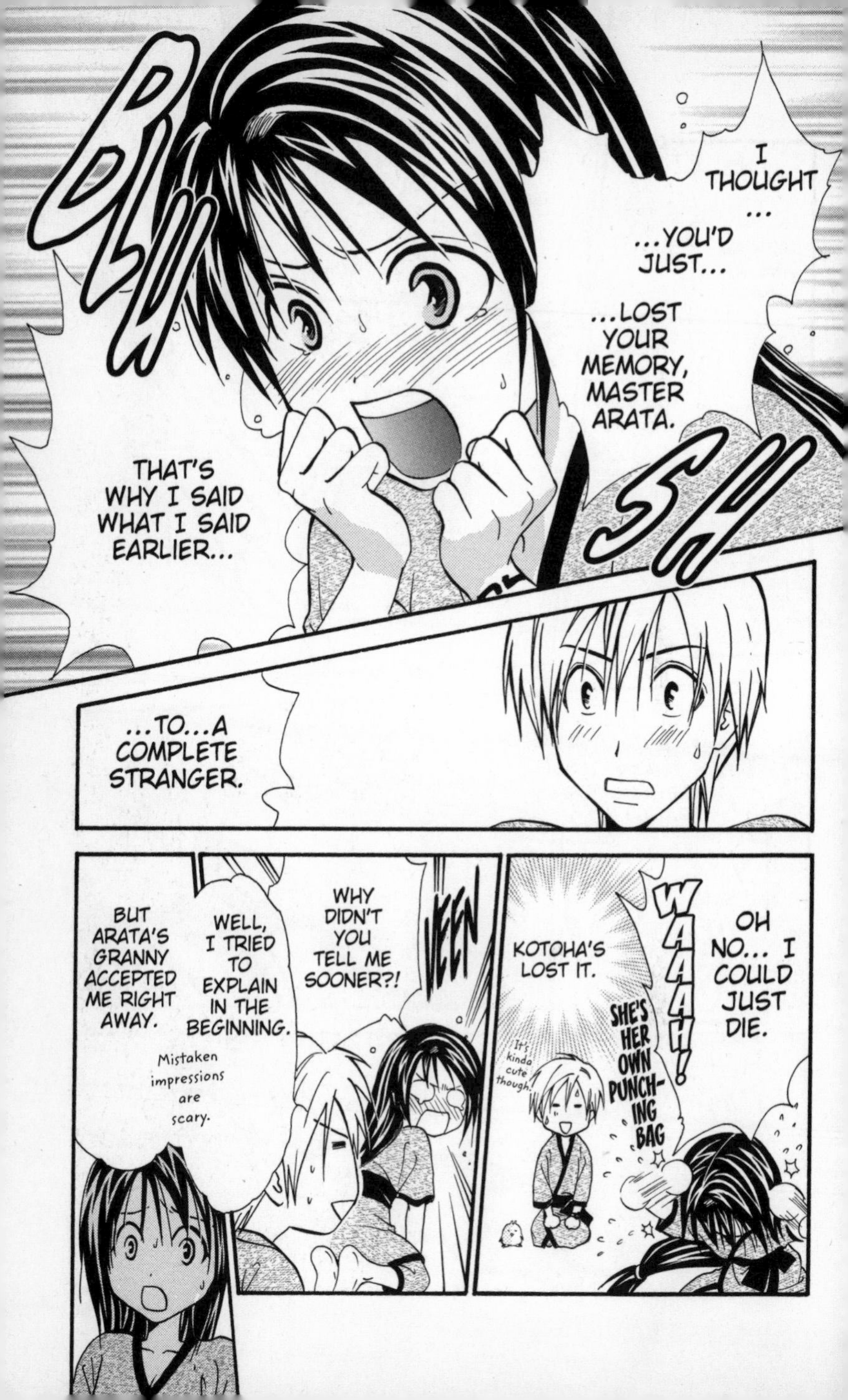
I THOUGHT...
...YOU'D JUST...
...LOST YOUR MEMORY, MASTER ARATA.
THAT'S WHY I SAID WHAT I SAID EARLIER...
...TO...A COMPLETE STRANGER.
OH NO... I COULD JUST DIE.
WAAAH!
SHE'S HER OWN PUNCHING BAG
KOTOHA'S LOST IT.
It's kinda cute though.
WHY DIDN'T YOU TELL ME SOONER?!
WELL, I TRIED TO EXPLAIN IN THE BEGINNING.
BUT ARATA'S GRANNY ACCEPTED ME RIGHT AWAY.
Mistaken impressions are scary.

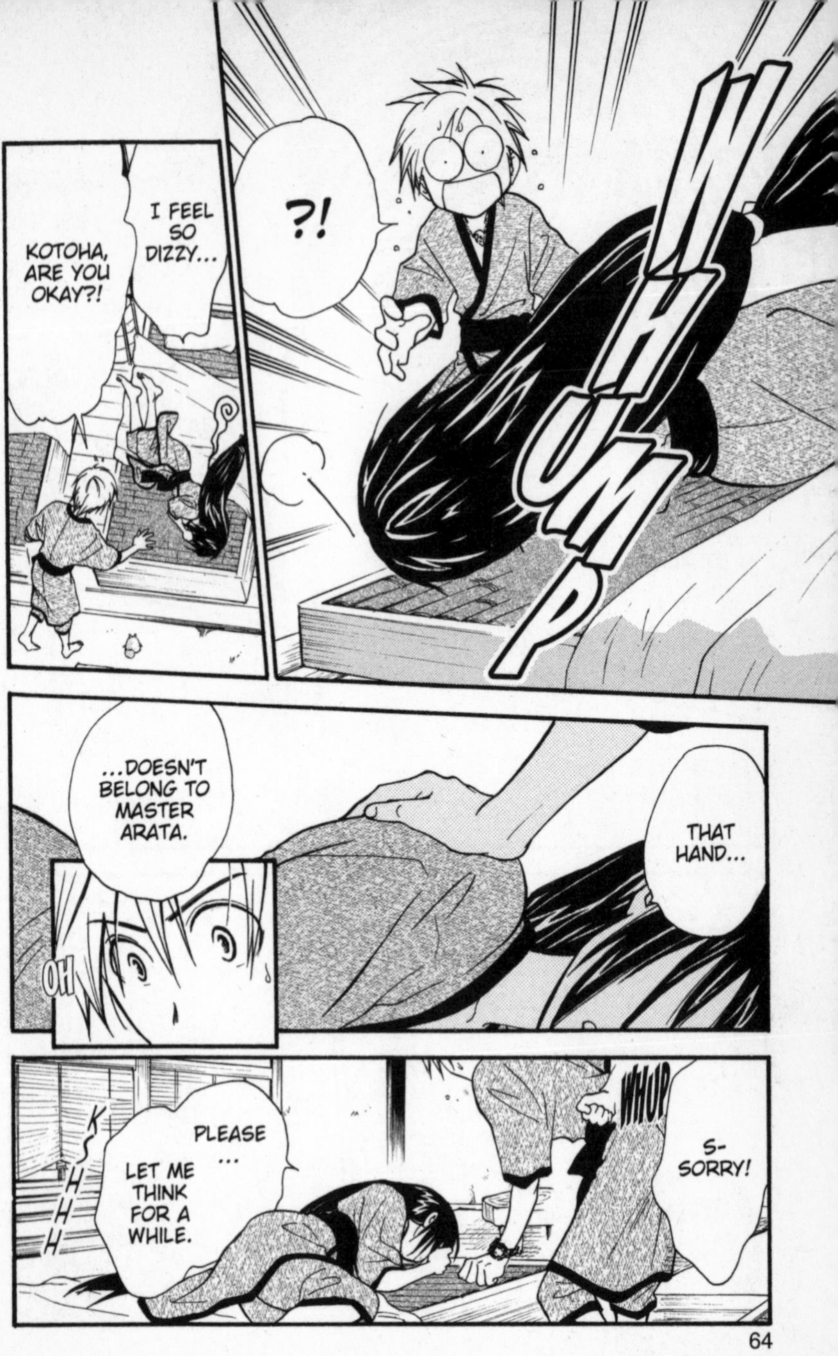
?!
WHUMP
I FEEL SO DIZZY...
KOTOHA, ARE YOU OKAY?!
THAT HAND...
...DOESN'T BELONG TO MASTER ARATA.
OH
S-SORRY!
WHUP
PLEASE... LET ME THINK FOR A WHILE.
KSHHHH

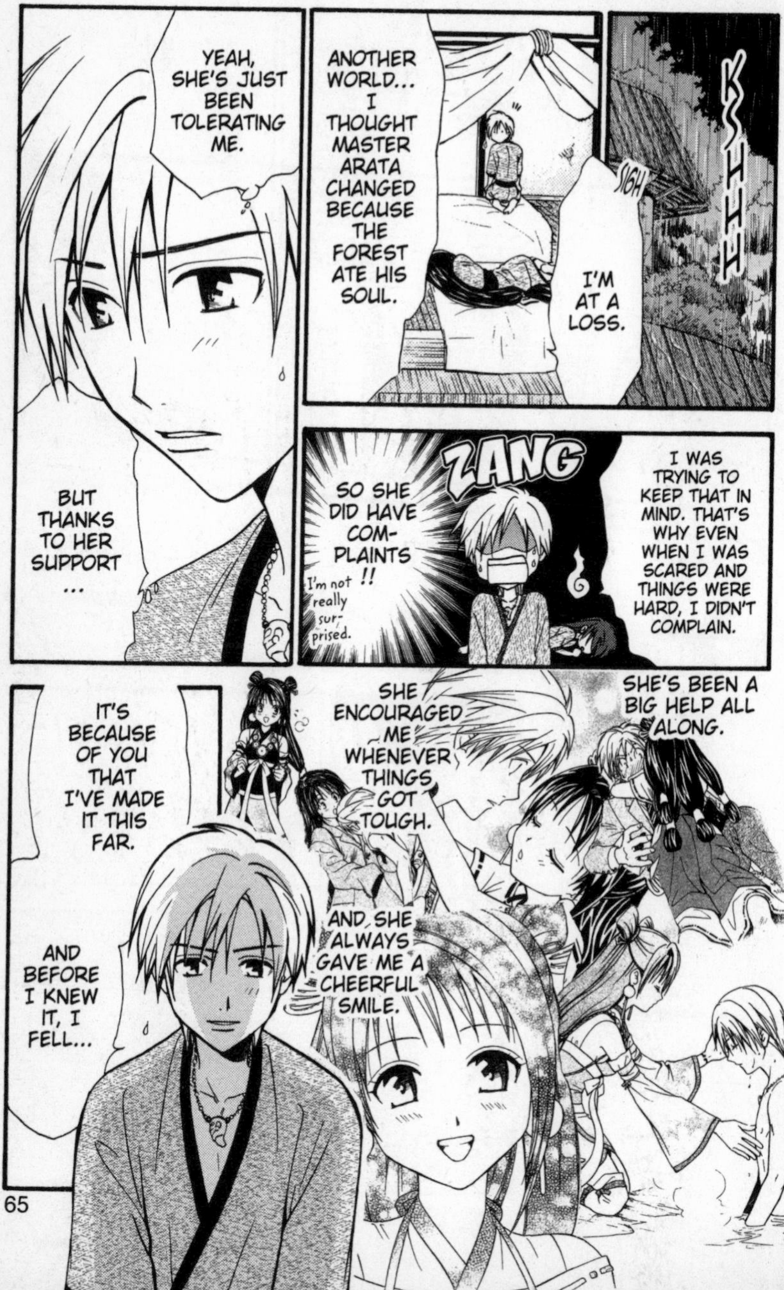
KSHHH
SIGH
I'M AT A LOSS.
ANOTHER WORLD... I THOUGHT MASTER ARATA CHANGED BECAUSE THE FOREST ATE HIS SOUL.
I WAS TRYING TO KEEP THAT IN MIND. THAT'S WHY EVEN WHEN I WAS SCARED AND THINGS WERE HARD, I DIDN'T COMPLAIN.
ZANG
SO SHE DID HAVE COM-PLAINTS !!
I'm not really sur-prised.
YEAH, SHE'S JUST BEEN TOLERATING ME.
BUT THANKS TO HER SUPPORT ...
SHE'S BEEN A BIG HELP ALL ALONG.
SHE ENCOURAGED ME WHENEVER THINGS GOT TOUGH.
AND SHE ALWAYS GAVE ME A CHEERFUL SMILE.
IT'S BECAUSE OF YOU THAT I'VE MADE IT THIS FAR.
AND BEFORE I KNEW IT, I FELL...

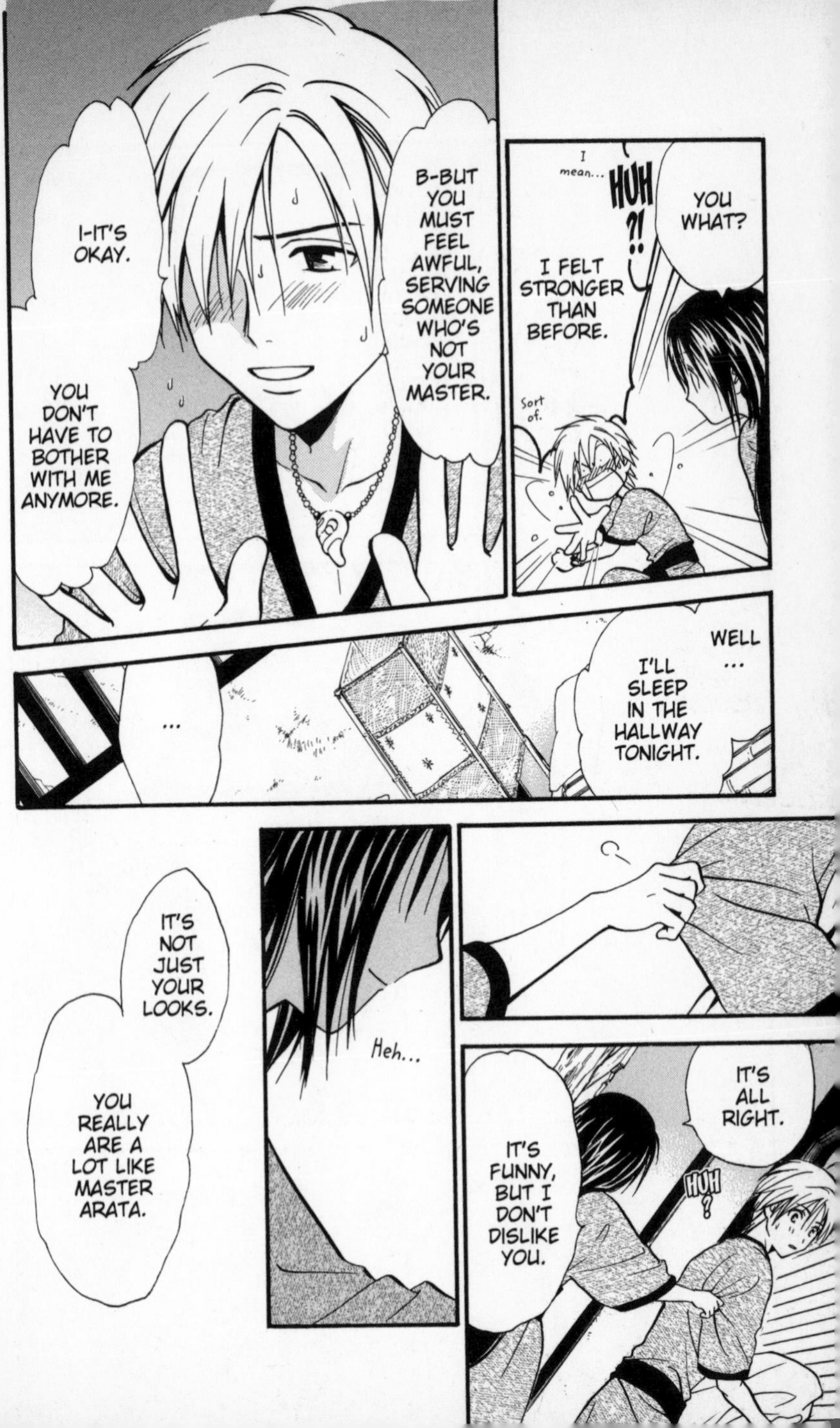
YOU WHAT?
HUH?!
I mean...
I FELT STRONGER THAN BEFORE.
Sort of.
B-BUT YOU MUST FEEL AWFUL, SERVING SOMEONE WHO'S NOT YOUR MASTER.
I-IT'S OKAY.
YOU DON'T HAVE TO BOTHER WITH ME ANYMORE.
WELL...
I'LL SLEEP IN THE HALLWAY TONIGHT.
...
IT'S ALL RIGHT.
HUH?
IT'S FUNNY, BUT I DON'T DISLIKE YOU.
Heh...
IT'S NOT JUST YOUR LOOKS.
YOU REALLY ARE A LOT LIKE MASTER ARATA.

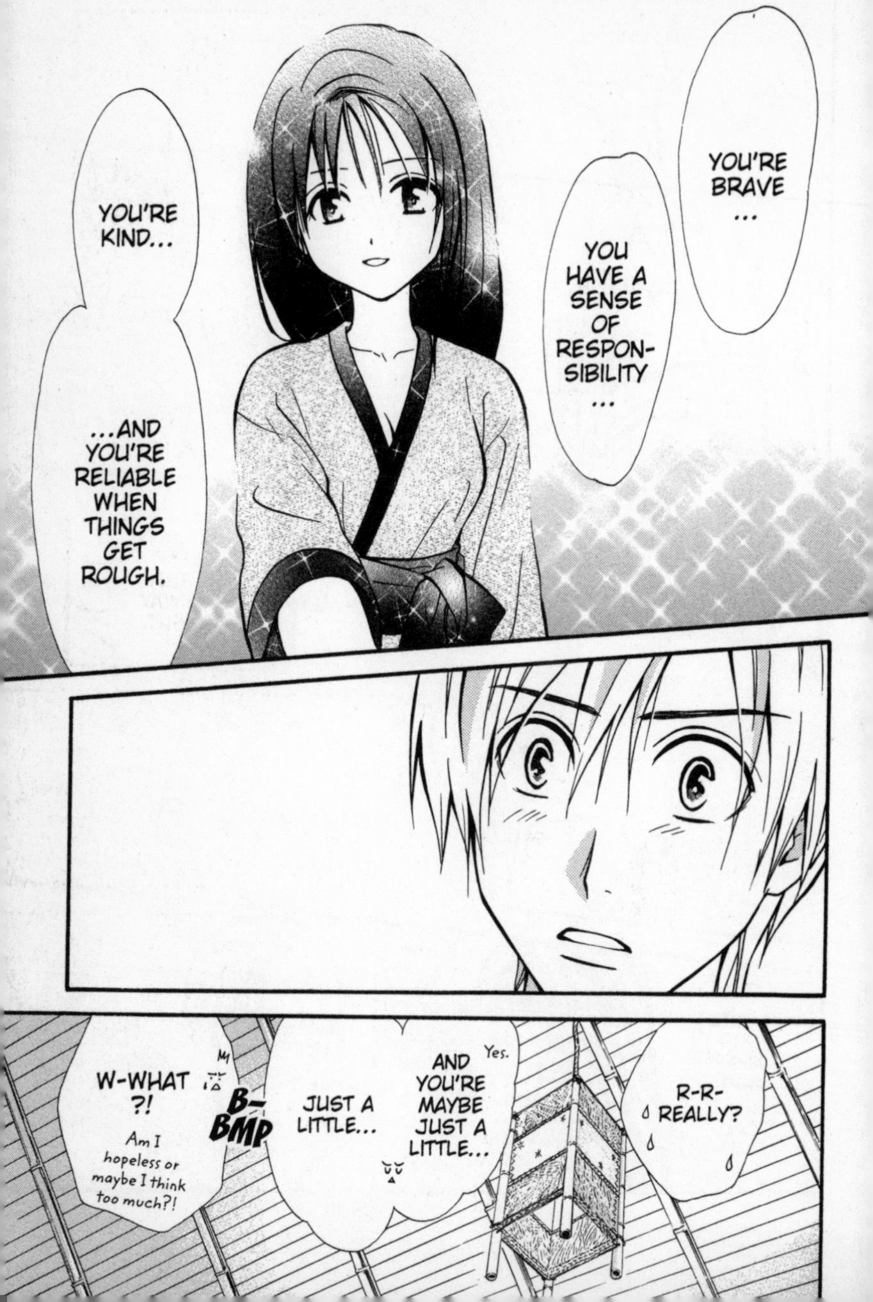
YOU'RE BRAVE ...
YOU HAVE A SENSE OF RESPON-SIBILITY ...
YOU'RE KIND...
...AND YOU'RE RELIABLE WHEN THINGS GET ROUGH.
R-R-REALLY?
Yes.
AND YOU'RE MAYBE JUST A LITTLE...
JUST A LITTLE...
B-BMP
W-WHAT ?!
Am I hopeless or maybe I think too much?!

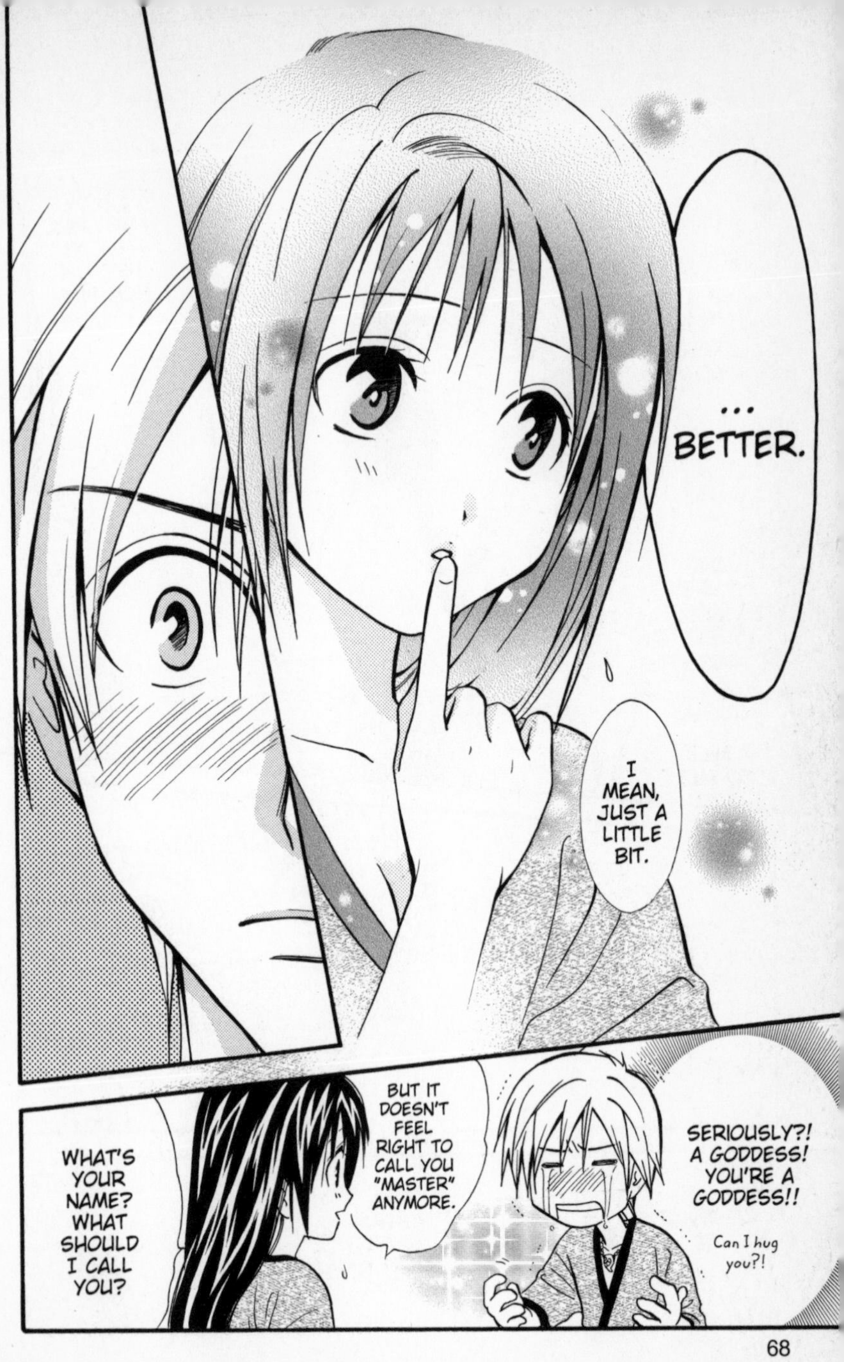
...BETTER.
I MEAN, JUST A LITTLE BIT.
SERIOUSLY?! A GODDESS! YOU'RE A GODDESS!!
Can I hug you?!
BUT IT DOESN'T FEEL RIGHT TO CALL YOU "MASTER" ANYMORE.
WHAT'S YOUR NAME? WHAT SHOULD I CALL YOU?

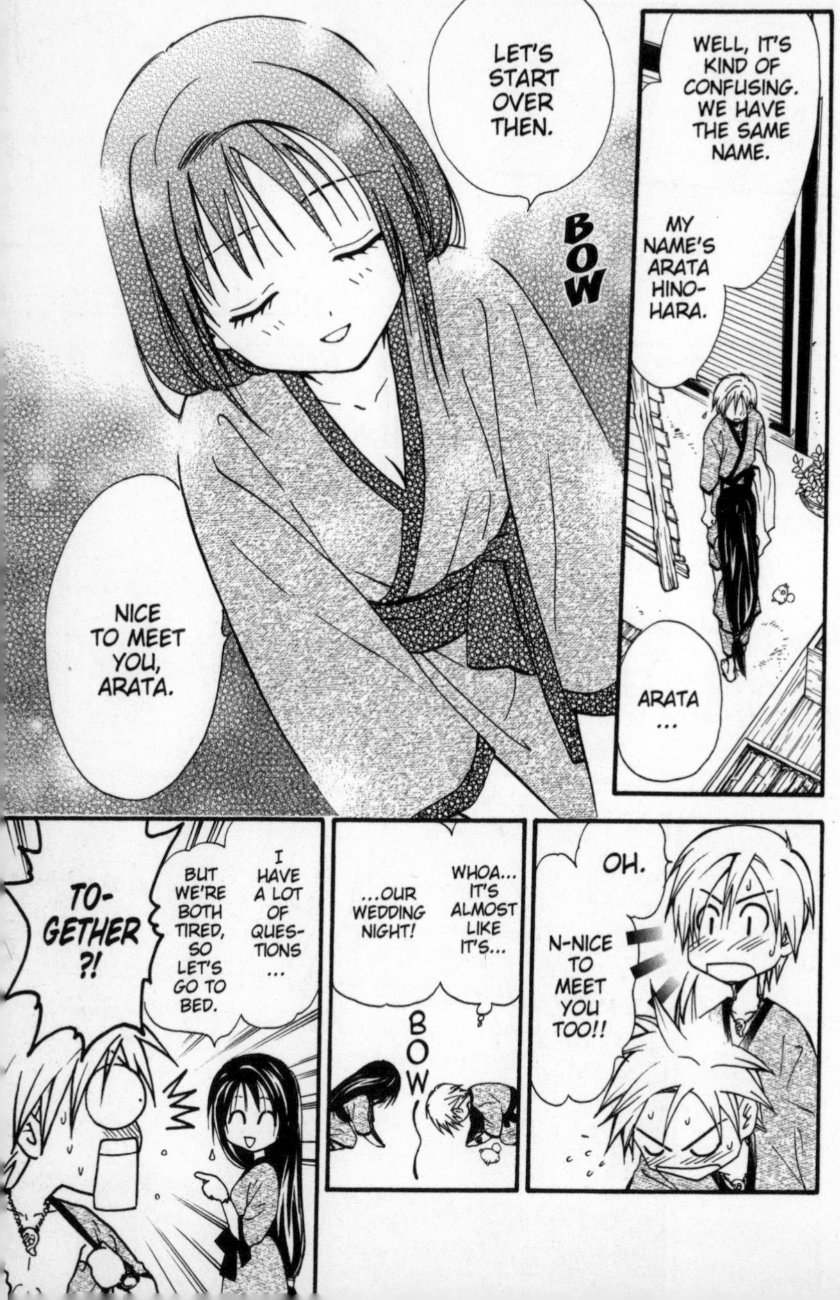
WELL, IT'S KIND OF CONFUSING. WE HAVE THE SAME NAME.
MY NAME'S ARATA HINO-HARA.
ARATA...
LET'S START OVER THEN.
BOW
NICE TO MEET YOU, ARATA.
OH.
N-NICE TO MEET YOU TOO!!
WHOA... IT'S ALMOST LIKE IT'S...
...OUR WEDDING NIGHT!
BOW!
I HAVE A LOT OF QUES-TIONS...
BUT WE'RE BOTH TIRED, SO LET'S GO TO BED.
TO-GETHER?!

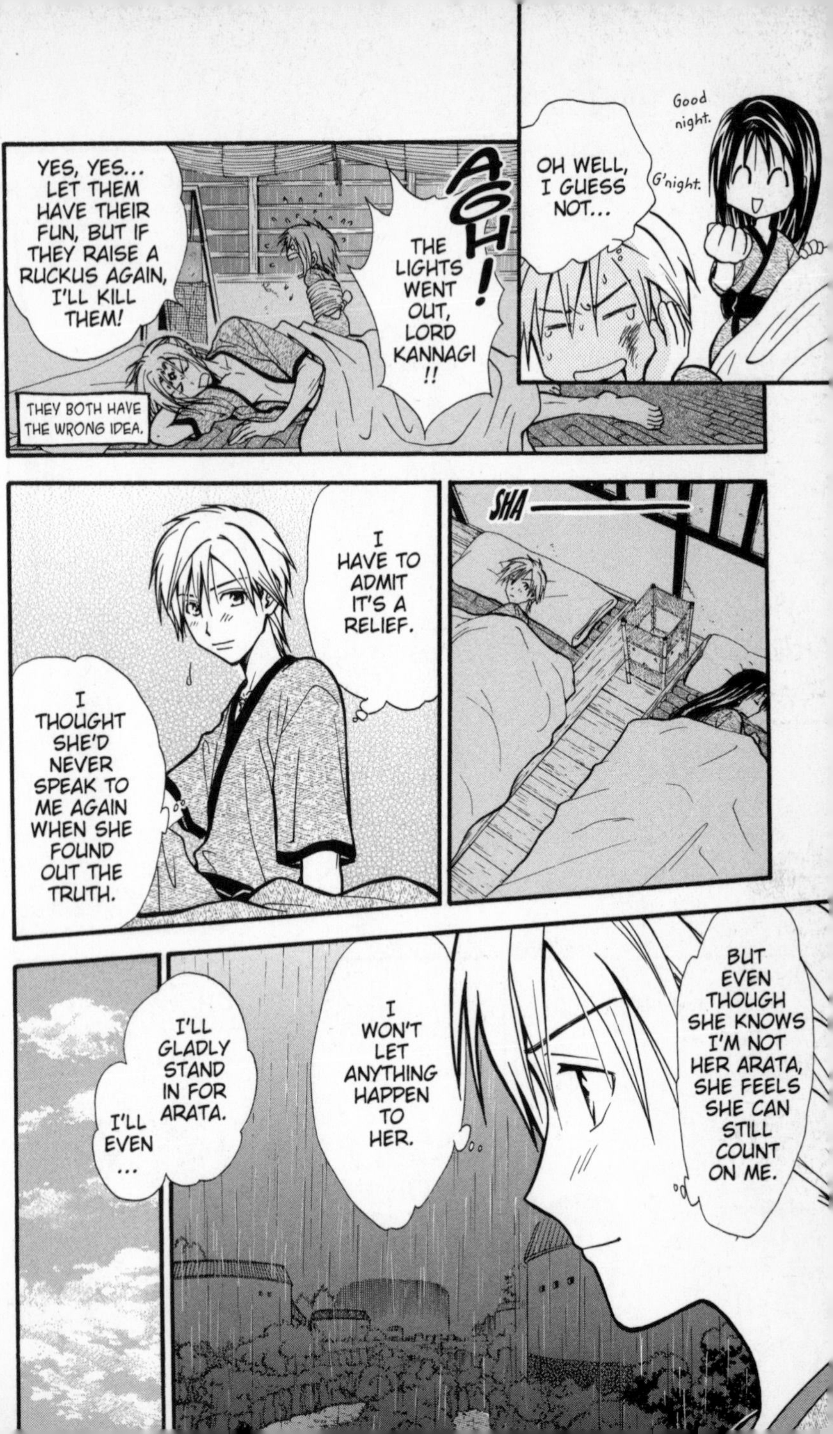

Good night.
G'night.
OH WELL, I GUESS NOT...
AGH!
THE LIGHTS WENT OUT, LORD KANNAGI!!
YES, YES... LET THEM HAVE THEIR FUN, BUT IF THEY RAISE A RUCKUS AGAIN, I'LL KILL THEM!
THEY BOTH HAVE THE WRONG IDEA.
SHA—
I HAVE TO ADMIT IT'S A RELIEF.
I THOUGHT SHE'D NEVER SPEAK TO ME AGAIN WHEN SHE FOUND OUT THE TRUTH.
BUT EVEN THOUGH SHE KNOWS I'M NOT HER ARATA, SHE FEELS SHE CAN STILL COUNT ON ME.
I WON'T LET ANYTHING HAPPEN TO HER.
I'LL GLADLY STAND IN FOR ARATA.
I'LL EVEN...

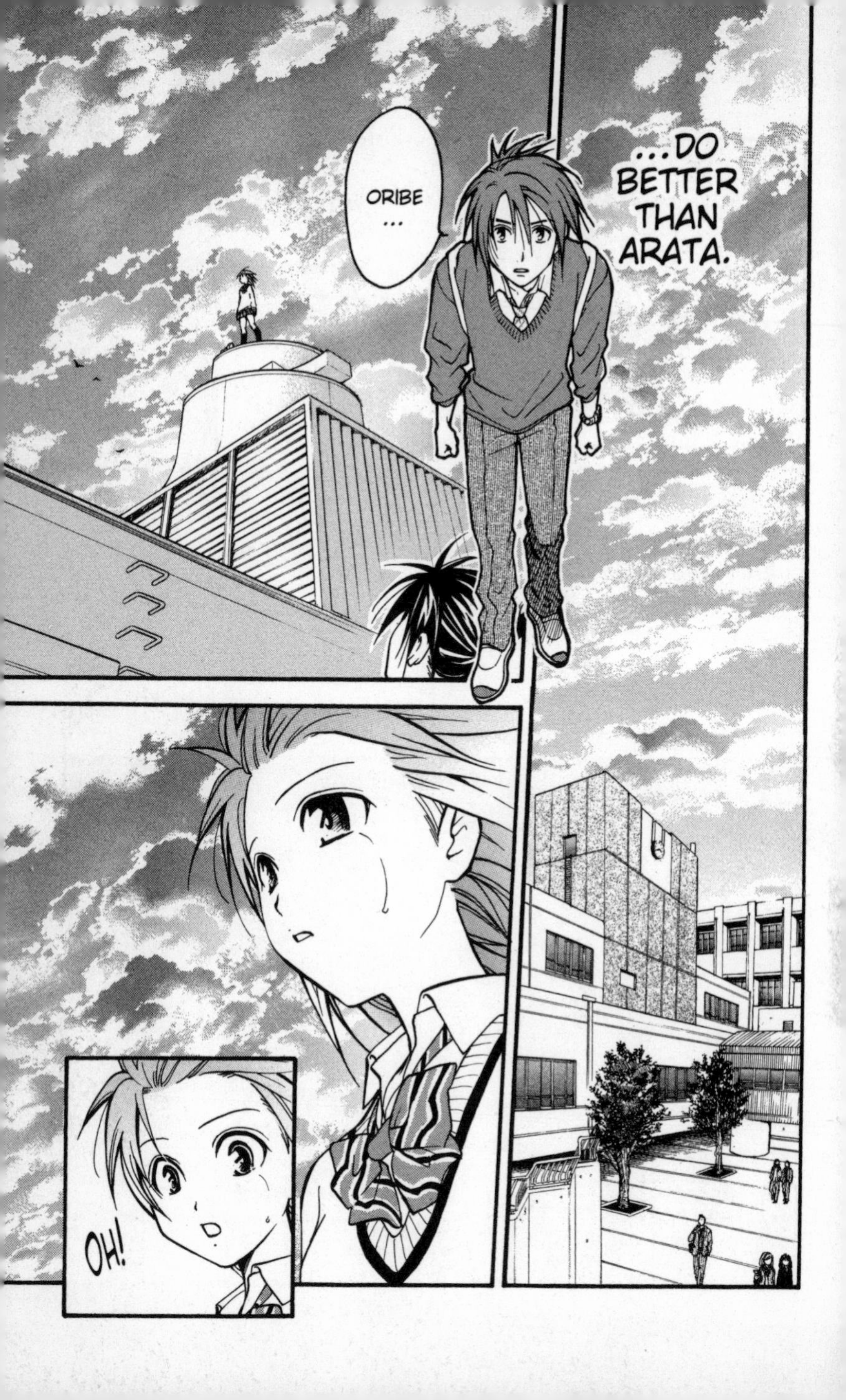
...DO BETTER THAN ARATA.
ORIBE ...
OH!

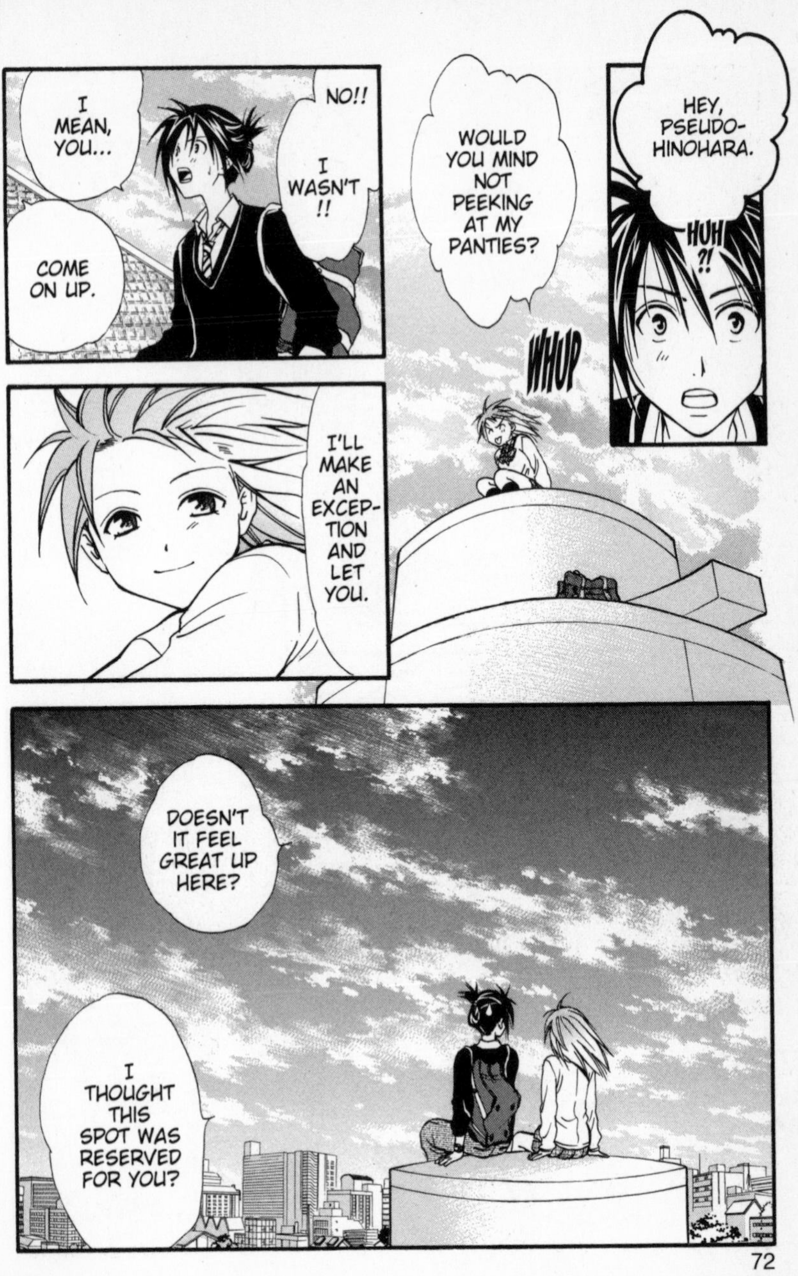
HEY, PSEUDO-HINOHARA.
HUH ?!
WOULD YOU MIND NOT PEEKING AT MY PANTIES?
WHUP
NO!!
I WASN'T !!
I MEAN, YOU...
COME ON UP.
I'LL MAKE AN EXCEPTION AND LET YOU.
DOESN'T IT FEEL GREAT UP HERE?
I THOUGHT THIS SPOT WAS RESERVED FOR YOU?

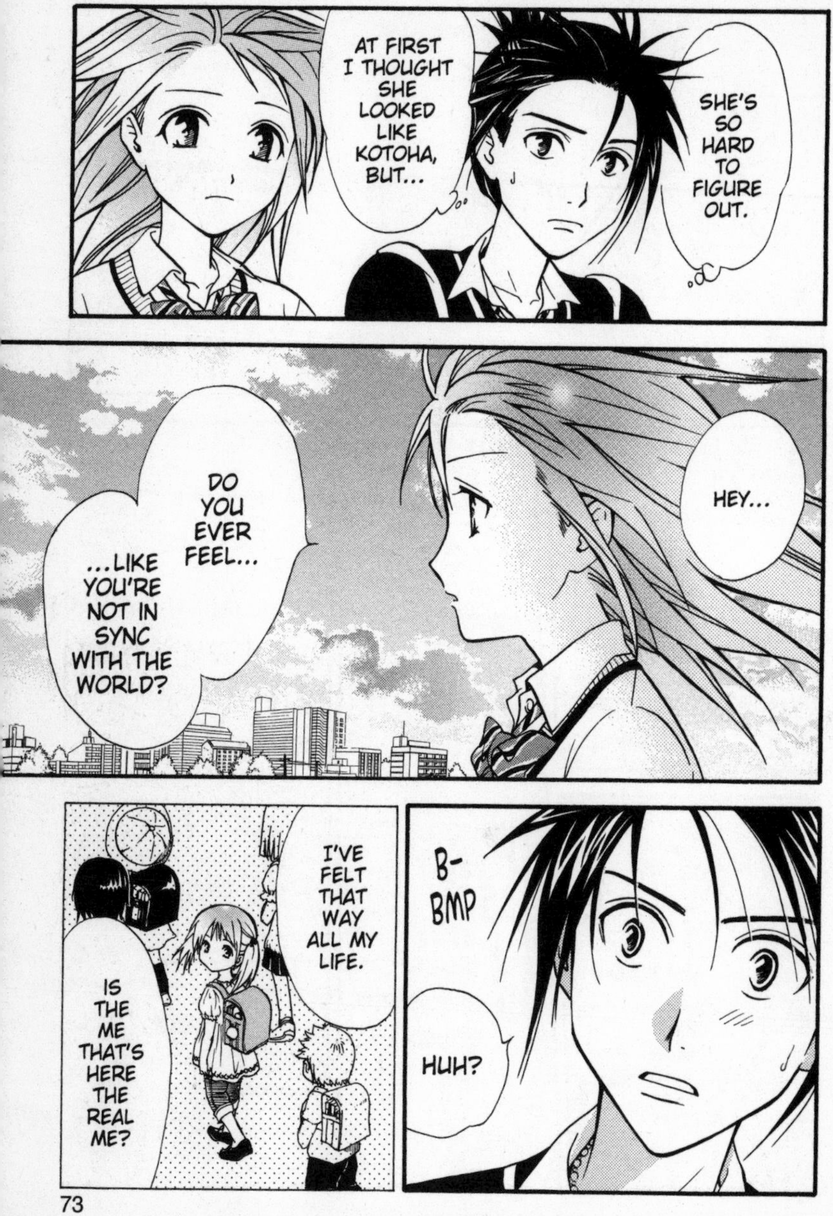
AT FIRST I THOUGHT SHE LOOKED LIKE KOTOHA, BUT...
SHE'S SO HARD TO FIGURE OUT.
HEY...
DO YOU EVER FEEL...
...LIKE YOU'RE NOT IN SYNC WITH THE WORLD?
B-BMP
HUH?
I'VE FELT THAT WAY ALL MY LIFE.
IS THE ME THAT'S HERE THE REAL ME?

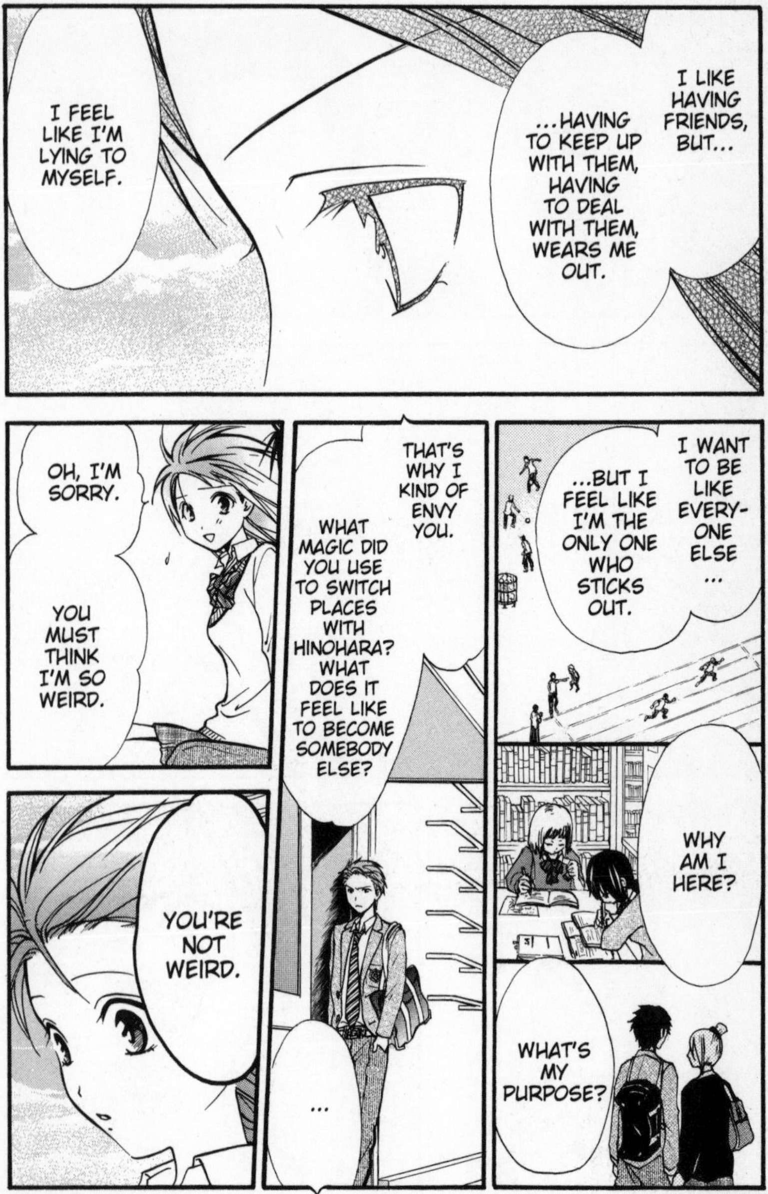
I LIKE HAVING FRIENDS, BUT...
...HAVING TO KEEP UP WITH THEM, HAVING TO DEAL WITH THEM, WEARS ME OUT.
I FEEL LIKE I'M LYING TO MYSELF.
I WANT TO BE LIKE EVERY-ONE ELSE...
...BUT I FEEL LIKE I'M THE ONLY ONE WHO STICKS OUT.
WHY AM I HERE?
WHAT'S MY PURPOSE?
THAT'S WHY I KIND OF ENVY YOU.
WHAT MAGIC DID YOU USE TO SWITCH PLACES WITH HINOHARA? WHAT DOES IT FEEL LIKE TO BECOME SOMEBODY ELSE?
...
OH, I'M SORRY.
YOU MUST THINK I'M SO WEIRD.
YOU'RE NOT WEIRD.

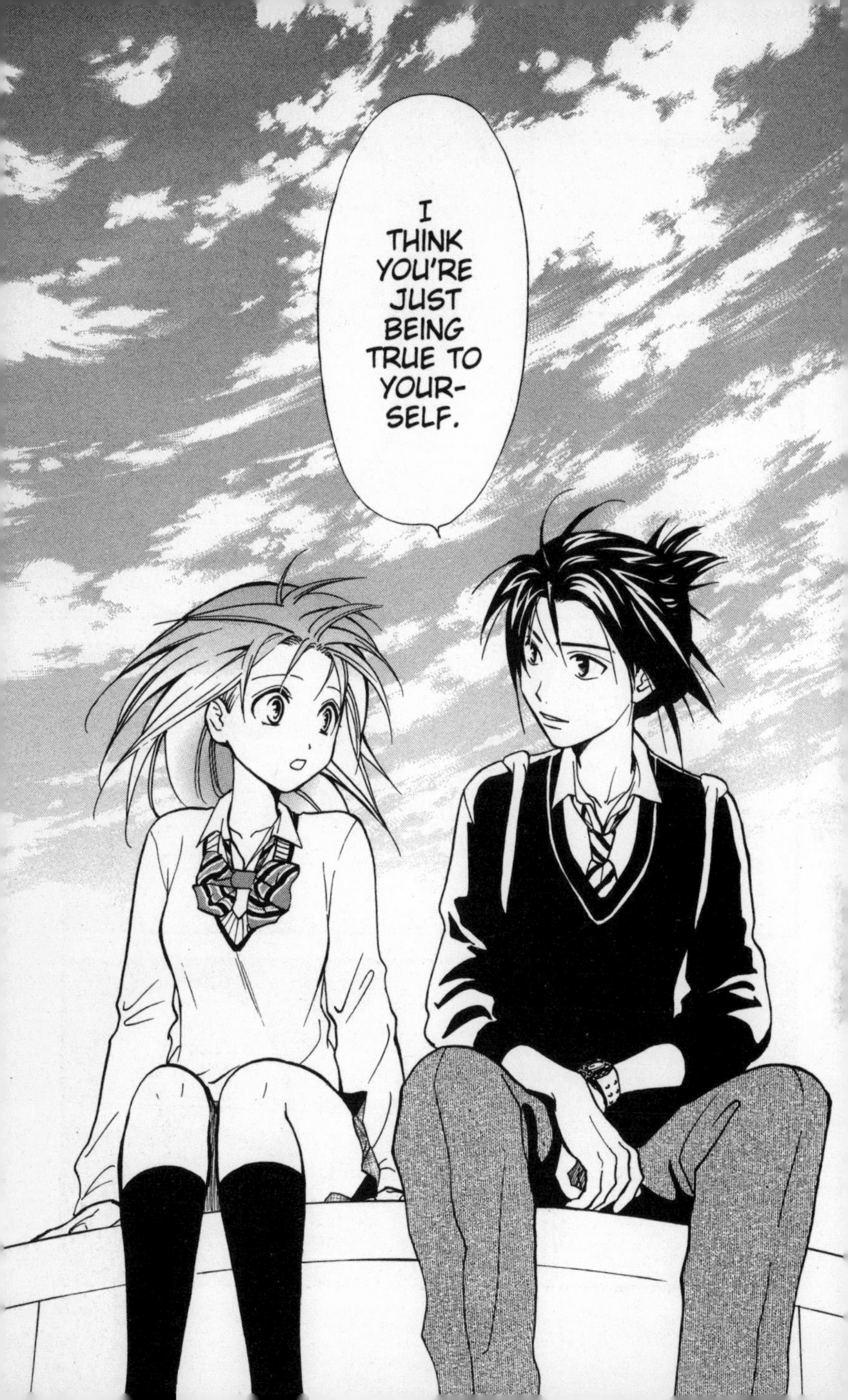
I THINK YOU'RE JUST BEING TRUE TO YOUR-SELF.

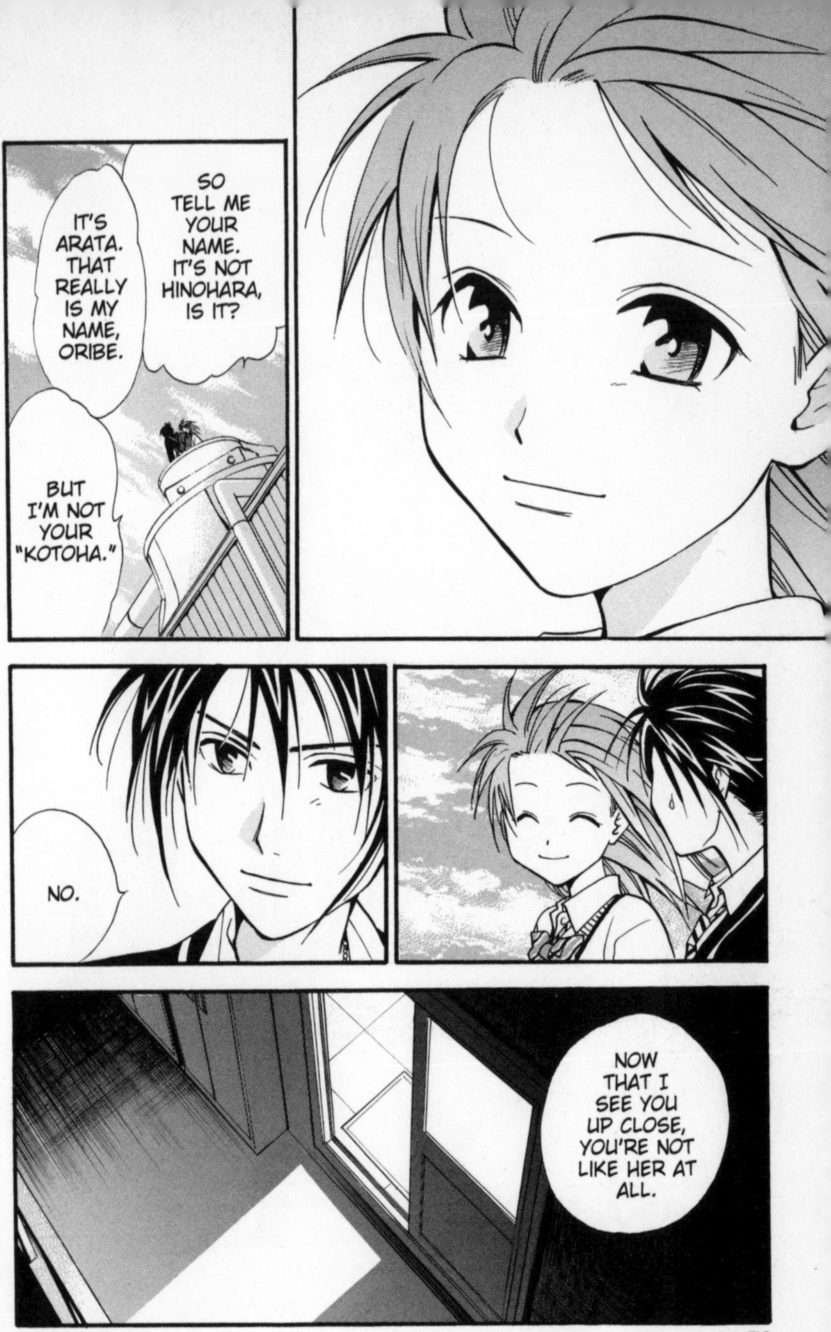
SO TELL ME YOUR NAME. IT'S NOT HINOHARA, IS IT?
IT'S ARATA. THAT REALLY IS MY NAME, ORIBE.
BUT I'M NOT YOUR "KOTOHA."
NO.
NOW THAT I SEE YOU UP CLOSE, YOU'RE NOT LIKE HER AT ALL.

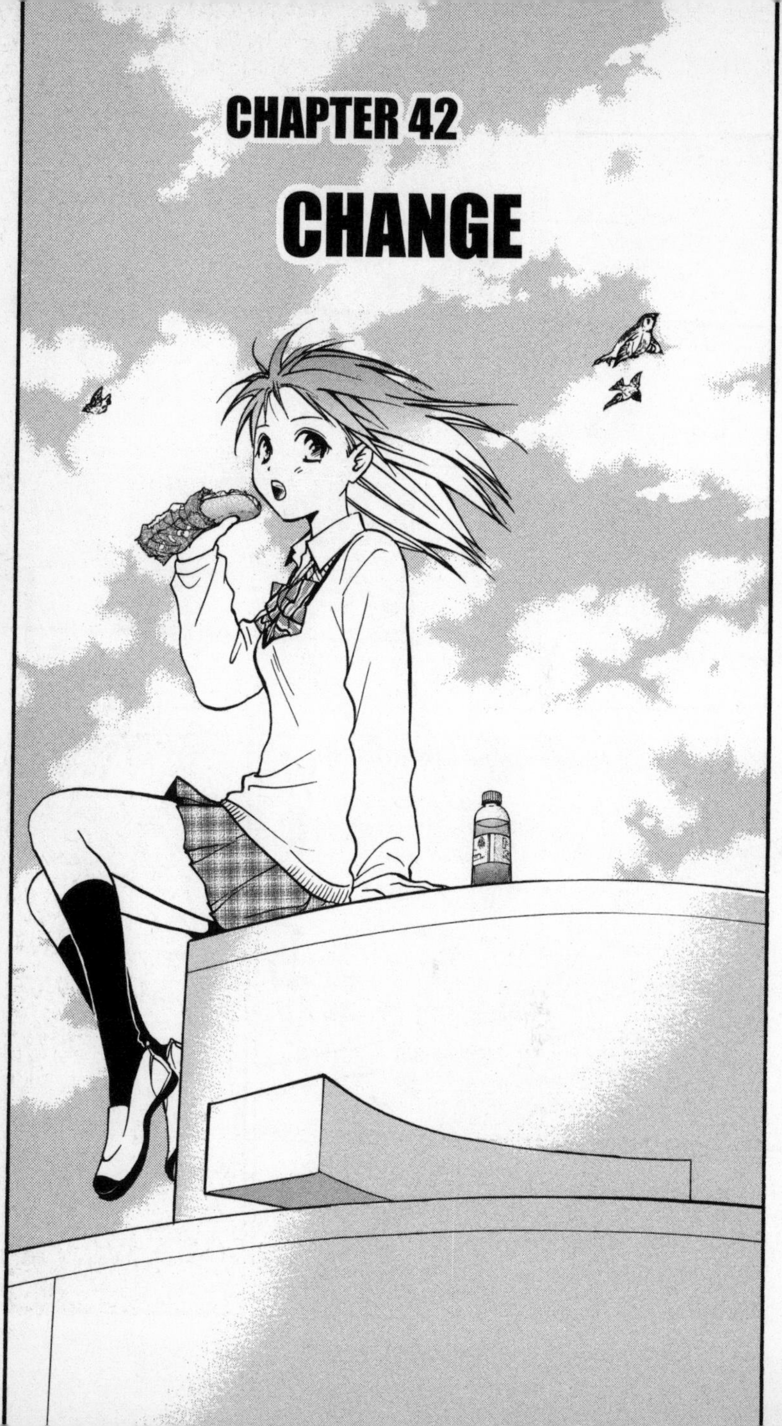
CHAPTER 42
CHANGE

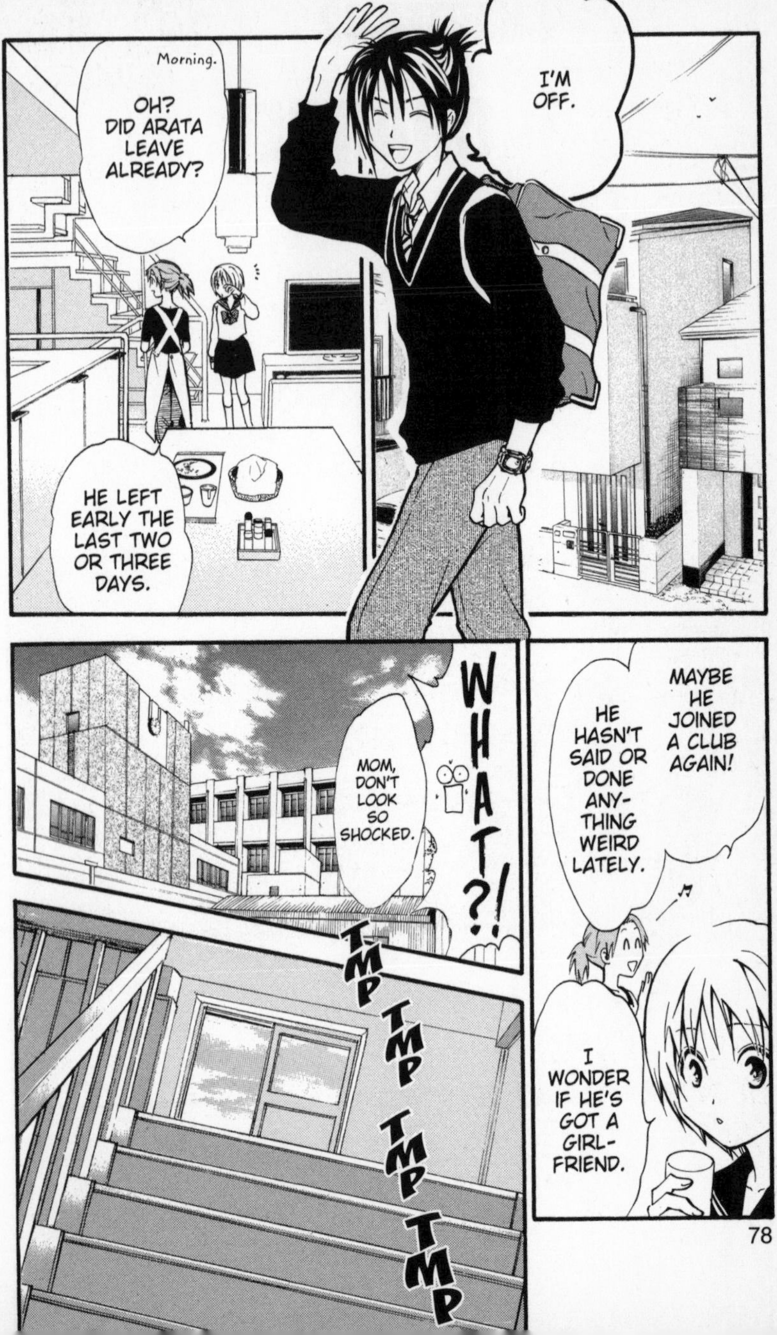

I'M OFF.
Morning.
OH? DID ARATA LEAVE ALREADY?
HE LEFT EARLY THE LAST TWO OR THREE DAYS.
MAYBE HE JOINED A CLUB AGAIN!
HE HASN'T SAID OR DONE ANYTHING WEIRD LATELY.
I WONDER IF HE'S GOT A GIRLFRIEND.
WHAT?!
MOM, DON'T LOOK SO SHOCKED.
TMP TMP TMP TMP TMP

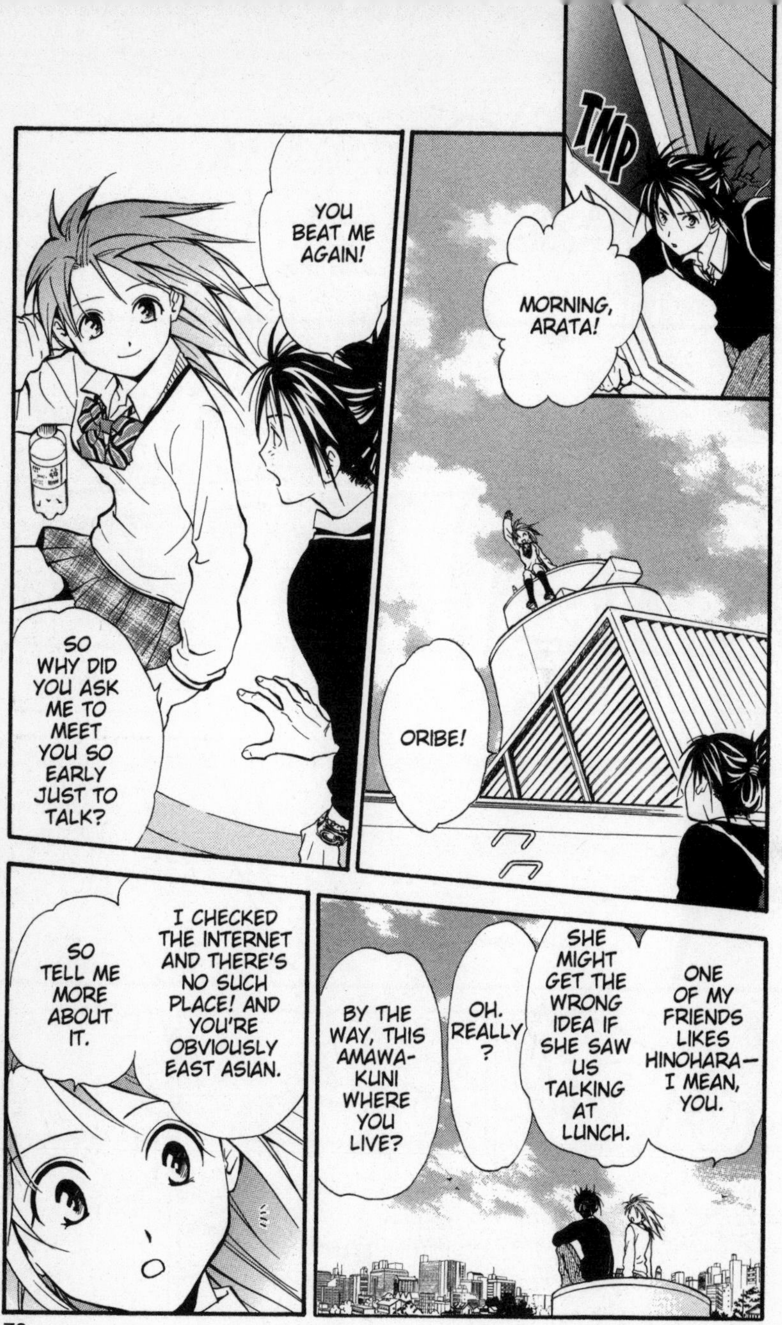
TMP
MORNING, ARATA!
ORIBE!
YOU BEAT ME AGAIN!
SO WHY DID YOU ASK ME TO MEET YOU SO EARLY JUST TO TALK?
ONE OF MY FRIENDS LIKES HINOHARA—I MEAN, YOU.
SHE MIGHT GET THE WRONG IDEA IF SHE SAW US TALKING AT LUNCH.
OH. REALLY?
BY THE WAY, THIS AMAWA-KUNI WHERE YOU LIVE?
I CHECKED THE INTERNET AND THERE'S NO SUCH PLACE! AND YOU'RE OBVIOUSLY EAST ASIAN.
SO TELL ME MORE ABOUT IT.

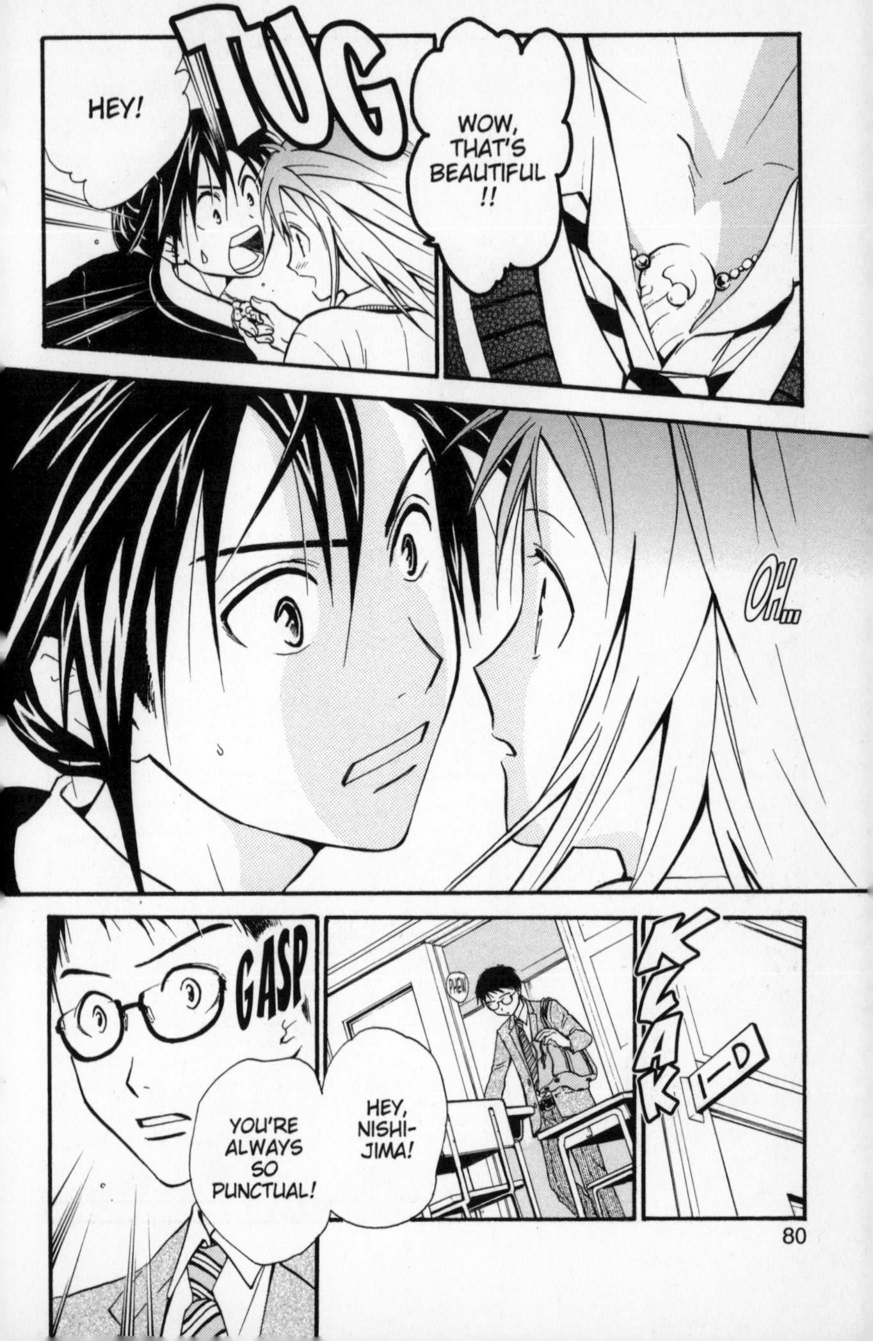
WOW, THAT'S BEAUTIFUL!!
TUG
HEY!
OH...
KLAK
I-D
PHEW
HEY, NISHI-JIMA!
YOU'RE ALWAYS SO PUNCTUAL!
GASP

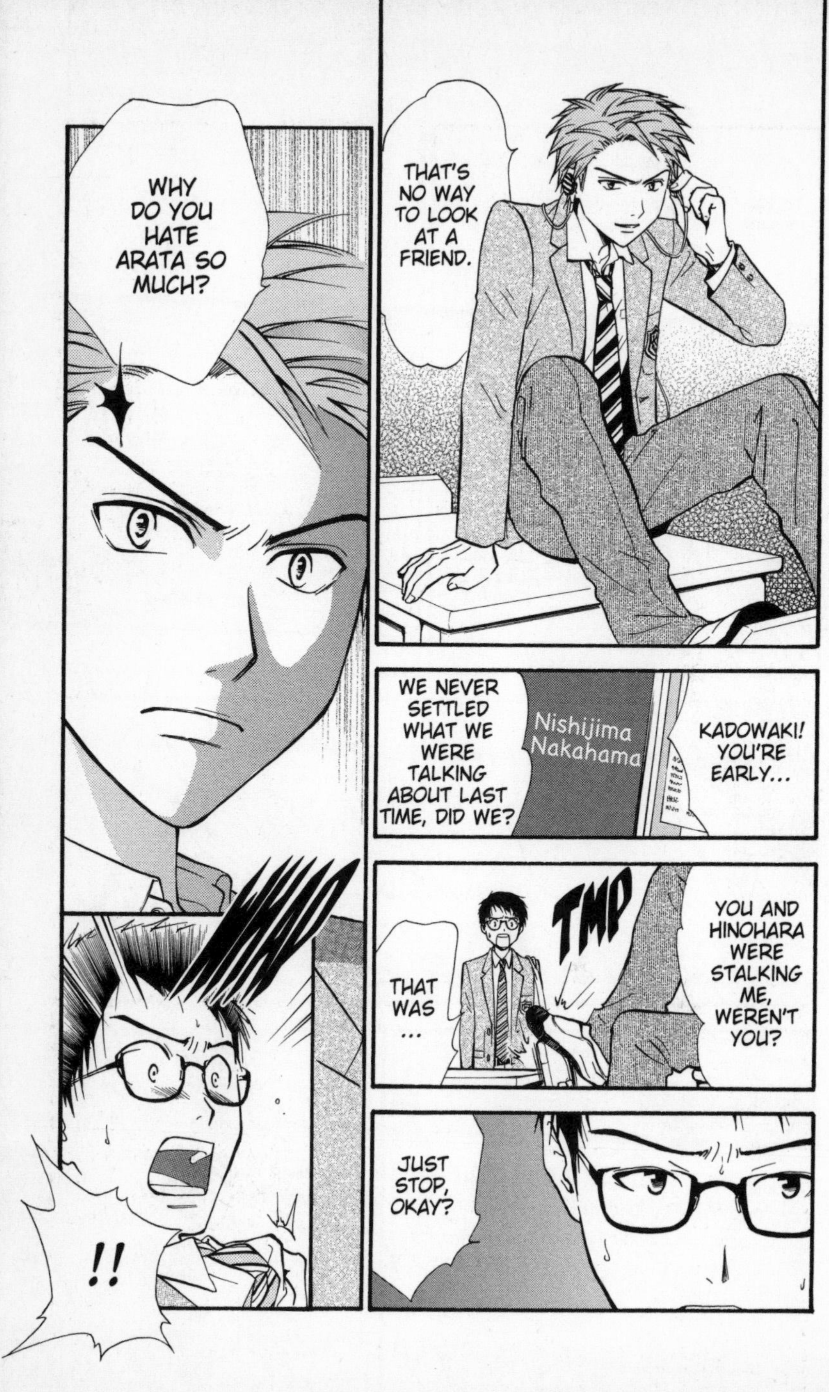
THAT'S NO WAY TO LOOK AT A FRIEND.
WHY DO YOU HATE ARATA SO MUCH?
KADOWAKI! YOU'RE EARLY...
Nishijima
Nakahama
WE NEVER SETTLED WHAT WE WERE TALKING ABOUT LAST TIME, DID WE?
YOU AND HINOHARA WERE STALKING ME, WEREN'T YOU?
TMP
THAT WAS ...
JUST STOP, OKAY?
!!

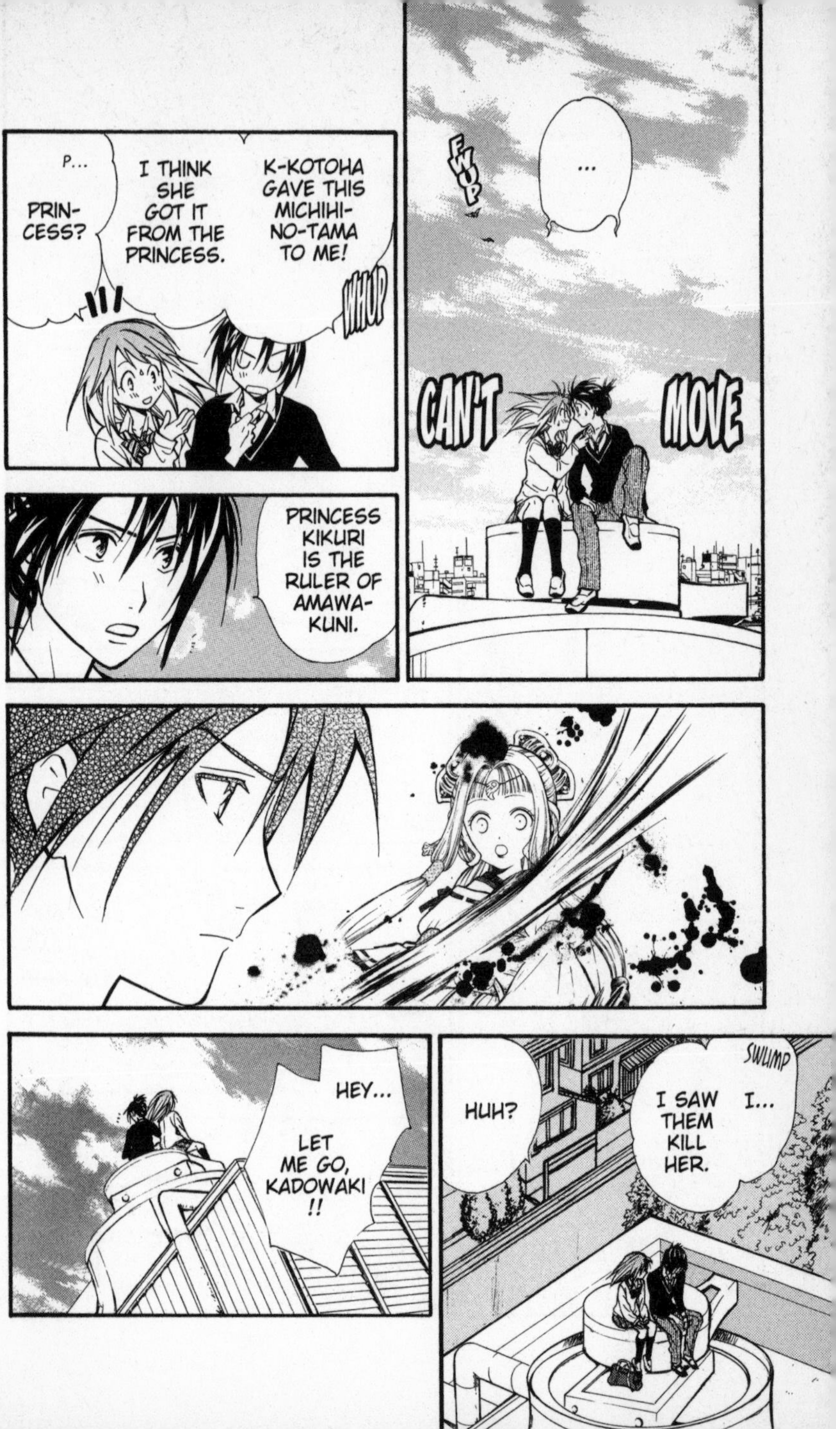
...
FWUP
CAN'T MOVE
K-KOTOHA GAVE THIS MICHIHI-NO-TAMA TO ME!
WHUP
I THINK SHE GOT IT FROM THE PRINCESS.
P...
PRIN-CESS?
PRINCESS KIKURI IS THE RULER OF AMAWA-KUNI.
SWUMP
I...
I SAW THEM KILL HER.
HUH?
HEY...
LET ME GO, KADOWAKI!!

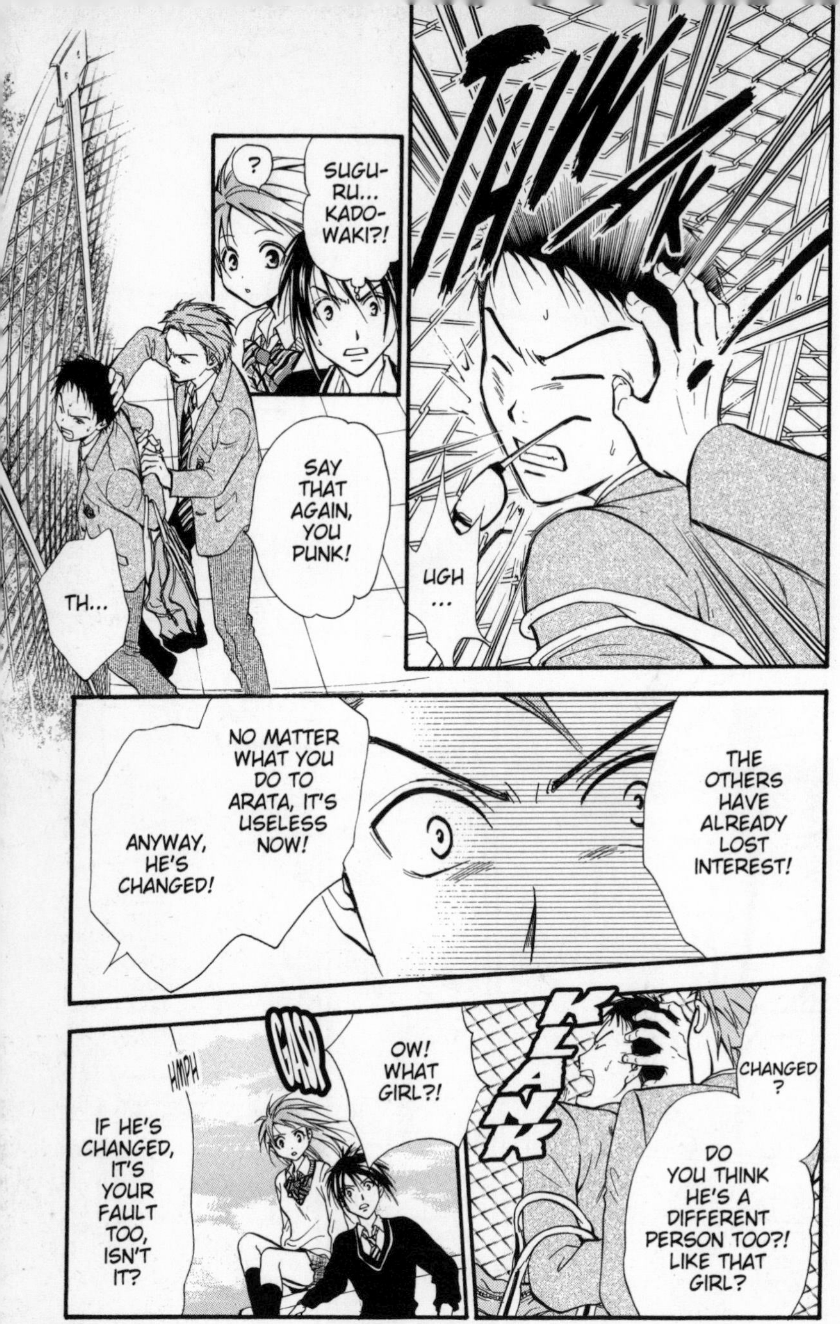
THWAK
UGH...
?
SUGURU... KADOWAKI?!
SAY THAT AGAIN, YOU PUNK!
TH...
THE OTHERS HAVE ALREADY LOST INTEREST!
NO MATTER WHAT YOU DO TO ARATA, IT'S USELESS NOW!
ANYWAY, HE'S CHANGED!
KLANK
CHANGED?
DO YOU THINK HE'S A DIFFERENT PERSON TOO?! LIKE THAT GIRL?
OW! WHAT GIRL?!
GASP
HMPH
IF HE'S CHANGED, IT'S YOUR FAULT TOO, ISN'T IT?

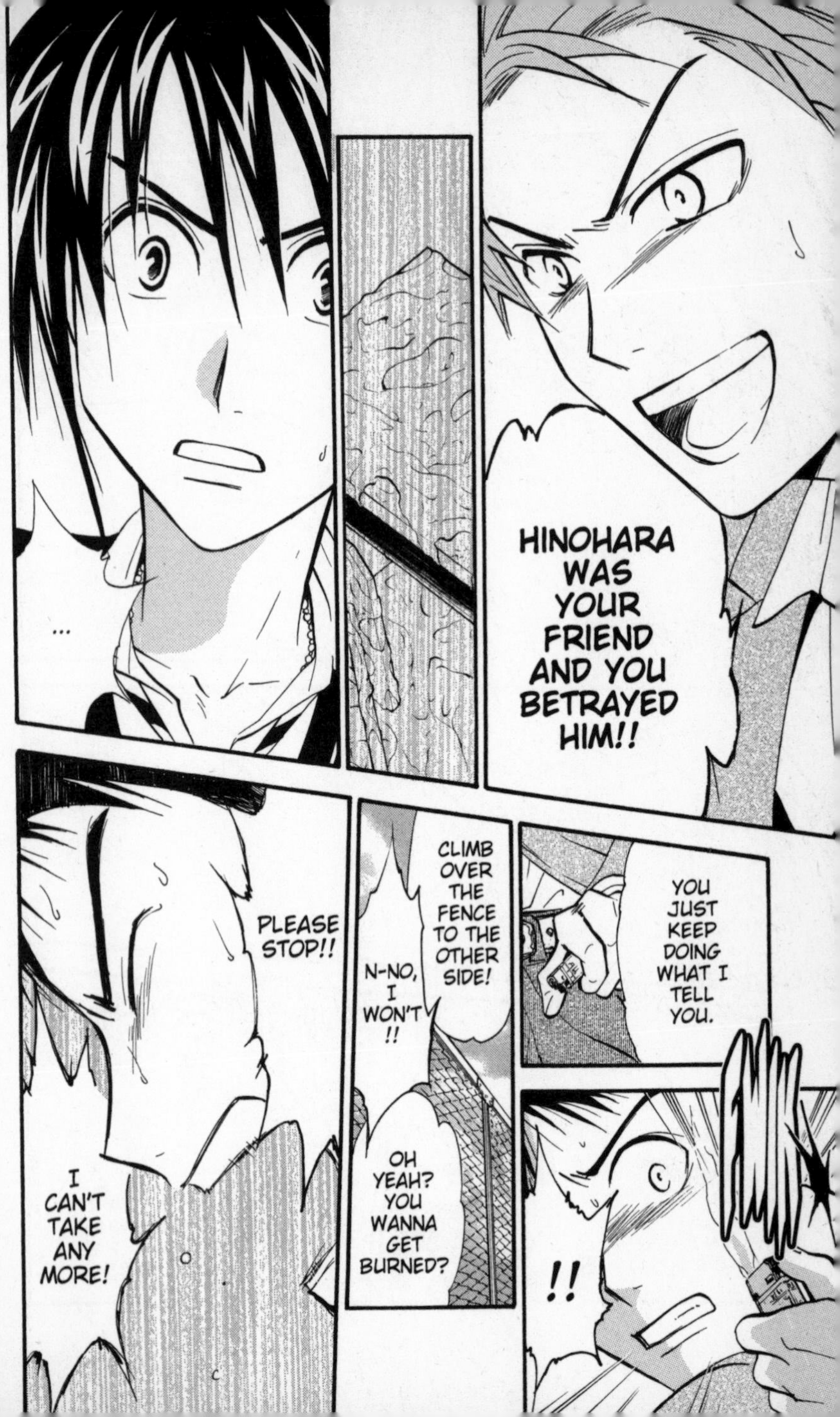
HINOHARA WAS YOUR FRIEND AND YOU BETRAYED HIM!!
...
YOU JUST KEEP DOING WHAT I TELL YOU.
!!
CLIMB OVER THE FENCE TO THE OTHER SIDE!
N-NO, I WON'T!!
OH YEAH? YOU WANNA GET BURNED?
PLEASE STOP!!
I CAN'T TAKE ANY MORE!

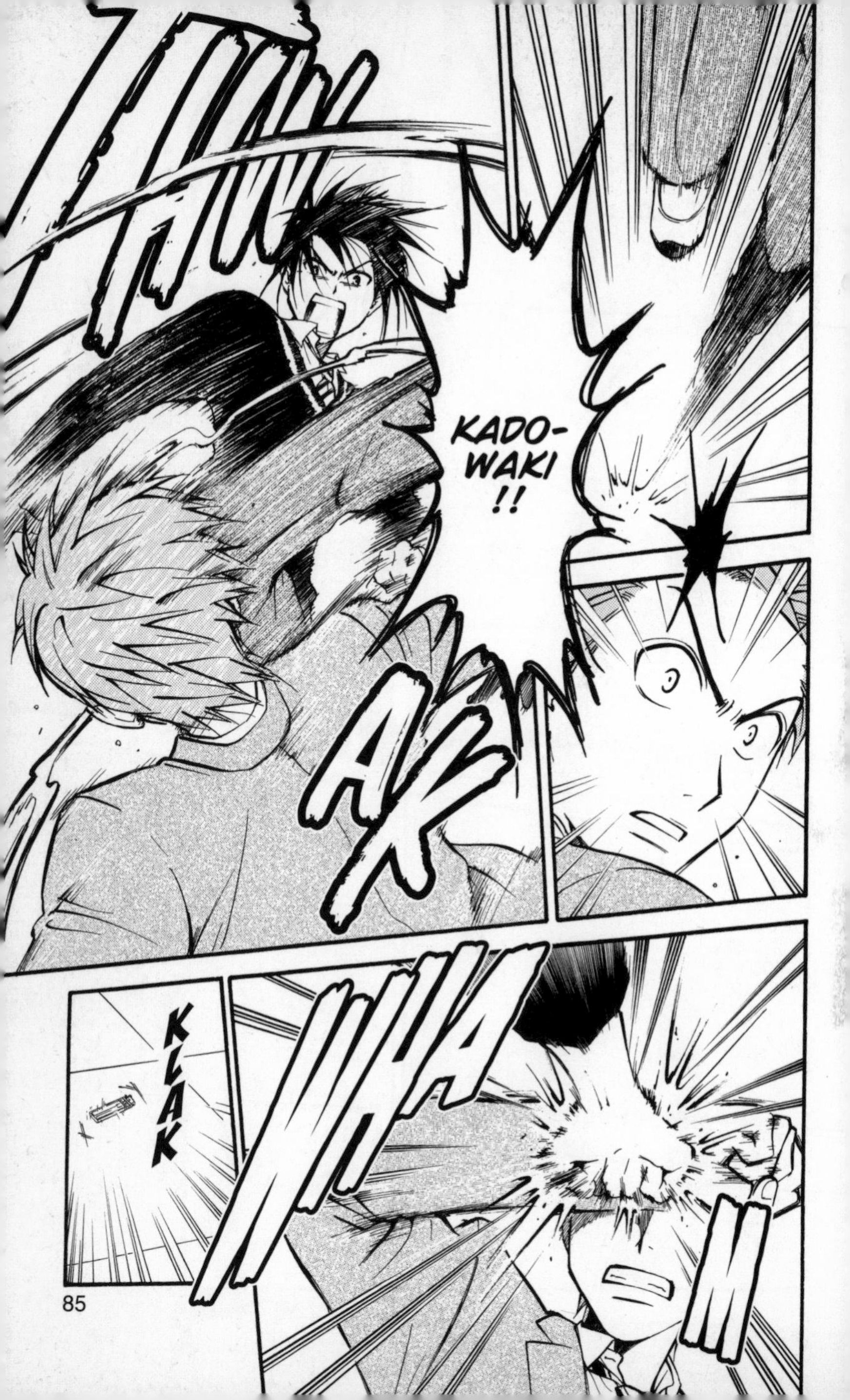
KADO-WAKI!!
WHAM
KLAK

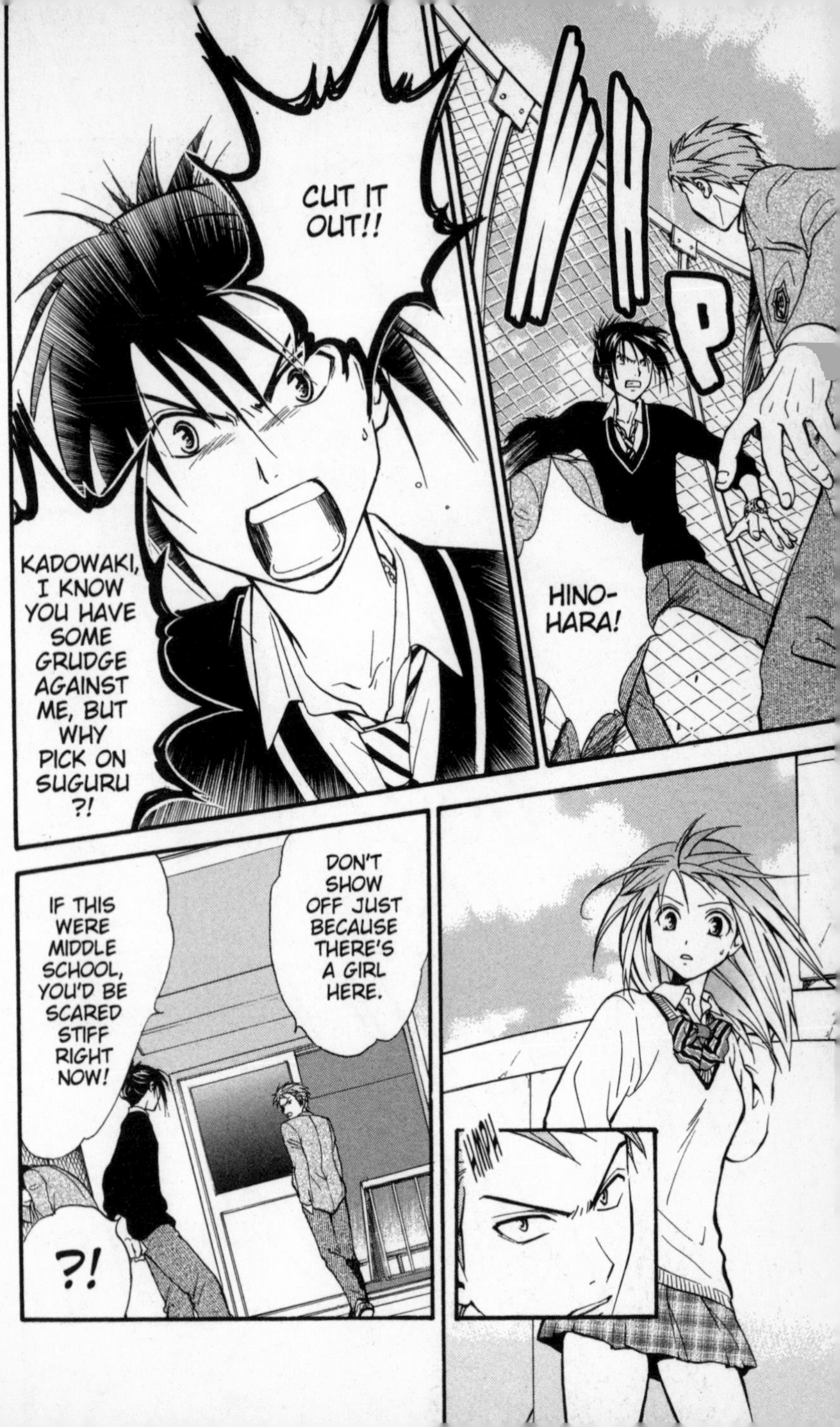
WHAP
HINO-HARA!
CUT IT OUT!!
KADOWAKI, I KNOW YOU HAVE SOME GRUDGE AGAINST ME, BUT WHY PICK ON SUGURU ?!
HMPH
DON'T SHOW OFF JUST BECAUSE THERE'S A GIRL HERE.
IF THIS WERE MIDDLE SCHOOL, YOU'D BE SCARED STIFF RIGHT NOW!
?!

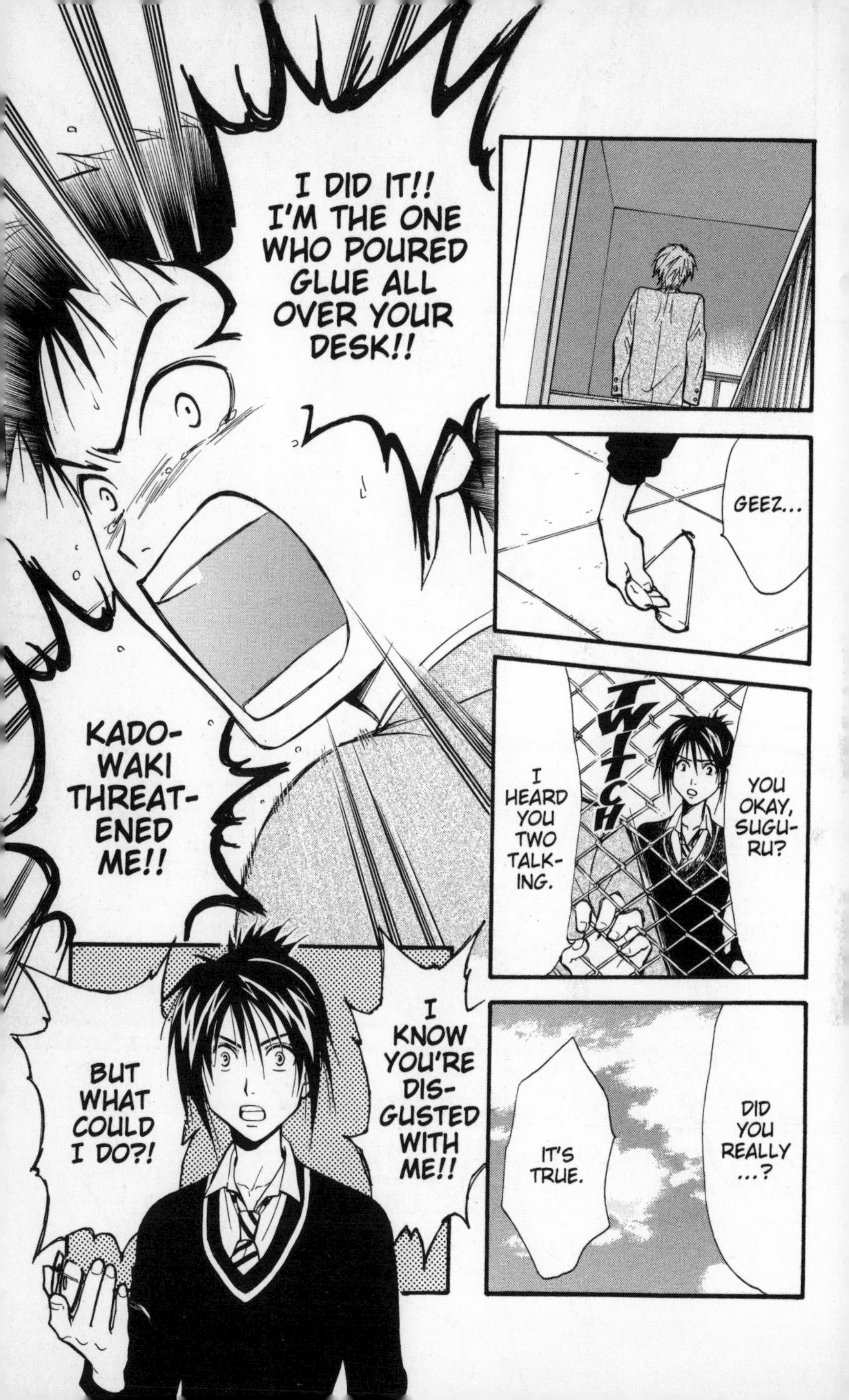
GEEZ...
TWITCH
YOU OKAY, SUGU-RU?
I HEARD YOU TWO TALK-ING.
DID YOU REALLY ...?
IT'S TRUE.
I DID IT!! I'M THE ONE WHO POURED GLUE ALL OVER YOUR DESK!!
KADO-WAKI THREAT-ENED ME!!
I KNOW YOU'RE DIS-GUSTED WITH ME!!
BUT WHAT COULD I DO?!

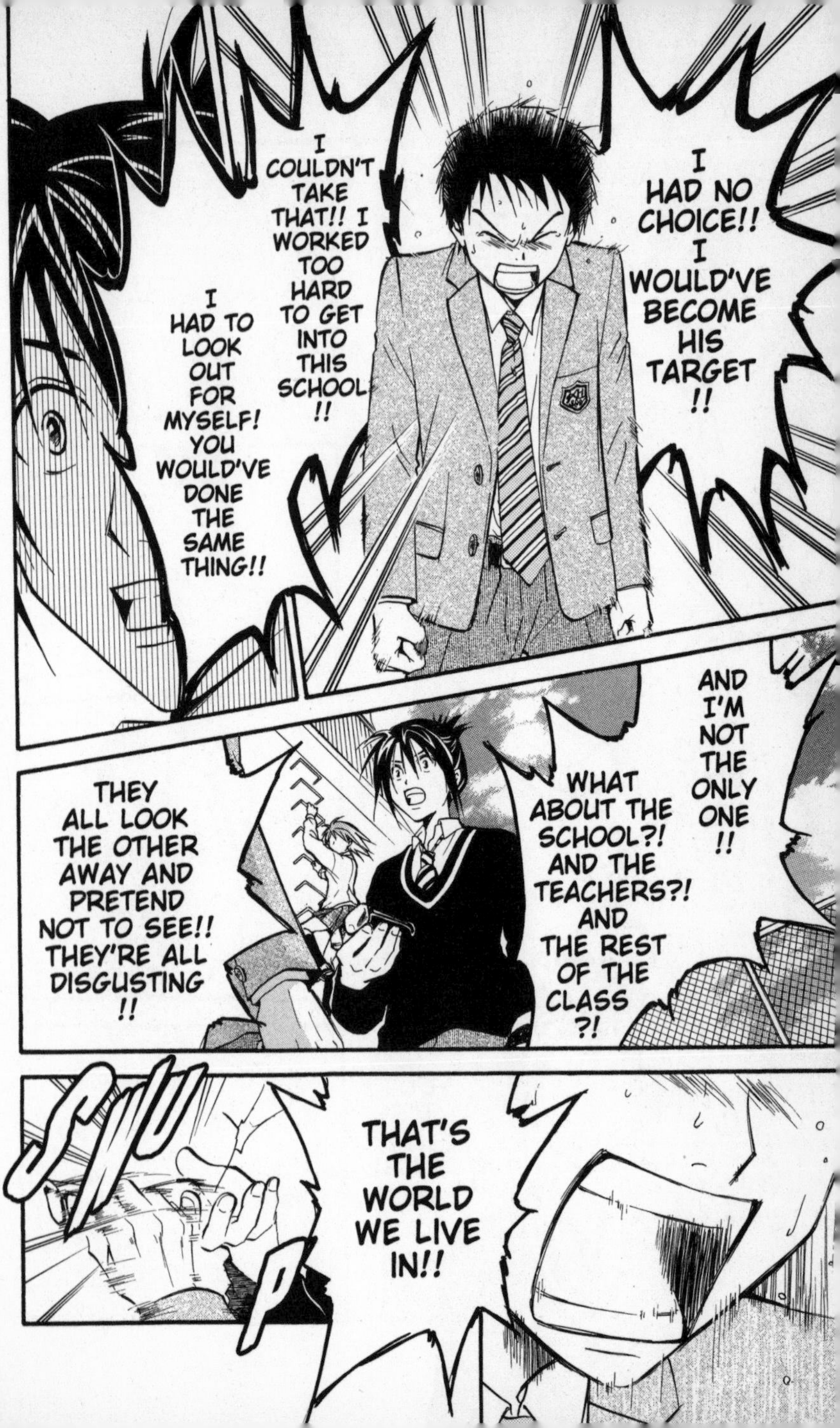
I HAD NO CHOICE!! I WOULD'VE BECOME HIS TARGET!!
I COULDN'T TAKE THAT!! I WORKED TOO HARD TO GET INTO THIS SCHOOL!!
I HAD TO LOOK OUT FOR MYSELF! YOU WOULD'VE DONE THE SAME THING!!
AND I'M NOT THE ONLY ONE!!
WHAT ABOUT THE SCHOOL?! AND THE TEACHERS?! AND THE REST OF THE CLASS?!
THEY ALL LOOK THE OTHER AWAY AND PRETEND NOT TO SEE!! THEY'RE ALL DISGUSTING!!
THAT'S THE WORLD WE LIVE IN!!

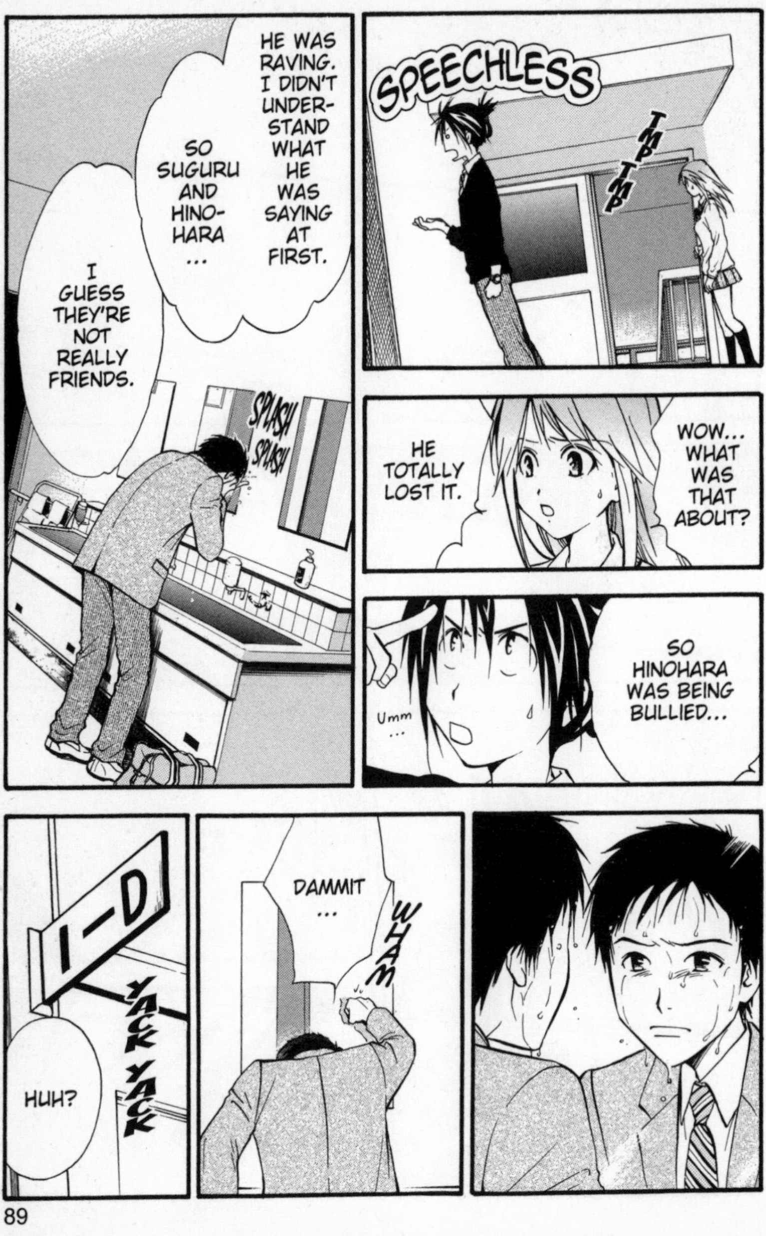
SPEECHLESS
TMP TMP
WOW... WHAT WAS THAT ABOUT?
HE TOTALLY LOST IT.
SO HINOHARA WAS BEING BULLIED...
Umm ...
HE WAS RAVING. I DIDN'T UNDER-STAND WHAT HE WAS SAYING AT FIRST.
SO SUGURU AND HINO-HARA ...
I GUESS THEY'RE NOT REALLY FRIENDS.
SPLASH SPLASH
DAMMIT ...
WHAM
I-D
YACK YACK
HUH?

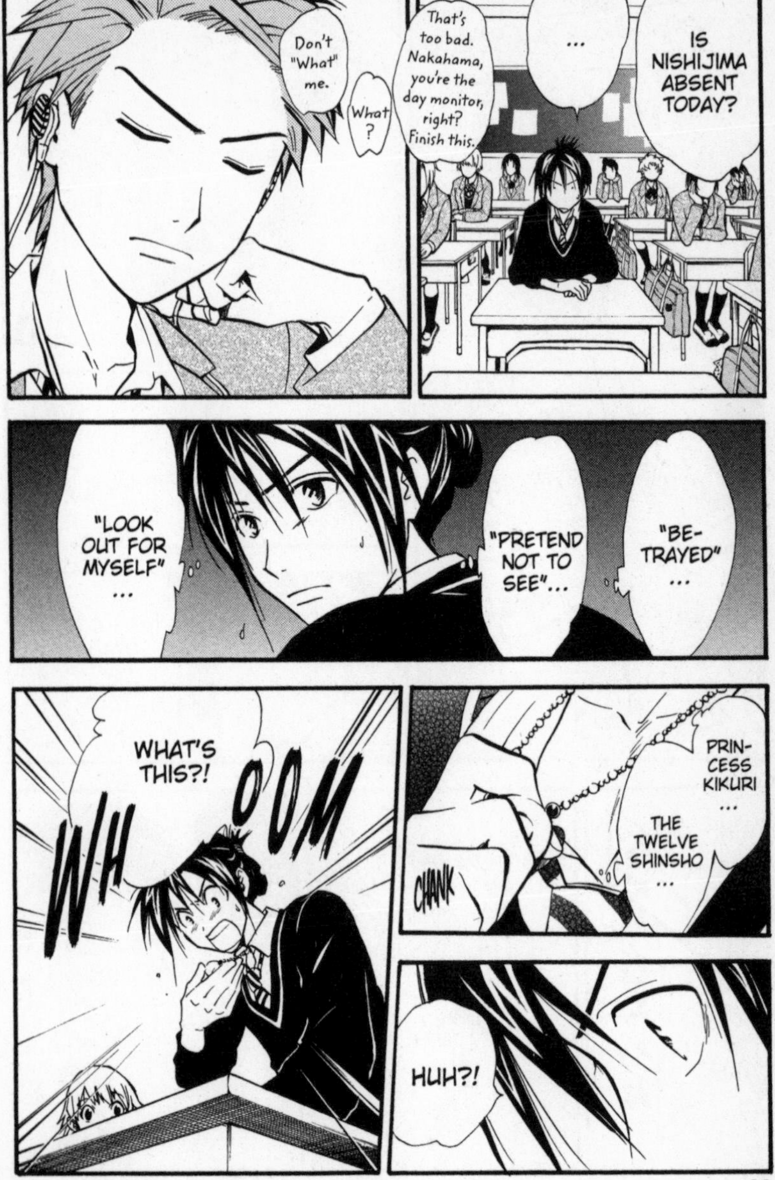
IS NISHIJIMA ABSENT TODAY?
...
That's too bad. Nakahama, you're the day monitor, right? Finish this.
What?
Don't "What" me.
"BE-TRAYED"...
"PRETEND NOT TO SEE"...
"LOOK OUT FOR MYSELF"...
PRIN-CESS KIKURI...
THE TWELVE SHINSHO...
CHANK
HUH?!
WHAT'S THIS?!
WHOOM

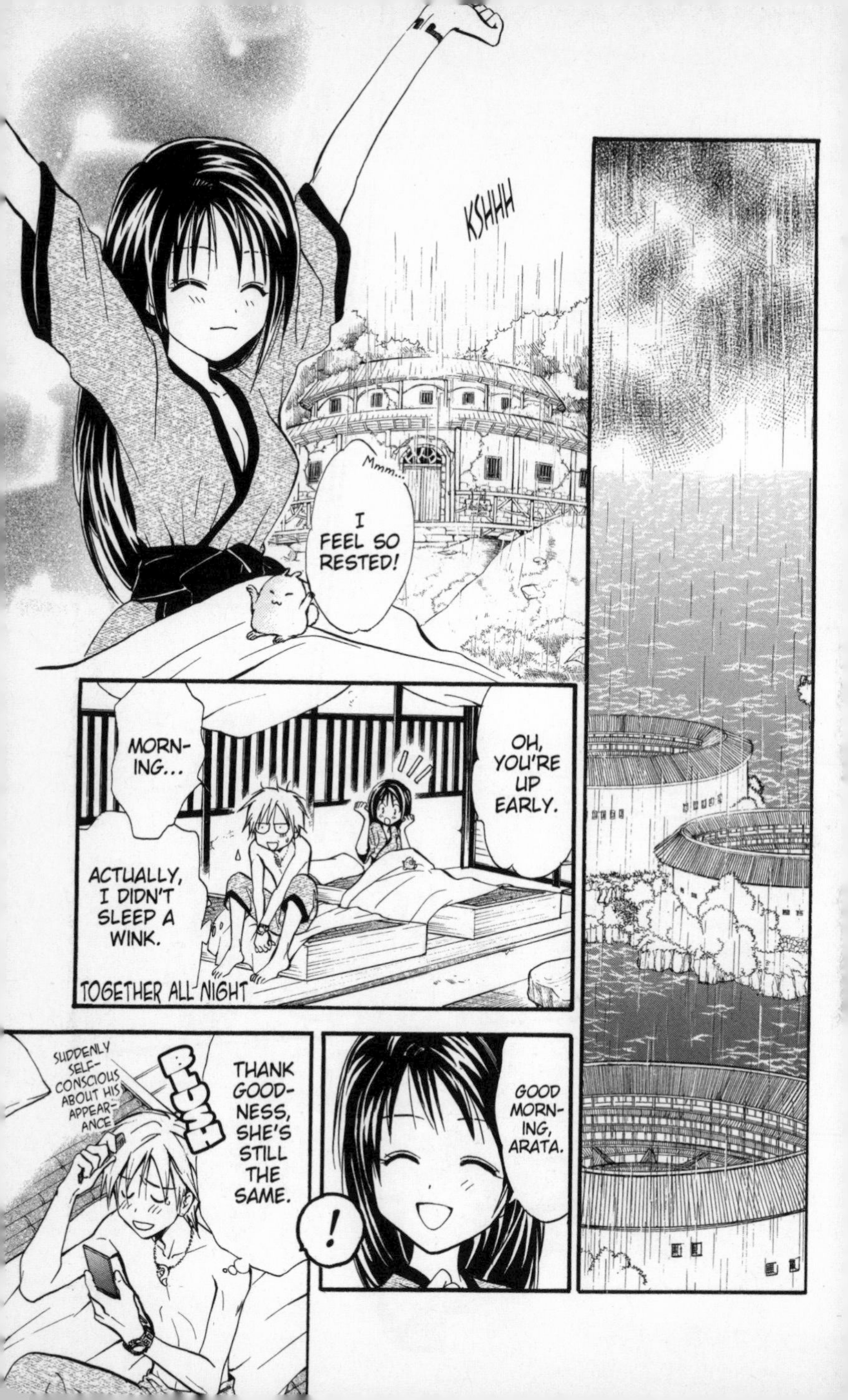
KSHHH
Mmm...
I FEEL SO RESTED!
OH, YOU'RE UP EARLY.
MORNING...
ACTUALLY, I DIDN'T SLEEP A WINK.
TOGETHER ALL NIGHT
GOOD MORNING, ARATA.
!
THANK GOODNESS, SHE'S STILL THE SAME.
SUDDENLY SELF-CONSCIOUS ABOUT HIS APPEARANCE

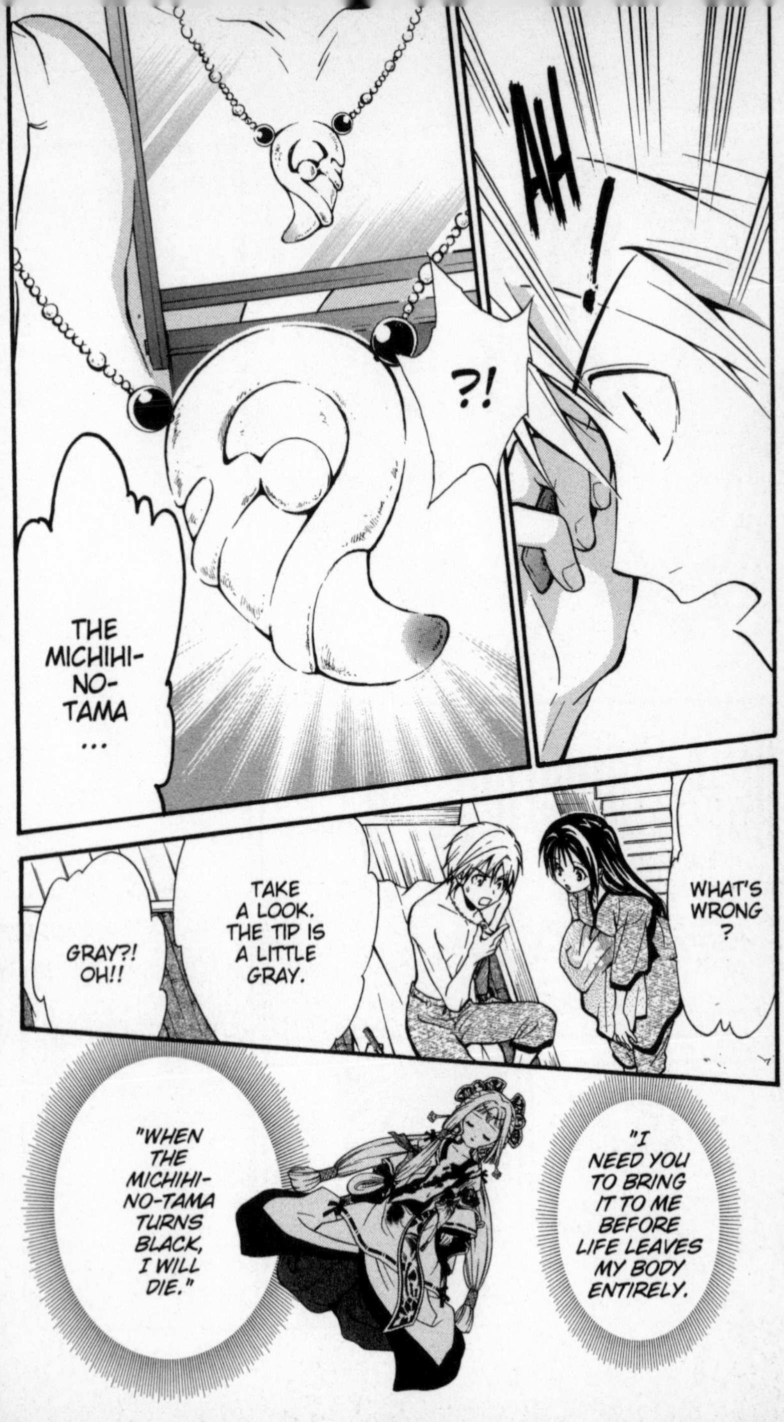
AH!
?!
THE MICHIHI-NO-TAMA...
WHAT'S WRONG?
TAKE A LOOK. THE TIP IS A LITTLE GRAY.
GRAY?! OH!!
"I NEED YOU TO BRING IT TO ME BEFORE LIFE LEAVES MY BODY ENTIRELY.
"WHEN THE MICHIHI-NO-TAMA TURNS BLACK, I WILL DIE."

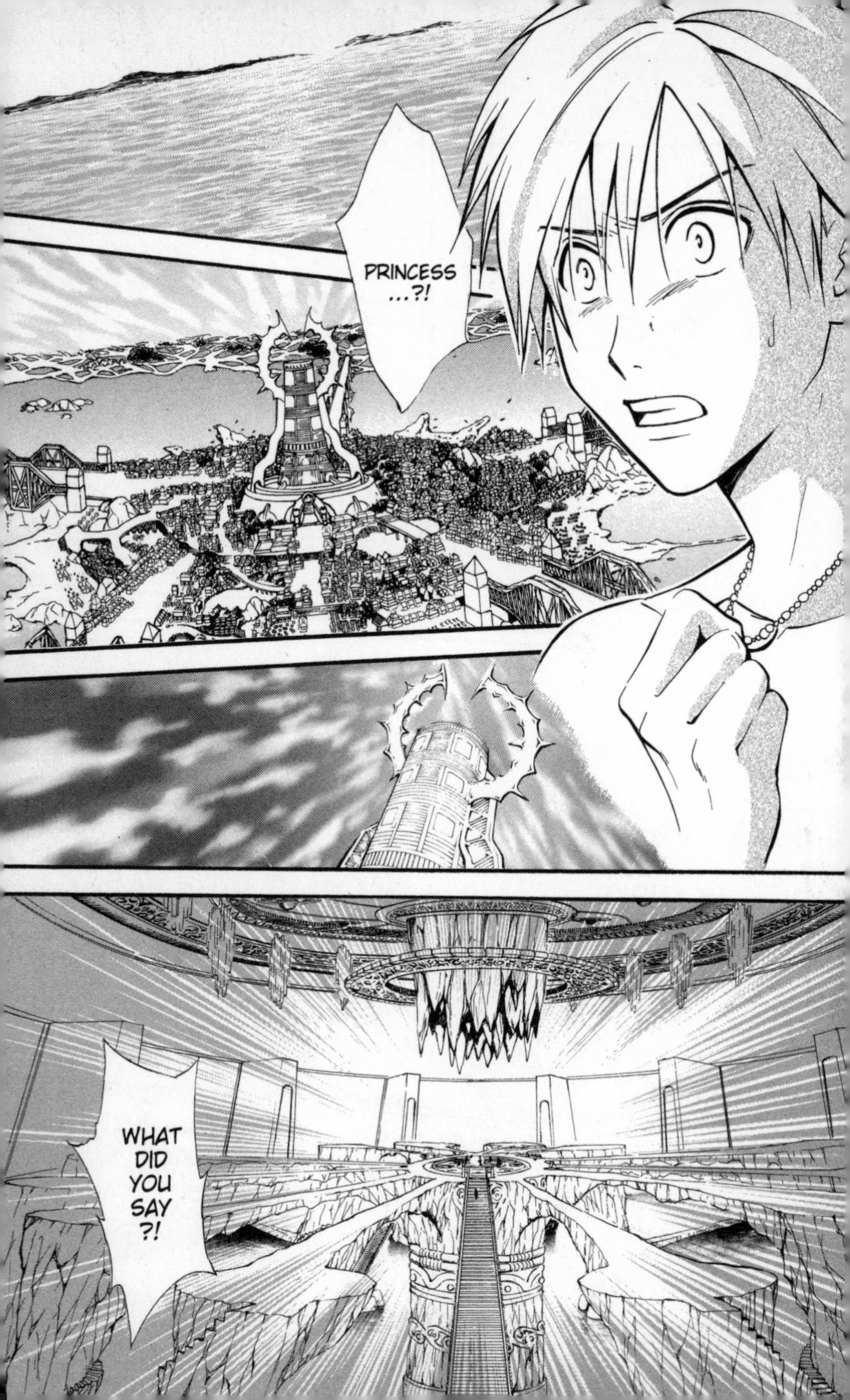
PRINCESS ...?!
WHAT DID YOU SAY ?!

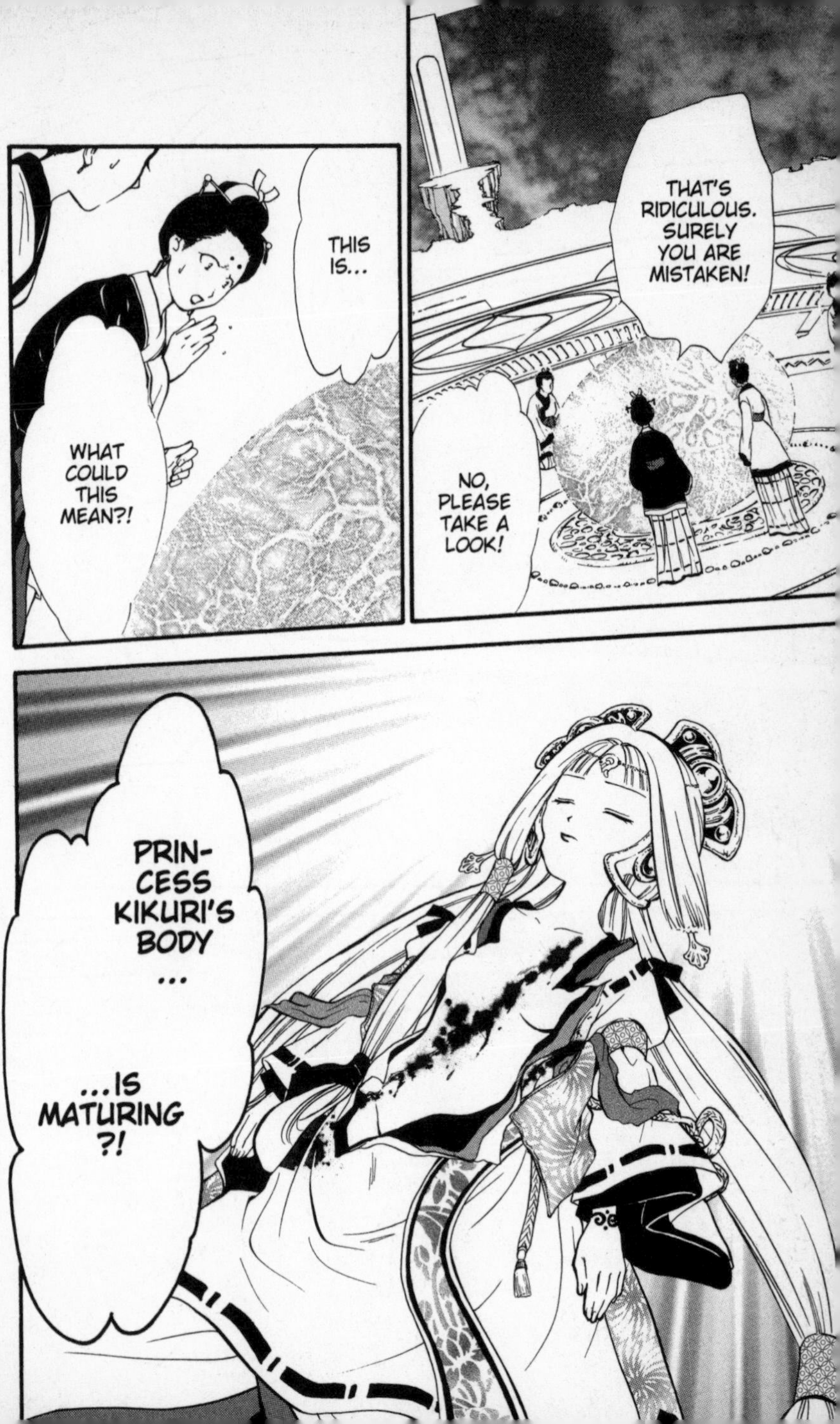
THAT'S RIDICULOUS. SURELY YOU ARE MISTAKEN!
NO, PLEASE TAKE A LOOK!
THIS IS...
WHAT COULD THIS MEAN?!
PRIN-CESS KIKURI'S BODY...
...IS MATURING?!

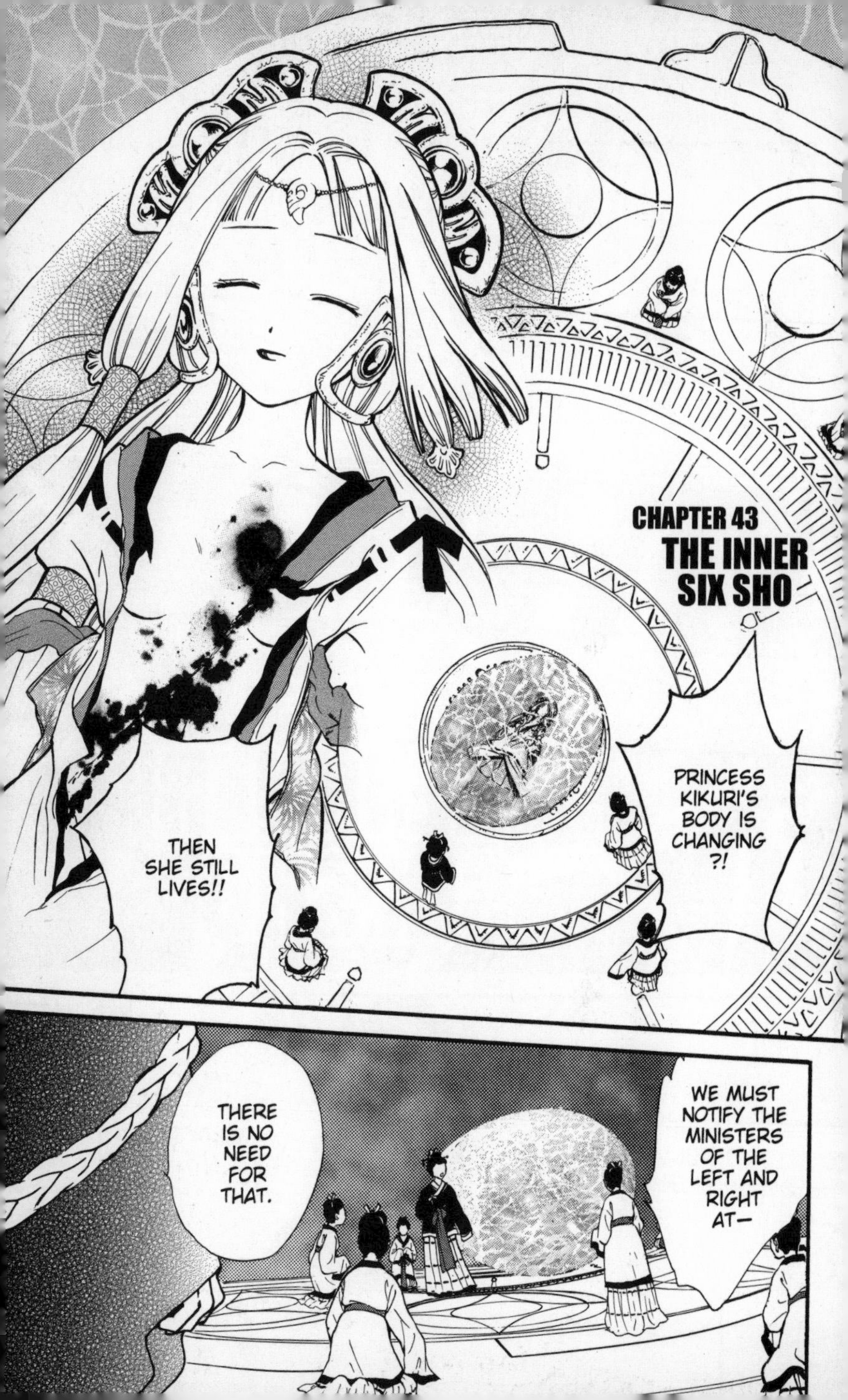
CHAPTER 43
THE INNER SIX SHO
PRINCESS KIKURI'S BODY IS CHANGING ?!
THEN SHE STILL LIVES!!
WE MUST NOTIFY THE MINISTERS OF THE LEFT AND RIGHT AT—
THERE IS NO NEED FOR THAT.

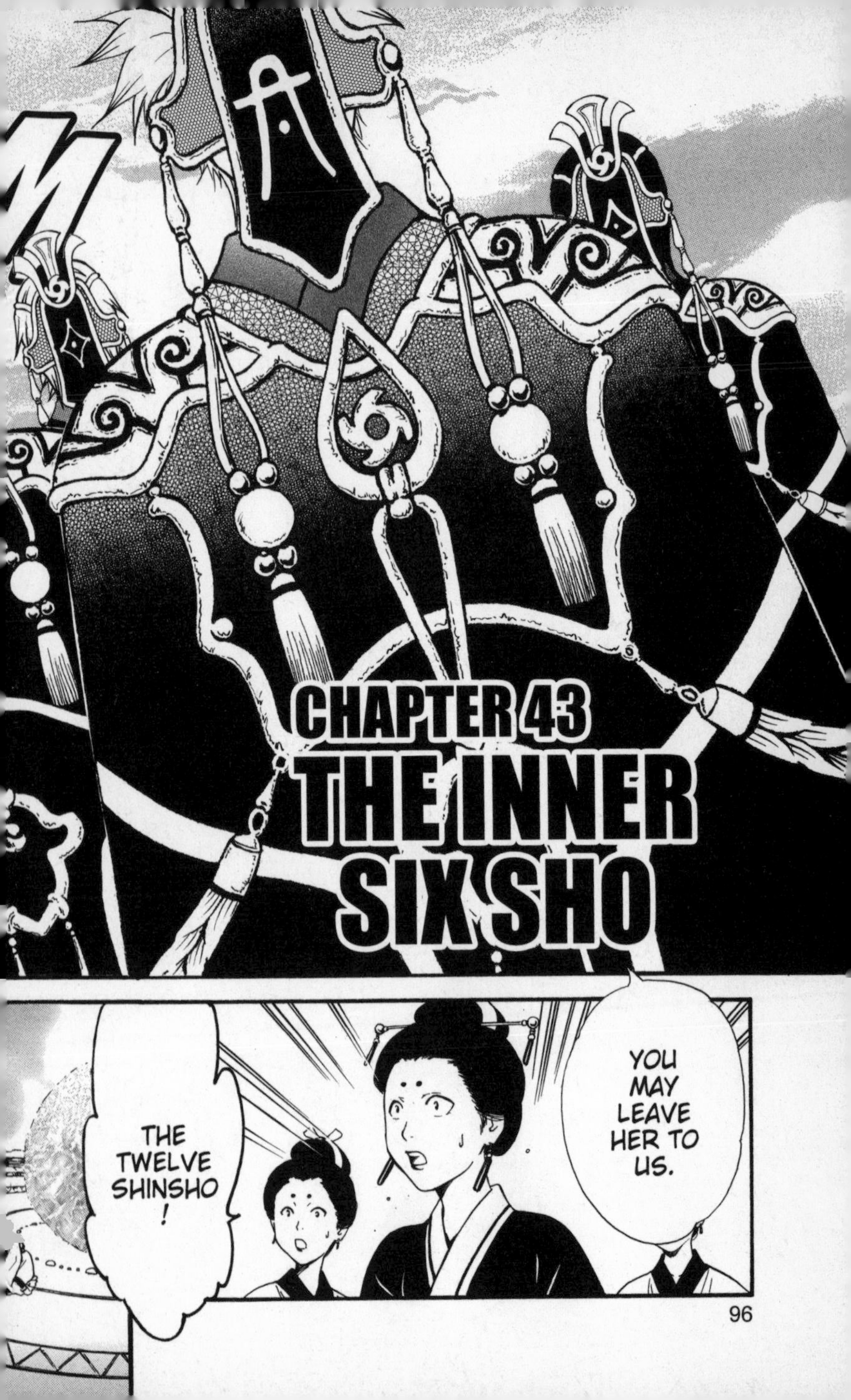
CHAPTER 43
THE INNER SIX SHO
YOU MAY LEAVE HER TO US.
THE TWELVE SHINSHO!

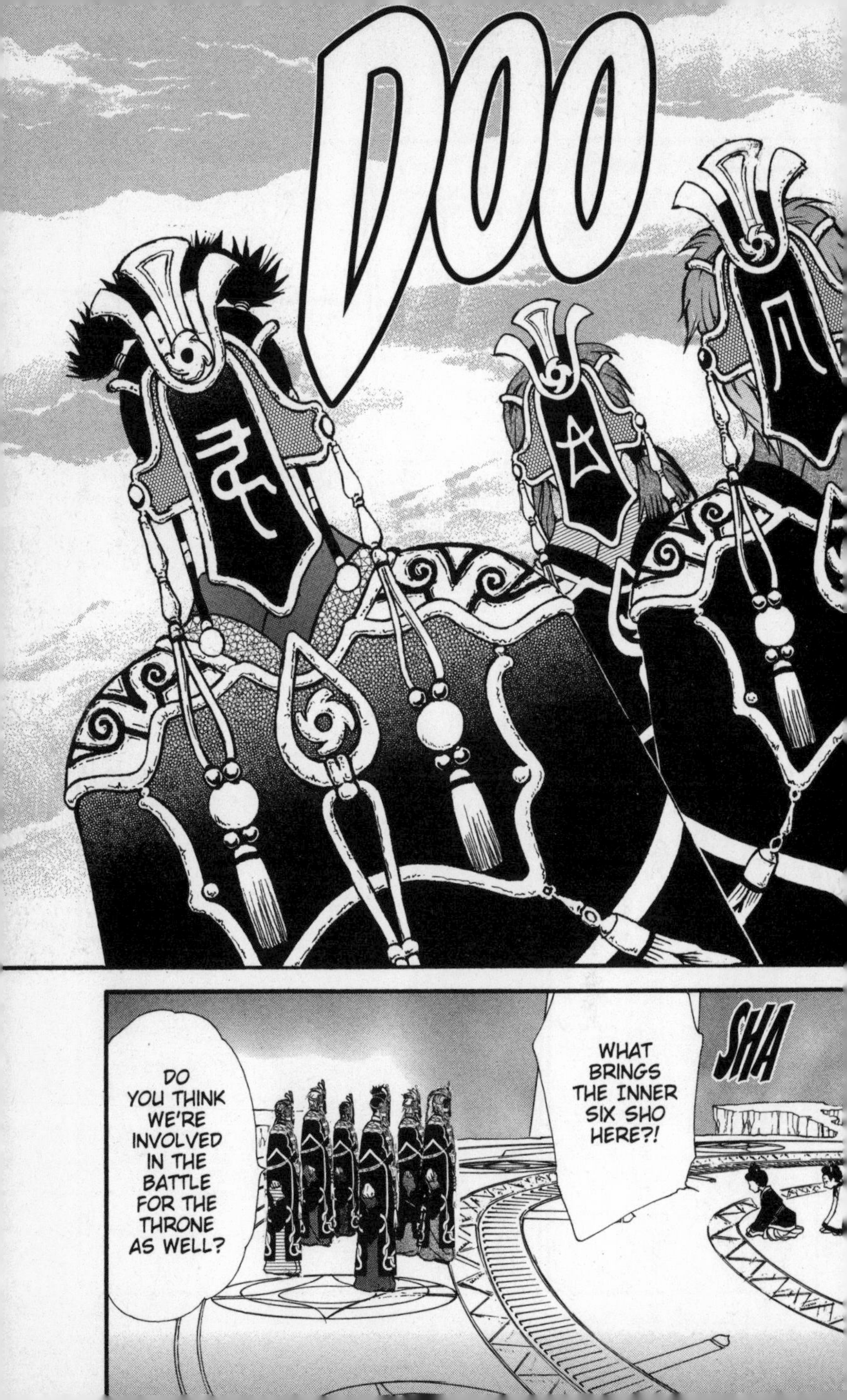
DOO
SHA
WHAT BRINGS THE INNER SIX SHO HERE?!
DO YOU THINK WE'RE INVOLVED IN THE BATTLE FOR THE THRONE AS WELL?

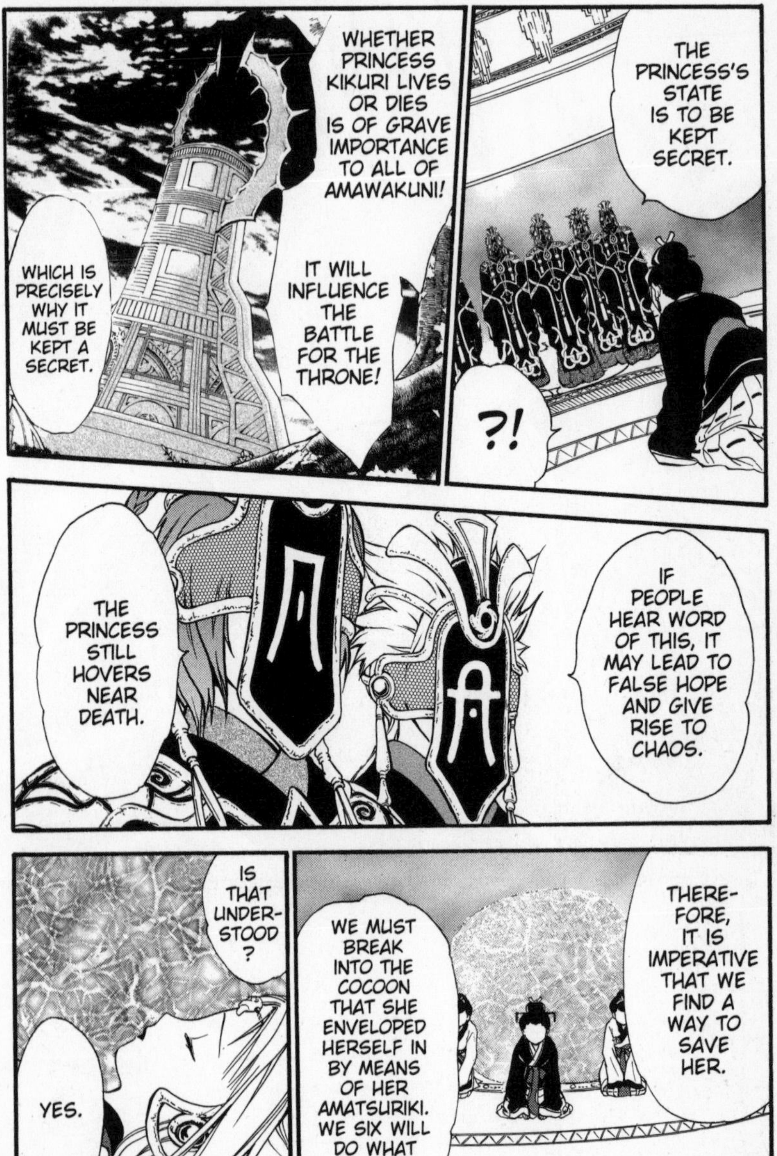
THE PRINCESS'S STATE IS TO BE KEPT SECRET.
?!
WHETHER PRINCESS KIKURI LIVES OR DIES IS OF GRAVE IMPORTANCE TO ALL OF AMAWAKUNI!
IT WILL INFLUENCE THE BATTLE FOR THE THRONE!
WHICH IS PRECISELY WHY IT MUST BE KEPT A SECRET.
THE PRINCESS STILL HOVERS NEAR DEATH.
IF PEOPLE HEAR WORD OF THIS, IT MAY LEAD TO FALSE HOPE AND GIVE RISE TO CHAOS.
THEREFORE, IT IS IMPERATIVE THAT WE FIND A WAY TO SAVE HER.
WE MUST BREAK INTO THE COCOON THAT SHE ENVELOPED HERSELF IN BY MEANS OF HER AMATSURIKI. WE SIX WILL DO WHAT WE CAN.
IS THAT UNDERSTOOD?
YES.

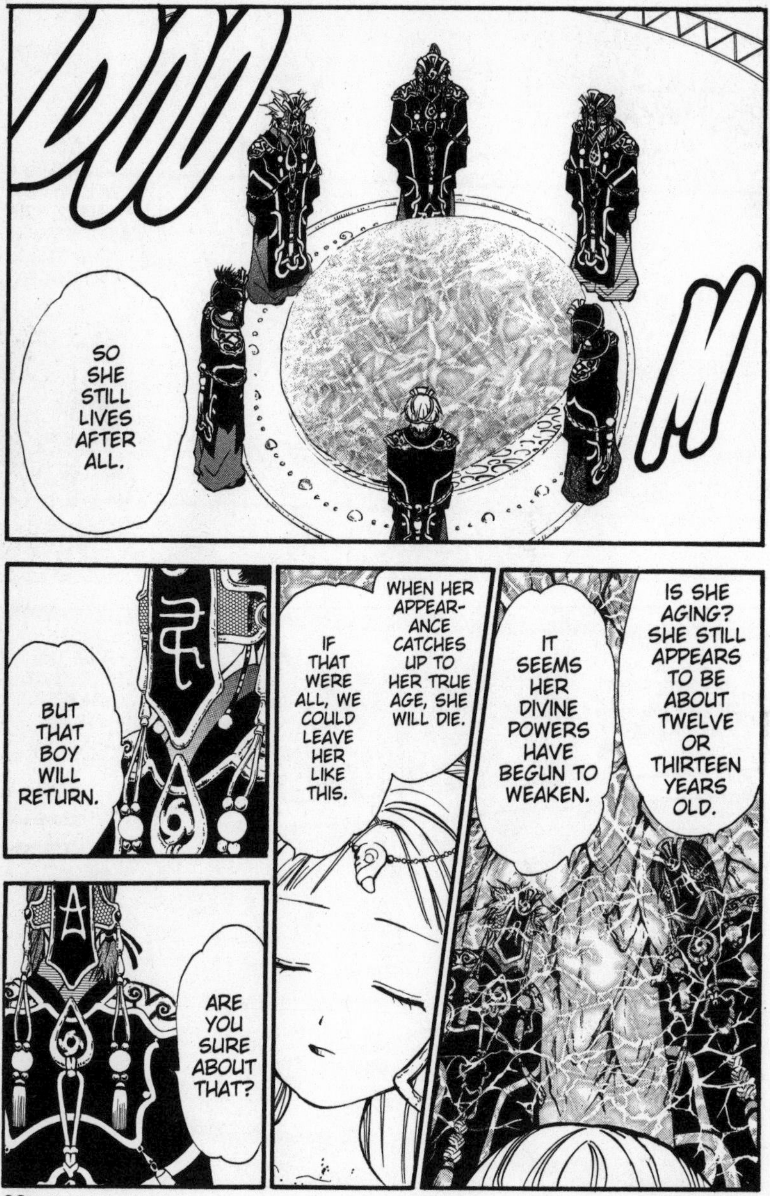
DOO
M
SO SHE STILL LIVES AFTER ALL.
IS SHE AGING? SHE STILL APPEARS TO BE ABOUT TWELVE OR THIRTEEN YEARS OLD.
IT SEEMS HER DIVINE POWERS HAVE BEGUN TO WEAKEN.
WHEN HER APPEAR-ANCE CATCHES UP TO HER TRUE AGE, SHE WILL DIE.
IF THAT WERE ALL, WE COULD LEAVE HER LIKE THIS.
BUT THAT BOY WILL RETURN.
ARE YOU SURE ABOUT THAT?

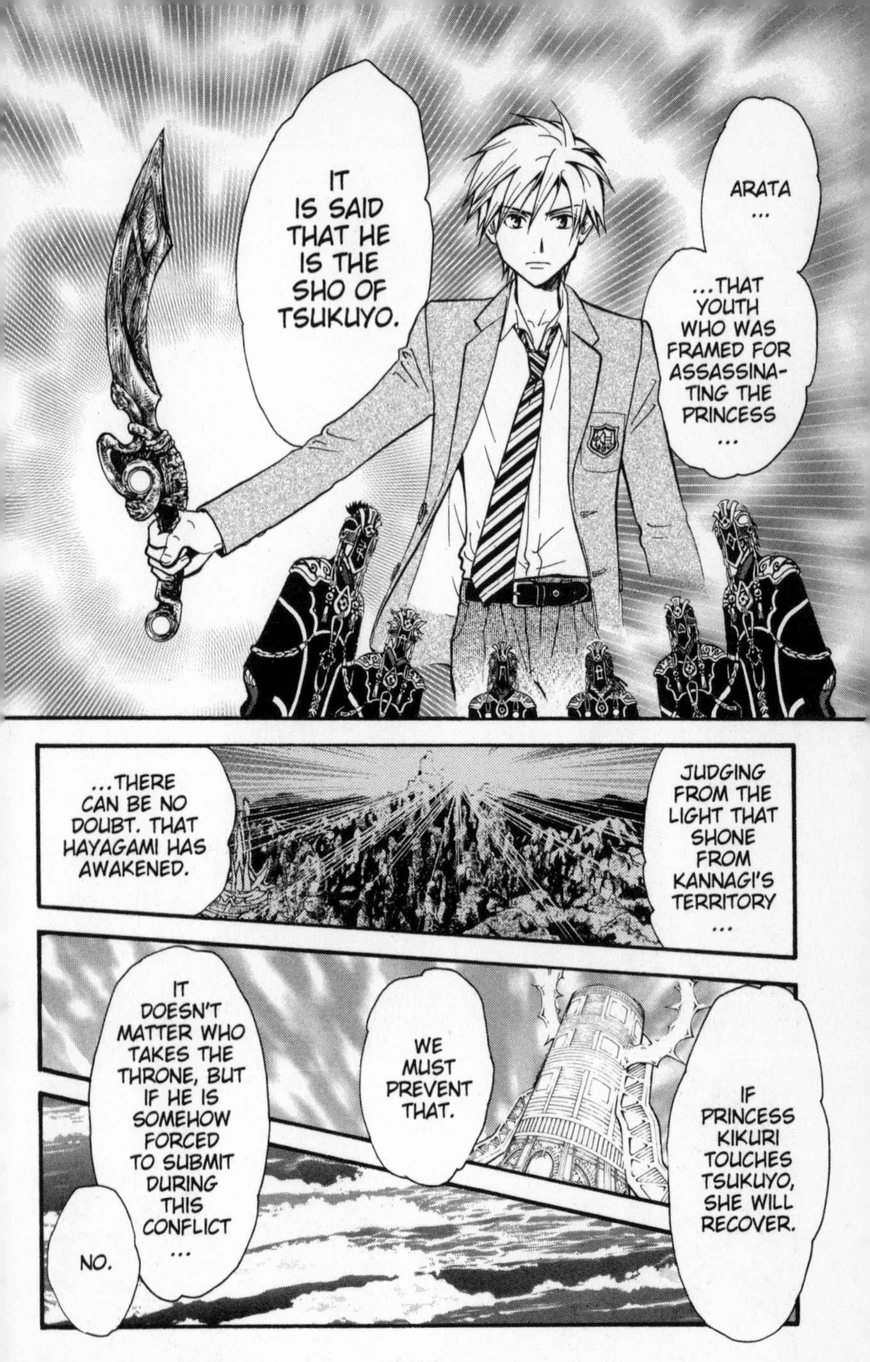
ARATA ...
...THAT YOUTH WHO WAS FRAMED FOR ASSASSINA-TING THE PRINCESS ...
IT IS SAID THAT HE IS THE SHO OF TSUKUYO.
JUDGING FROM THE LIGHT THAT SHONE FROM KANNAGI'S TERRITORY ...
...THERE CAN BE NO DOUBT. THAT HAYAGAMI HAS AWAKENED.
IF PRINCESS KIKURI TOUCHES TSUKUYO, SHE WILL RECOVER.
WE MUST PREVENT THAT.
IT DOESN'T MATTER WHO TAKES THE THRONE, BUT IF HE IS SOMEHOW FORCED TO SUBMIT DURING THIS CONFLICT ...
NO.

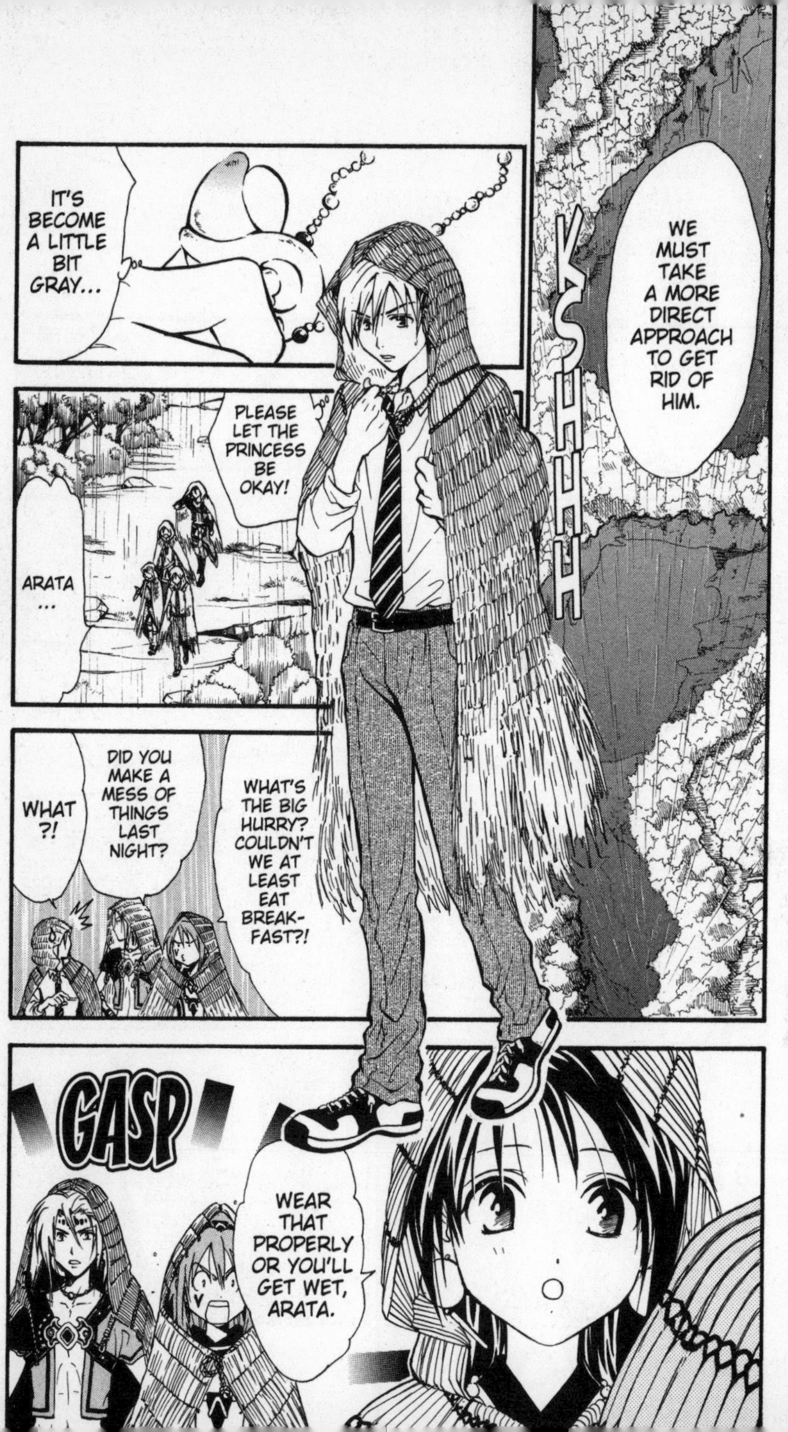
WE MUST TAKE A MORE DIRECT APPROACH TO GET RID OF HIM.
KASHHHHH
IT'S BECOME A LITTLE BIT GRAY...
PLEASE LET THE PRINCESS BE OKAY!
ARATA...
WHAT'S THE BIG HURRY? COULDN'T WE AT LEAST EAT BREAK-FAST?!
DID YOU MAKE A MESS OF THINGS LAST NIGHT?
WHAT?!
GASP
WEAR THAT PROPERLY OR YOU'LL GET WET, ARATA.

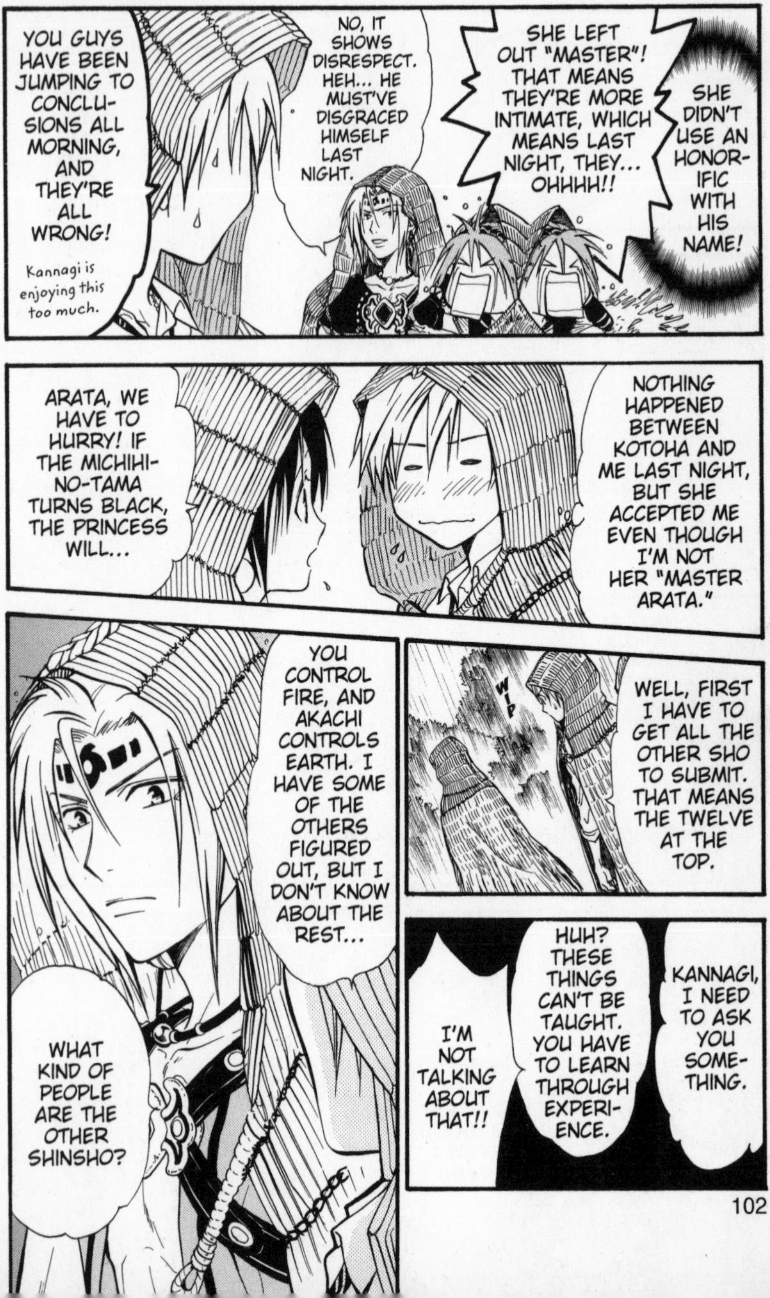

SHE DIDN'T USE AN HONORIFIC WITH HIS NAME!
SHE LEFT OUT "MASTER"! THAT MEANS THEY'RE MORE INTIMATE, WHICH MEANS LAST NIGHT, THEY... OHHHH!!
NO, IT SHOWS DISRESPECT. HEH... HE MUST'VE DISGRACED HIMSELF LAST NIGHT.
YOU GUYS HAVE BEEN JUMPING TO CONCLUSIONS ALL MORNING, AND THEY'RE ALL WRONG!
Kannagi is enjoying this too much.
NOTHING HAPPENED BETWEEN KOTOHA AND ME LAST NIGHT, BUT SHE ACCEPTED ME EVEN THOUGH I'M NOT HER "MASTER ARATA."
ARATA, WE HAVE TO HURRY! IF THE MICHIHI-NO-TAMA TURNS BLACK, THE PRINCESS WILL...
WELL, FIRST I HAVE TO GET ALL THE OTHER SHO TO SUBMIT. THAT MEANS THE TWELVE AT THE TOP.
WIP
KANNAGI, I NEED TO ASK YOU SOMETHING.
HUH? THESE THINGS CAN'T BE TAUGHT. YOU HAVE TO LEARN THROUGH EXPERIENCE.
I'M NOT TALKING ABOUT THAT!!
YOU CONTROL FIRE, AND AKACHI CONTROLS EARTH. I HAVE SOME OF THE OTHERS FIGURED OUT, BUT I DON'T KNOW ABOUT THE REST...
WHAT KIND OF PEOPLE ARE THE OTHER SHINSHO?

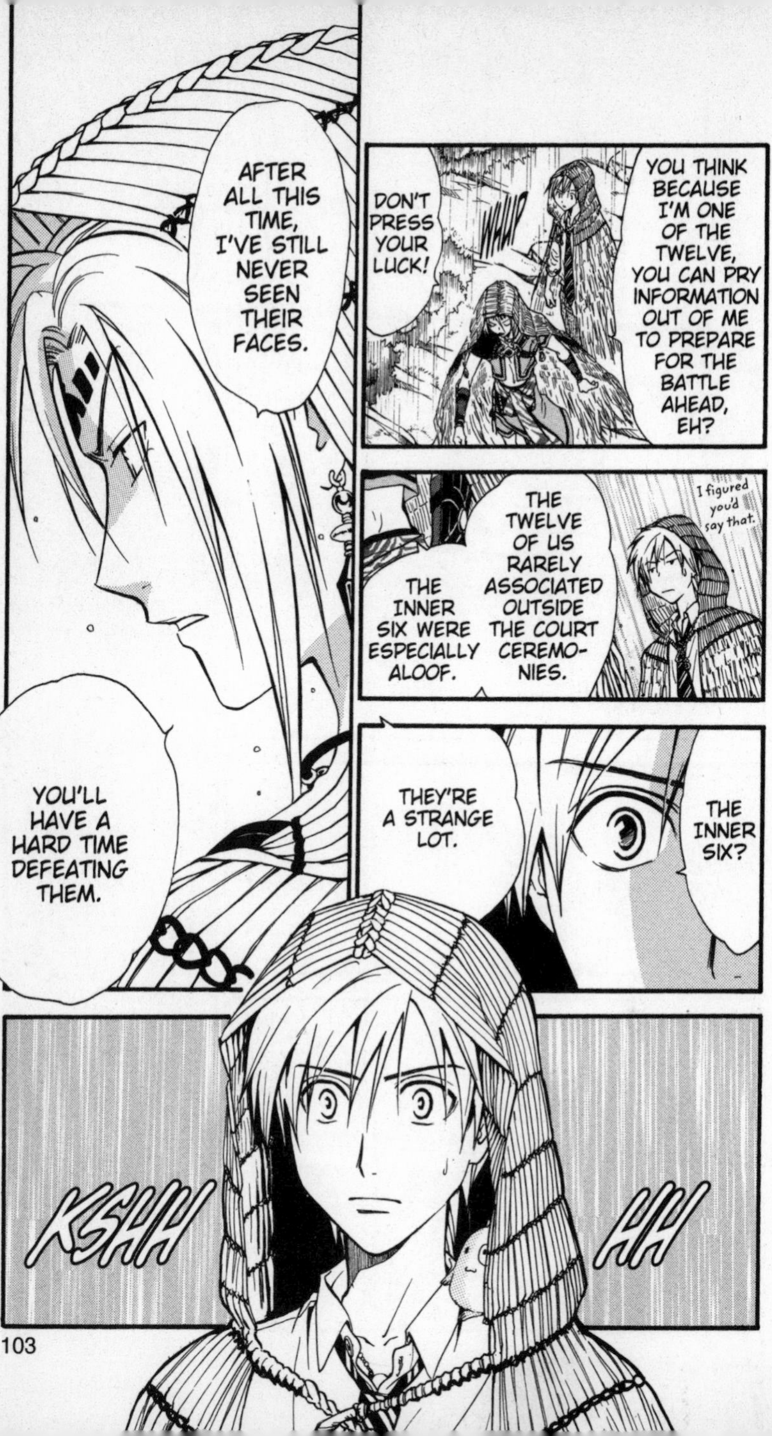
YOU THINK BECAUSE I'M ONE OF THE TWELVE, YOU CAN PRY INFORMATION OUT OF ME TO PREPARE FOR THE BATTLE AHEAD, EH?
WHAP
DON'T PRESS YOUR LUCK!
I figured you'd say that.
THE TWELVE OF US RARELY ASSOCIATED OUTSIDE THE COURT CEREMONIES.
THE INNER SIX WERE ESPECIALLY ALOOF.
THE INNER SIX?
THEY'RE A STRANGE LOT.
AFTER ALL THIS TIME, I'VE STILL NEVER SEEN THEIR FACES.
YOU'LL HAVE A HARD TIME DEFEATING THEM.
KSHH HH

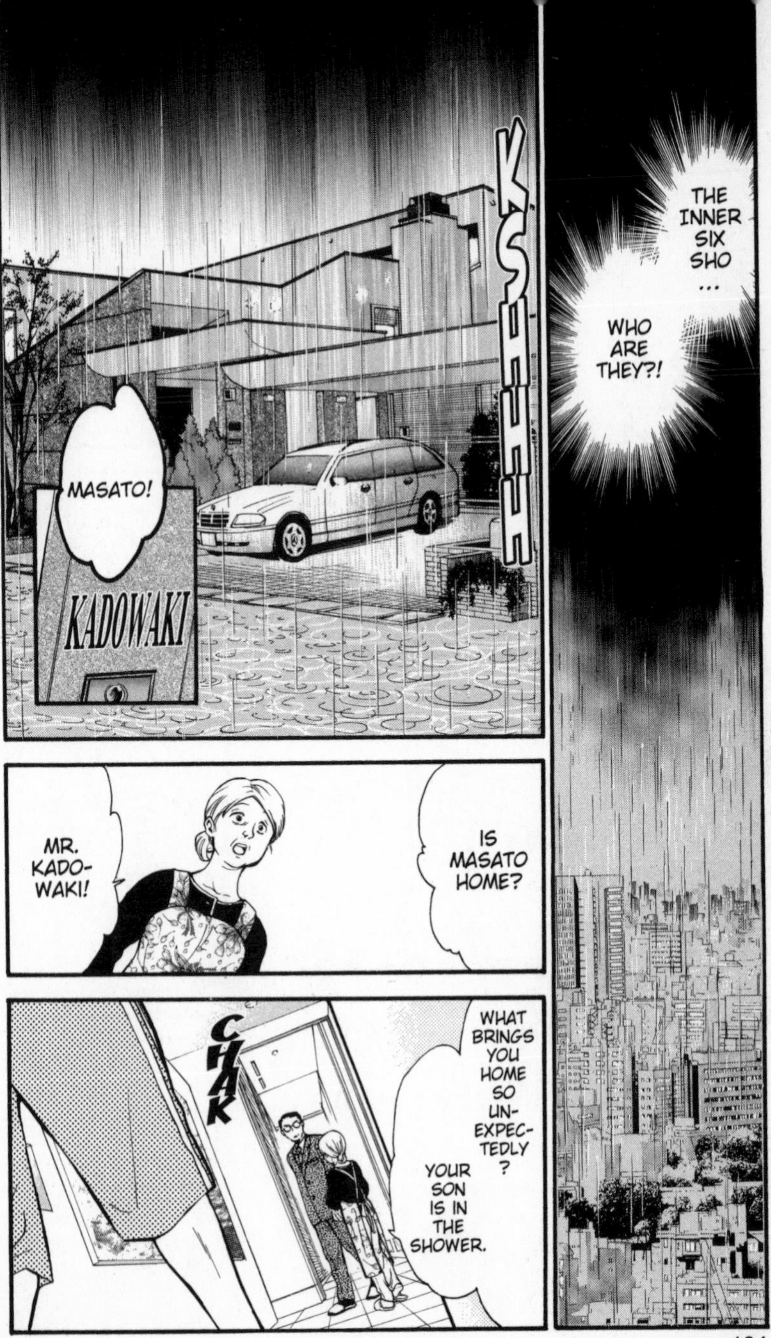
THE INNER SIX SHO ...
WHO ARE THEY?!
KSHHHHH
MASATO!
KADOWAKI
IS MASATO HOME?
MR. KADO-WAKI!
CHAK
WHAT BRINGS YOU HOME SO UN-EXPEC-TEDLY?
YOUR SON IS IN THE SHOWER.

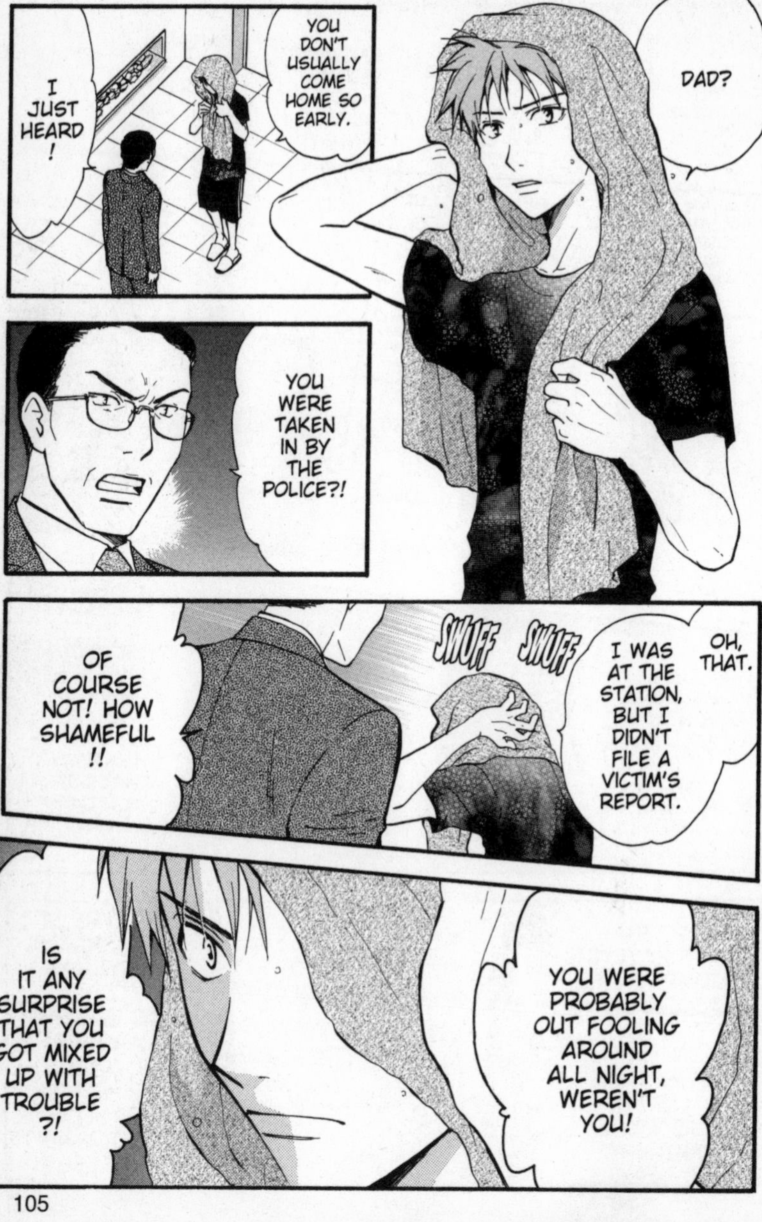
DAD?
YOU DON'T USUALLY COME HOME SO EARLY.
I JUST HEARD!
YOU WERE TAKEN IN BY THE POLICE?!
SWUFF SWUFF
OH, THAT.
I WAS AT THE STATION, BUT I DIDN'T FILE A VICTIM'S REPORT.
OF COURSE NOT! HOW SHAMEFUL!!
YOU WERE PROBABLY OUT FOOLING AROUND ALL NIGHT, WEREN'T YOU!
IS IT ANY SURPRISE THAT YOU GOT MIXED UP WITH TROUBLE?!

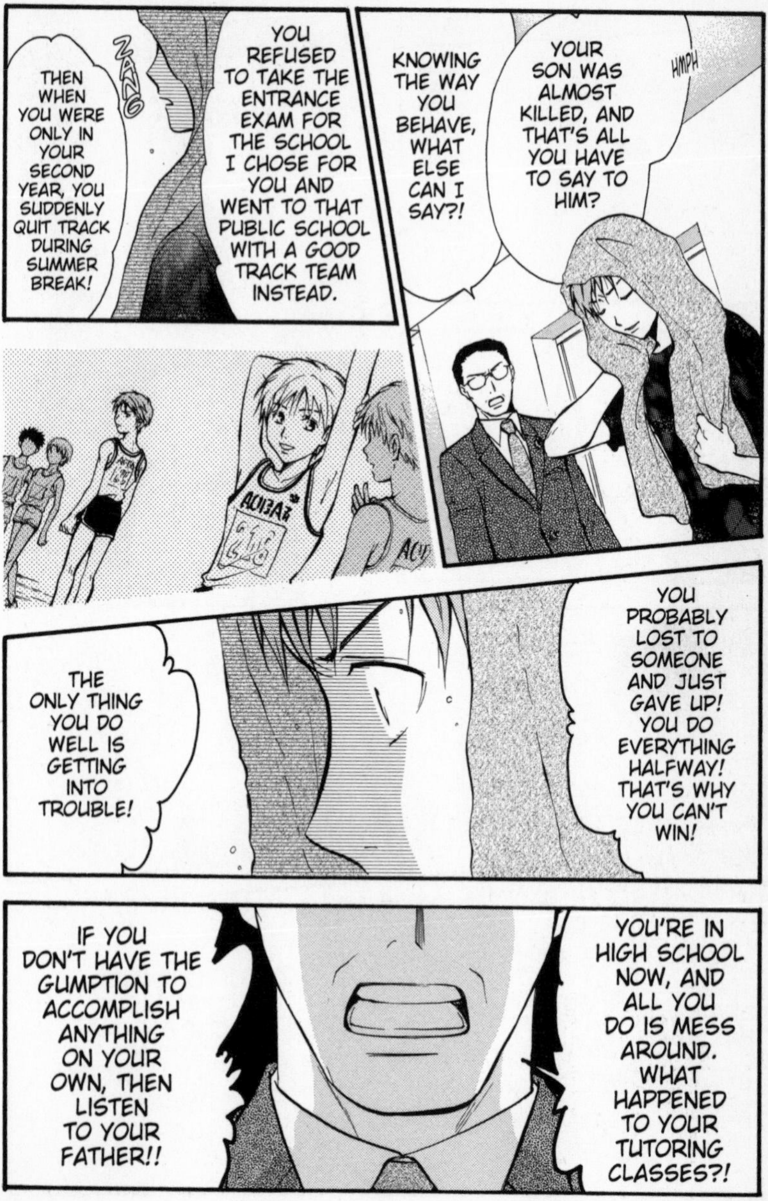
HMPH
YOUR SON WAS ALMOST KILLED, AND THAT'S ALL YOU HAVE TO SAY TO HIM?
KNOWING THE WAY YOU BEHAVE, WHAT ELSE CAN I SAY?!
YOU REFUSED TO TAKE THE ENTRANCE EXAM FOR THE SCHOOL I CHOSE FOR YOU AND WENT TO THAT PUBLIC SCHOOL WITH A GOOD TRACK TEAM INSTEAD.
ZANG
THEN WHEN YOU WERE ONLY IN YOUR SECOND YEAR, YOU SUDDENLY QUIT TRACK DURING SUMMER BREAK!
YOU PROBABLY LOST TO SOMEONE AND JUST GAVE UP! YOU DO EVERYTHING HALFWAY! THAT'S WHY YOU CAN'T WIN!
THE ONLY THING YOU DO WELL IS GETTING INTO TROUBLE!
YOU'RE IN HIGH SCHOOL NOW, AND ALL YOU DO IS MESS AROUND. WHAT HAPPENED TO YOUR TUTORING CLASSES?!
IF YOU DON'T HAVE THE GUMPTION TO ACCOMPLISH ANYTHING ON YOUR OWN, THEN LISTEN TO YOUR FATHER!!

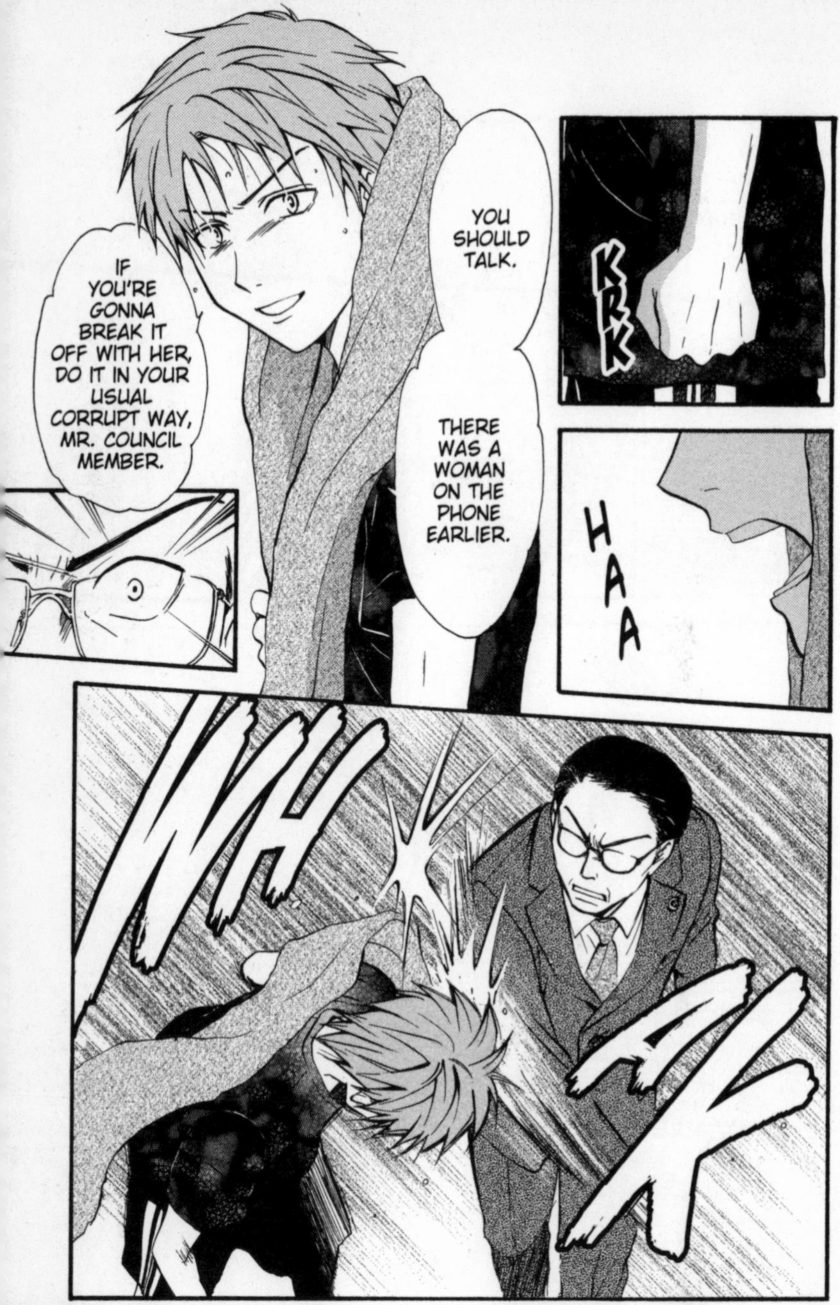
YOU SHOULD TALK.
THERE WAS A WOMAN ON THE PHONE EARLIER.
IF YOU'RE GONNA BREAK IT OFF WITH HER, DO IT IN YOUR USUAL CORRUPT WAY, MR. COUNCIL MEMBER.
KRK
HAA
WHAAK

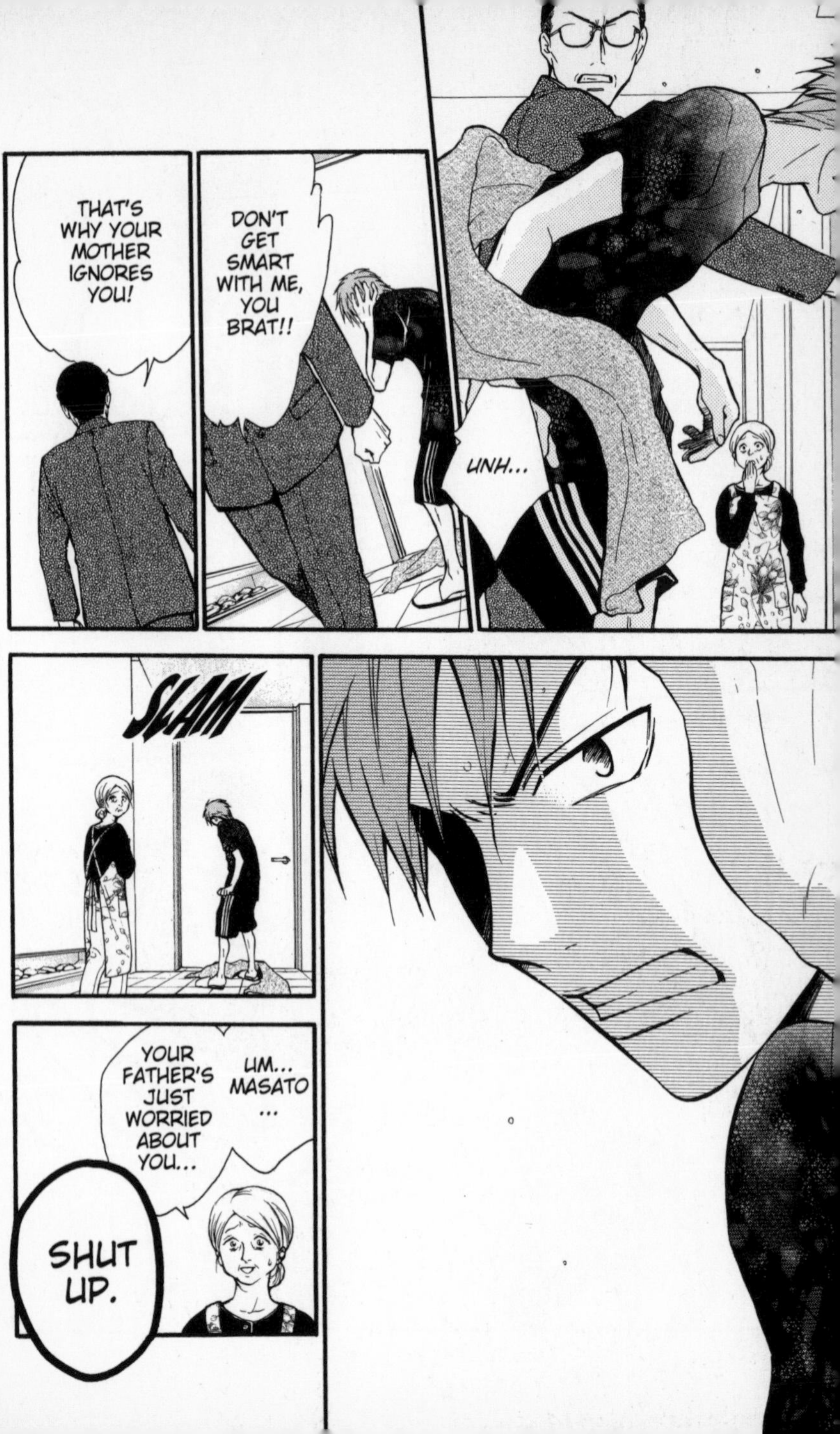
UNH...
DON'T GET SMART WITH ME, YOU BRAT!!
THAT'S WHY YOUR MOTHER IGNORES YOU!
SLAM
UM... MASATO...
YOUR FATHER'S JUST WORRIED ABOUT YOU...
SHUT UP.

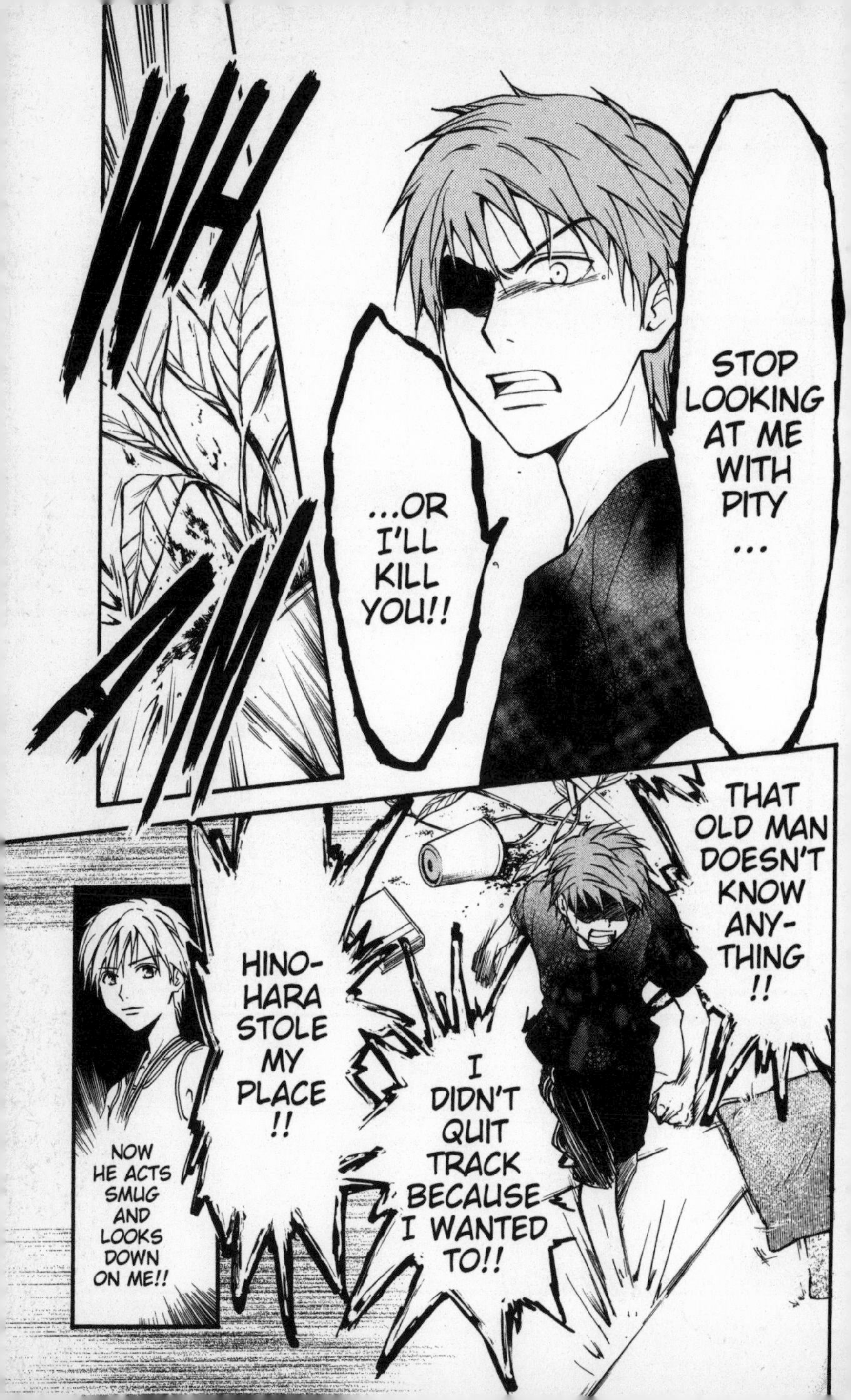
STOP LOOKING AT ME WITH PITY...
...OR I'LL KILL YOU!!
WHAM
THAT OLD MAN DOESN'T KNOW ANY-THING!!
I DIDN'T QUIT TRACK BECAUSE I WANTED TO!!
HINO-HARA STOLE MY PLACE!!
NOW HE ACTS SMUG AND LOOKS DOWN ON ME!!

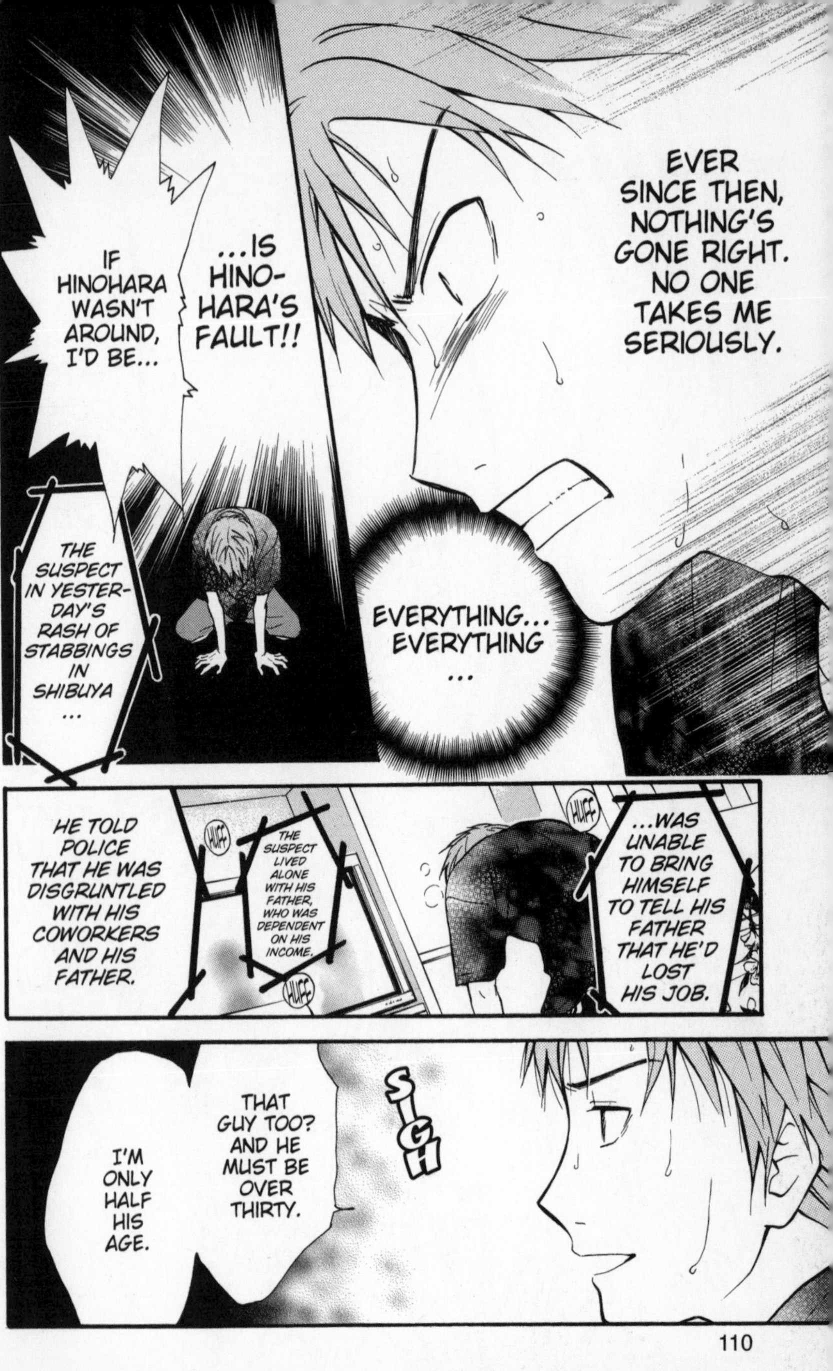
EVER SINCE THEN, NOTHING'S GONE RIGHT. NO ONE TAKES ME SERIOUSLY.
EVERYTHING... EVERYTHING ...
...IS HINO-HARA'S FAULT!!
IF HINOHARA WASN'T AROUND, I'D BE...
THE SUSPECT IN YESTER-DAY'S RASH OF STABBINGS IN SHIBUYA ...
HUFF
...WAS UNABLE TO BRING HIMSELF TO TELL HIS FATHER THAT HE'D LOST HIS JOB.
HUFF
THE SUSPECT LIVED ALONE WITH HIS FATHER, WHO WAS DEPENDENT ON HIS INCOME.
HUFF
HE TOLD POLICE THAT HE WAS DISGRUNTLED WITH HIS COWORKERS AND HIS FATHER.
SIGH
THAT GUY TOO? AND HE MUST BE OVER THIRTY.
I'M ONLY HALF HIS AGE.

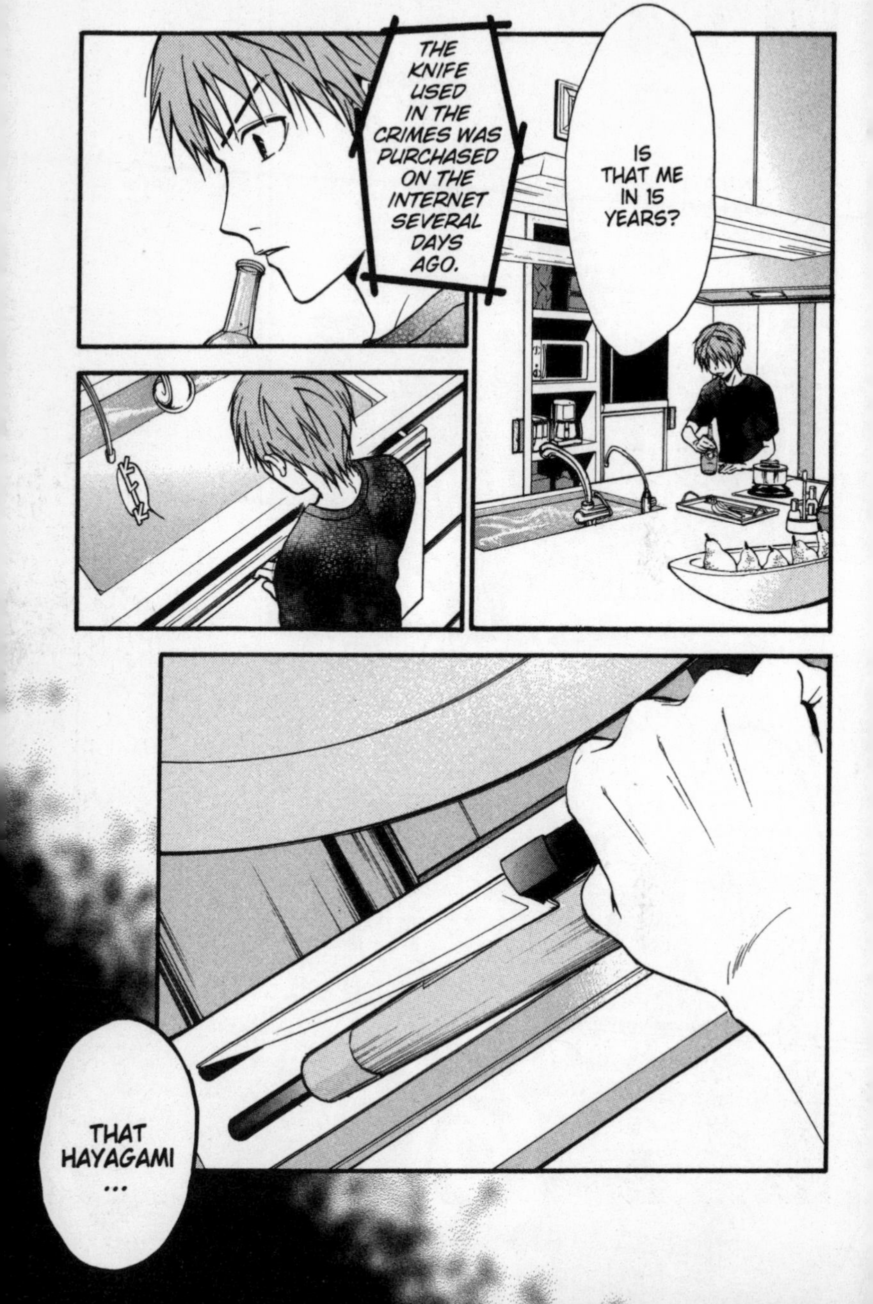
IS THAT ME IN 15 YEARS?
THE KNIFE USED IN THE CRIMES WAS PURCHASED ON THE INTERNET SEVERAL DAYS AGO.
THAT HAYAGAMI ...

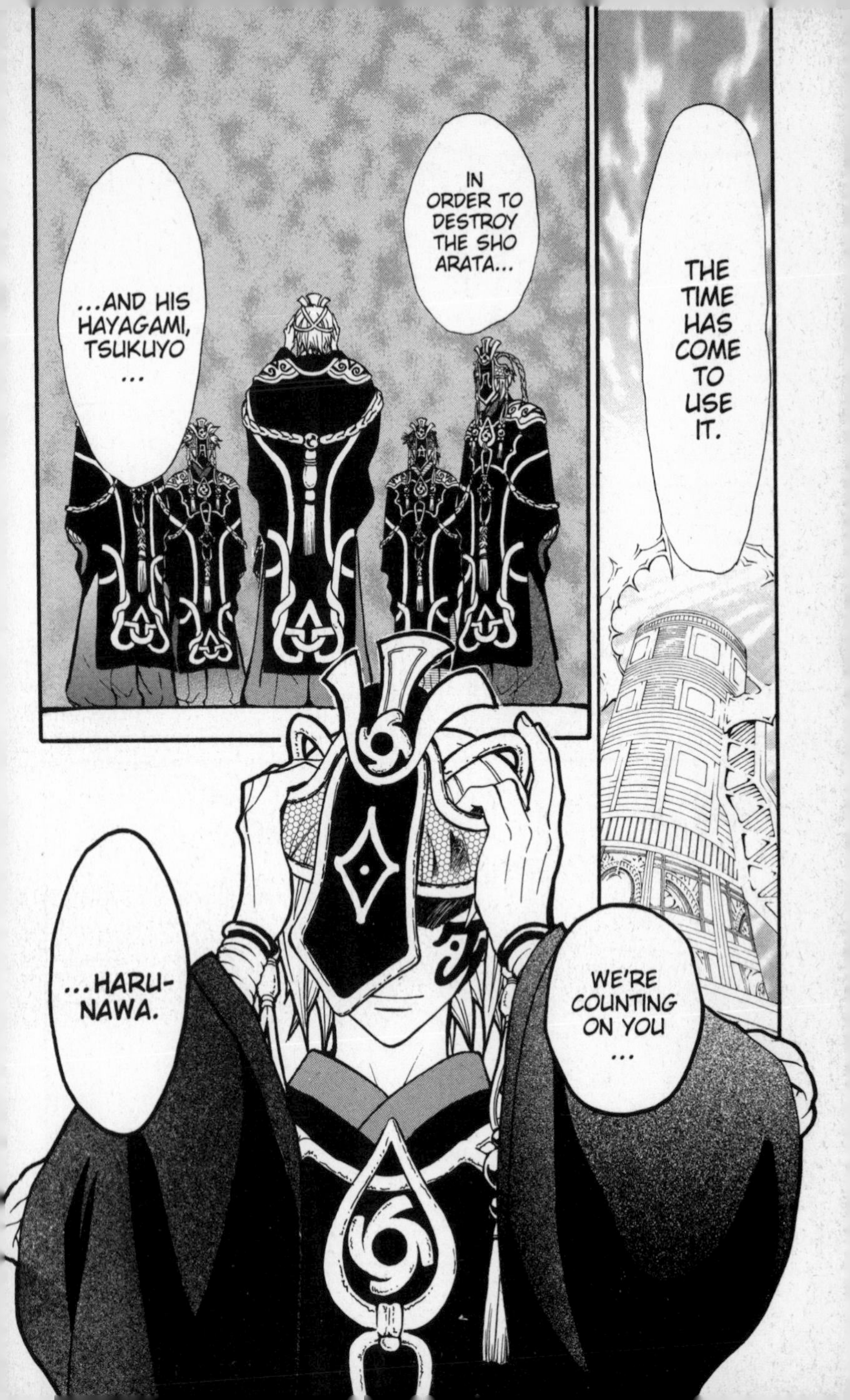
THE TIME HAS COME TO USE IT.
IN ORDER TO DESTROY THE SHO ARATA...
...AND HIS HAYAGAMI, TSUKUYO...
WE'RE COUNTING ON YOU...
...HARUNAWA.

Arata
THE LEGEND

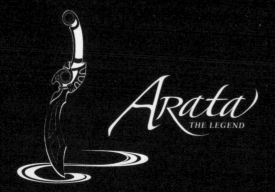

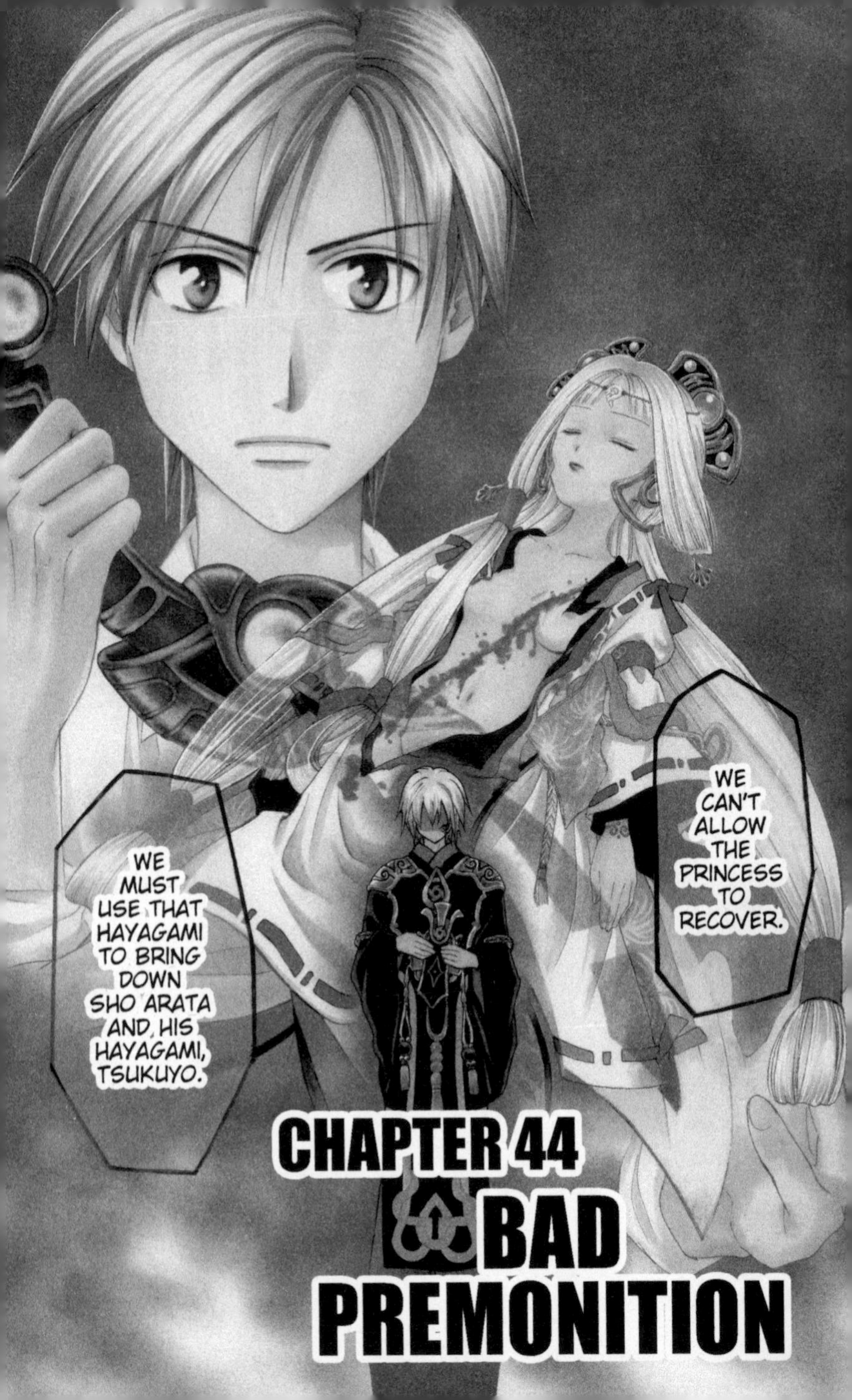
WE CAN'T ALLOW THE PRINCESS TO RECOVER.
WE MUST USE THAT HAYAGAMI TO BRING DOWN SHO ARATA AND HIS HAYAGAMI, TSUKUYO.
CHAPTER 44
BAD PREMONITION

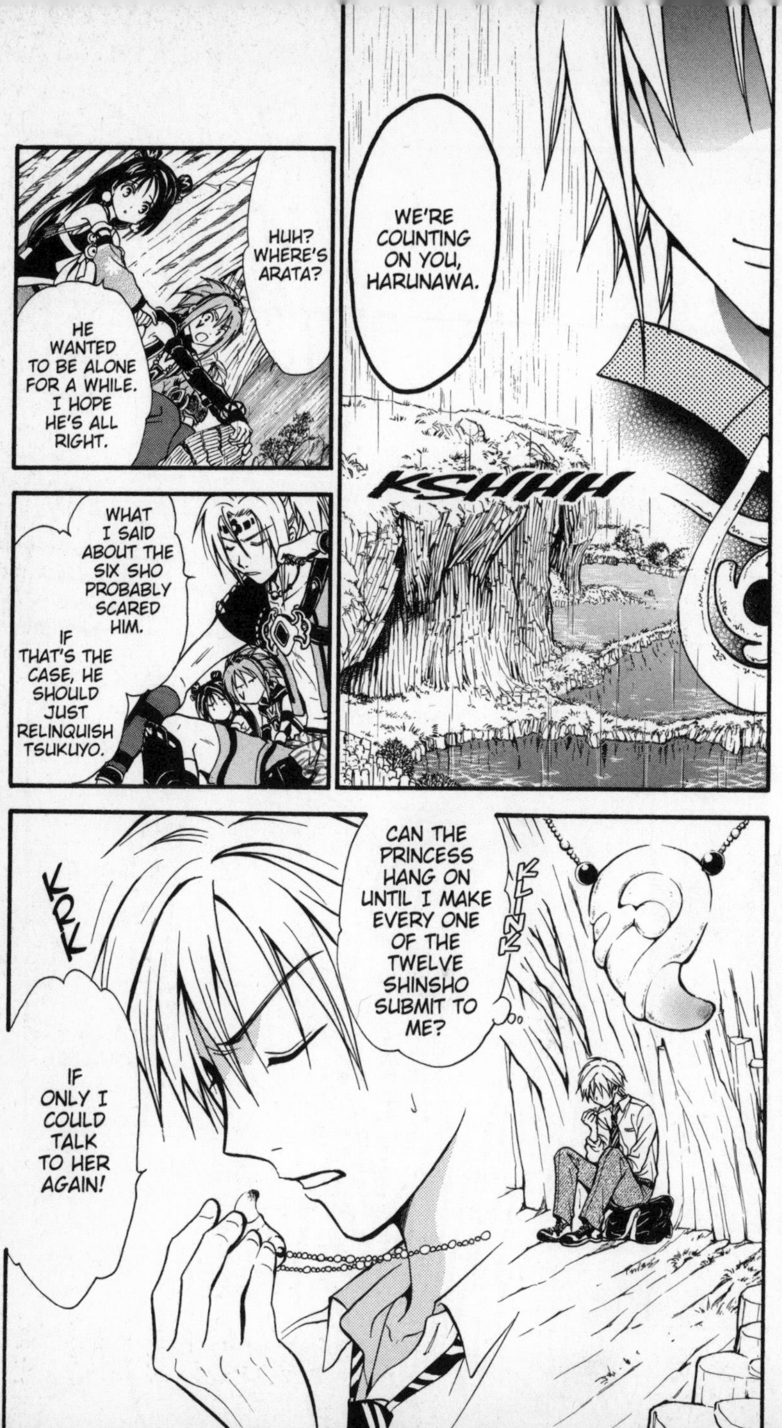
WE'RE COUNTING ON YOU, HARUNAWA.
KSHHH
HUH? WHERE'S ARATA?
HE WANTED TO BE ALONE FOR A WHILE. I HOPE HE'S ALL RIGHT.
WHAT I SAID ABOUT THE SIX SHO PROBABLY SCARED HIM.
IF THAT'S THE CASE, HE SHOULD JUST RELINQUISH TSUKUYO.
CAN THE PRINCESS HANG ON UNTIL I MAKE EVERY ONE OF THE TWELVE SHINSHO SUBMIT TO ME?
KLINK
KRK
IF ONLY I COULD TALK TO HER AGAIN!

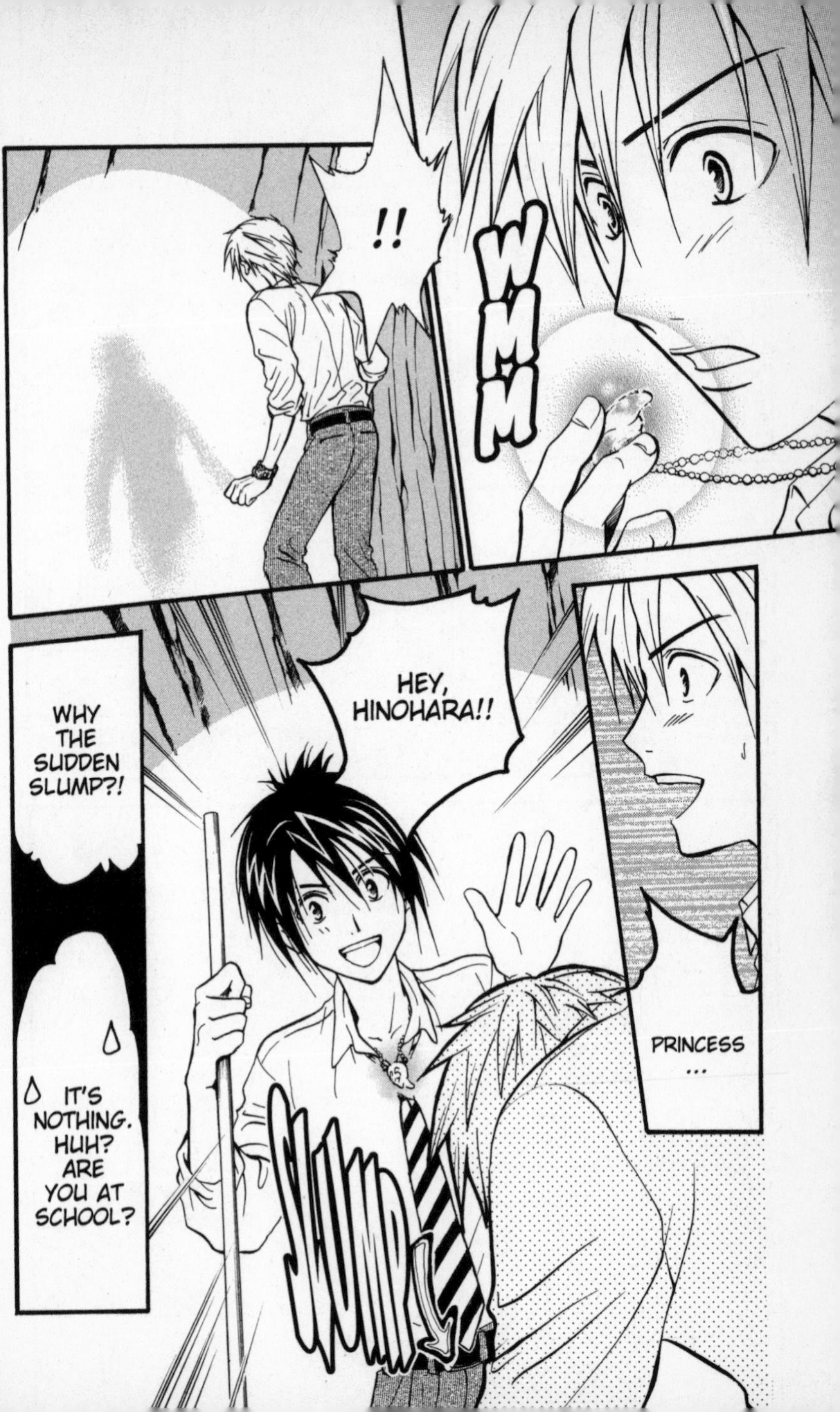
WHMM
!!
PRINCESS...
HEY, HINOHARA!!
WHY THE SUDDEN SLUMP?!
IT'S NOTHING. HUH? ARE YOU AT SCHOOL?

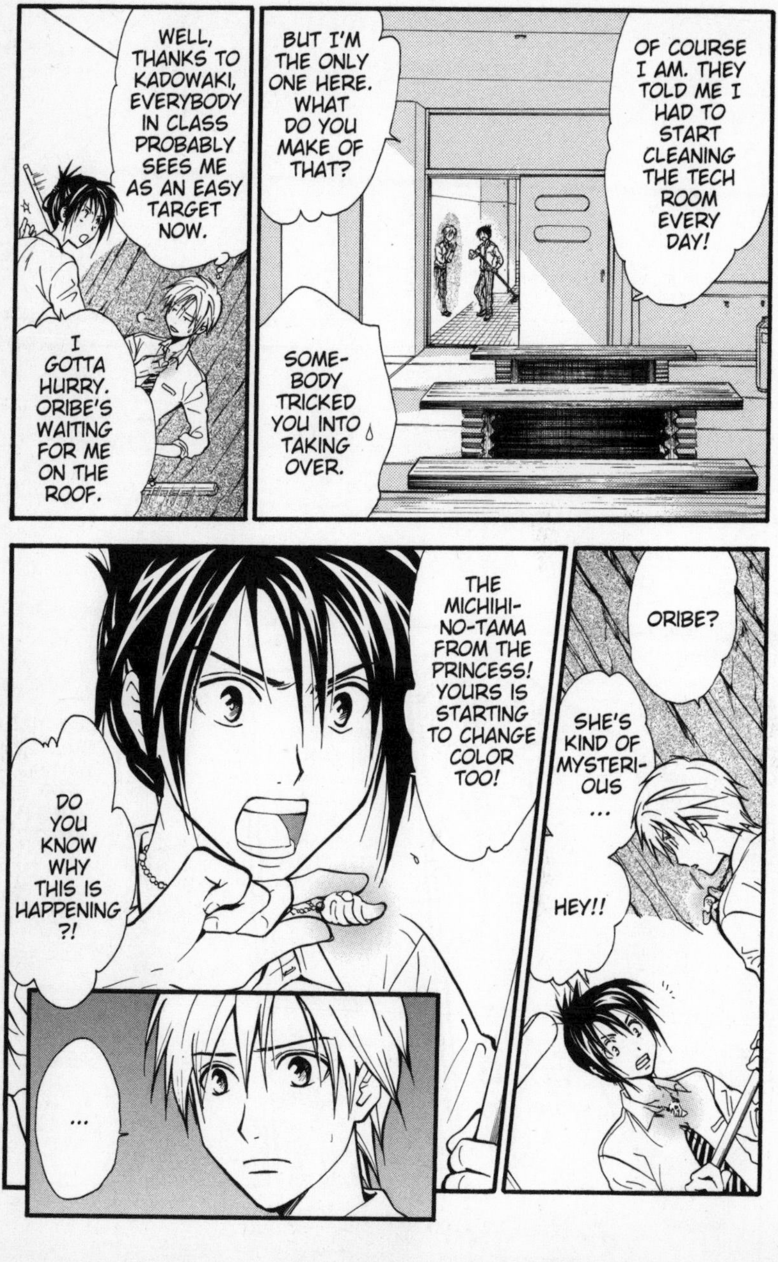
OF COURSE I AM. THEY TOLD ME I HAD TO START CLEANING THE TECH ROOM EVERY DAY!
BUT I'M THE ONLY ONE HERE. WHAT DO YOU MAKE OF THAT?
SOME-BODY TRICKED YOU INTO TAKING OVER.
WELL, THANKS TO KADOWAKI, EVERYBODY IN CLASS PROBABLY SEES ME AS AN EASY TARGET NOW.
I GOTTA HURRY. ORIBE'S WAITING FOR ME ON THE ROOF.
ORIBE?
SHE'S KIND OF MYSTERI-OUS...
HEY!!
THE MICHIHI-NO-TAMA FROM THE PRINCESS! YOURS IS STARTING TO CHANGE COLOR TOO!
DO YOU KNOW WHY THIS IS HAPPENING?!
...

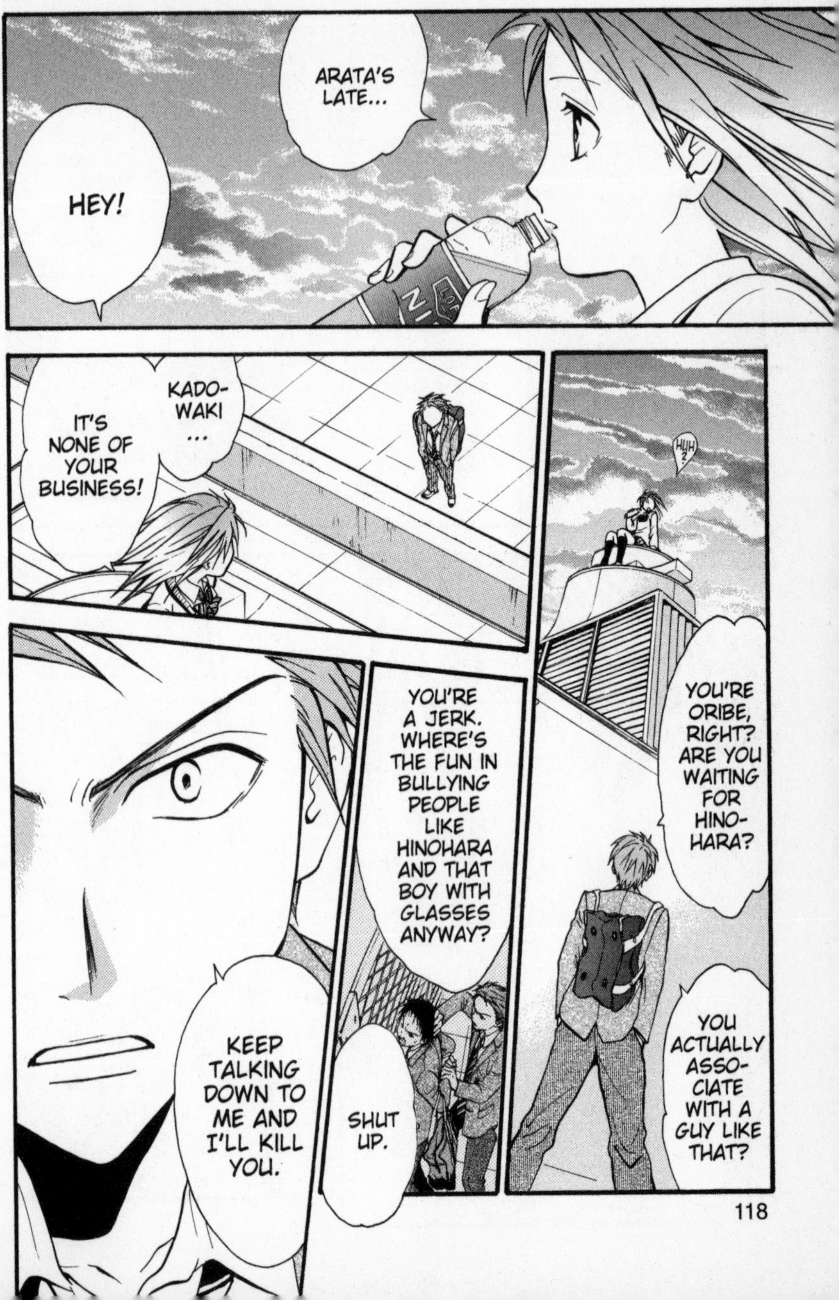
ARATA'S LATE...
HEY!
HUH?
YOU'RE ORIBE, RIGHT? ARE YOU WAITING FOR HINO-HARA?
YOU ACTUALLY ASSO-CIATE WITH A GUY LIKE THAT?
KADO-WAKI ...
IT'S NONE OF YOUR BUSINESS!
YOU'RE A JERK. WHERE'S THE FUN IN BULLYING PEOPLE LIKE HINOHARA AND THAT BOY WITH GLASSES ANYWAY?
SHUT UP.
KEEP TALKING DOWN TO ME AND I'LL KILL YOU.

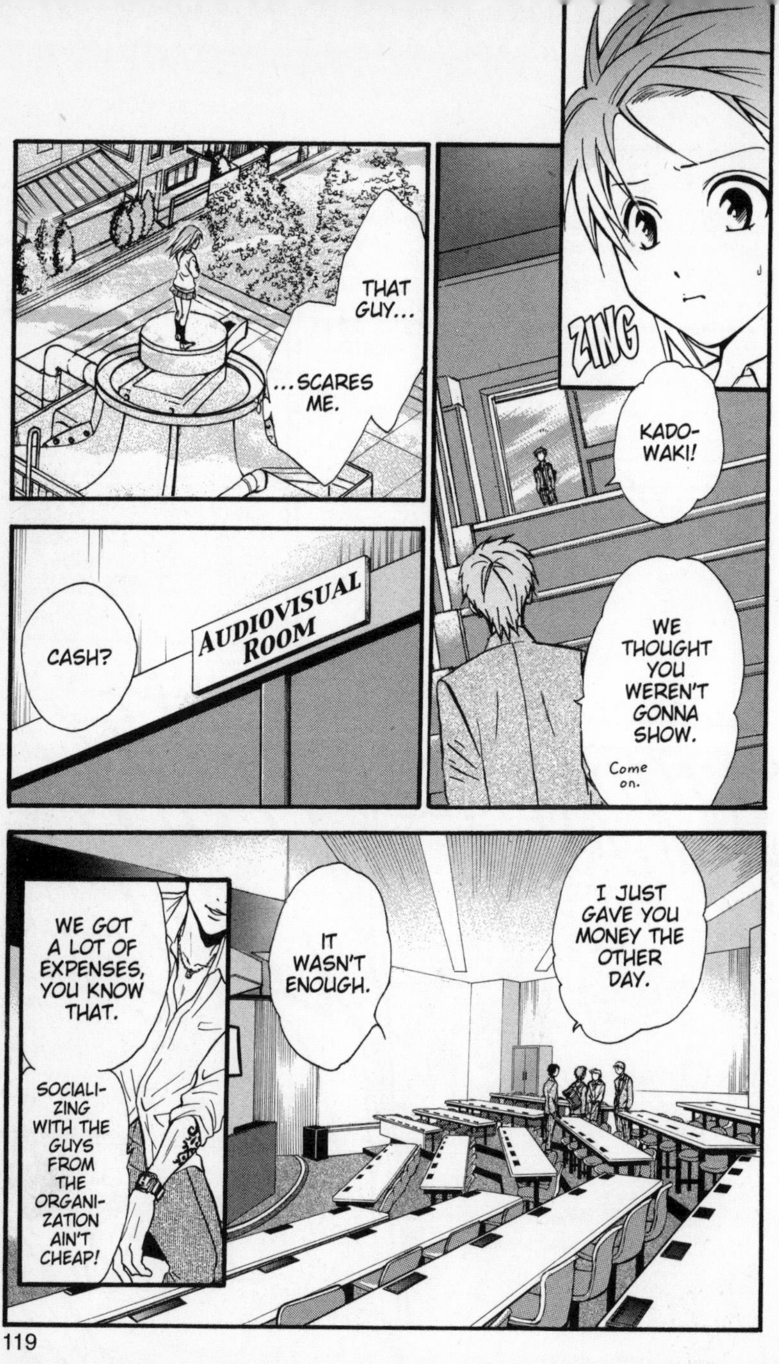
ZING
KADO-WAKI!
WE THOUGHT YOU WEREN'T GONNA SHOW.
Come on.
THAT GUY...
...SCARES ME.
AUDIOVISUAL ROOM
CASH?
I JUST GAVE YOU MONEY THE OTHER DAY.
IT WASN'T ENOUGH.
WE GOT A LOT OF EXPENSES, YOU KNOW THAT.
SOCIALI-ZING WITH THE GUYS FROM THE ORGANI-ZATION AIN'T CHEAP!

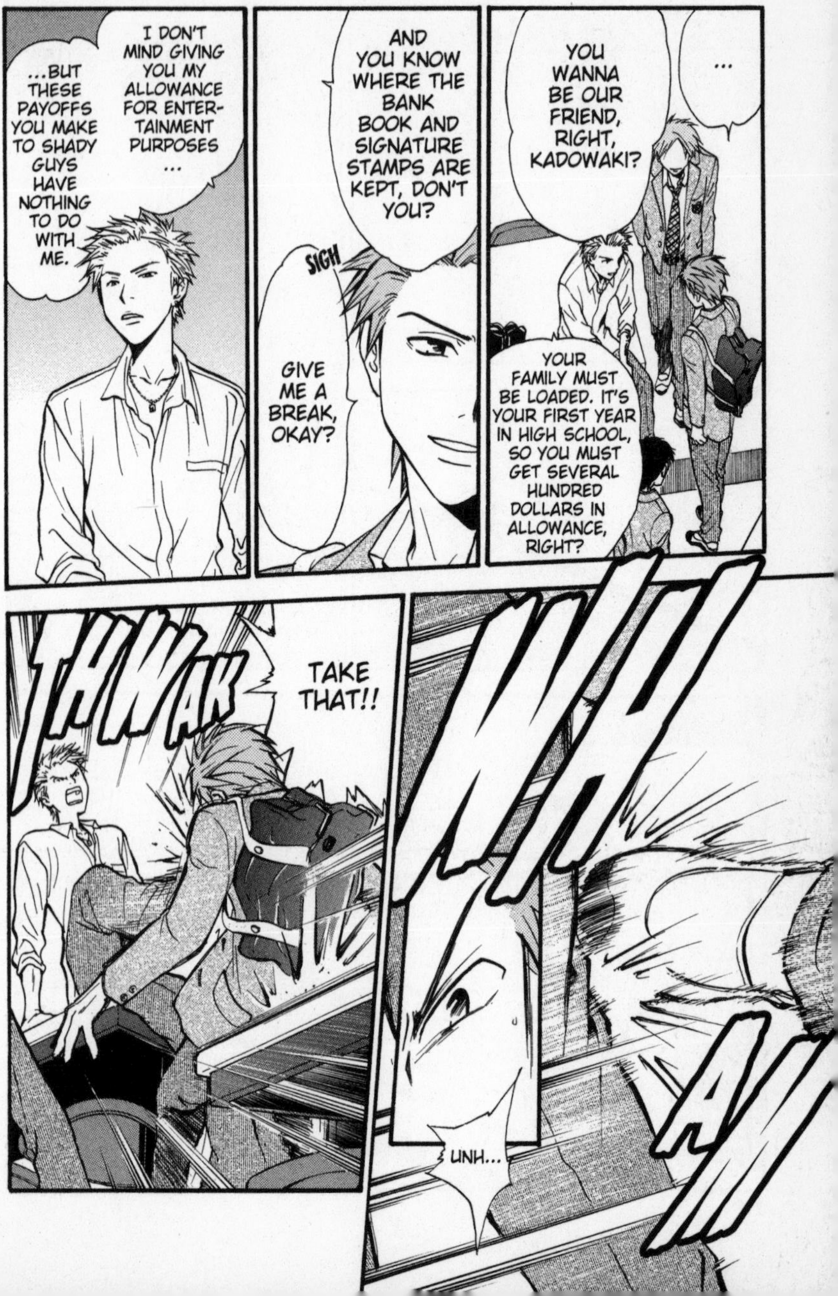
...
YOU WANNA BE OUR FRIEND, RIGHT, KADOWAKI?
YOUR FAMILY MUST BE LOADED. IT'S YOUR FIRST YEAR IN HIGH SCHOOL, SO YOU MUST GET SEVERAL HUNDRED DOLLARS IN ALLOWANCE, RIGHT?
AND YOU KNOW WHERE THE BANK BOOK AND SIGNATURE STAMPS ARE KEPT, DON'T YOU?
SIGH
GIVE ME A BREAK, OKAY?
I DON'T MIND GIVING YOU MY ALLOWANCE FOR ENTERTAINMENT PURPOSES ...
...BUT THESE PAYOFFS YOU MAKE TO SHADY GUYS HAVE NOTHING TO DO WITH ME.
WHAM
UNH...
TAKE THAT!!
THWAK

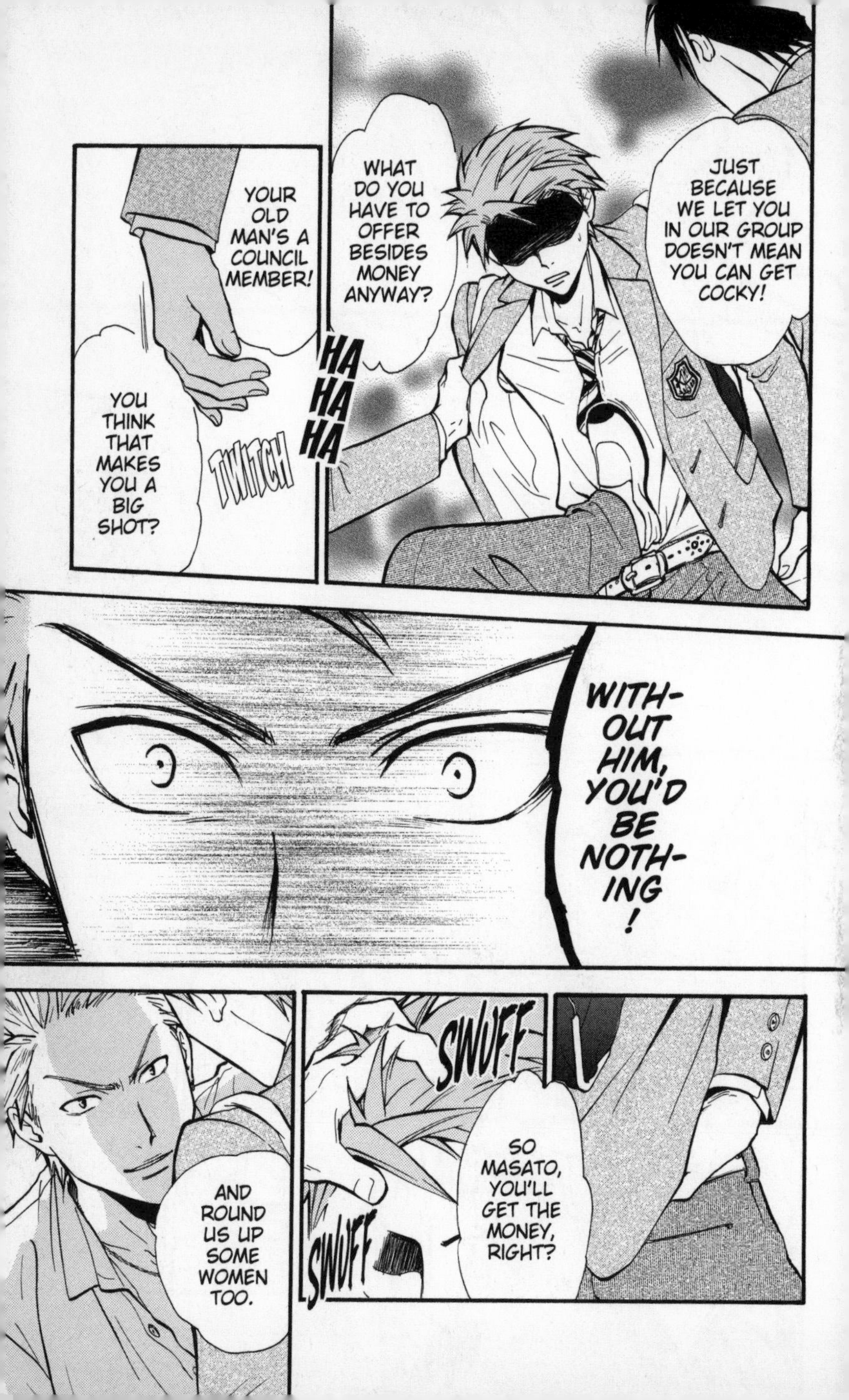
JUST BECAUSE WE LET YOU IN OUR GROUP DOESN'T MEAN YOU CAN GET COCKY!
WHAT DO YOU HAVE TO OFFER BESIDES MONEY ANYWAY?
HA HA HA
YOUR OLD MAN'S A COUNCIL MEMBER!
YOU THINK THAT MAKES YOU A BIG SHOT?
TWITCH
WITH-OUT HIM, YOU'D BE NOTH-ING!
SNUFF
SO MASATO, YOU'LL GET THE MONEY, RIGHT?
SNUFF
AND ROUND US UP SOME WOMEN TOO.

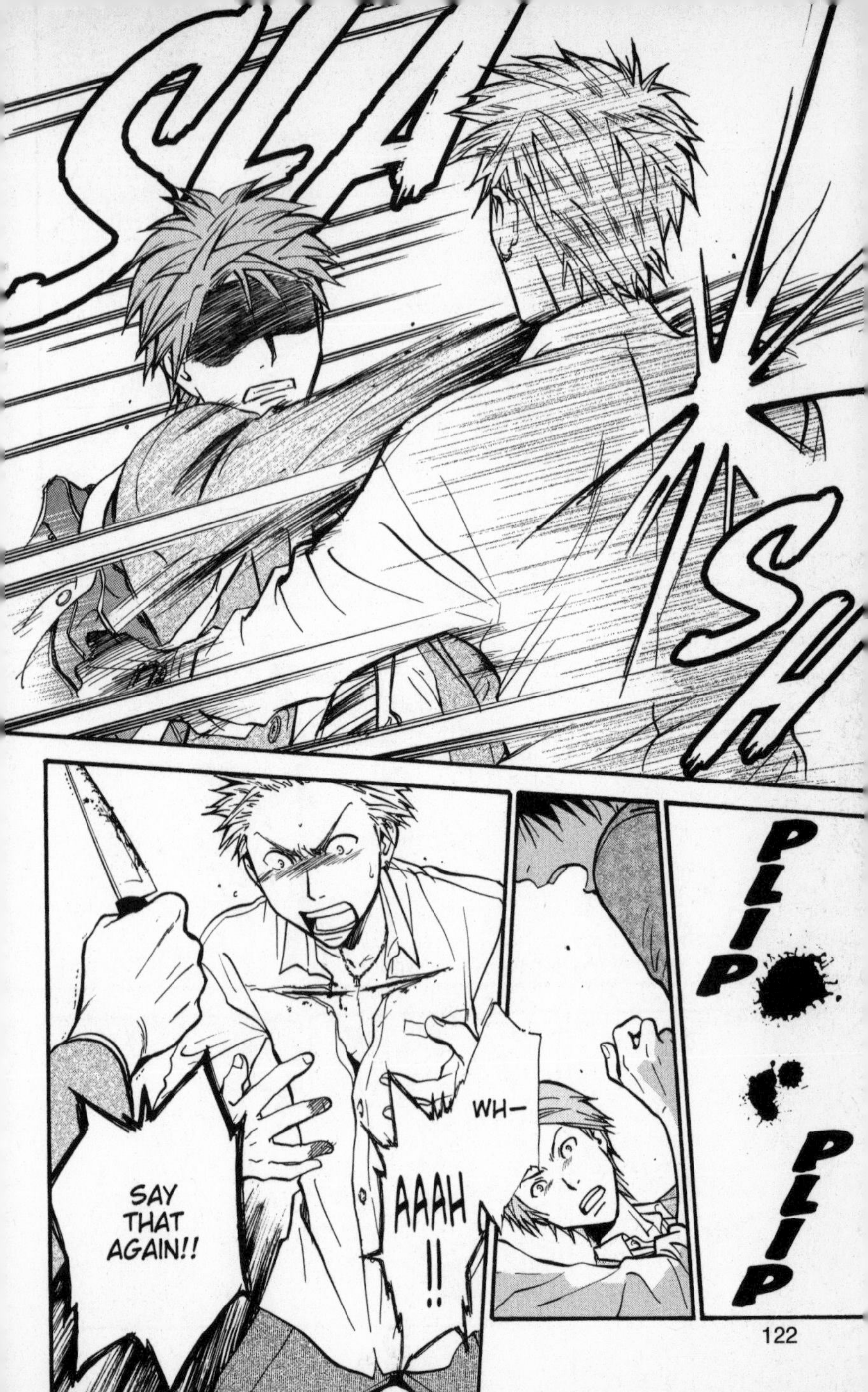
SLASH
PLIP
PLIP
WH—
AAAH!!
SAY THAT AGAIN!!

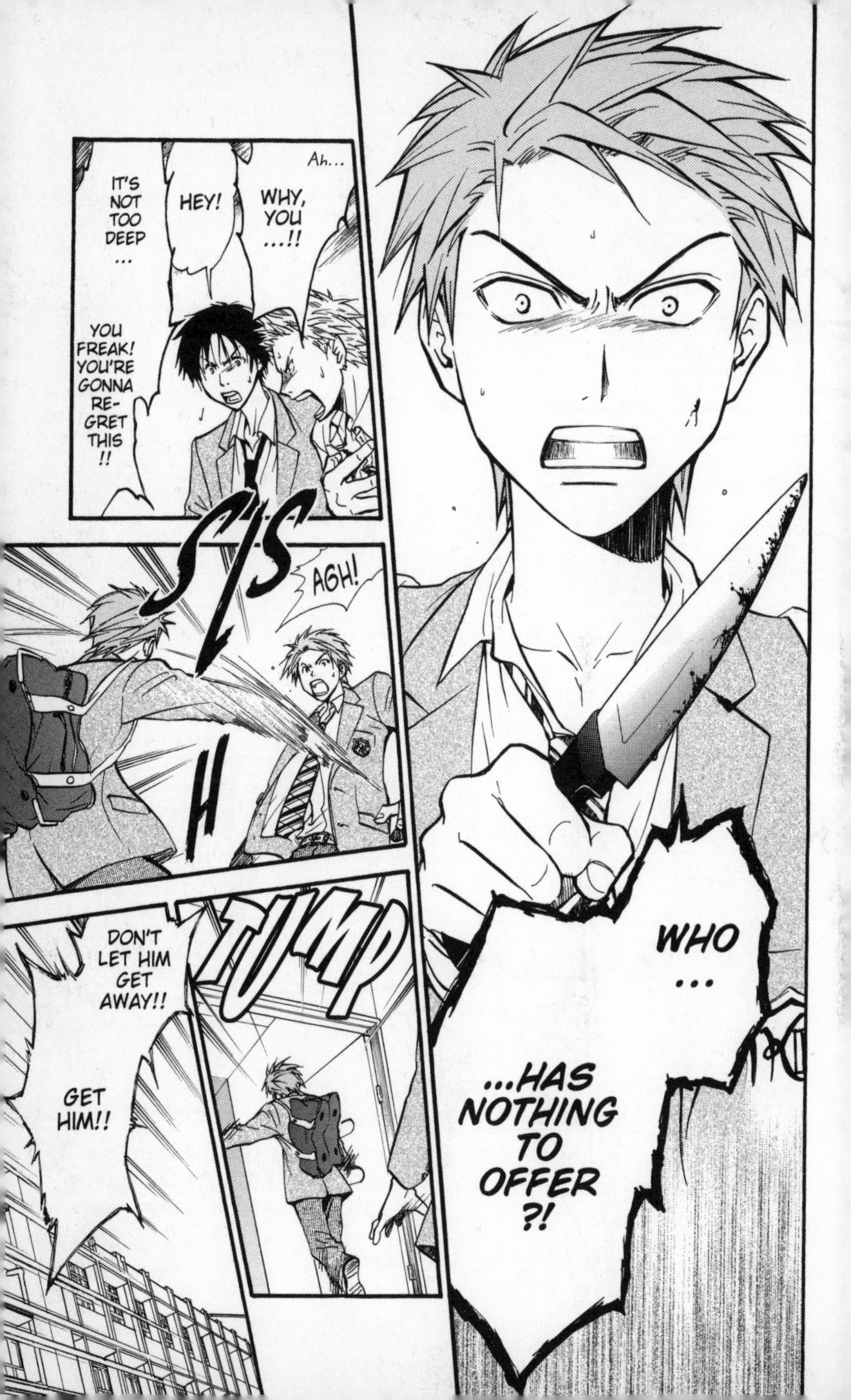
WHO ...
...HAS NOTHING TO OFFER ?!
Ah...
WHY, YOU ...!!
HEY!
IT'S NOT TOO DEEP ...
YOU FREAK! YOU'RE GONNA RE-GRET THIS !!
AGH!
TUMP
DON'T LET HIM GET AWAY!!
GET HIM!!

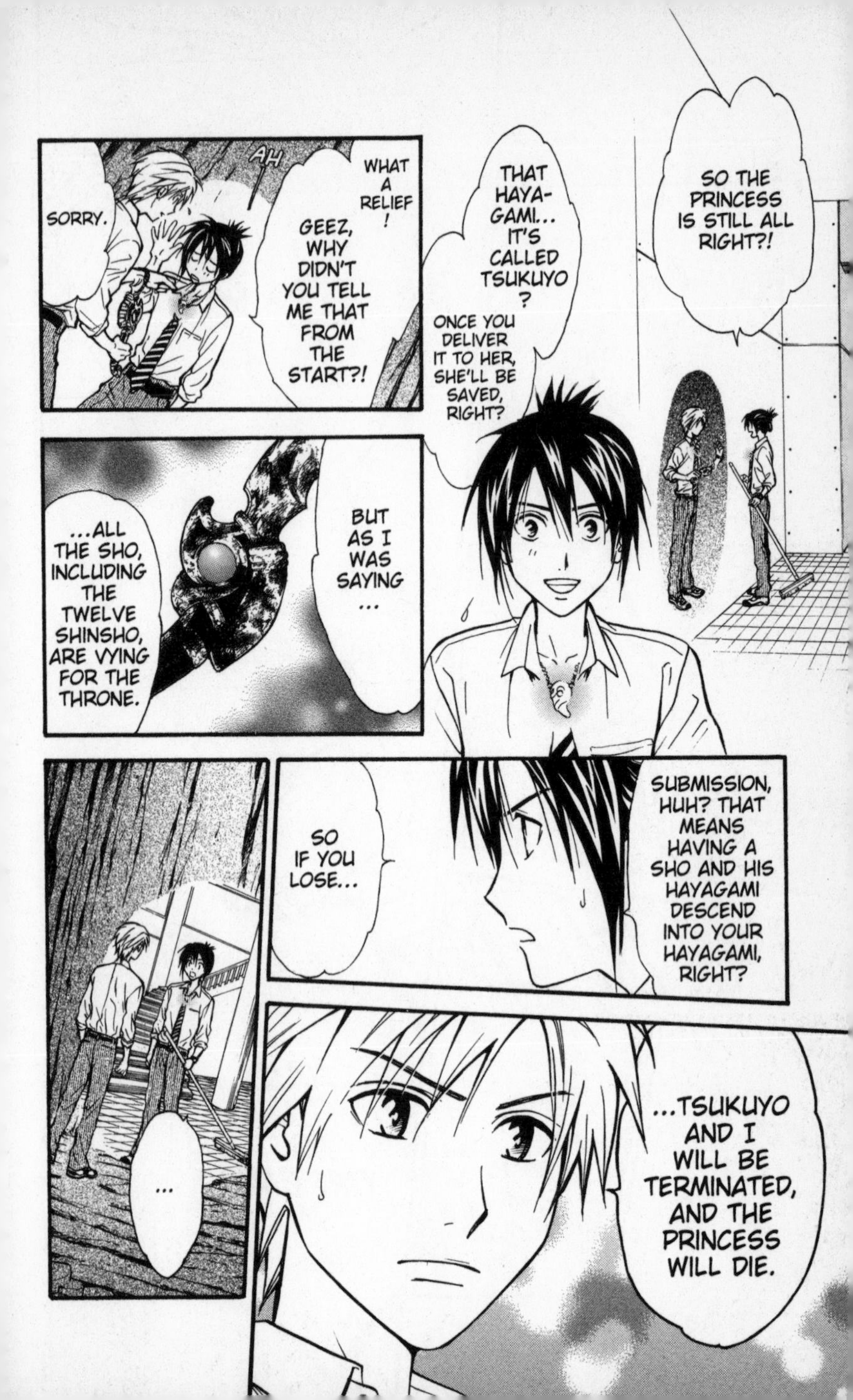
SO THE PRINCESS IS STILL ALL RIGHT?!
THAT HAYA-GAMI... IT'S CALLED TSUKUYO?
ONCE YOU DELIVER IT TO HER, SHE'LL BE SAVED, RIGHT?
WHAT A RELIEF!
GEEZ, WHY DIDN'T YOU TELL ME THAT FROM THE START?!
AH
SORRY.
BUT AS I WAS SAYING...
...ALL THE SHO, INCLUDING THE TWELVE SHINSHO, ARE VYING FOR THE THRONE.
SUBMISSION, HUH? THAT MEANS HAVING A SHO AND HIS HAYAGAMI DESCEND INTO YOUR HAYAGAMI, RIGHT?
SO IF YOU LOSE...
...TSUKUYO AND I WILL BE TERMINATED, AND THE PRINCESS WILL DIE.
...

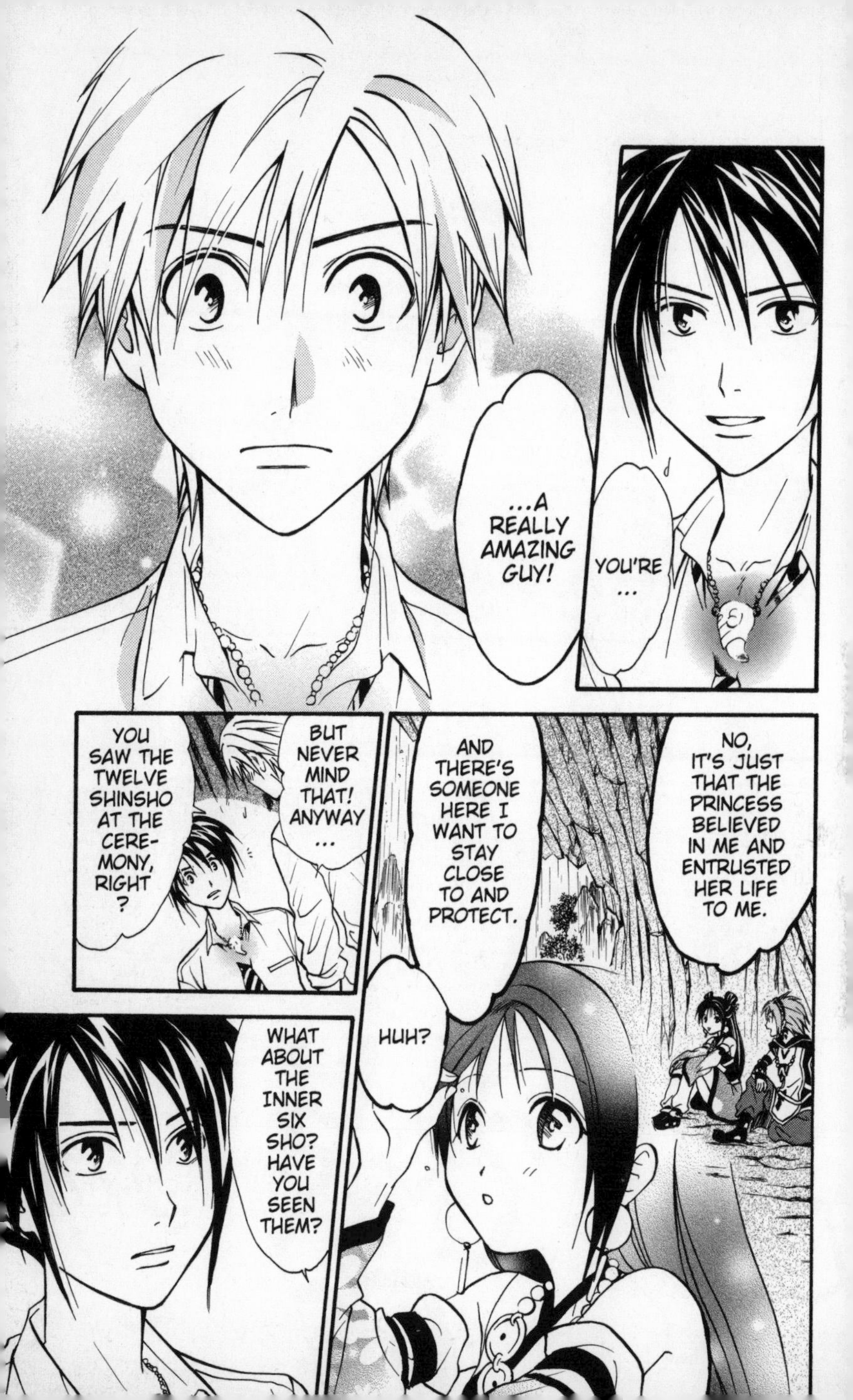
YOU'RE ...
...A REALLY AMAZING GUY!
NO, IT'S JUST THAT THE PRINCESS BELIEVED IN ME AND ENTRUSTED HER LIFE TO ME.
AND THERE'S SOMEONE HERE I WANT TO STAY CLOSE TO AND PROTECT.
HUH?
BUT NEVER MIND THAT! ANYWAY ...
YOU SAW THE TWELVE SHINSHO AT THE CERE-MONY, RIGHT?
WHAT ABOUT THE INNER SIX SHO? HAVE YOU SEEN THEM?

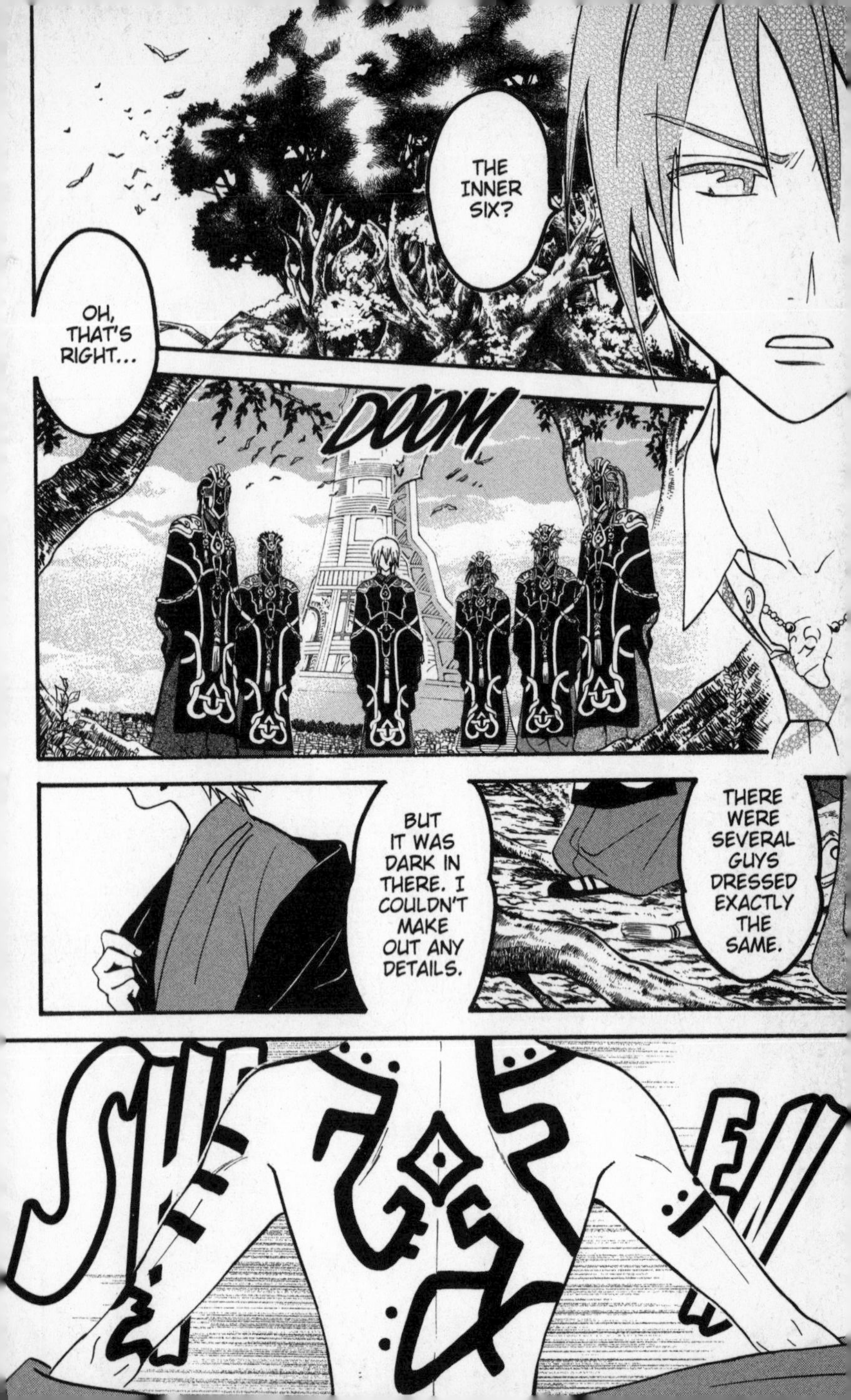
THE INNER SIX?
OH, THAT'S RIGHT...
DOOM
THERE WERE SEVERAL GUYS DRESSED EXACTLY THE SAME.
BUT IT WAS DARK IN THERE. I COULDN'T MAKE OUT ANY DETAILS.

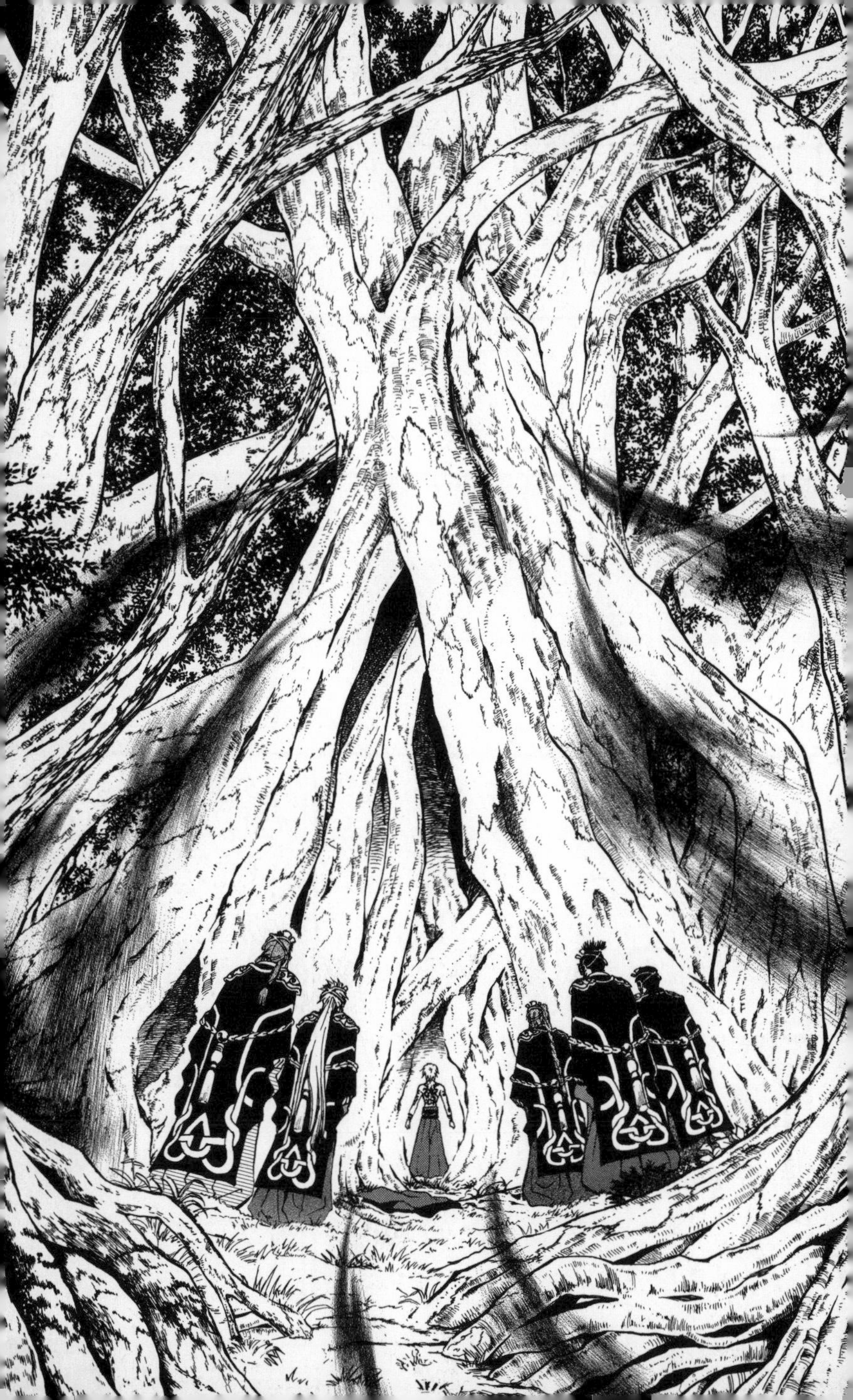

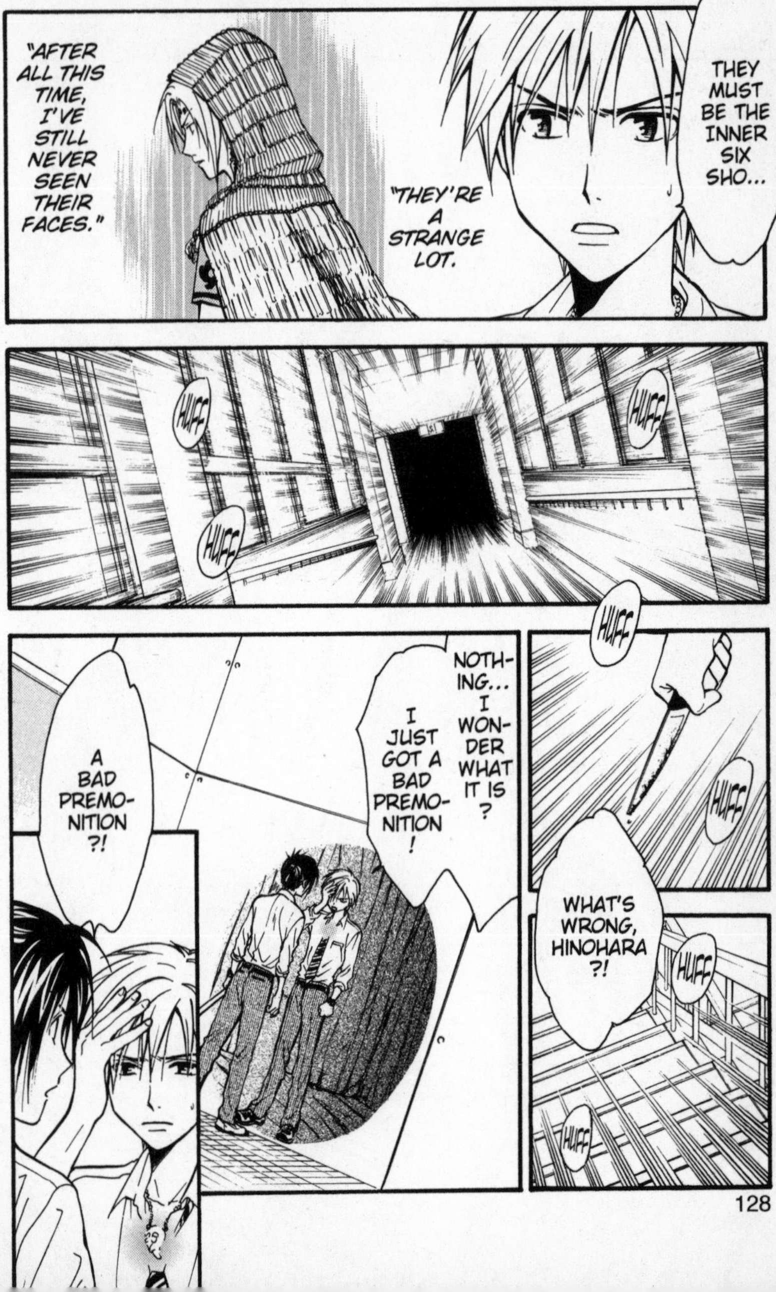
THEY MUST BE THE INNER SIX SHO...
"THEY'RE A STRANGE LOT.
"AFTER ALL THIS TIME, I'VE STILL NEVER SEEN THEIR FACES."
HUFF
HUFF
HUFF
HUFF
HUFF
WHAT'S WRONG, HINOHARA?!
HUFF
HUFF
NOTHING... I WONDER WHAT IT IS?
I JUST GOT A BAD PREMONITION!
A BAD PREMONITION?!

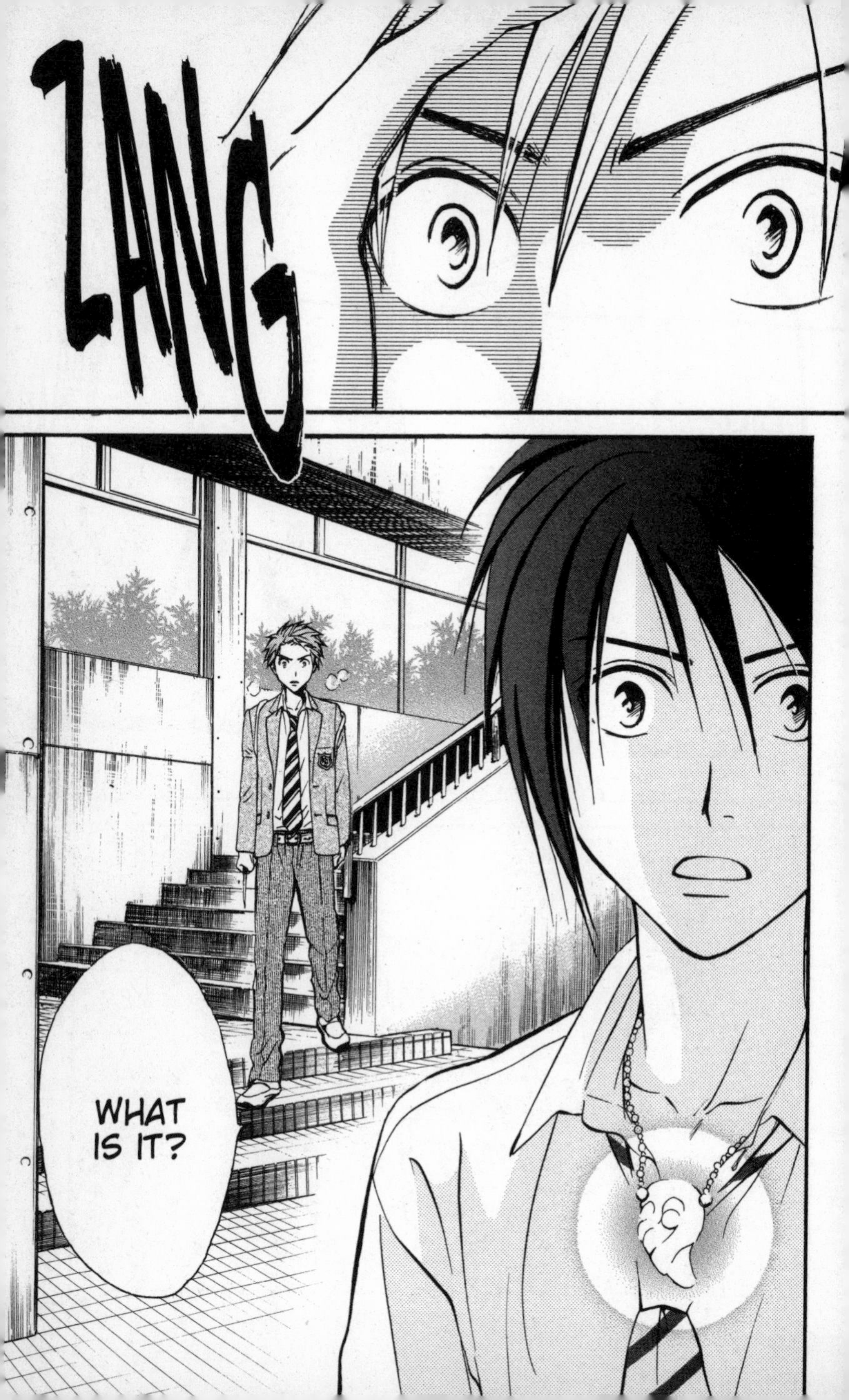
ZANG
WHAT IS IT?

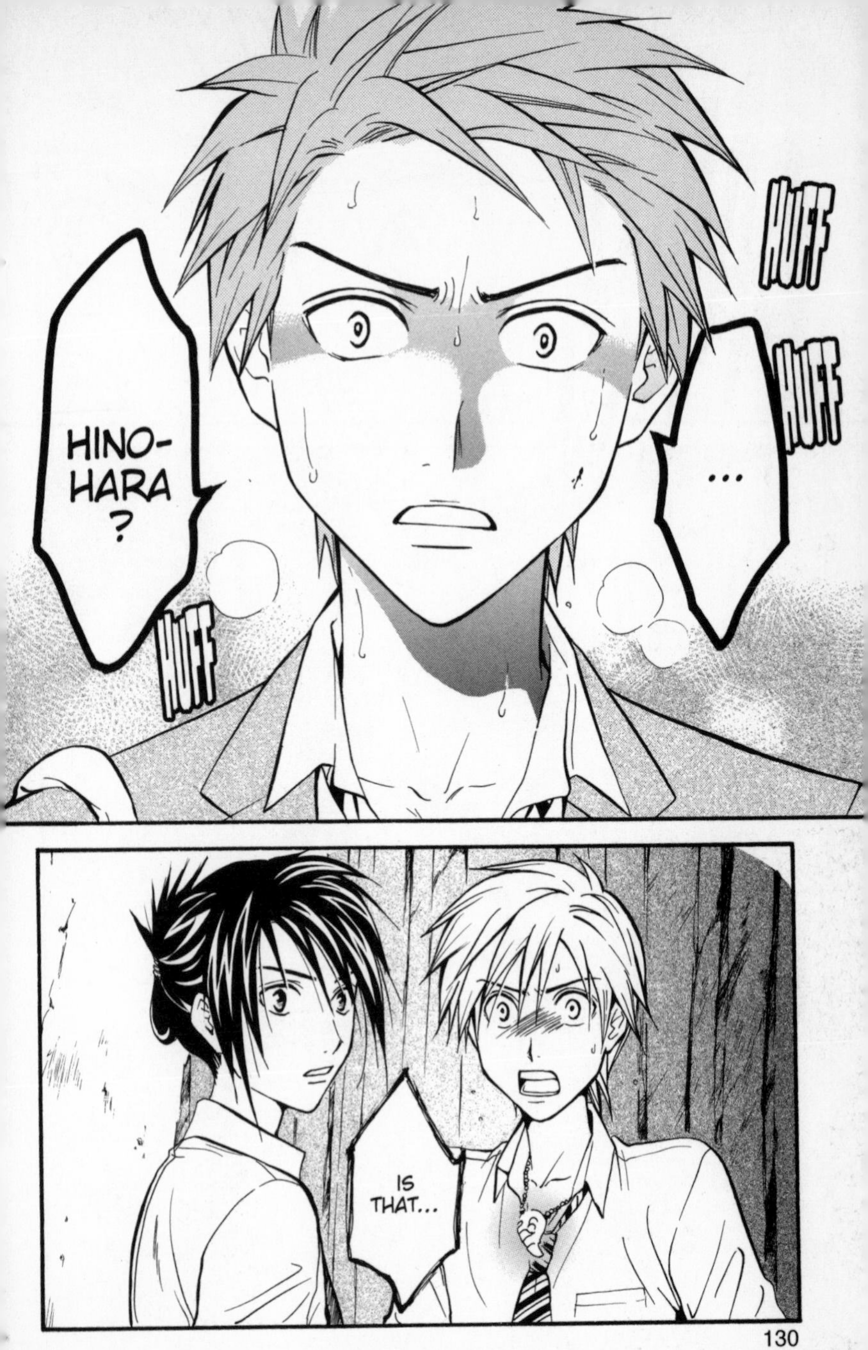
HUFF
HUFF
...
HINO-HARA?
HUFF
IS THAT...

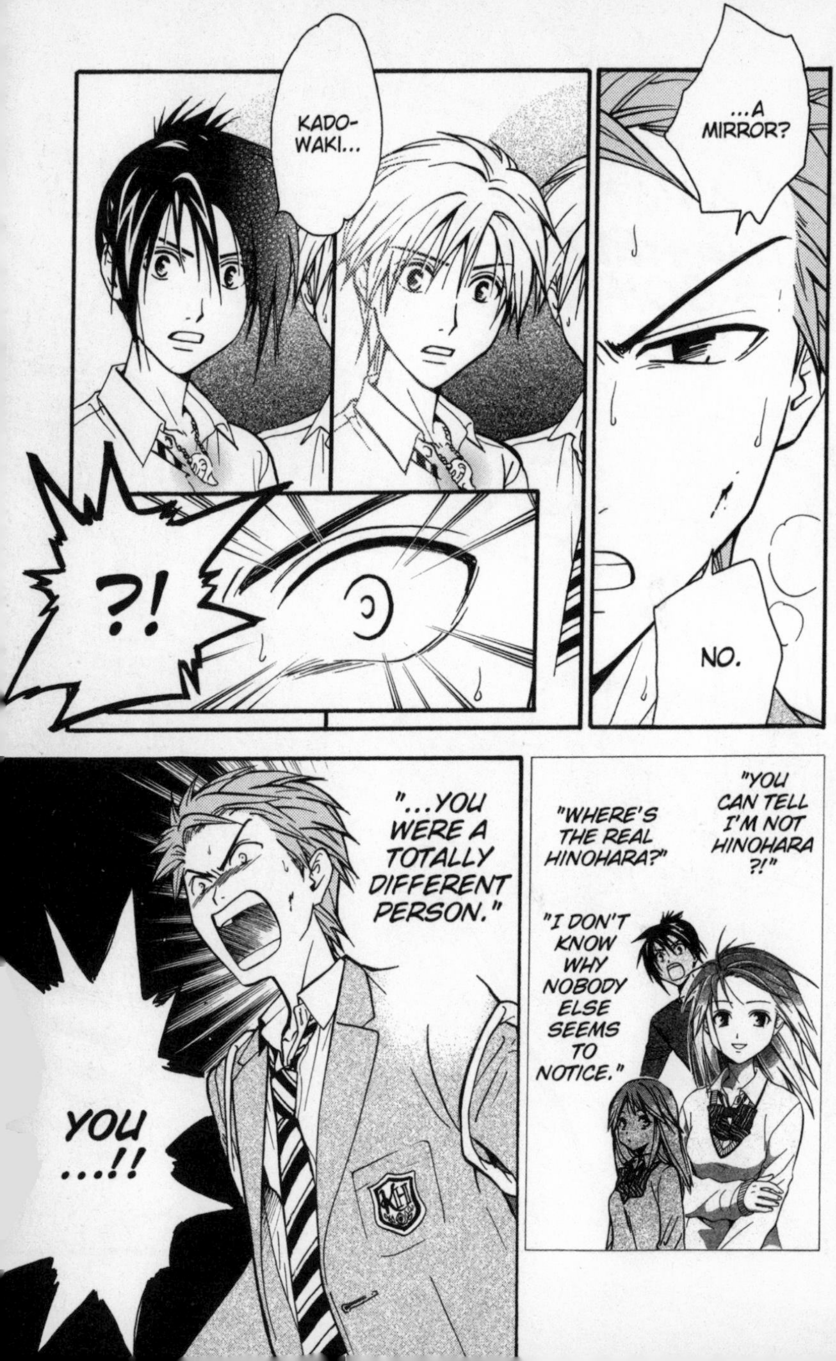
...A MIRROR?
NO.
KADO-WAKI...
?!
"YOU CAN TELL I'M NOT HINOHARA?!"
"WHERE'S THE REAL HINOHARA?"
"I DON'T KNOW WHY NOBODY ELSE SEEMS TO NOTICE."
"...YOU WERE A TOTALLY DIFFERENT PERSON."
YOU...!!

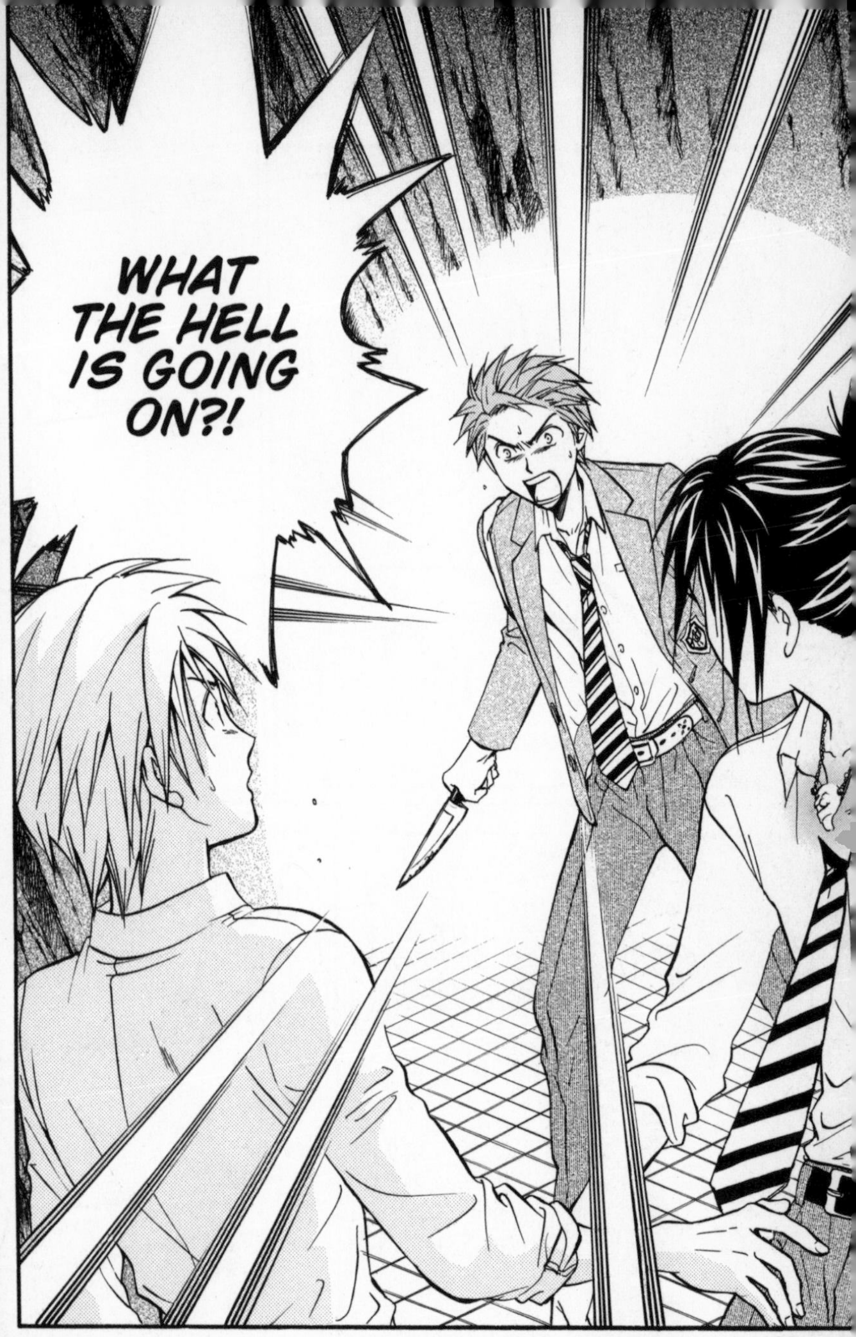
WHAT THE HELL IS GOING ON?!

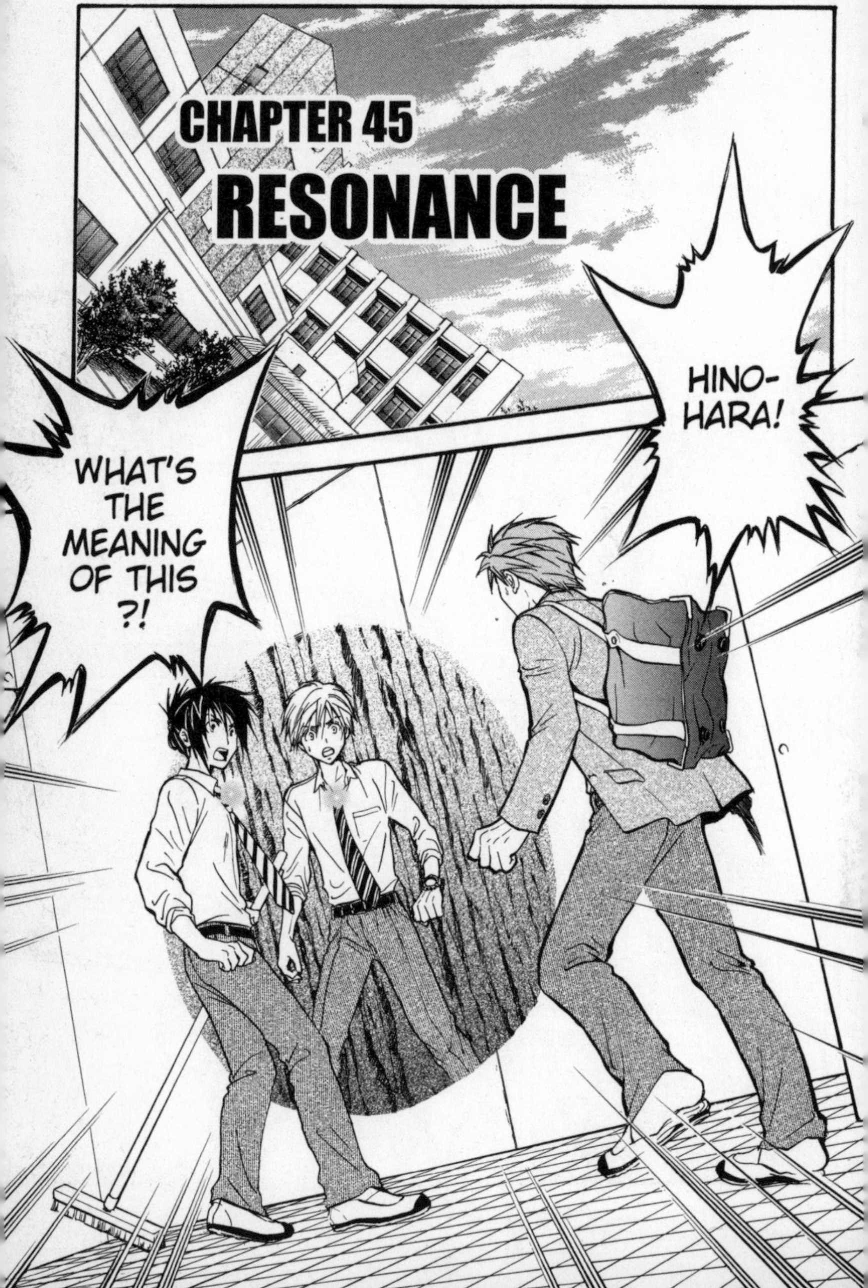
CHAPTER 45
RESONANCE
HINO-HARA!
WHAT'S THE MEANING OF THIS?!

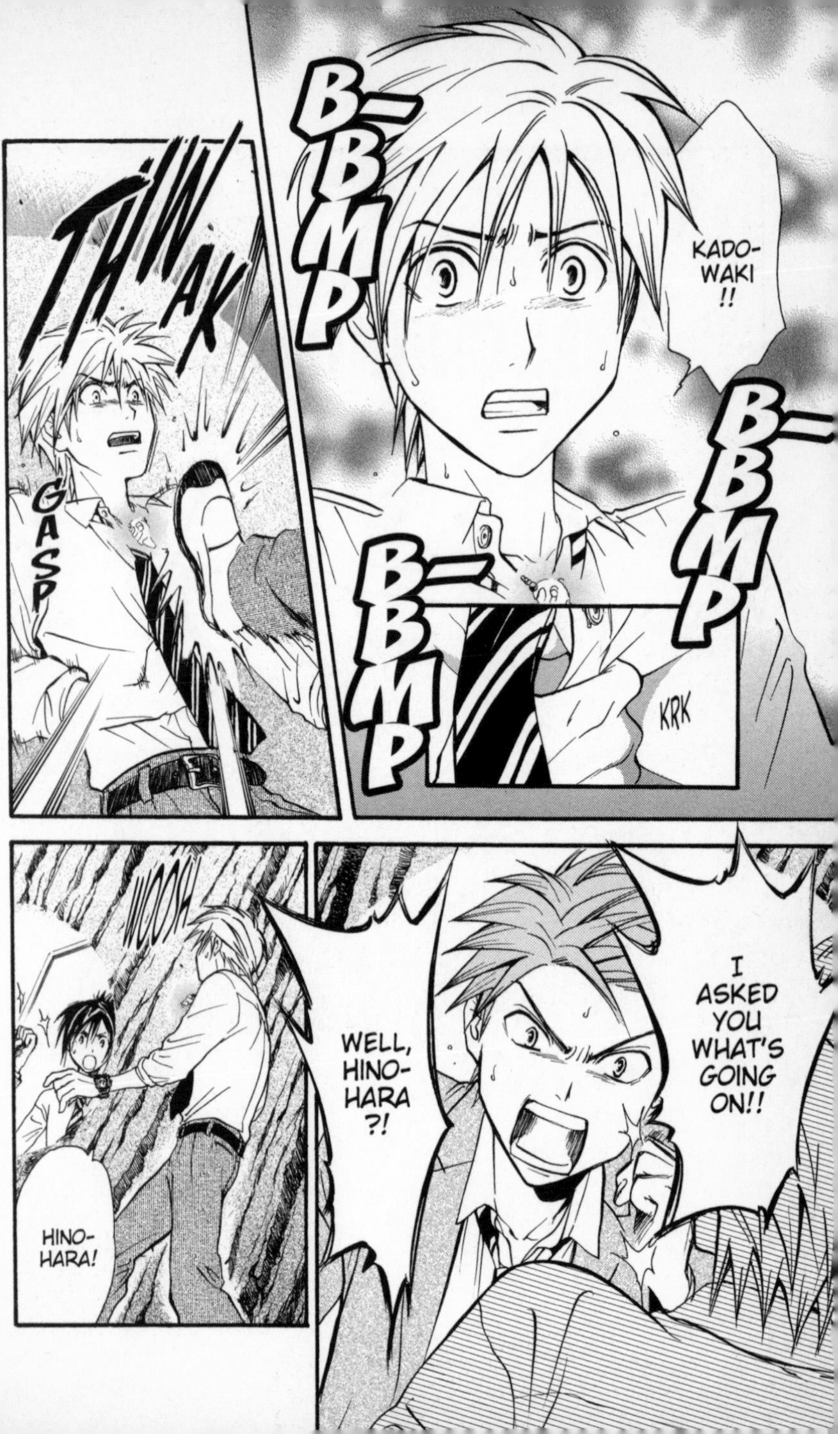
KADO-WAKI!!
B-BMP
B-BMP
B-BMP
KRK
THWAK
GASP
I ASKED YOU WHAT'S GOING ON!!
WELL, HINO-HARA?!
WHOOSH
HINO-HARA!

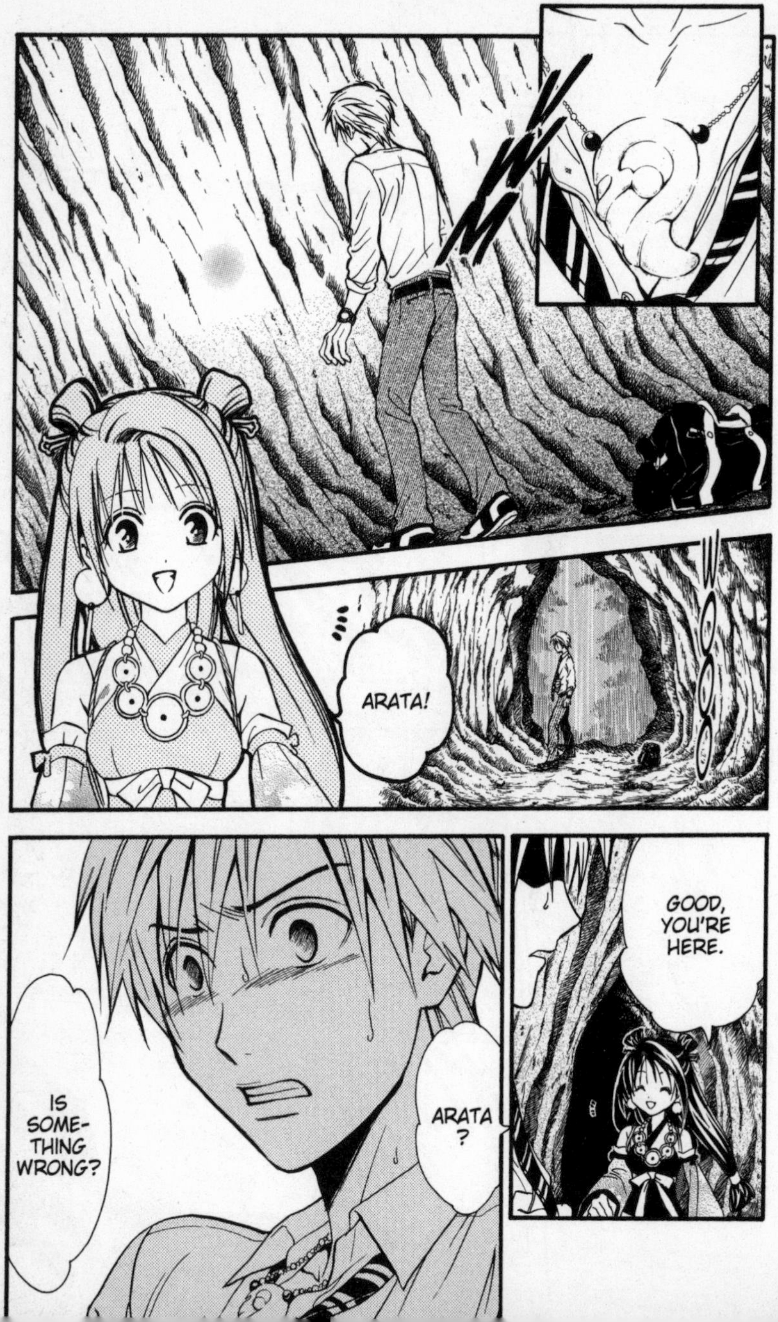
ARATA!
GOOD, YOU'RE HERE.
ARATA?
IS SOMETHING WRONG?

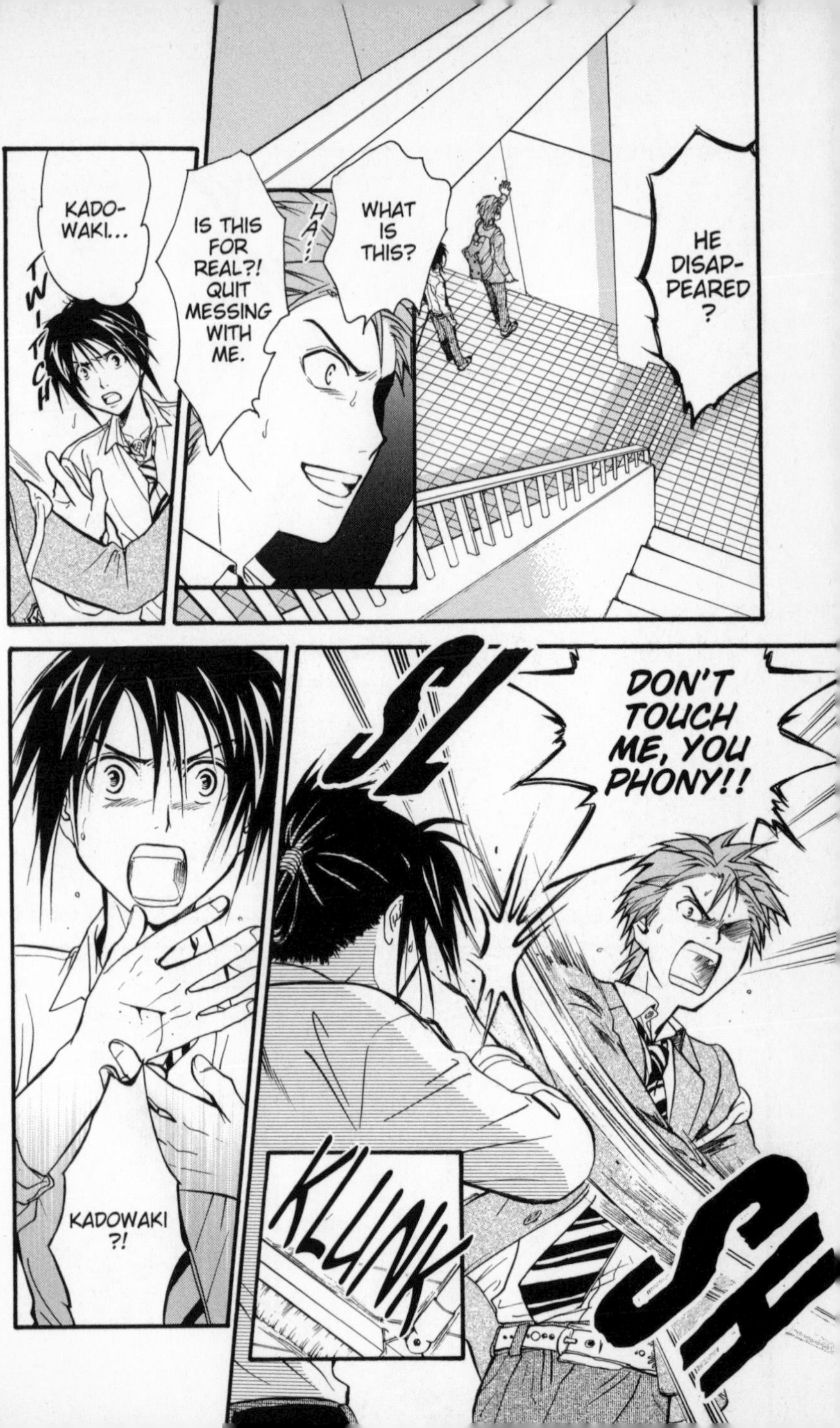
HE DISAPPEARED?
WHAT IS THIS?
HA..!
IS THIS FOR REAL?! QUIT MESSING WITH ME.
KADO-WAKI...
TWITCH
SH
DON'T TOUCH ME, YOU PHONY!!
SH
KLUNK
KADOWAKI?!

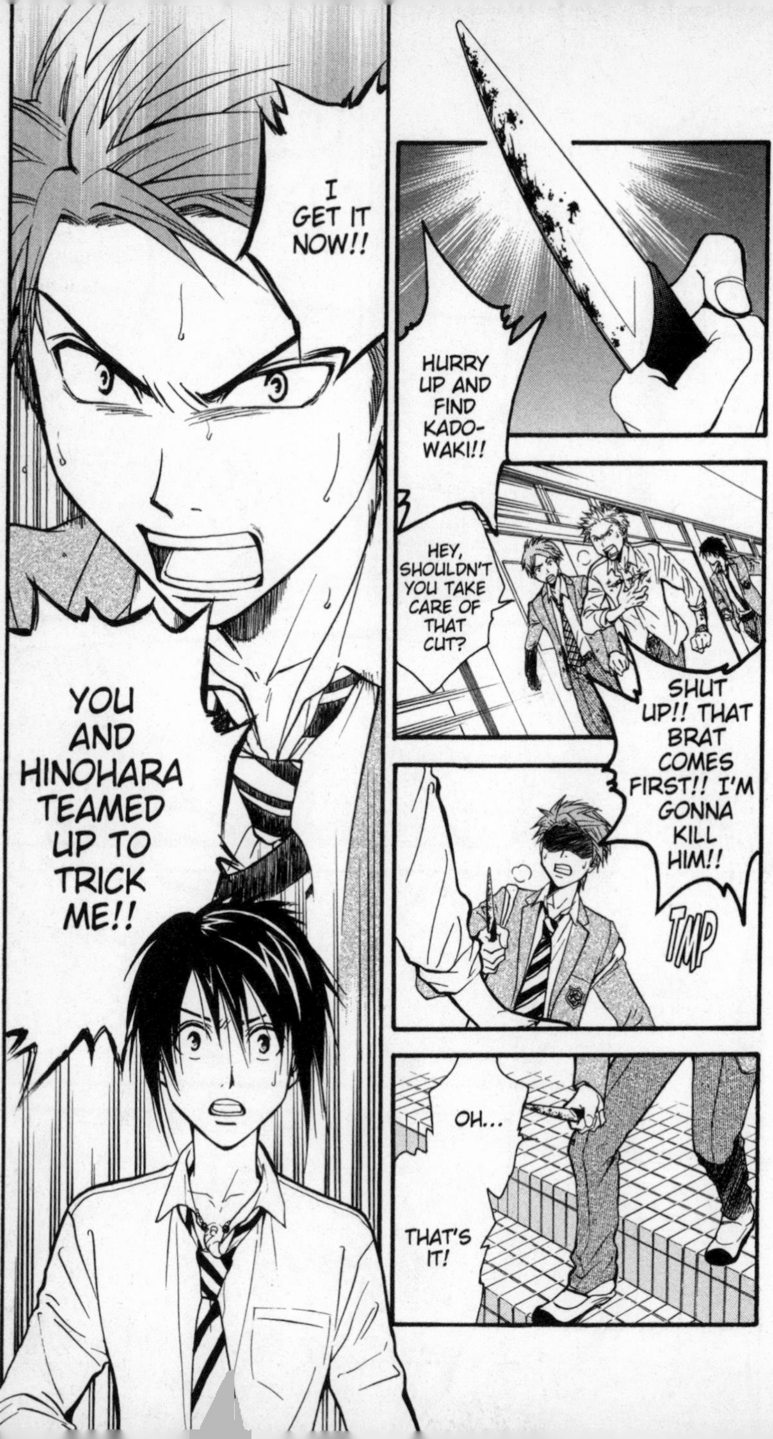
HURRY UP AND FIND KADO-WAKI!!
HEY, SHOULDN'T YOU TAKE CARE OF THAT CUT?
SHUT UP!! THAT BRAT COMES FIRST!! I'M GONNA KILL HIM!!
TMP
OH...
THAT'S IT!
I GET IT NOW!!
YOU AND HINOHARA TEAMED UP TO TRICK ME!!

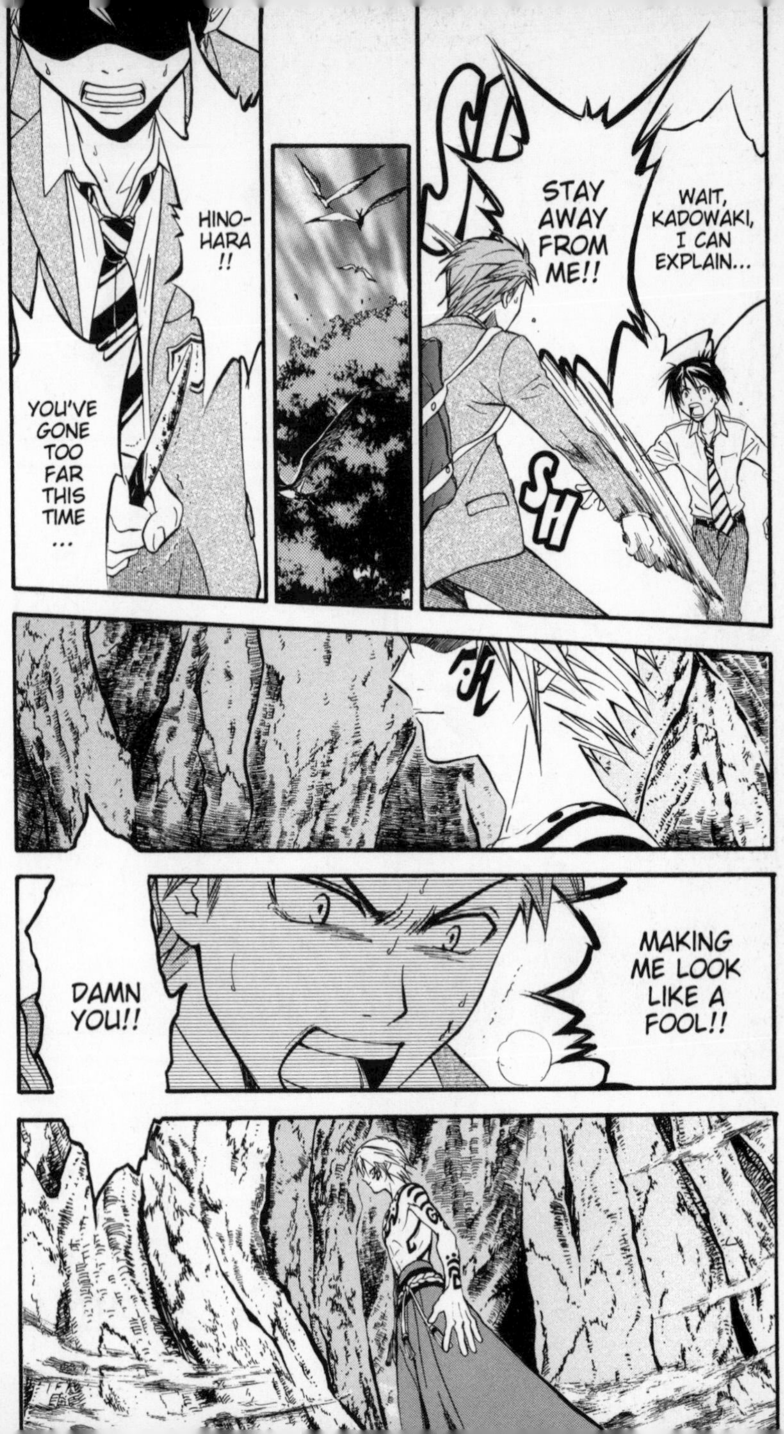
WAIT, KADOWAKI, I CAN EXPLAIN...
STAY AWAY FROM ME!!
SH
HINO-HARA!!
YOU'VE GONE TOO FAR THIS TIME...
MAKING ME LOOK LIKE A FOOL!!
DAMN YOU!!

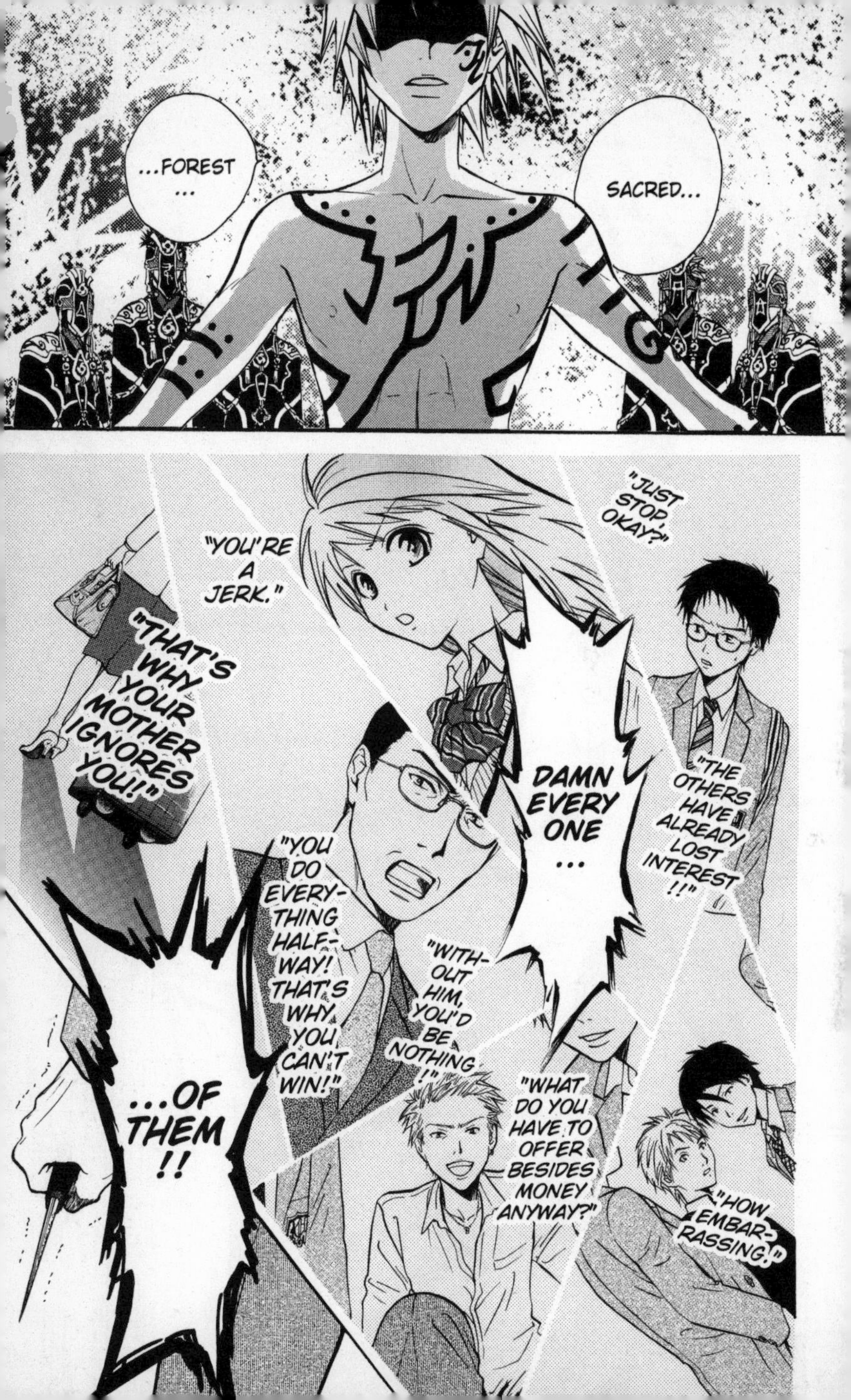
SACRED...
...FOREST ...
"JUST STOP, OKAY?"
"YOU'RE A JERK."
"THE OTHERS HAVE ALREADY LOST INTEREST!!"
DAMN EVERY ONE ...
"THAT'S WHY YOUR MOTHER IGNORES YOU!"
"YOU DO EVERY-THING HALF-WAY! THAT'S WHY YOU CAN'T WIN!"
"WITH-OUT HIM, YOU'D BE NOTHING!"
"HOW EMBAR-RASSING."
"WHAT DO YOU HAVE TO OFFER BESIDES MONEY ANYWAY?"
...OF THEM!!

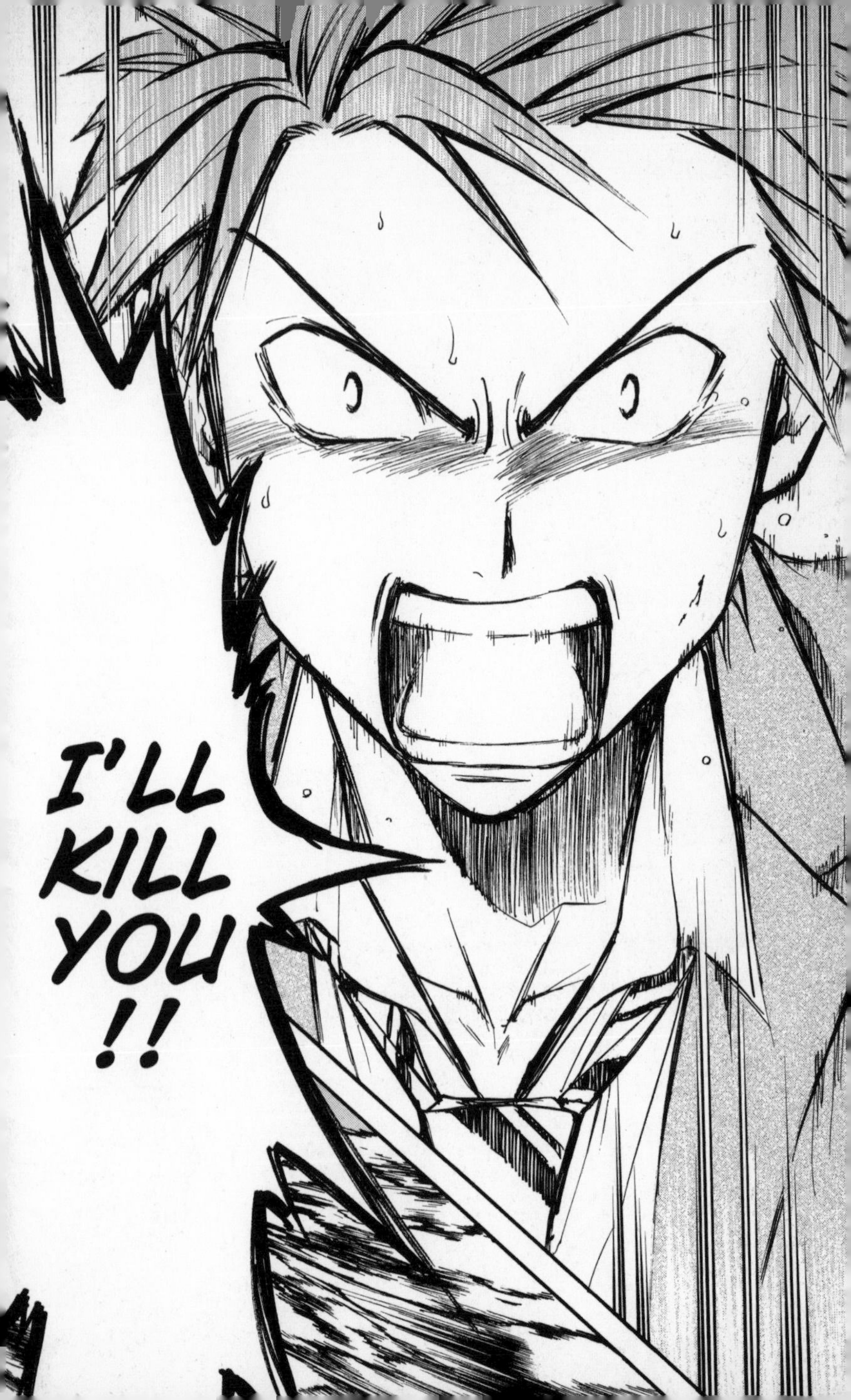
I'LL KILL YOU!!

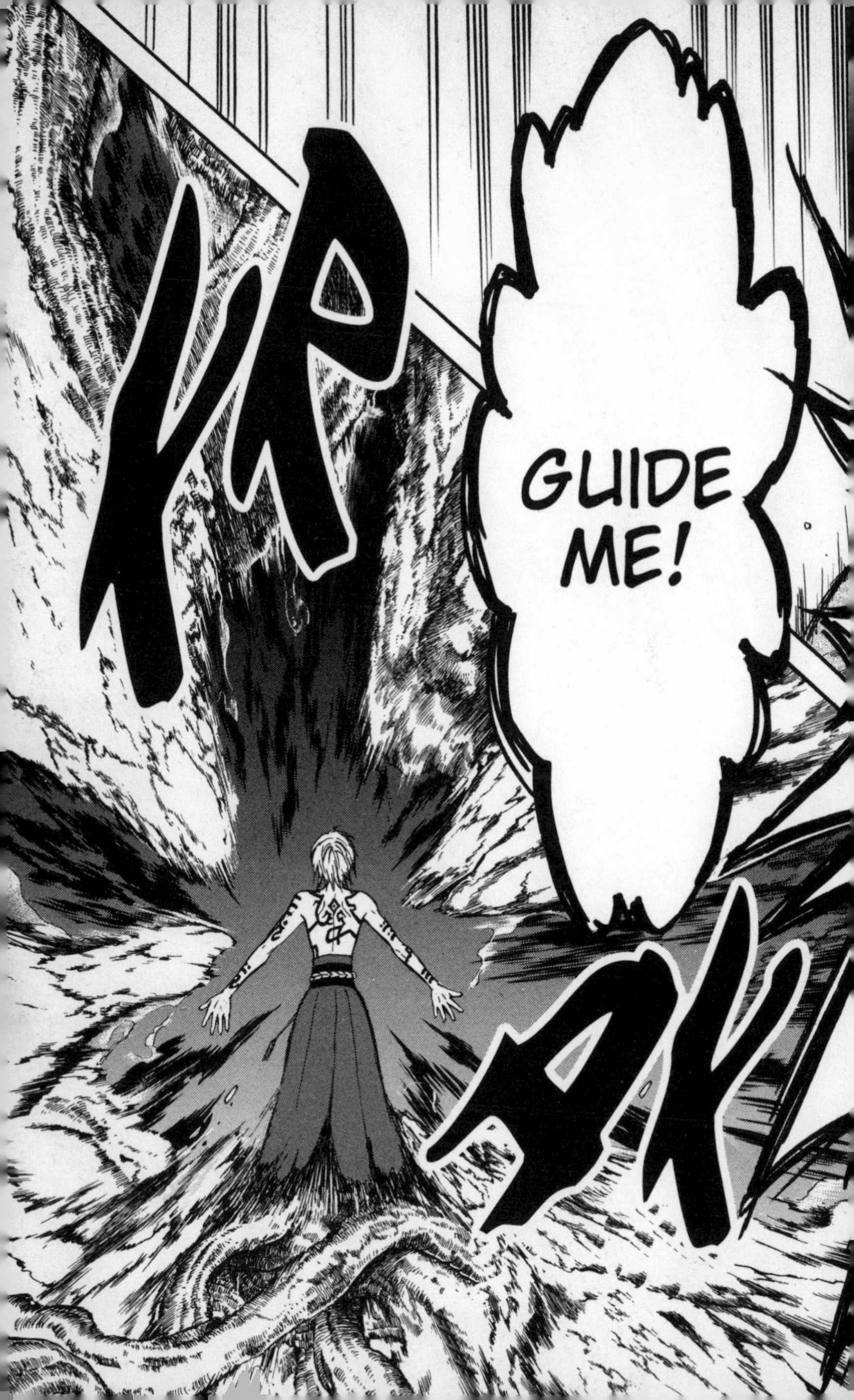
GUIDE ME!

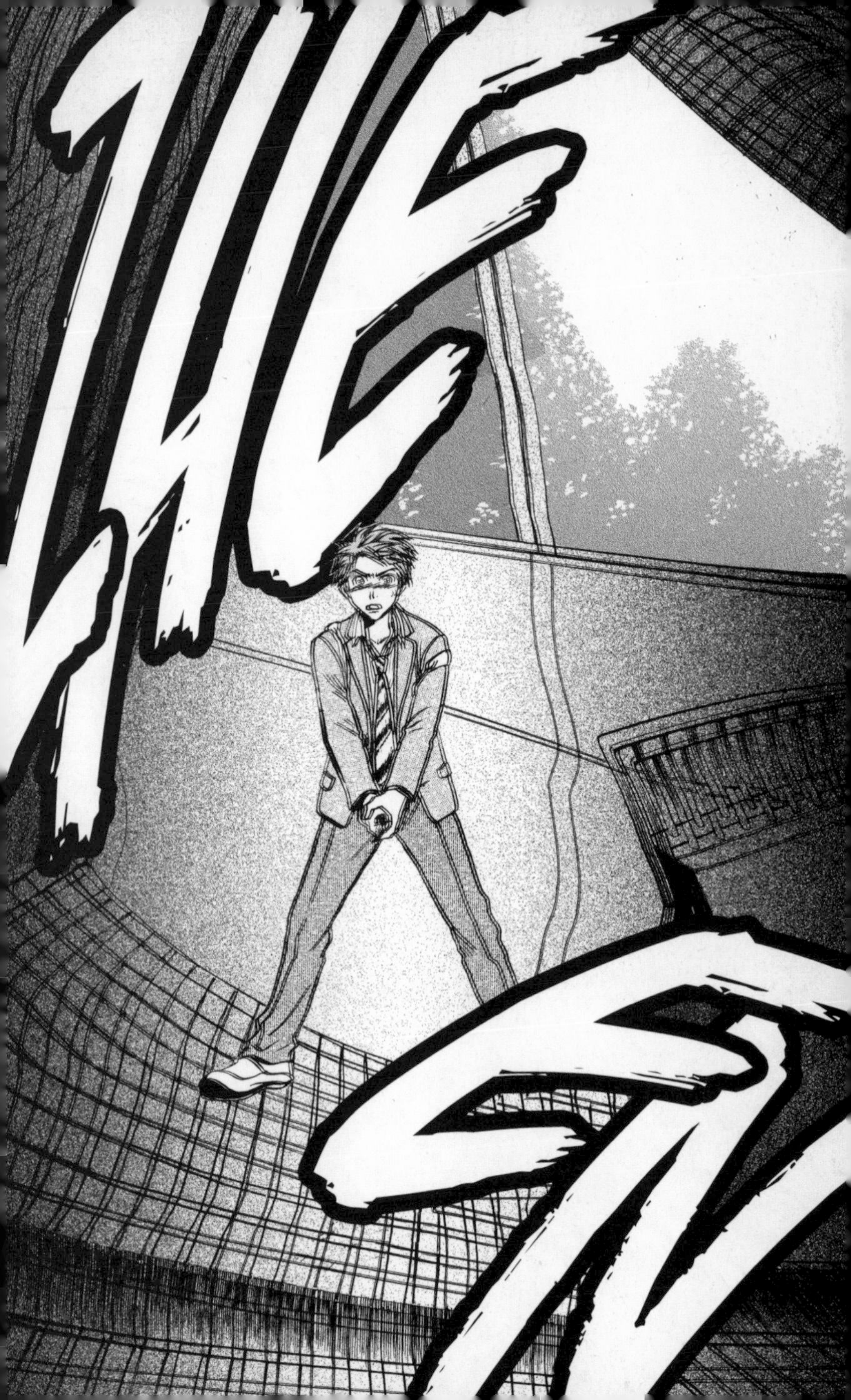

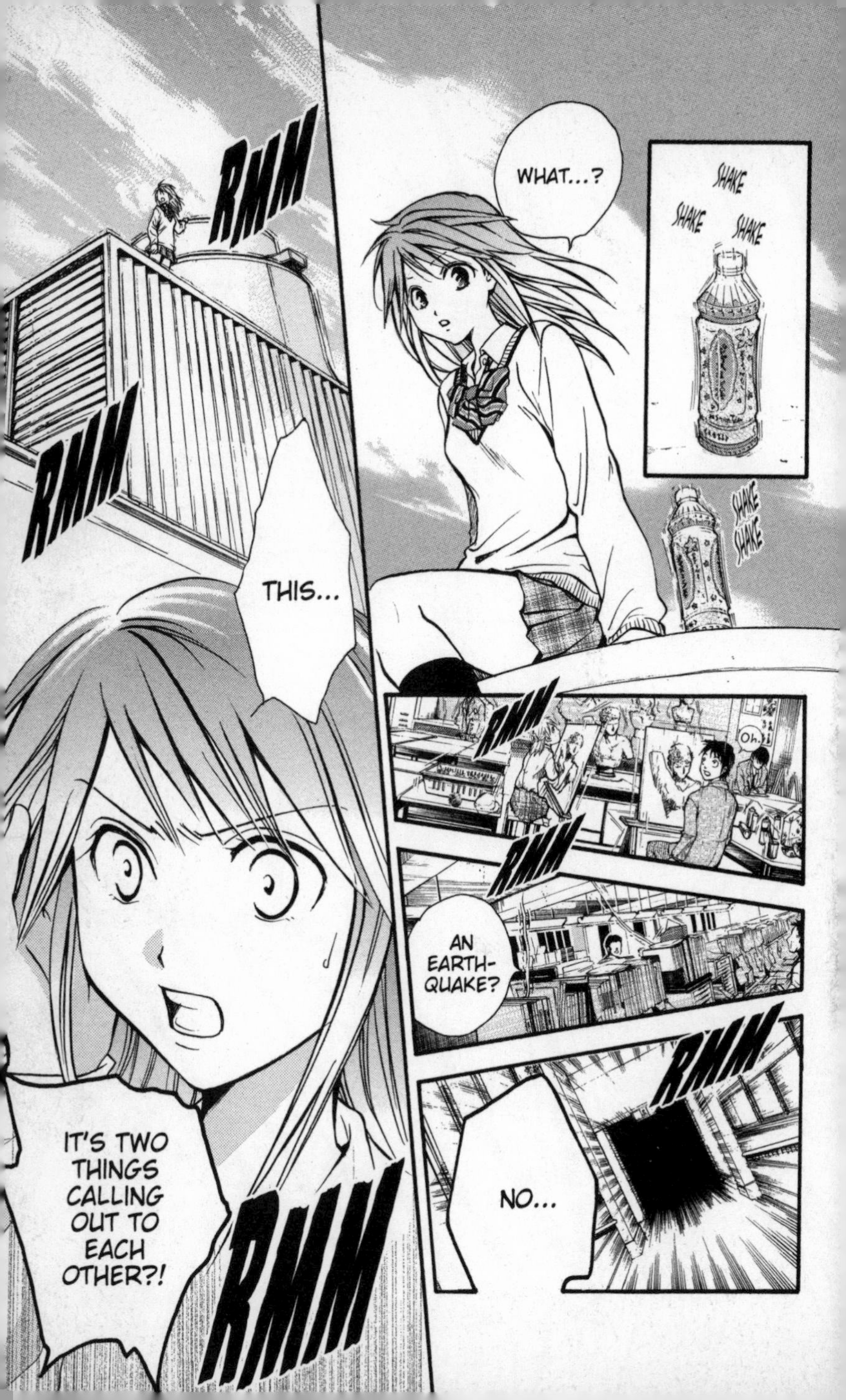
SHAKE
SHAKE
SHAKE
WHAT...?
SHAKE SHAKE
RMM
Oh.
RMM
AN EARTH-QUAKE?
RMM
NO...
RMM
RMM
THIS...
IT'S TWO THINGS CALLING OUT TO EACH OTHER?!
RMM

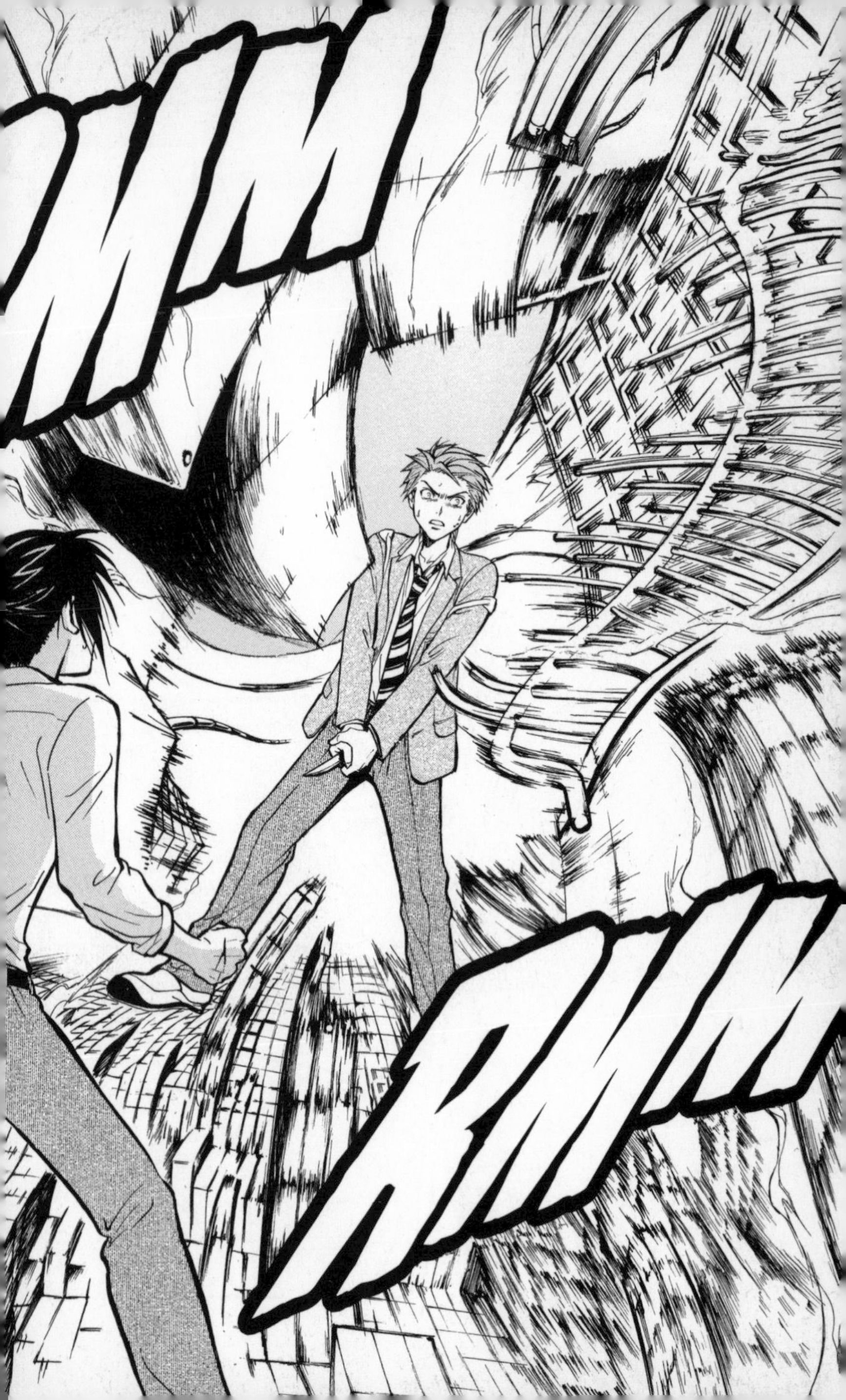

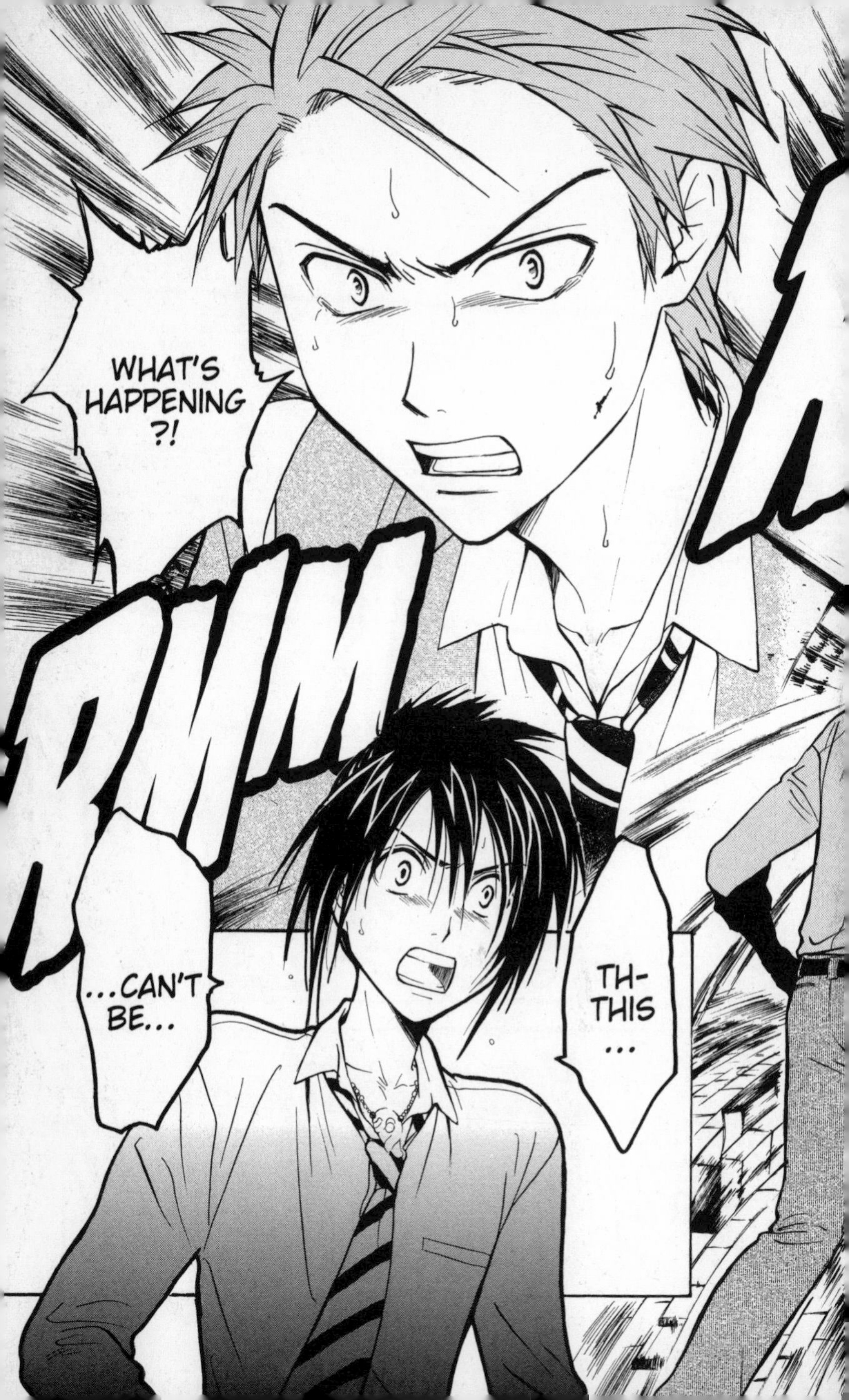
WHAT'S HAPPENING ?!
TH- THIS ...
...CAN'T BE...

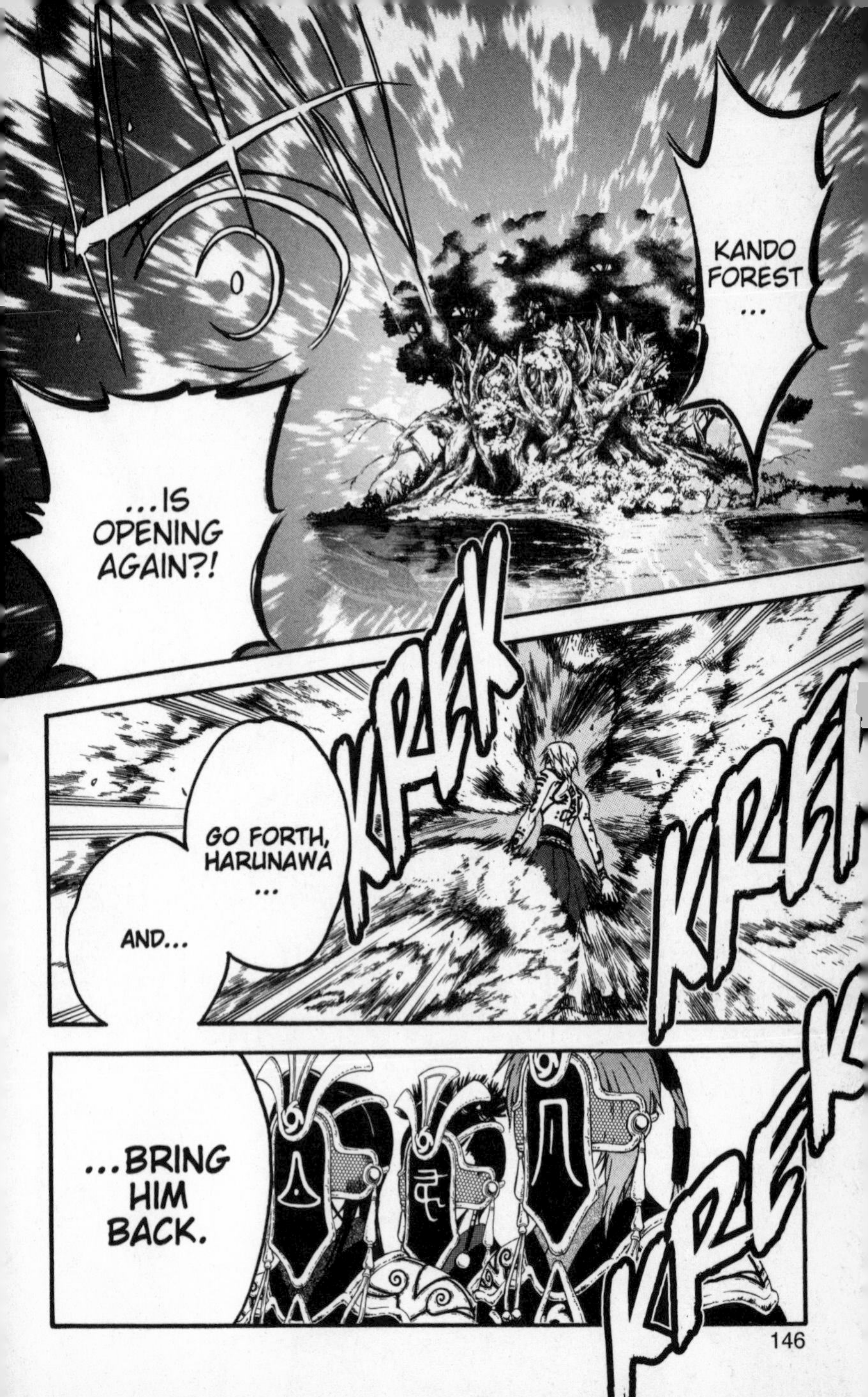

KANDO FOREST ...
...IS OPENING AGAIN?!
KREK
KREK
GO FORTH, HARUNAWA ...
AND...
KREK
...BRING HIM BACK.

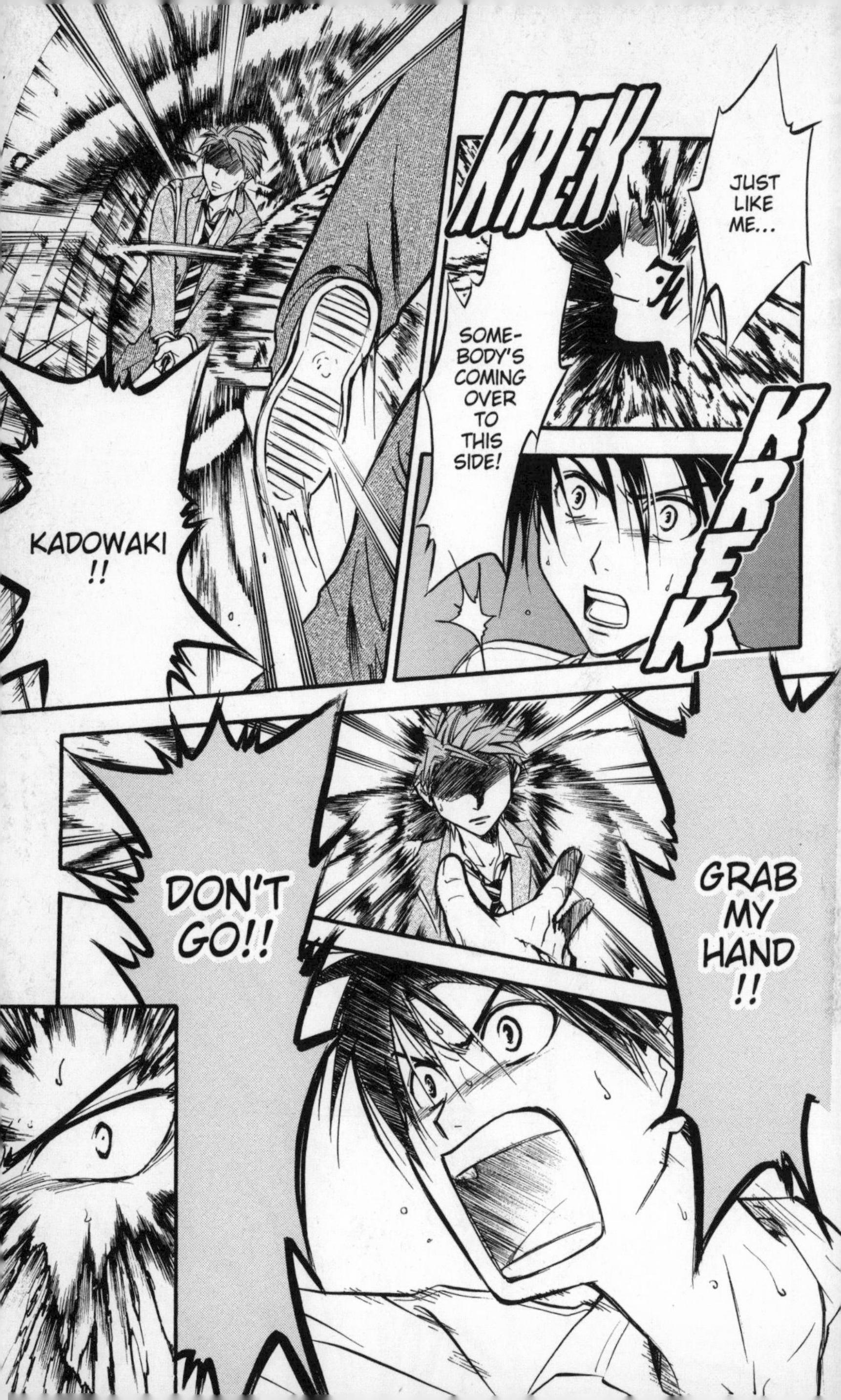
KREK
JUST LIKE ME...
SOMEBODY'S COMING OVER TO THIS SIDE!
KREK
KADOWAKI !!
GRAB MY HAND !!
DON'T GO!!

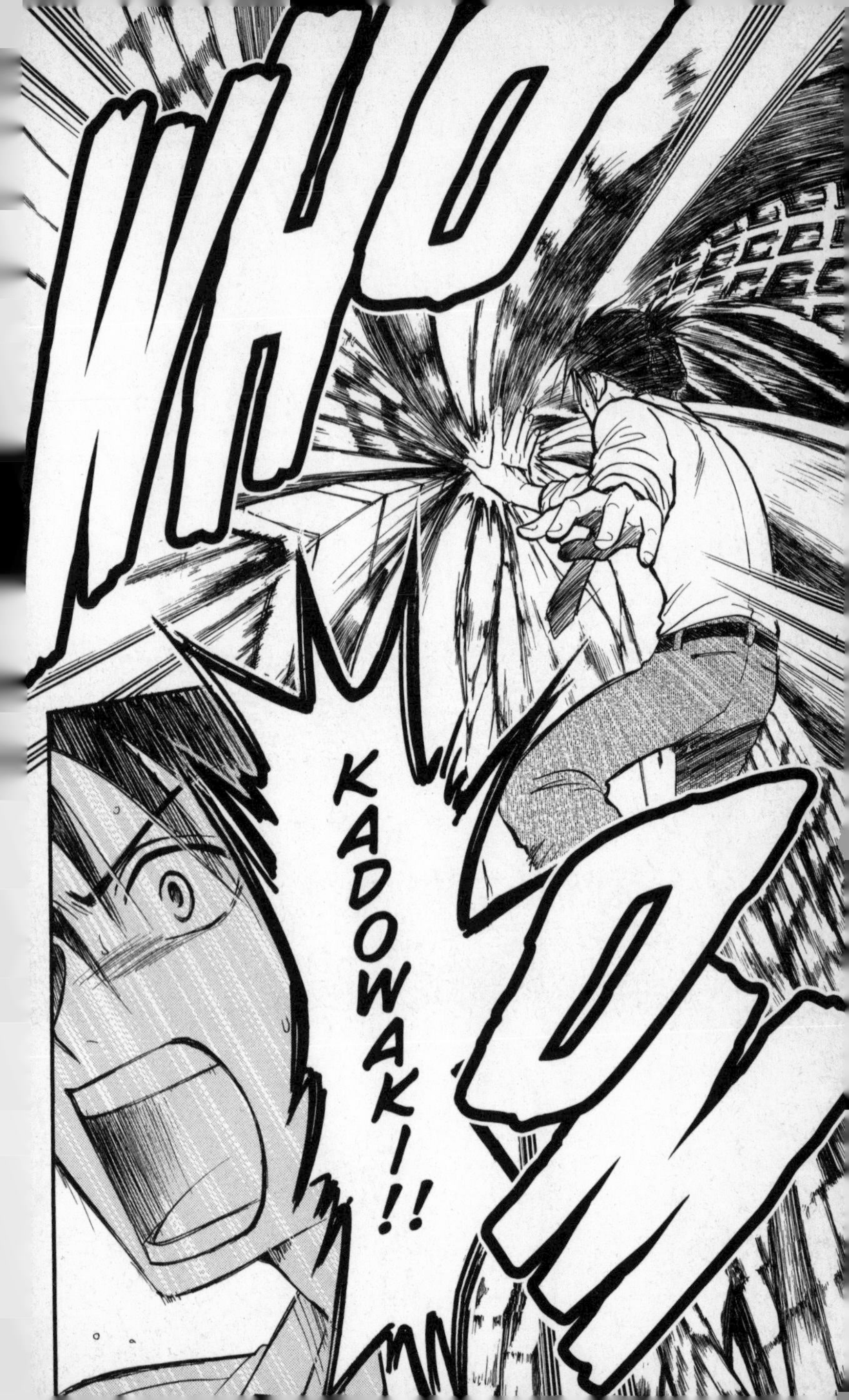
KADOWAKI!!

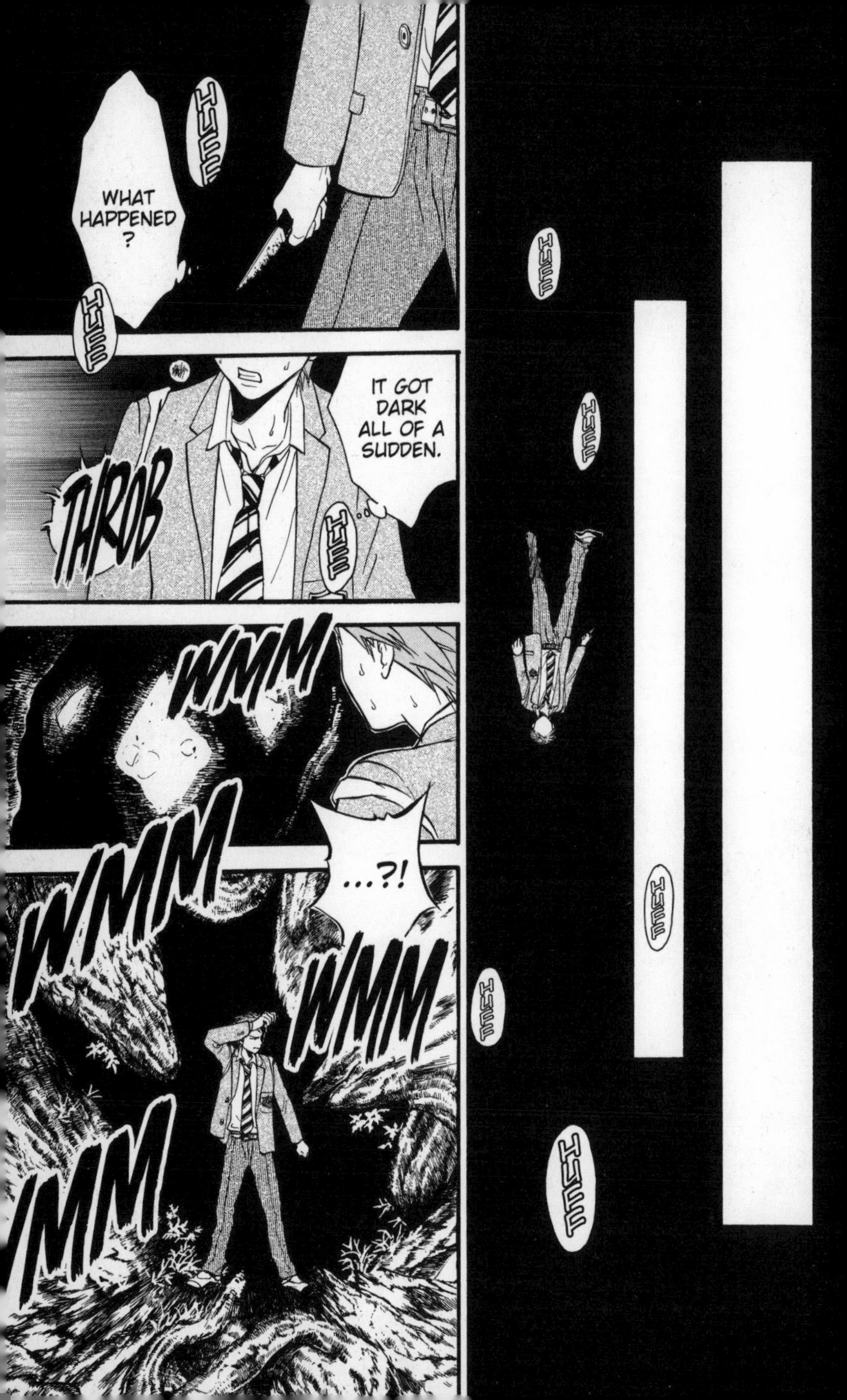
HUFF
HUFF
HUFF
HUFF
HUFF
HUFF
WHAT HAPPENED?
HUFF
IT GOT DARK ALL OF A SUDDEN.
HUFF
THROB
WMM
...?!
WMM
WMM
WMM

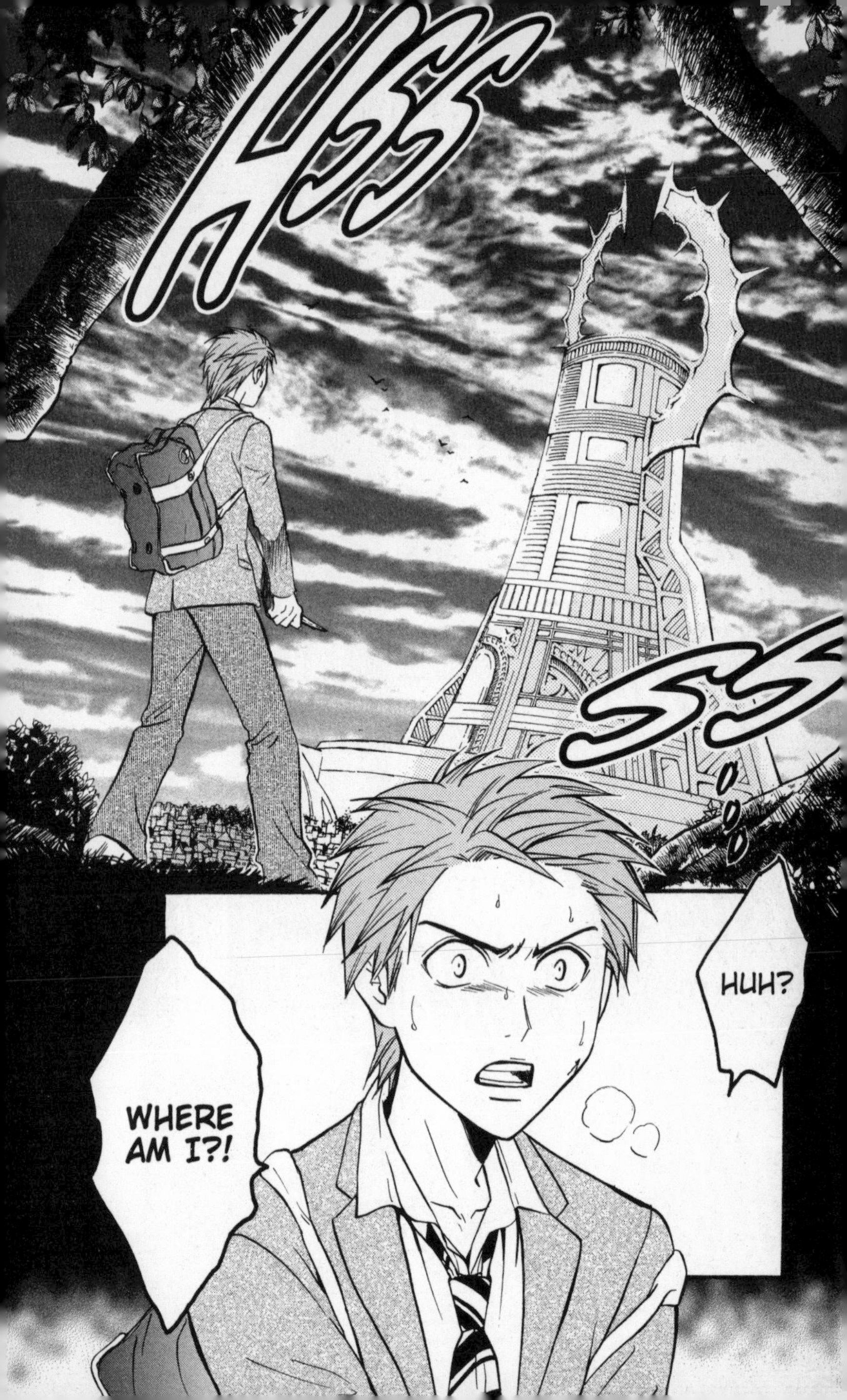
HSSS
SS
HUH?
WHERE AM I?!

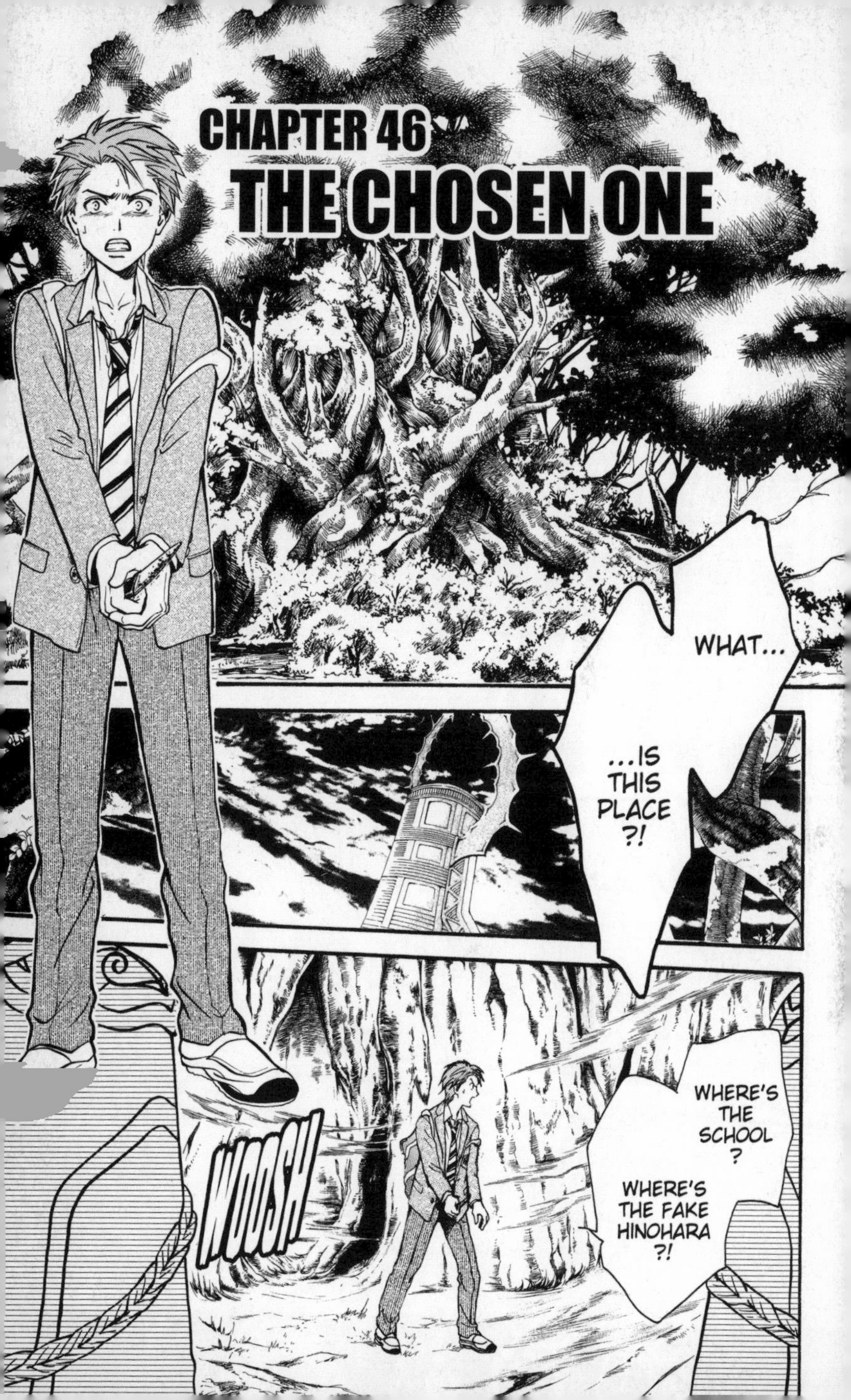
CHAPTER 46
THE CHOSEN ONE
WHAT...
...IS THIS PLACE ?!
WHERE'S THE SCHOOL ?
WHERE'S THE FAKE HINOHARA ?!
WOOSH

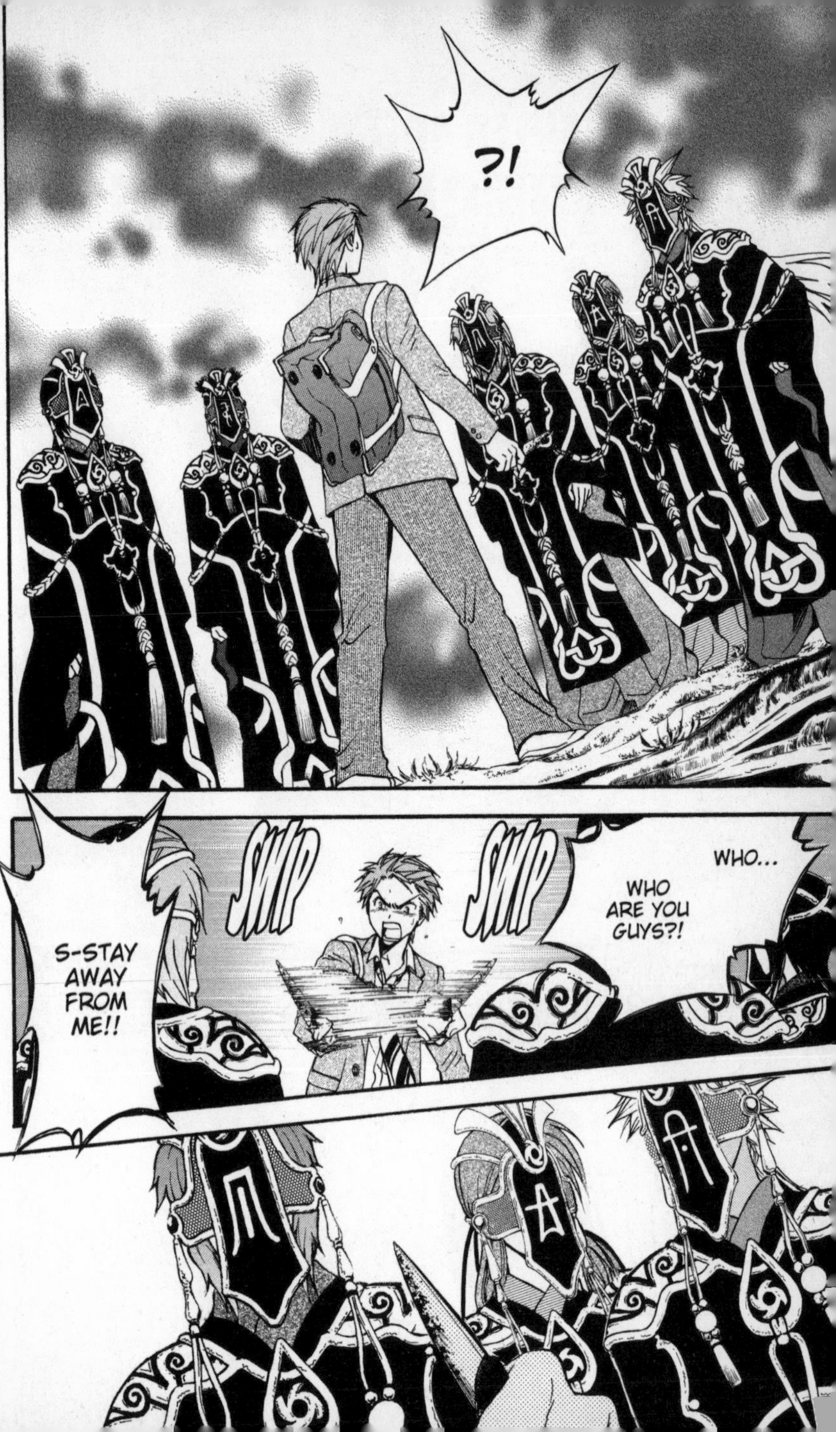
?!
WHO...
WHO ARE YOU GUYS?!
S-STAY AWAY FROM ME!!

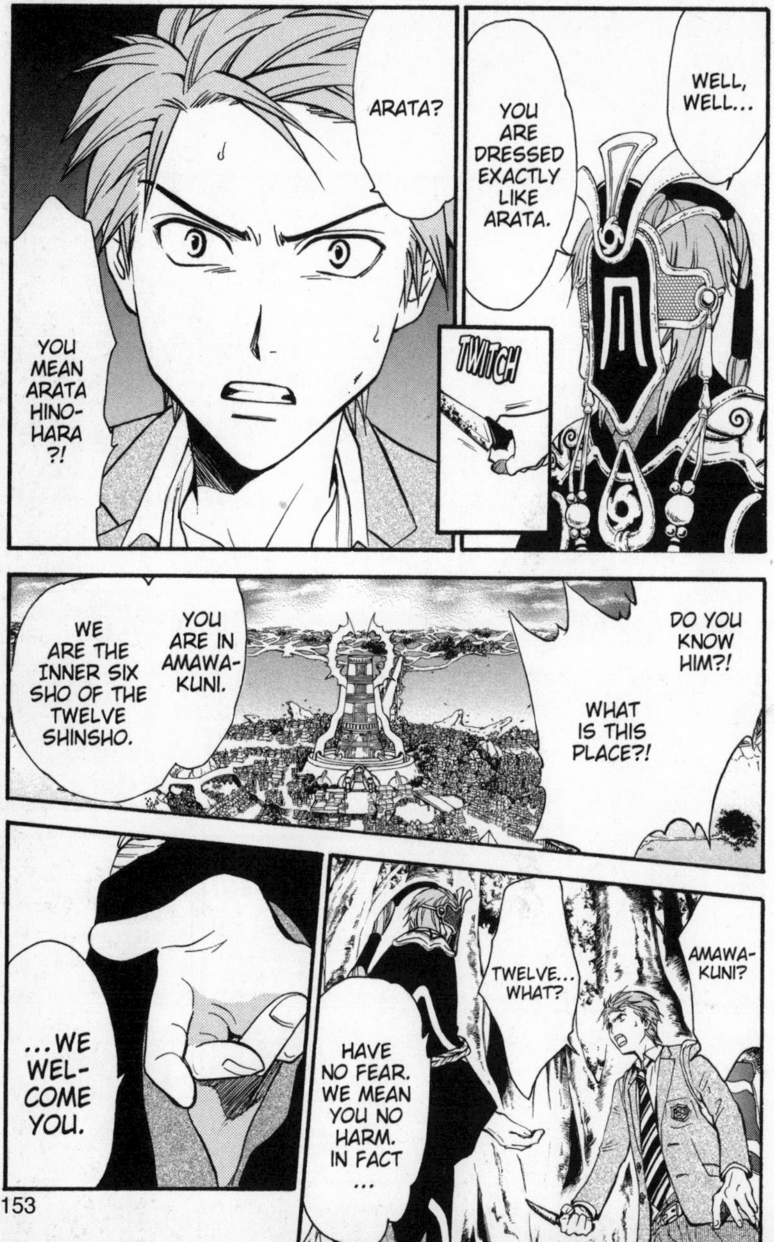
WELL, WELL...
YOU ARE DRESSED EXACTLY LIKE ARATA.
TWITCH
ARATA?
YOU MEAN ARATA HINO-HARA?!
DO YOU KNOW HIM?!
WHAT IS THIS PLACE?!
YOU ARE IN AMAWA-KUNI.
WE ARE THE INNER SIX SHO OF THE TWELVE SHINSHO.
AMAWA-KUNI?
TWELVE... WHAT?
HAVE NO FEAR. WE MEAN YOU NO HARM. IN FACT ...
...WE WEL-COME YOU.

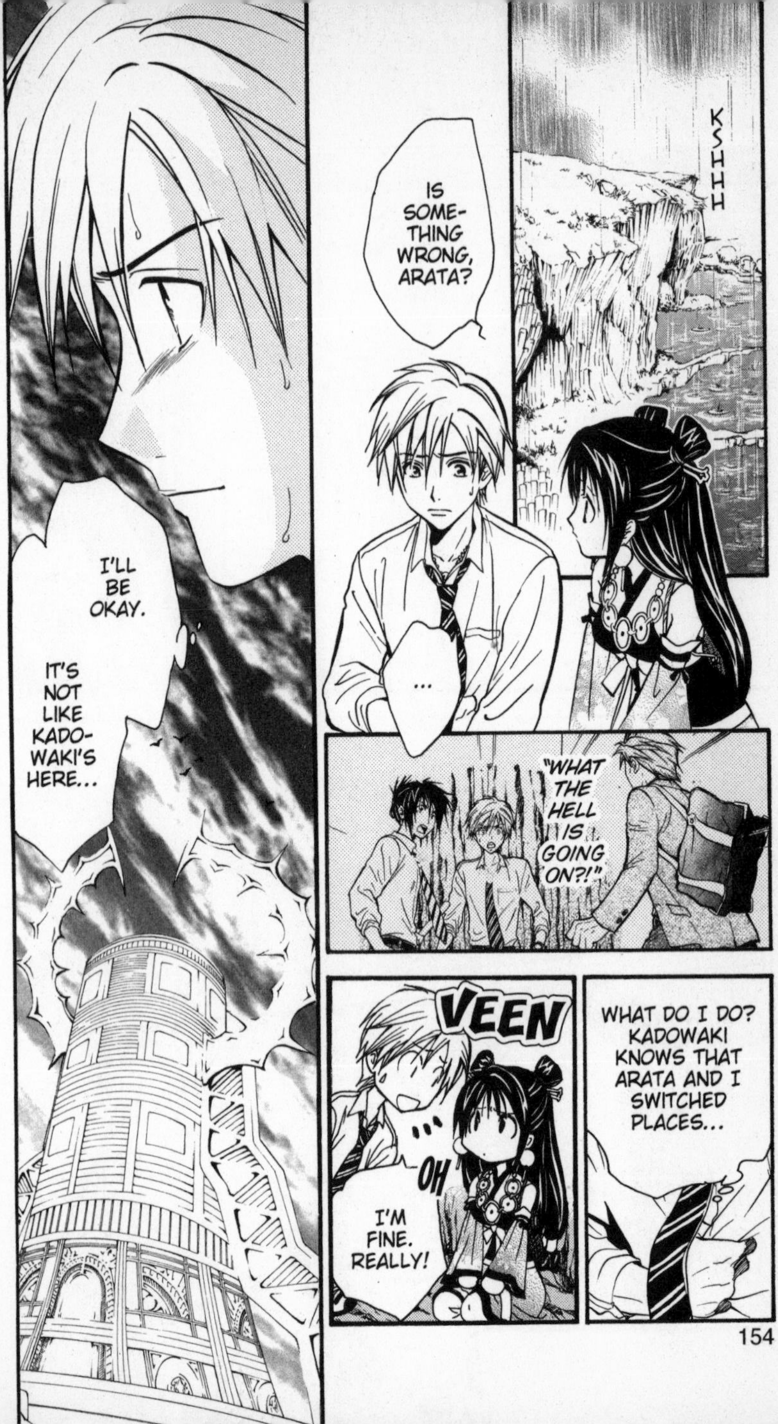
KSHHH
IS SOMETHING-THING WRONG, ARATA?
...
"WHAT THE HELL IS GOING ON?!"
WHAT DO I DO? KADOWAKI KNOWS THAT ARATA AND I SWITCHED PLACES...
VEEN
...
OH
I'M FINE. REALLY!
I'LL BE OKAY.
IT'S NOT LIKE KADO-WAKI'S HERE...

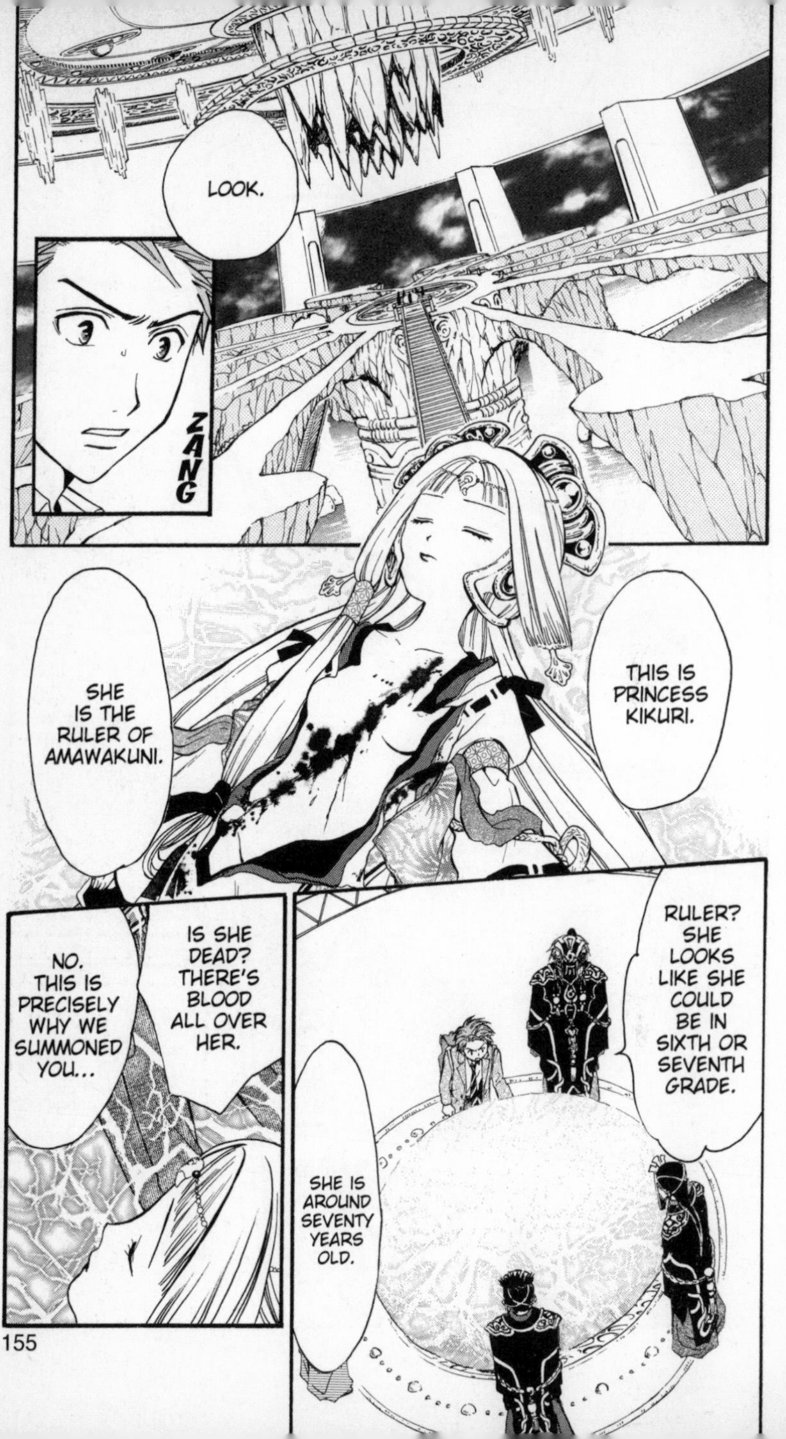
LOOK.
ZANG
THIS IS PRINCESS KIKURI.
SHE IS THE RULER OF AMAWAKUNI.
RULER? SHE LOOKS LIKE SHE COULD BE IN SIXTH OR SEVENTH GRADE.
SHE IS AROUND SEVENTY YEARS OLD.
IS SHE DEAD? THERE'S BLOOD ALL OVER HER.
NO. THIS IS PRECISELY WHY WE SUMMONED YOU...

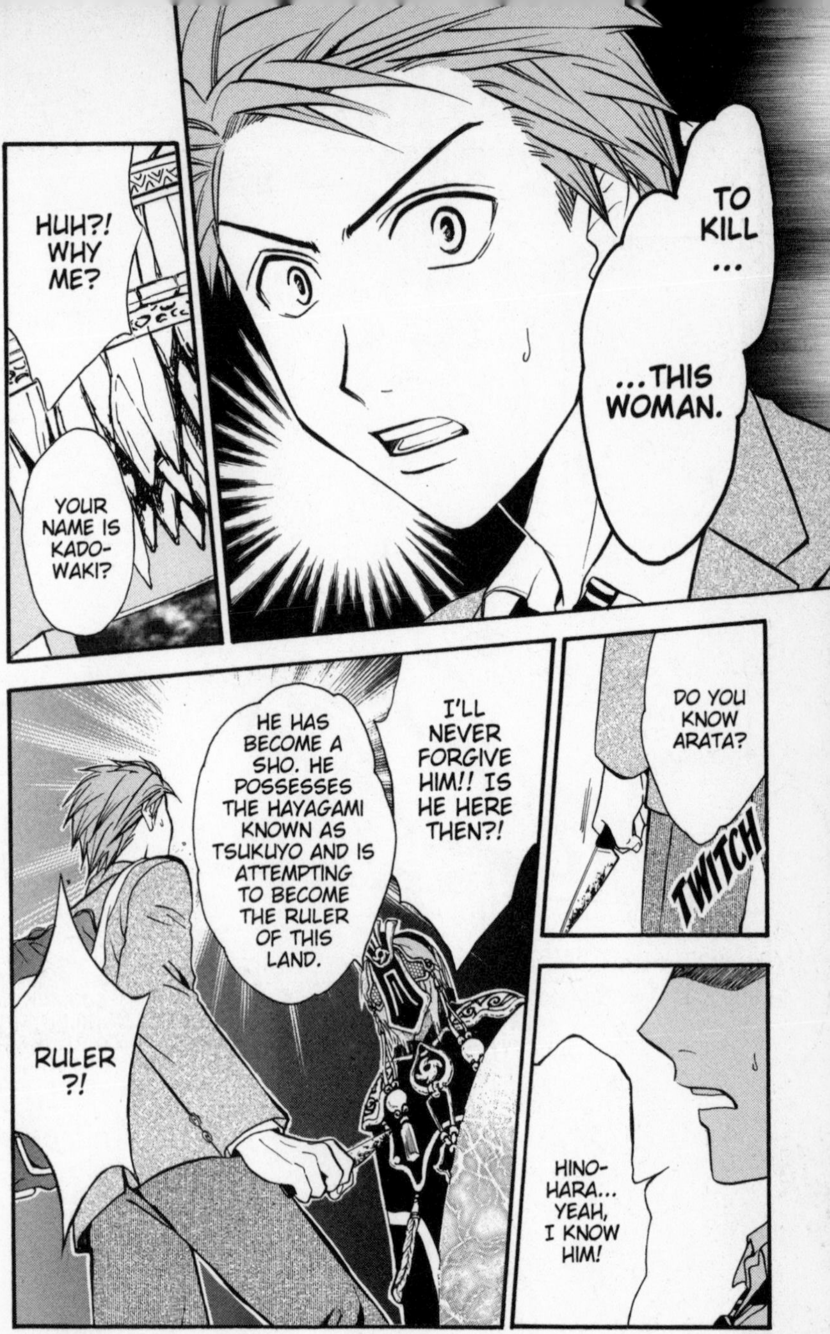
TO KILL ...
...THIS WOMAN.
HUH?! WHY ME?
YOUR NAME IS KADO-WAKI?
DO YOU KNOW ARATA?
TWITCH
HINO-HARA... YEAH, I KNOW HIM!
I'LL NEVER FORGIVE HIM!! IS HE HERE THEN?!
HE HAS BECOME A SHO. HE POSSESSES THE HAYAGAMI KNOWN AS TSUKUYO AND IS ATTEMPTING TO BECOME THE RULER OF THIS LAND.
RULER ?!

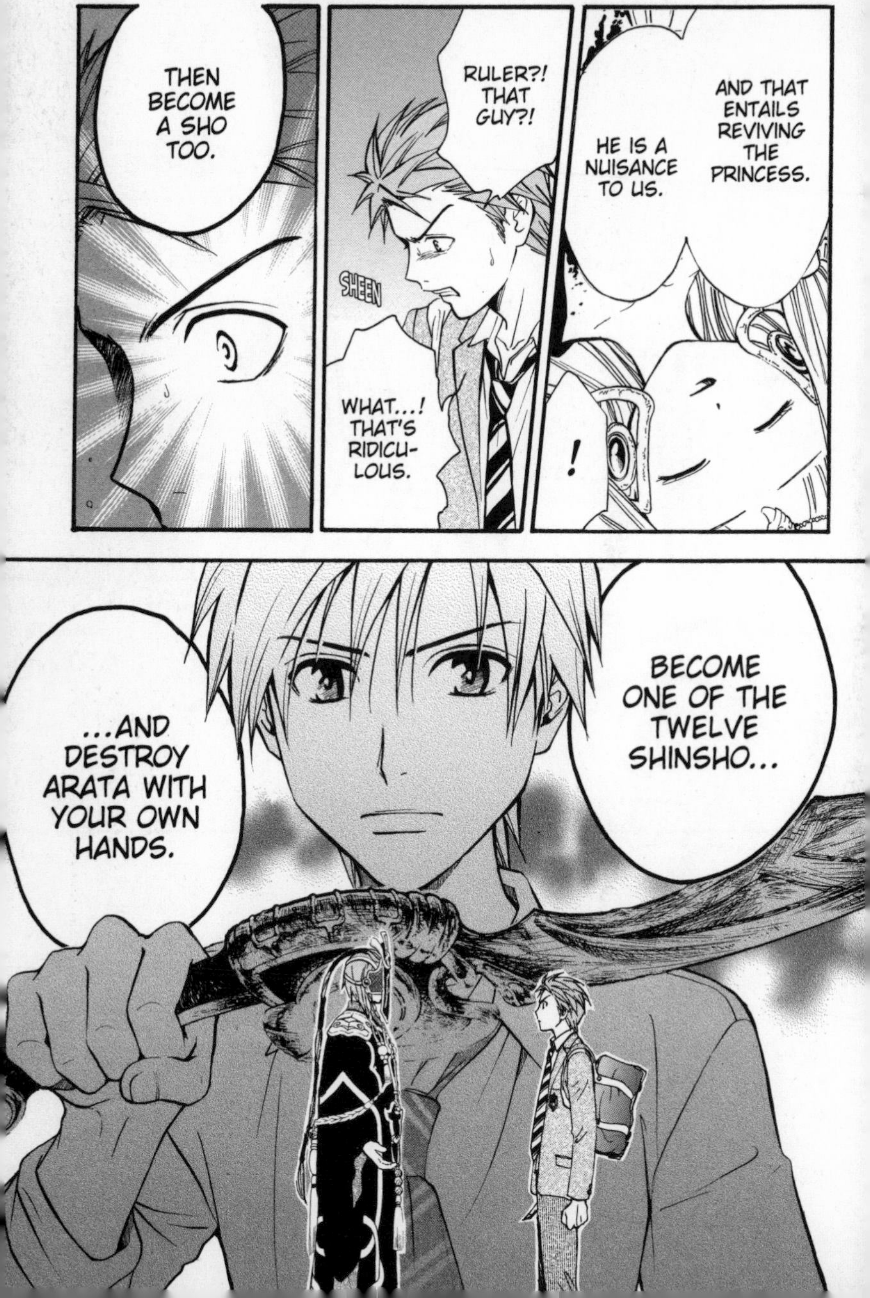
AND THAT ENTAILS REVIVING THE PRINCESS.
HE IS A NUISANCE TO US.
!
RULER?! THAT GUY?!
SHEEN
WHAT...! THAT'S RIDICU-LOUS.
THEN BECOME A SHO TOO.
BECOME ONE OF THE TWELVE SHINSHO...
...AND DESTROY ARATA WITH YOUR OWN HANDS.

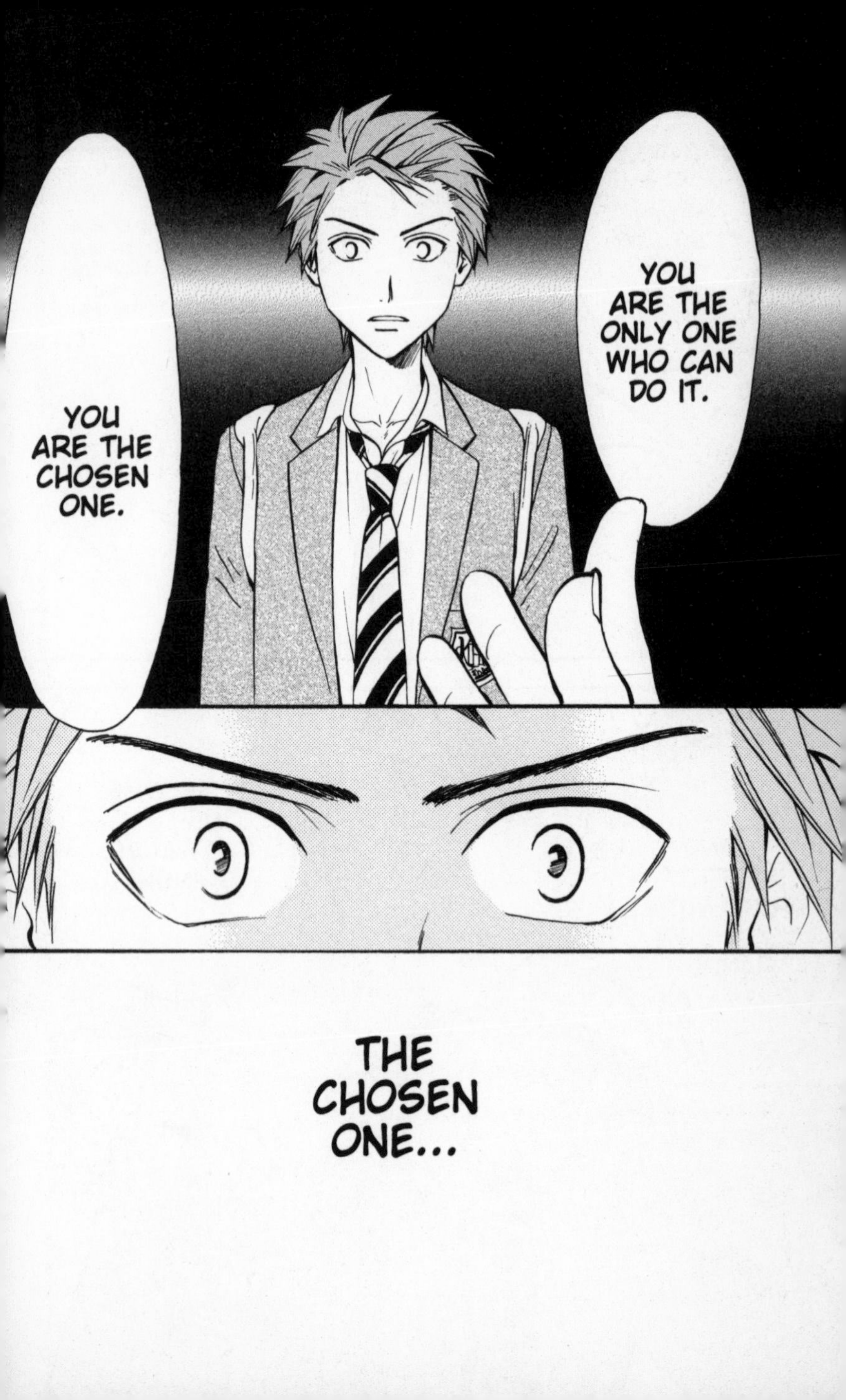
YOU ARE THE ONLY ONE WHO CAN DO IT.
YOU ARE THE CHOSEN ONE.
THE CHOSEN ONE...

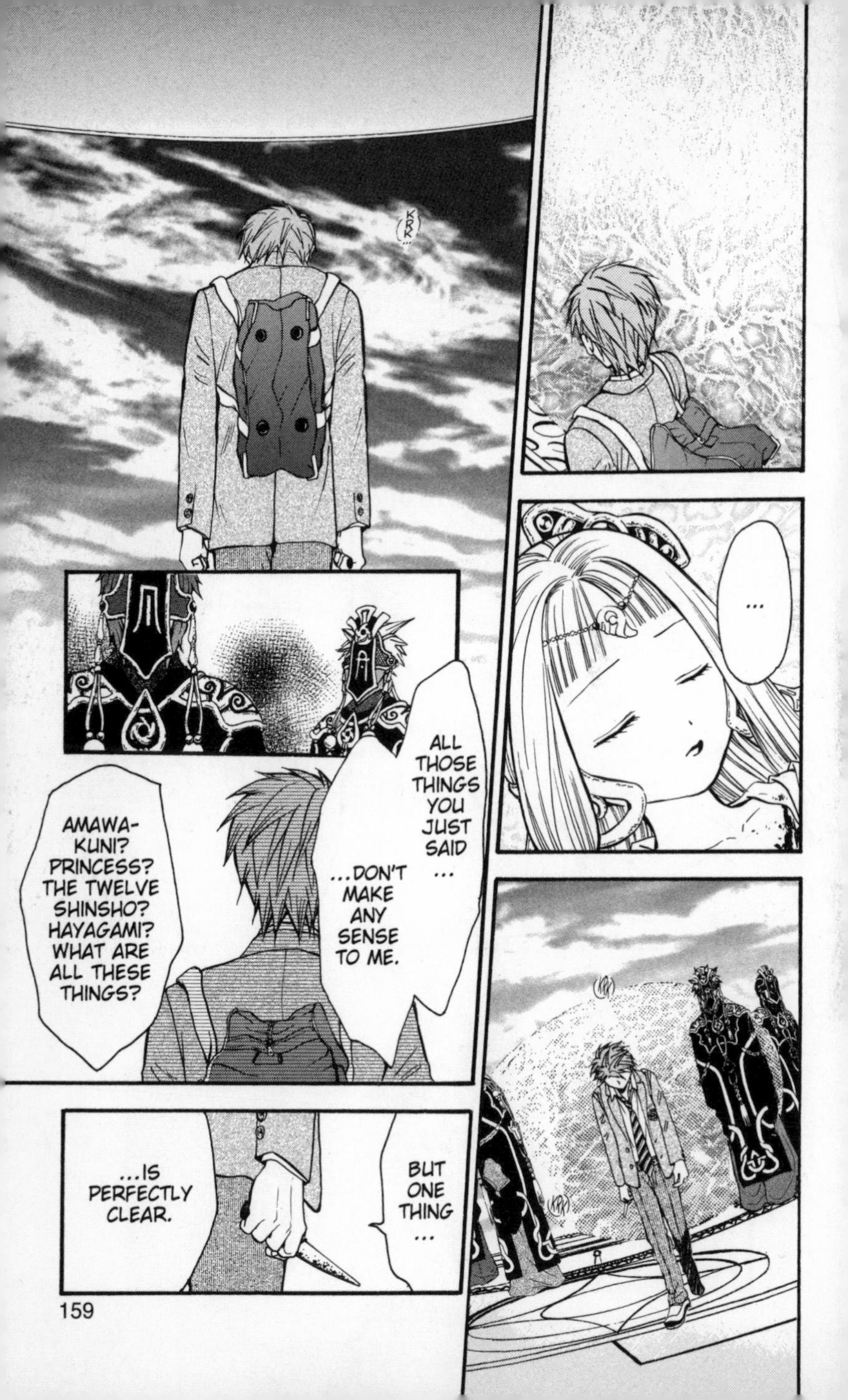

(KRK...)
...
AMAWA-KUNI? PRINCESS? THE TWELVE SHINSHO? HAYAGAMI? WHAT ARE ALL THESE THINGS?
ALL THOSE THINGS YOU JUST SAID...
...DON'T MAKE ANY SENSE TO ME.
(KRK)
(KRK)
BUT ONE THING...
...IS PERFECTLY CLEAR.

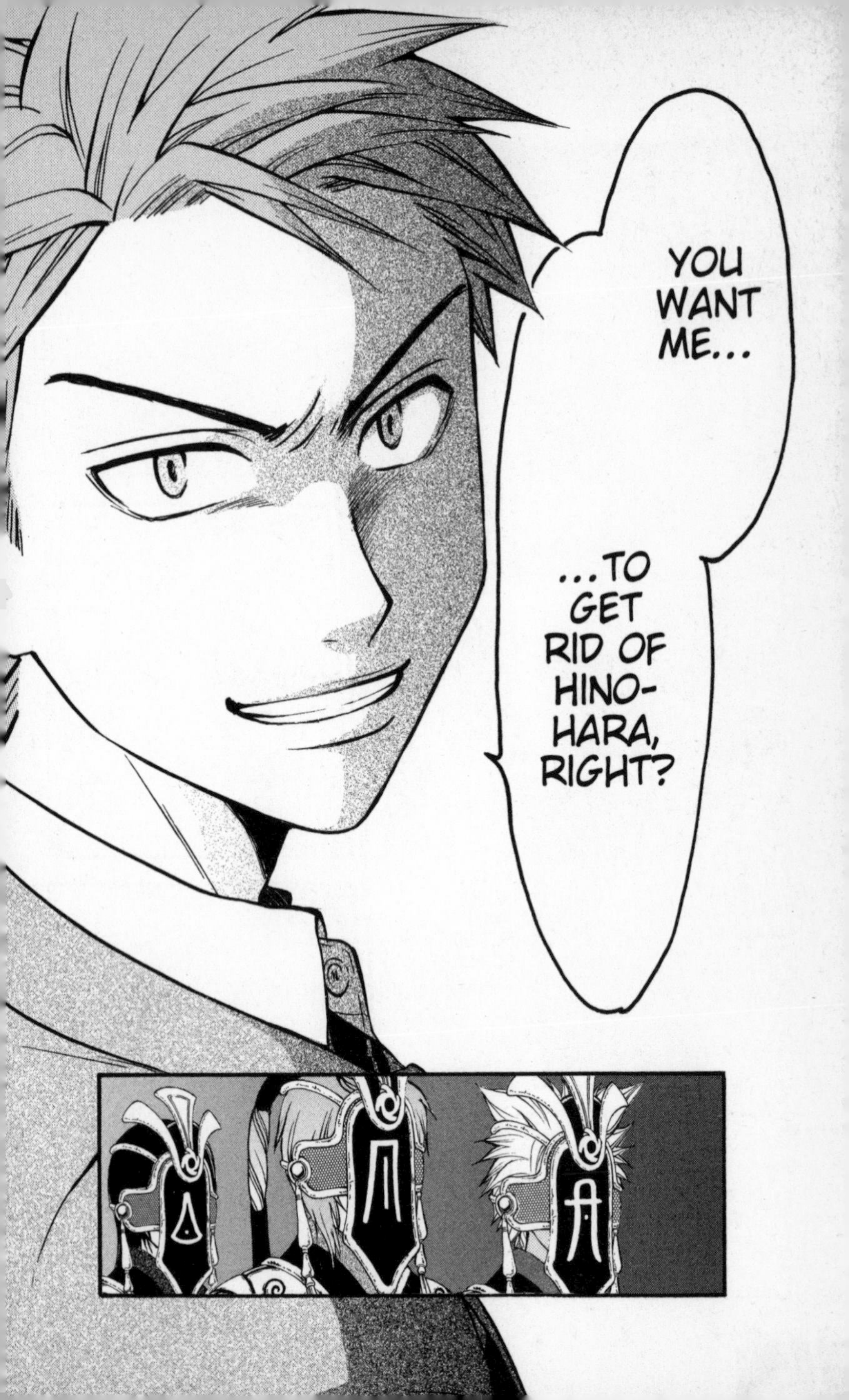
YOU WANT ME...
...TO GET RID OF HINO-HARA, RIGHT?

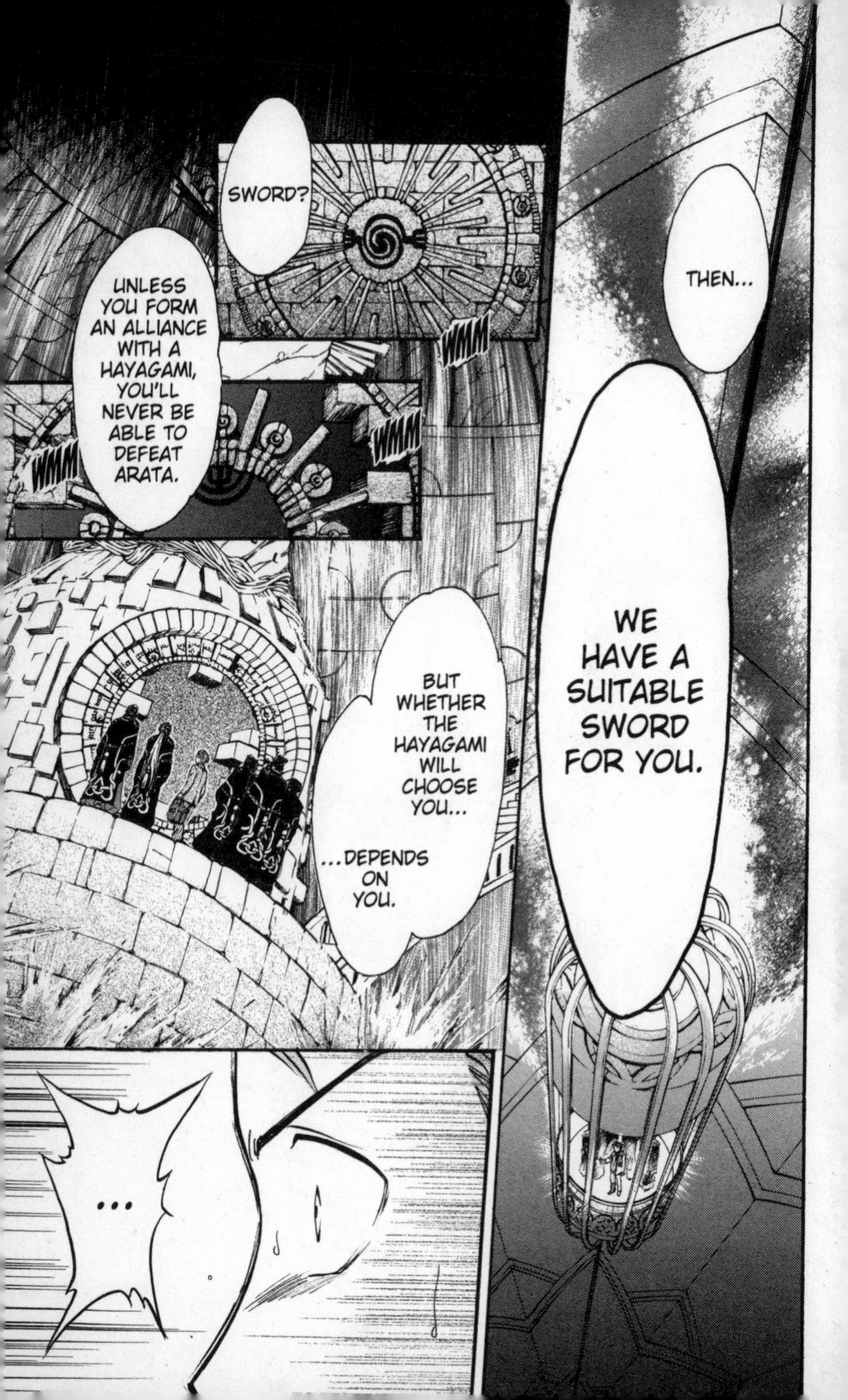
THEN...
WE HAVE A SUITABLE SWORD FOR YOU.
SWORD?
WMM
UNLESS YOU FORM AN ALLIANCE WITH A HAYAGAMI, YOU'LL NEVER BE ABLE TO DEFEAT ARATA.
WMM
WMM
BUT WHETHER THE HAYAGAMI WILL CHOOSE YOU...
...DEPENDS ON YOU.
...

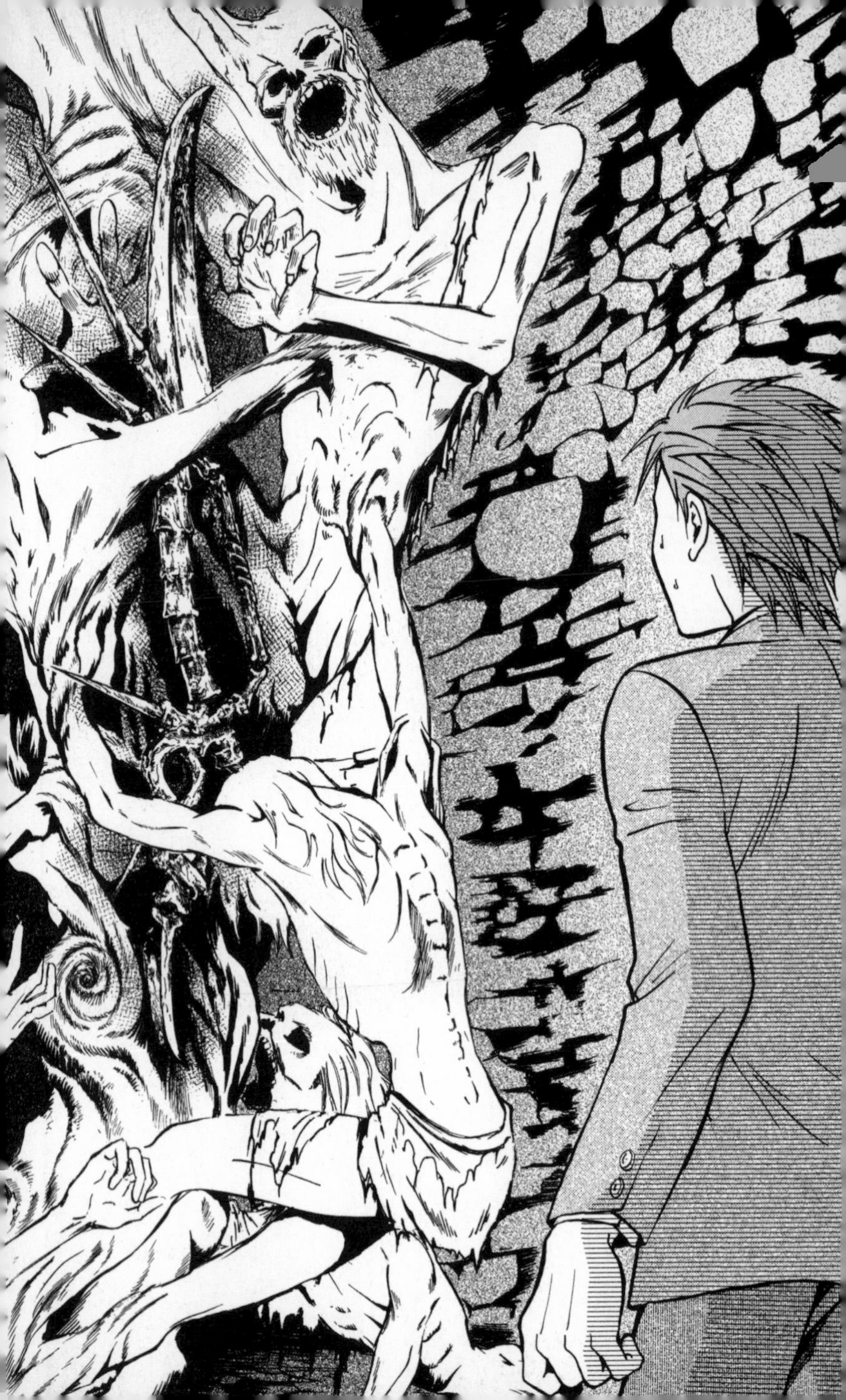

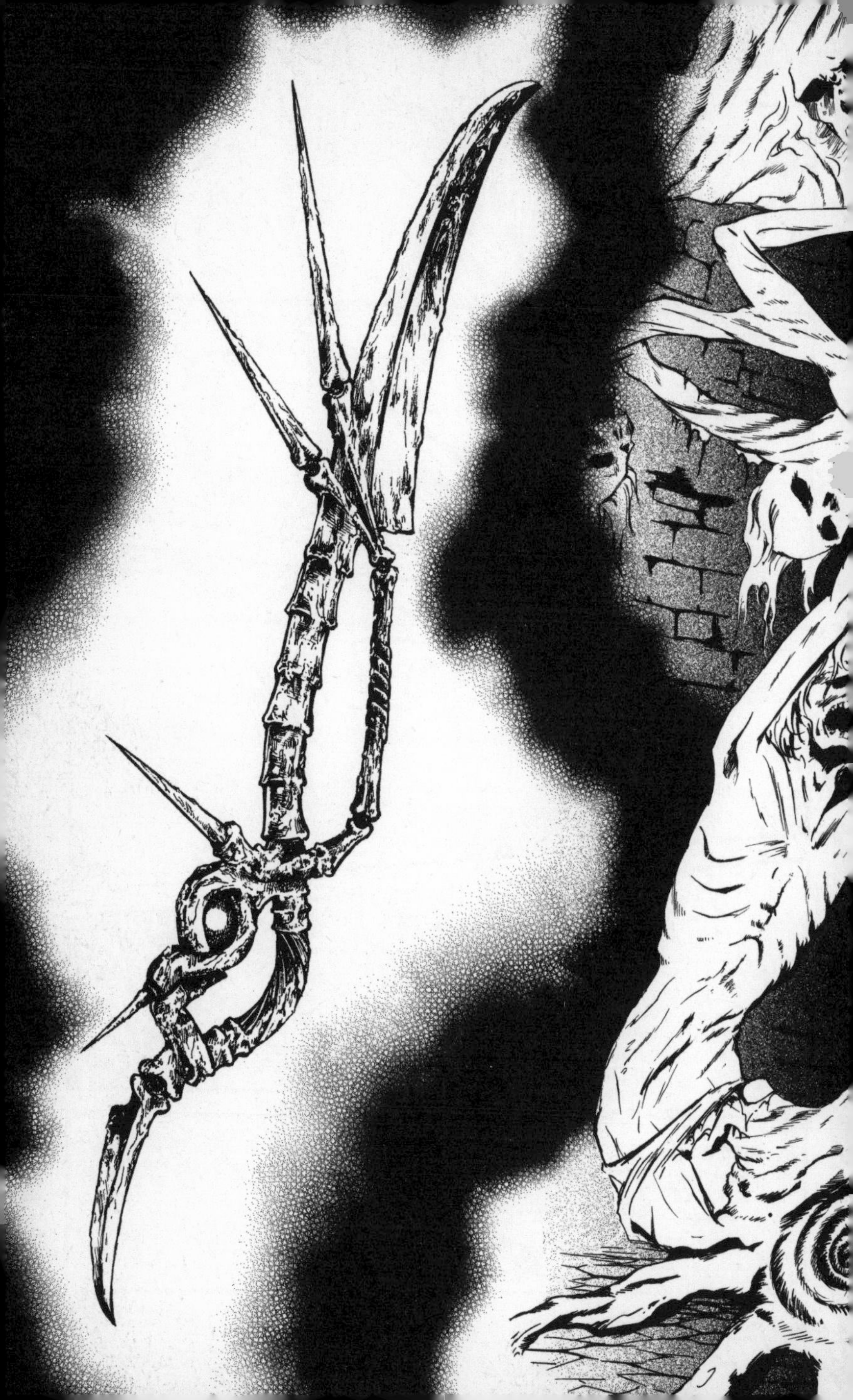

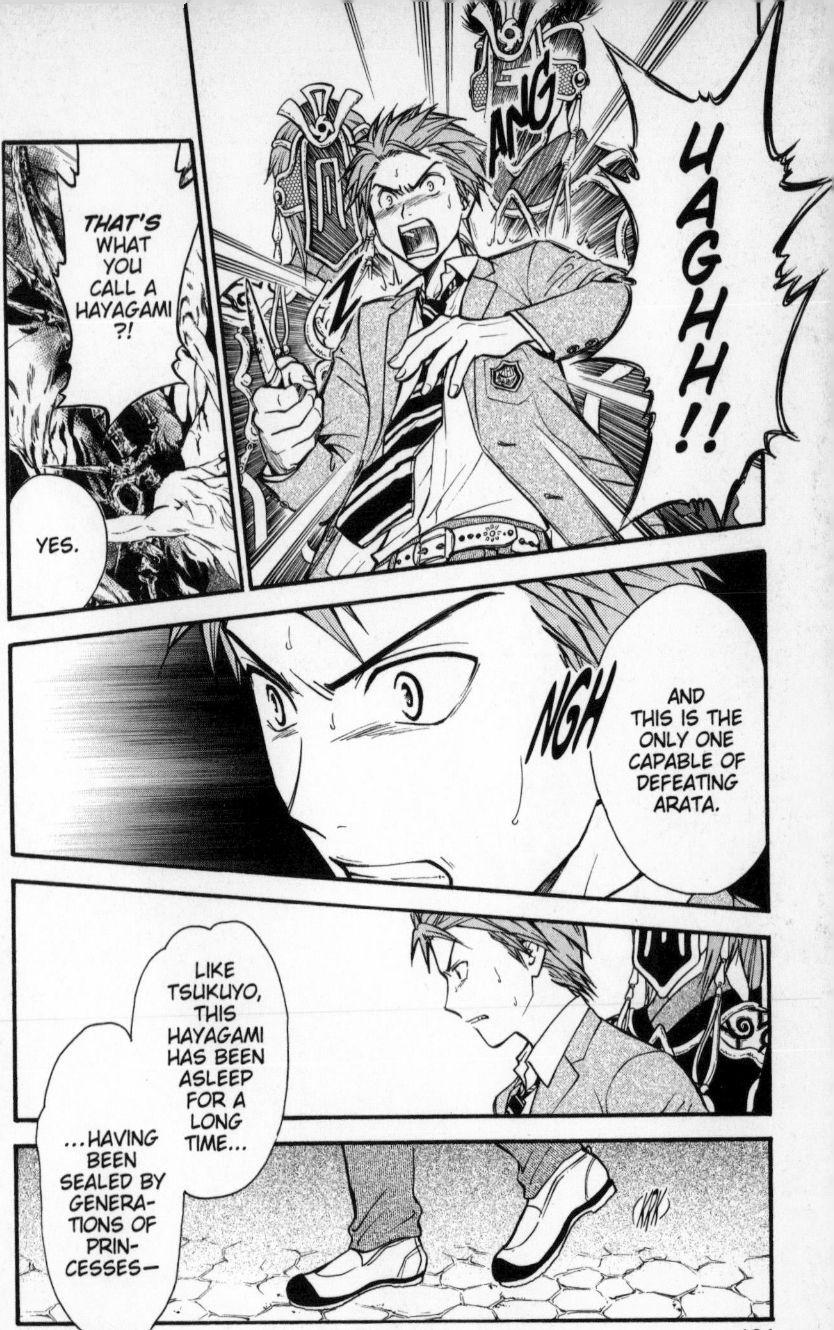
ANG
UAGHH!!
THAT'S WHAT YOU CALL A HAYAGAMI?!
YES.
NGH
AND THIS IS THE ONLY ONE CAPABLE OF DEFEATING ARATA.
LIKE TSUKUYO, THIS HAYAGAMI HAS BEEN ASLEEP FOR A LONG TIME...
...HAVING BEEN SEALED BY GENERATIONS OF PRINCESSES—

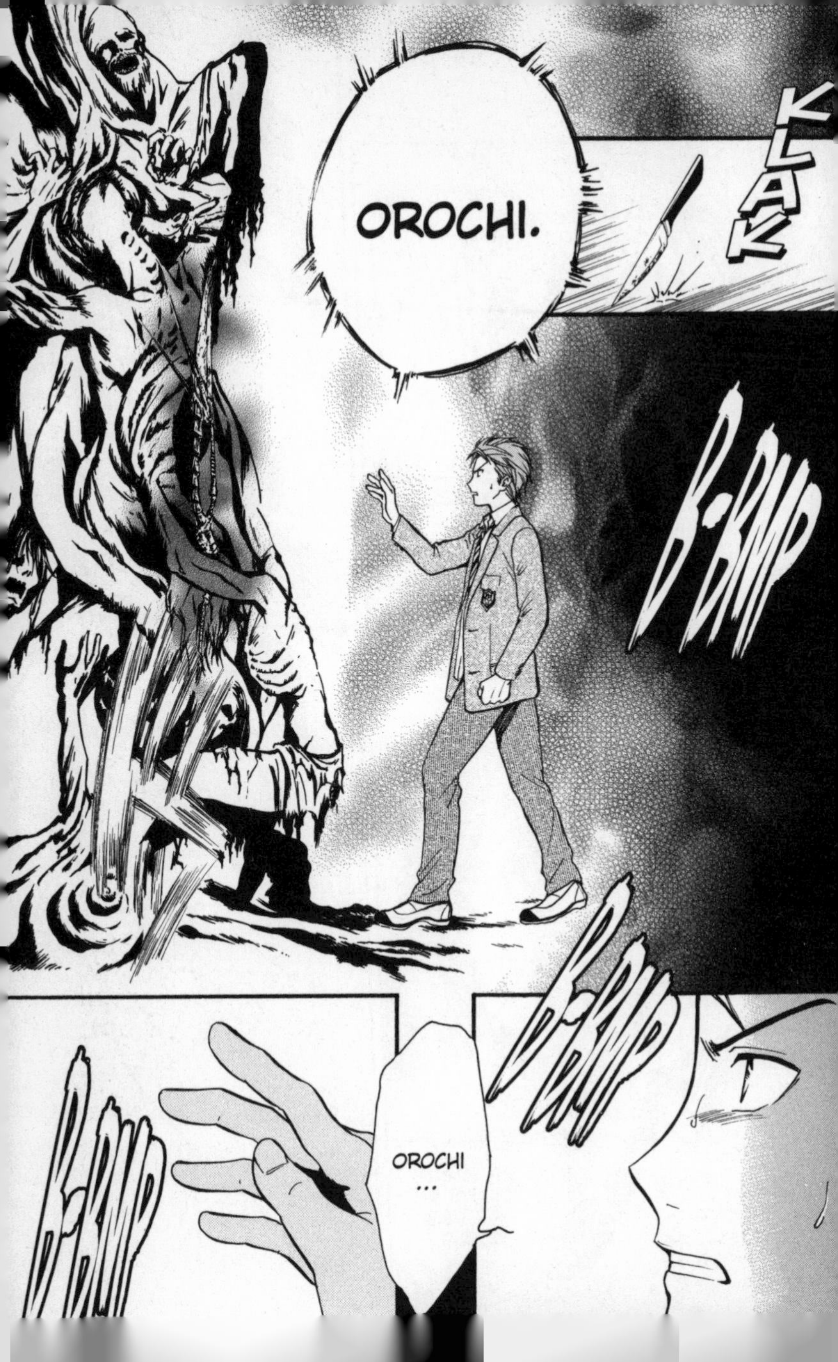
KLAK
OROCHI.
B-BMP
OROCHI ...

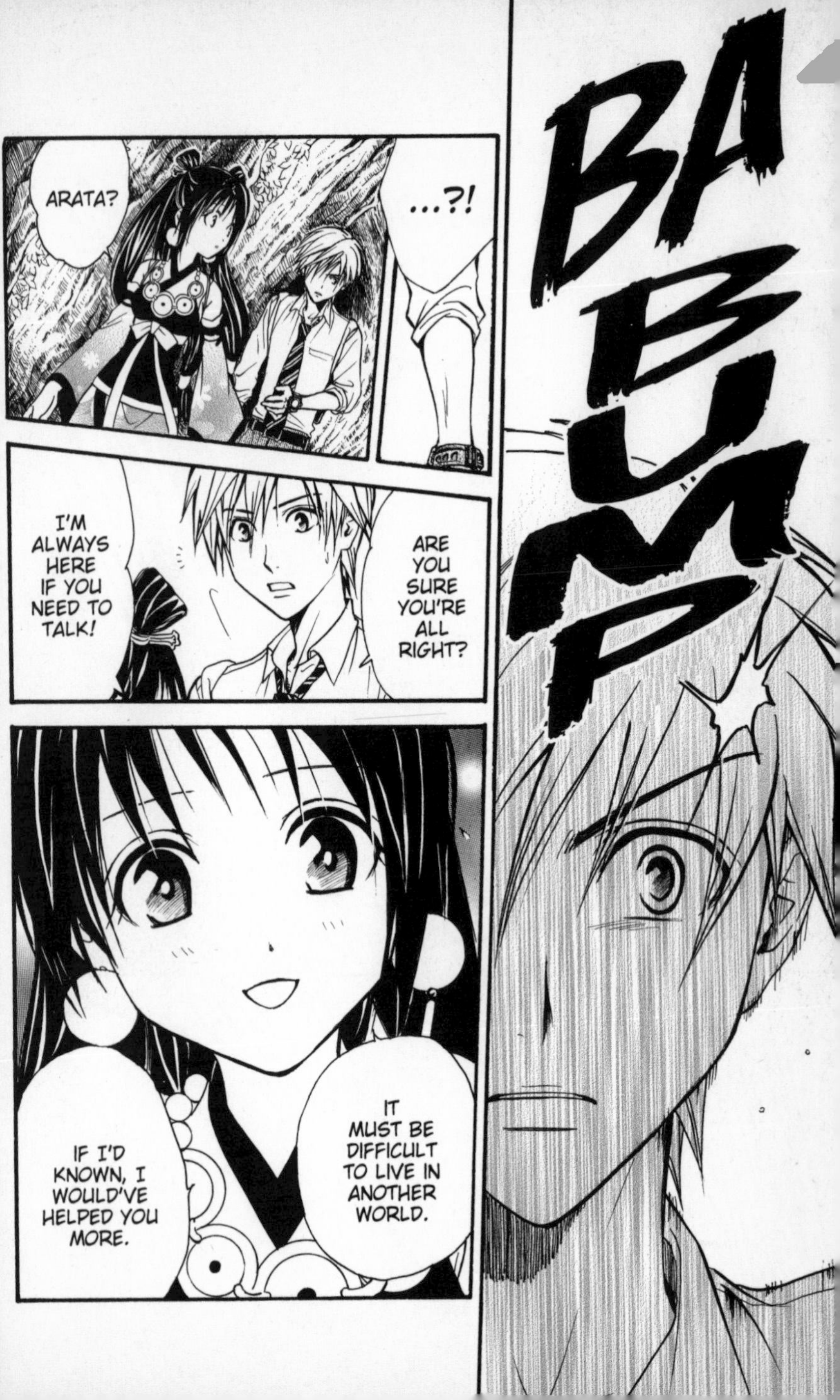
BA-BUMP
...?!
ARATA?
ARE YOU SURE YOU'RE ALL RIGHT?
I'M ALWAYS HERE IF YOU NEED TO TALK!
IT MUST BE DIFFICULT TO LIVE IN ANOTHER WORLD.
IF I'D KNOWN, I WOULD'VE HELPED YOU MORE.

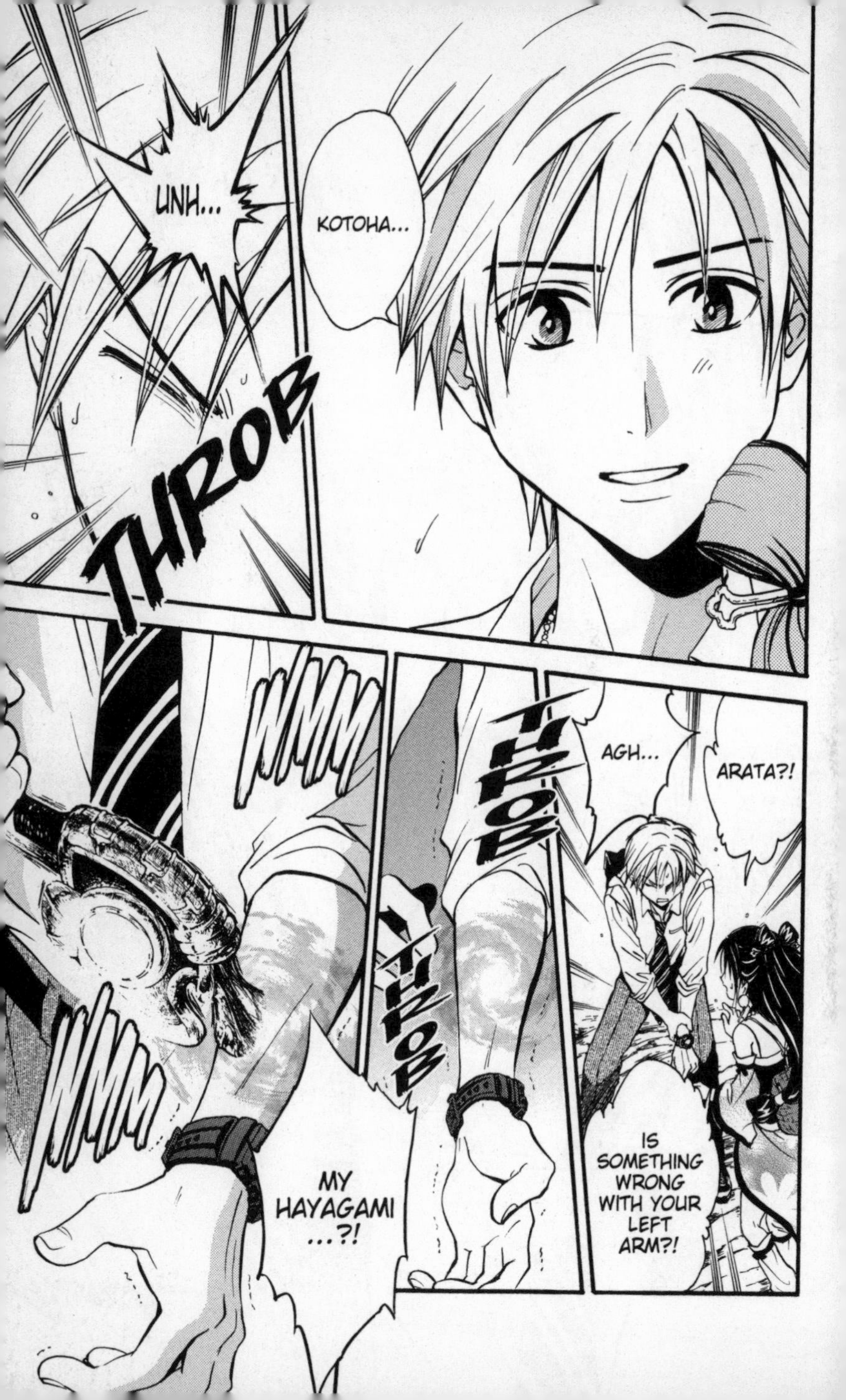
KOTOHA...
UNH...
THROB
ARATA?!
AGH...
IS SOMETHING WRONG WITH YOUR LEFT ARM?!
THROB
THROB
NMMM
NMMM
MY HAYAGAMI ...?!

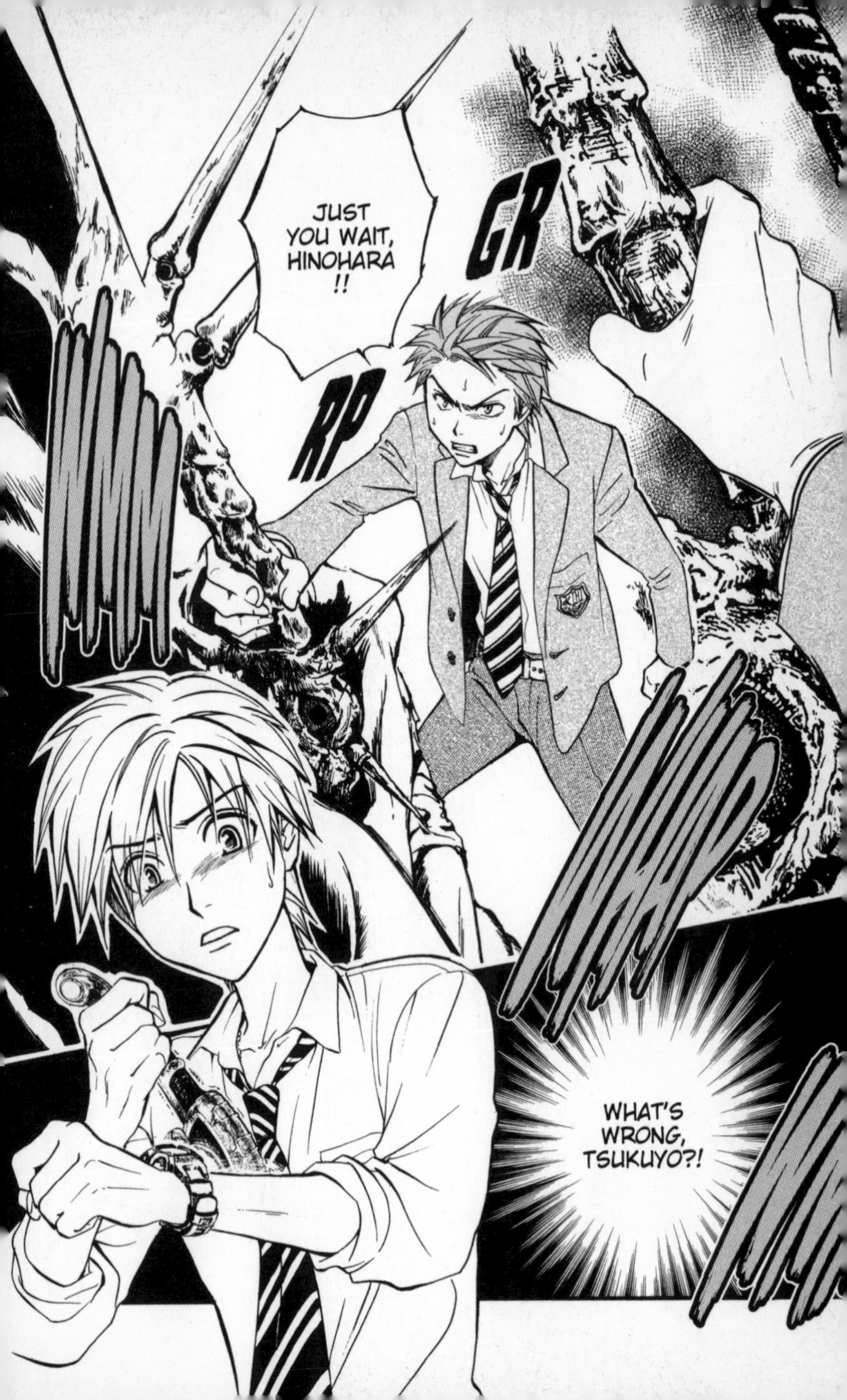
GR
RP
JUST YOU WAIT, HINOHARA!!
WHAT'S WRONG, TSUKUYO?!

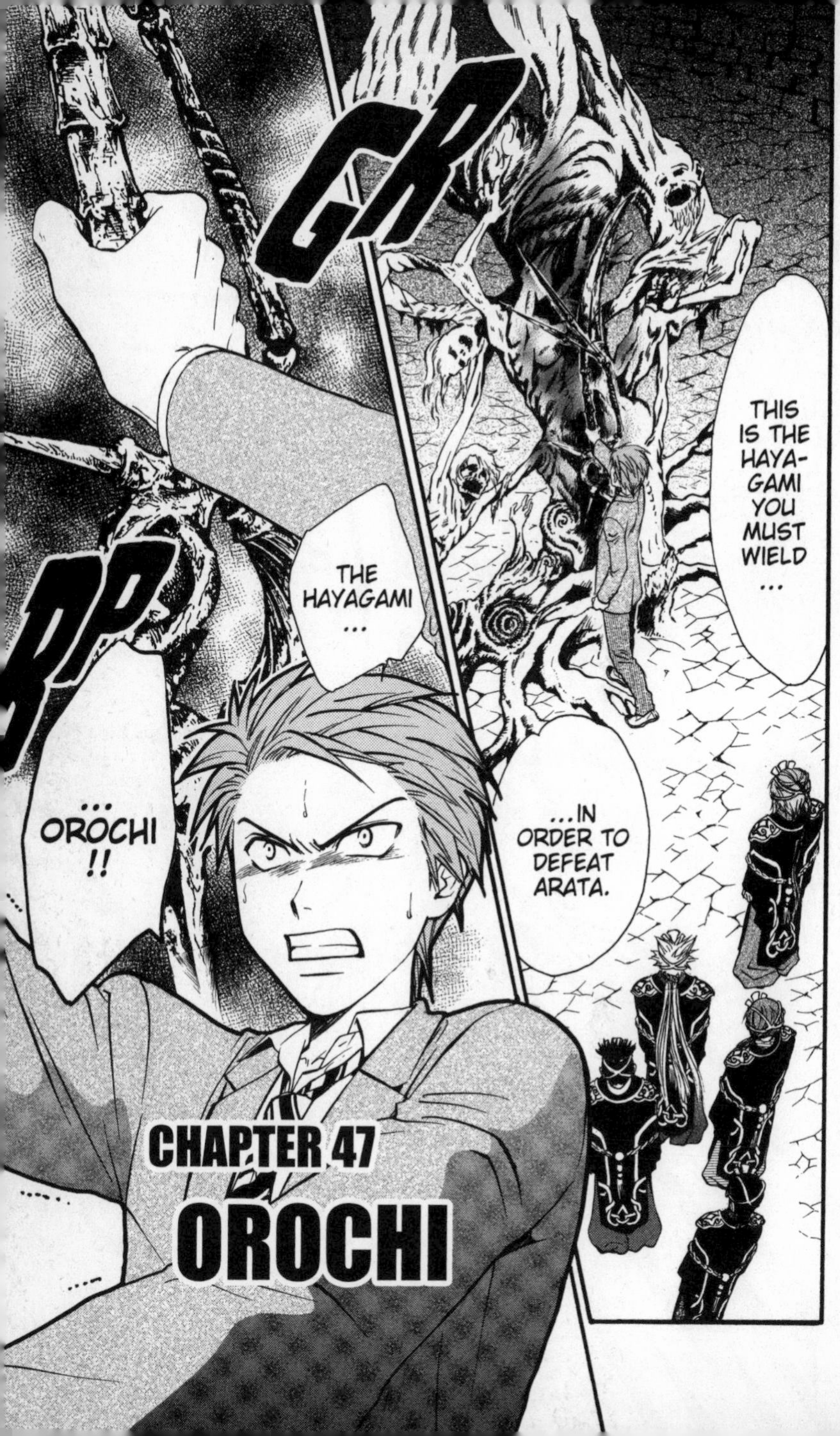
THIS IS THE HAYA-GAMI YOU MUST WIELD ...
...IN ORDER TO DEFEAT ARATA.
THE HAYAGAMI ...
... OROCHI !!
CHAPTER 47
OROCHI

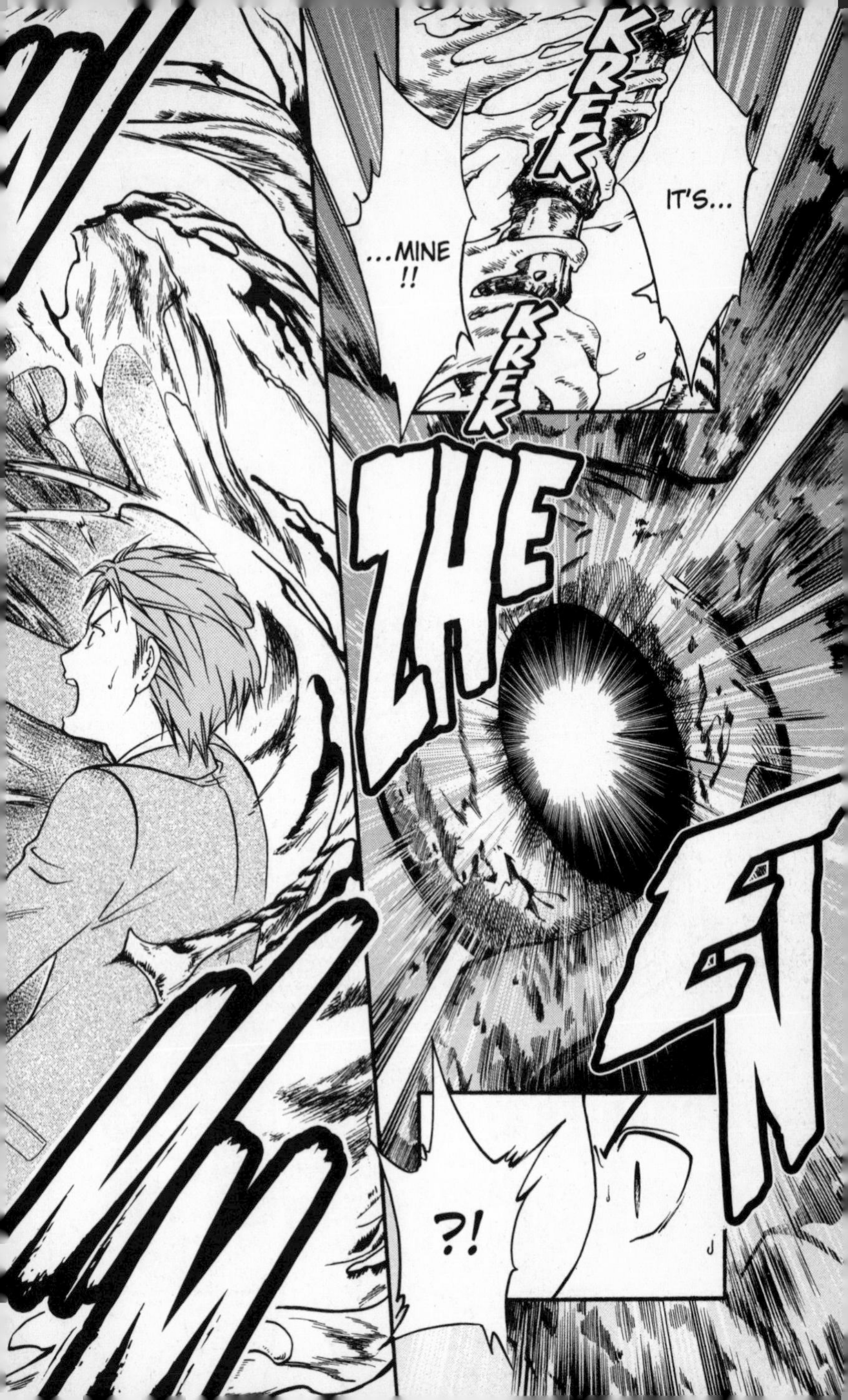
IT'S...
...MINE !!
KREK
KREK
ZHE
EN
?!

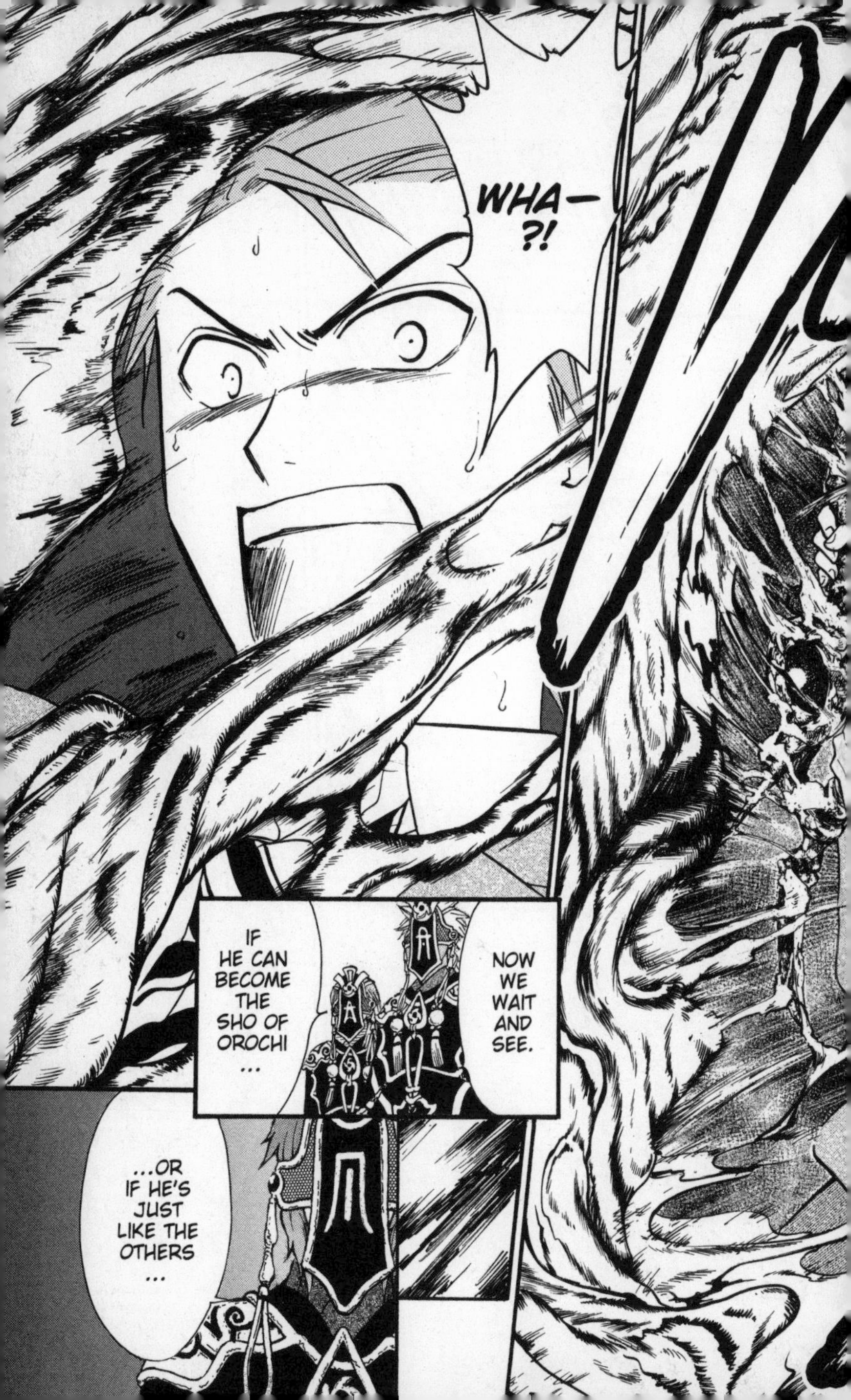
WHA— ?!
NOW WE WAIT AND SEE.
IF HE CAN BECOME THE SHO OF OROCHI ...
...OR IF HE'S JUST LIKE THE OTHERS ...

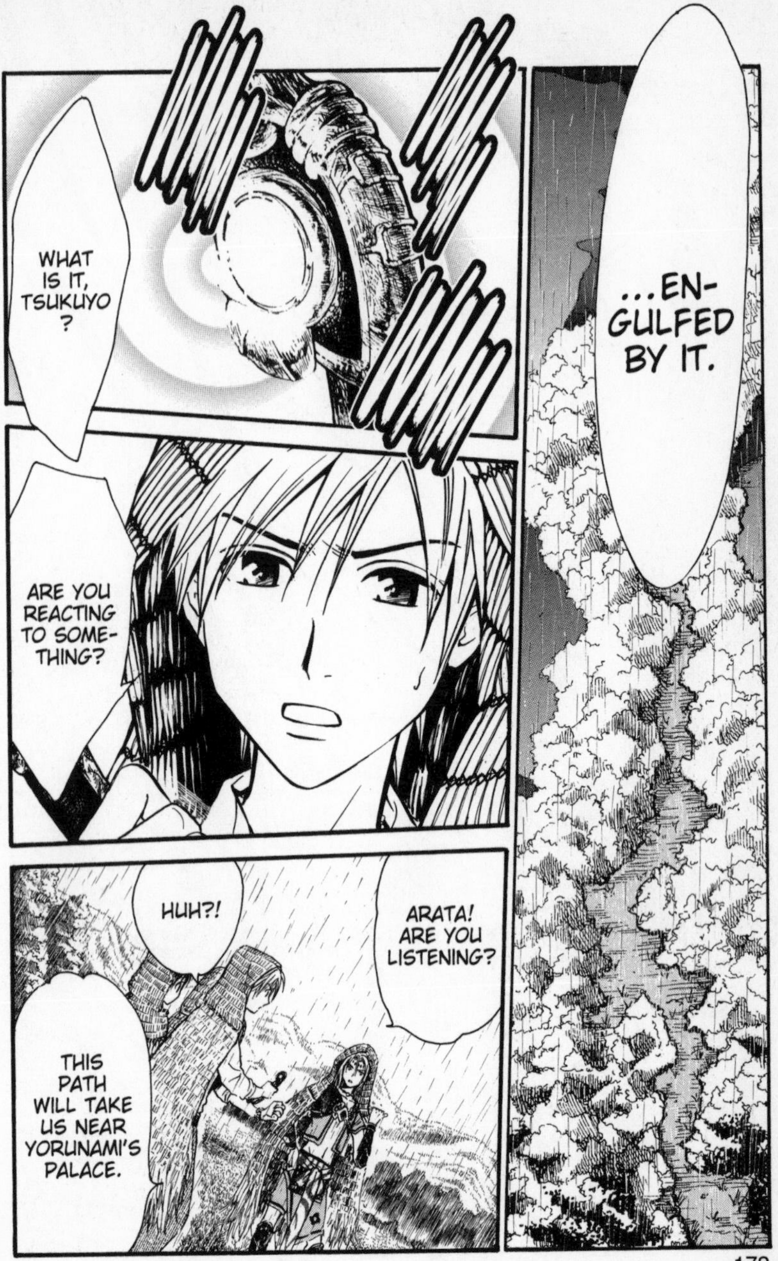
...EN-GULFED BY IT.
WHAT IS IT, TSUKUYO?
ARE YOU REACTING TO SOME-THING?
ARATA! ARE YOU LISTENING?
HUH?!
THIS PATH WILL TAKE US NEAR YORUNAMI'S PALACE.

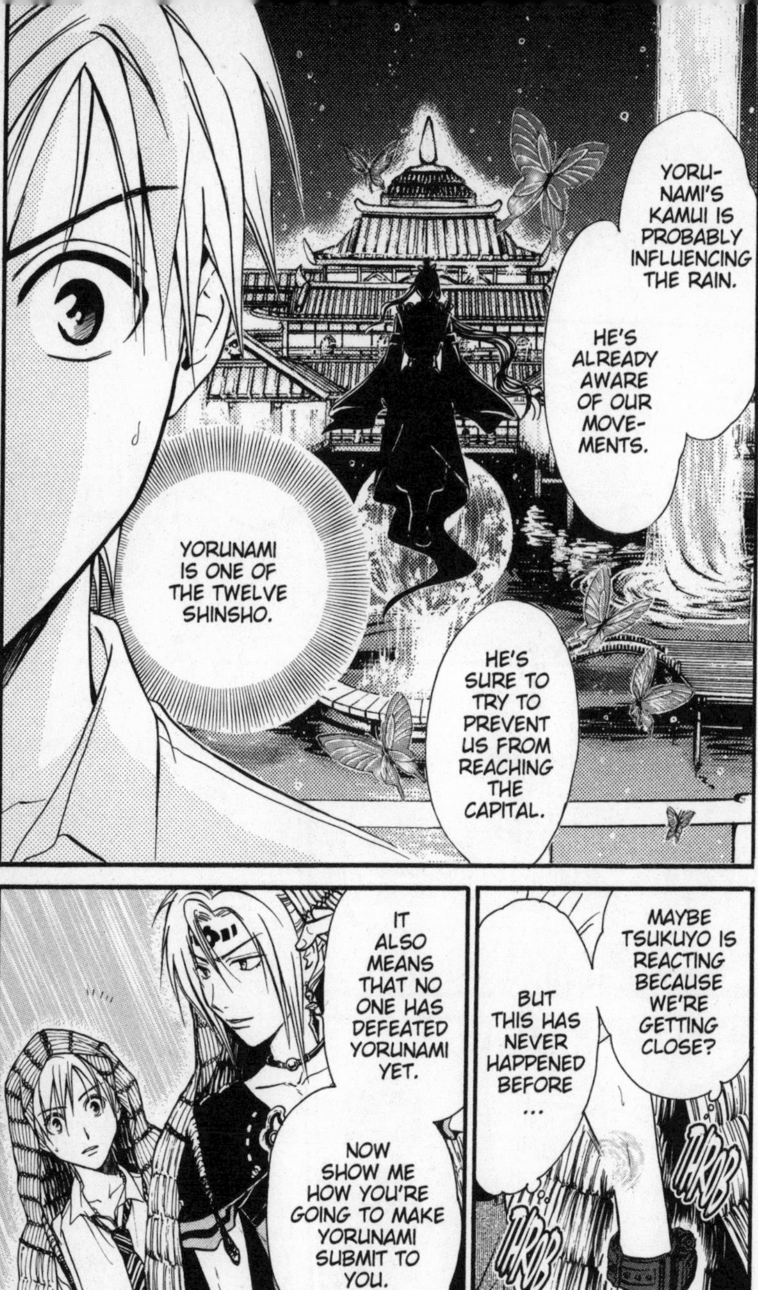
YORU-NAMI'S KAMUI IS PROBABLY INFLUENCING THE RAIN.
HE'S ALREADY AWARE OF OUR MOVE-MENTS.
HE'S SURE TO TRY TO PREVENT US FROM REACHING THE CAPITAL.
YORUNAMI IS ONE OF THE TWELVE SHINSHO.
MAYBE TSUKUYO IS REACTING BECAUSE WE'RE GETTING CLOSE?
BUT THIS HAS NEVER HAPPENED BEFORE ...
THROB
THROB
IT ALSO MEANS THAT NO ONE HAS DEFEATED YORUNAMI YET.
NOW SHOW ME HOW YOU'RE GOING TO MAKE YORUNAMI SUBMIT TO YOU.

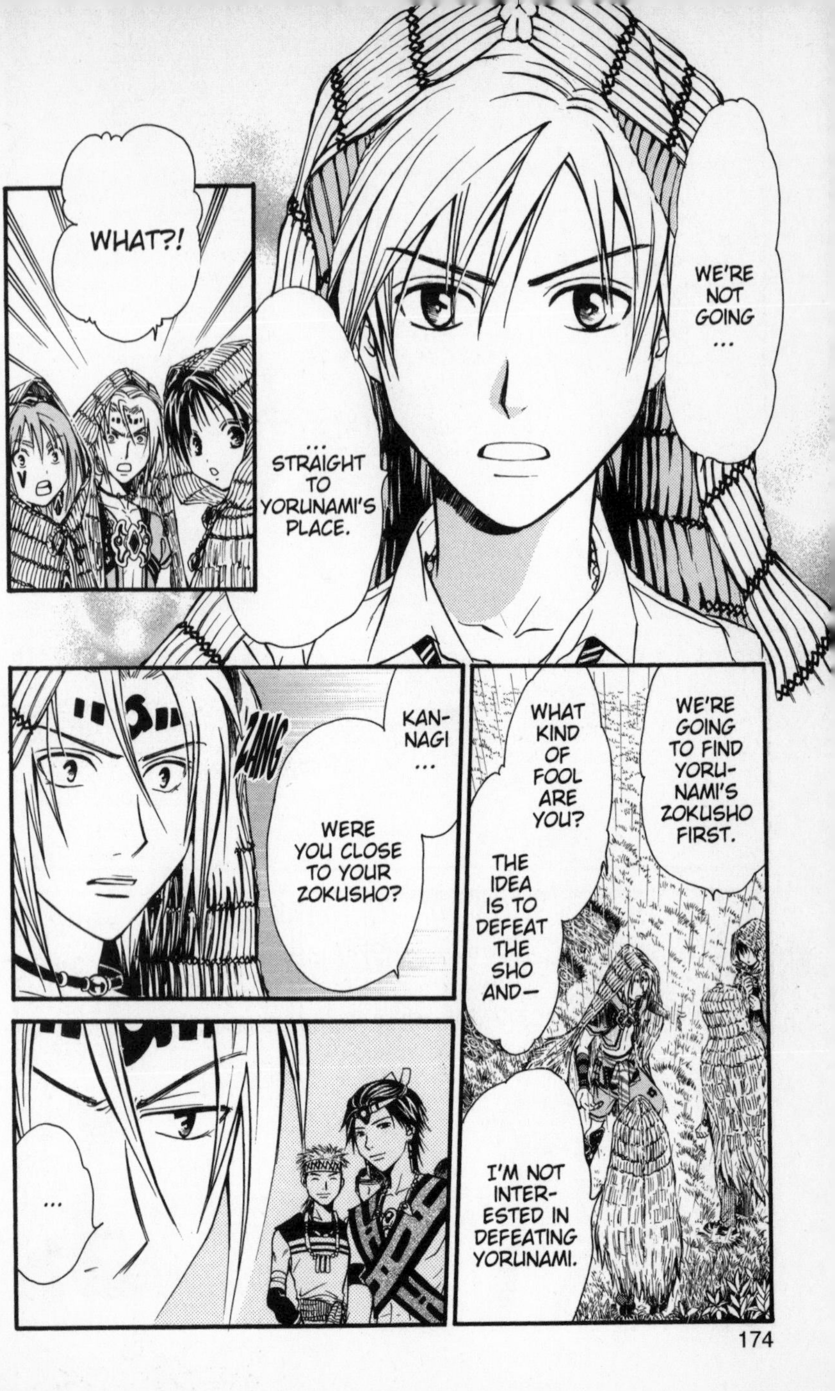
WE'RE NOT GOING ...
... STRAIGHT TO YORUNAMI'S PLACE.
WHAT?!
WE'RE GOING TO FIND YORUNAMI'S ZOKUSHO FIRST.
WHAT KIND OF FOOL ARE YOU?
THE IDEA IS TO DEFEAT THE SHO AND—
I'M NOT INTERESTED IN DEFEATING YORUNAMI.
ZANG
KANNAGI ...
WERE YOU CLOSE TO YOUR ZOKUSHO?
...

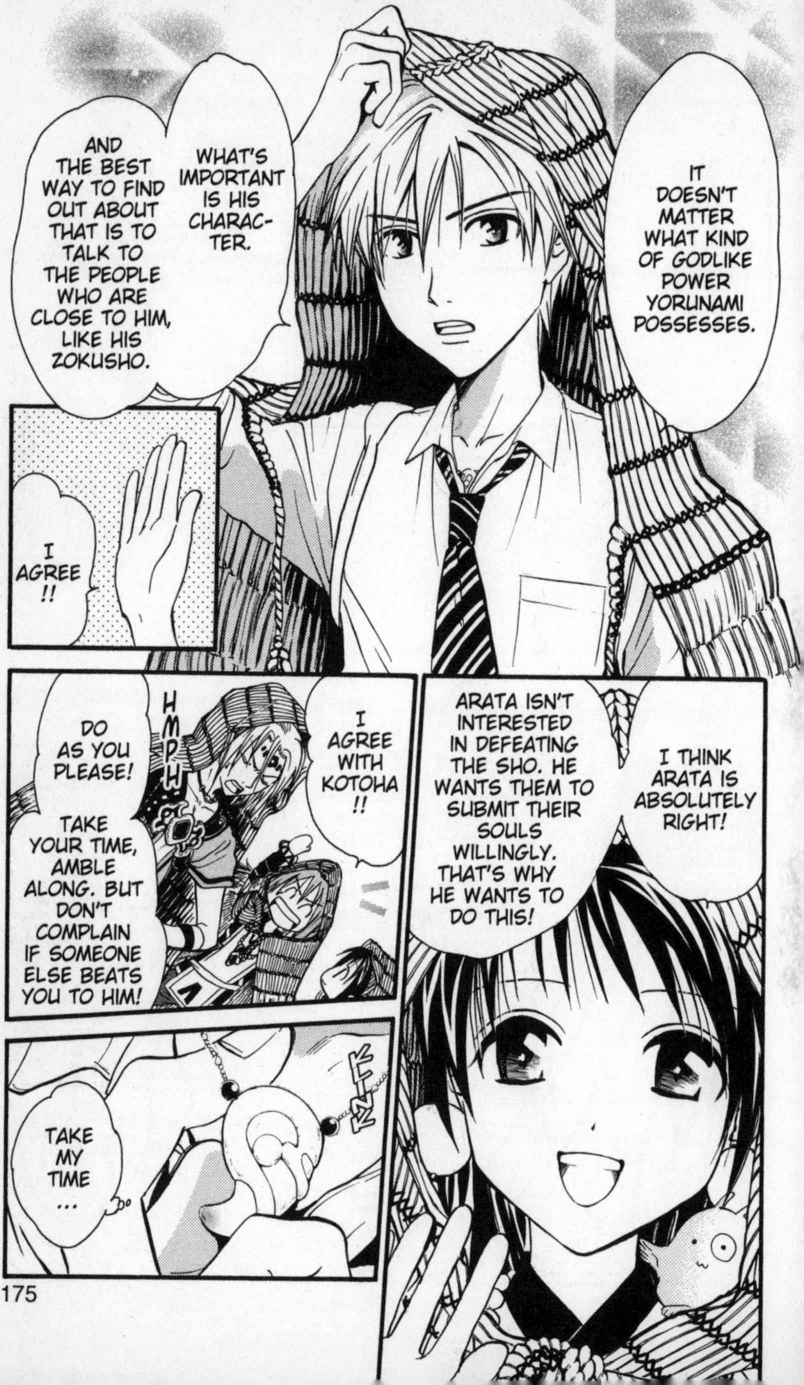
IT DOESN'T MATTER WHAT KIND OF GODLIKE POWER YORUNAMI POSSESSES.
WHAT'S IMPORTANT IS HIS CHARAC-TER.
AND THE BEST WAY TO FIND OUT ABOUT THAT IS TO TALK TO THE PEOPLE WHO ARE CLOSE TO HIM, LIKE HIS ZOKUSHO.
I AGREE !!
I THINK ARATA IS ABSOLUTELY RIGHT!
ARATA ISN'T INTERESTED IN DEFEATING THE SHO. HE WANTS THEM TO SUBMIT THEIR SOULS WILLINGLY. THAT'S WHY HE WANTS TO DO THIS!
I AGREE WITH KOTOHA !!
HMPH
DO AS YOU PLEASE!
TAKE YOUR TIME, AMBLE ALONG. BUT DON'T COMPLAIN IF SOMEONE ELSE BEATS YOU TO HIM!
TAKE MY TIME ...

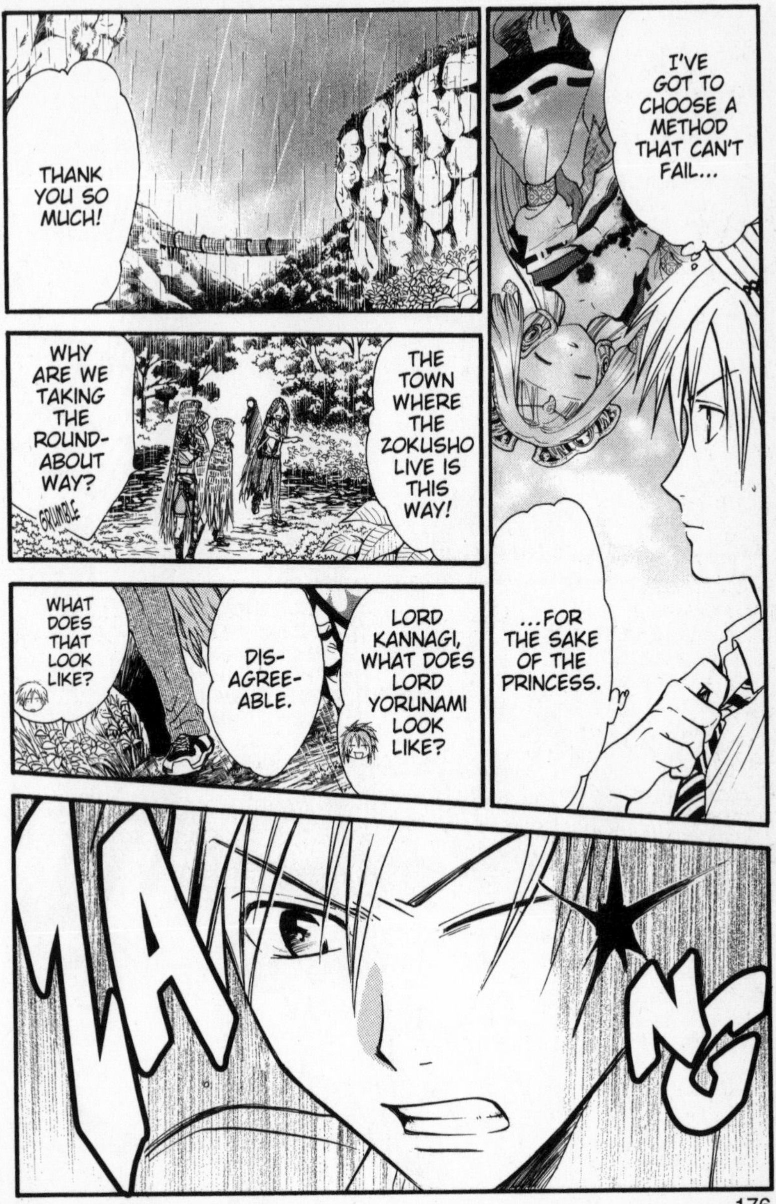
I'VE GOT TO CHOOSE A METHOD THAT CAN'T FAIL...
...FOR THE SAKE OF THE PRINCESS.
THANK YOU SO MUCH!
THE TOWN WHERE THE ZOKUSHO LIVE IS THIS WAY!
WHY ARE WE TAKING THE ROUND-ABOUT WAY?
GRUMBLE
LORD KANNAGI, WHAT DOES LORD YORUNAMI LOOK LIKE?
DIS-AGREE-ABLE.
WHAT DOES THAT LOOK LIKE?
WANG

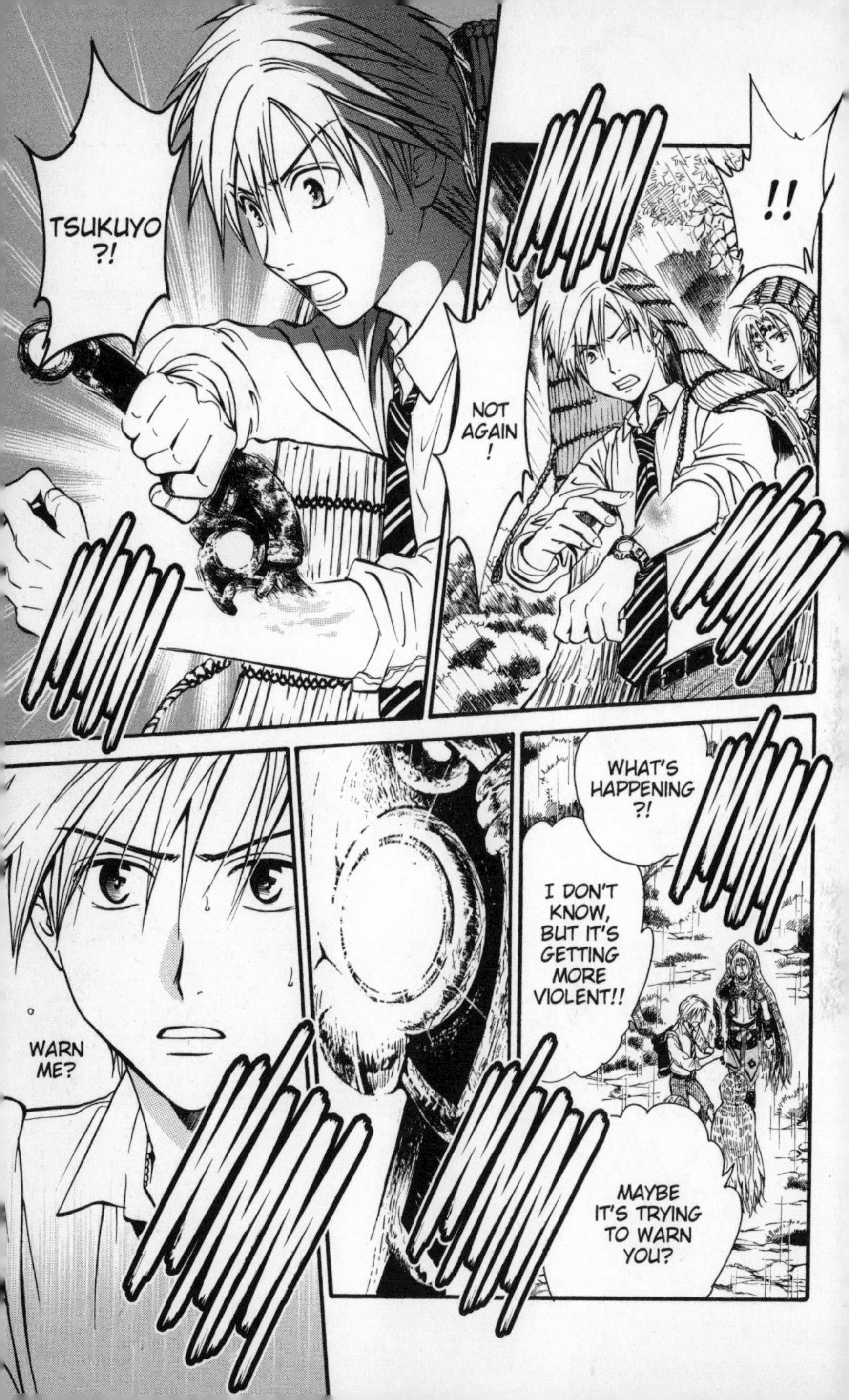
!!
NOT AGAIN!
TSUKUYO?!
WHAT'S HAPPENING?!
I DON'T KNOW, BUT IT'S GETTING MORE VIOLENT!!
MAYBE IT'S TRYING TO WARN YOU?
WARN ME?

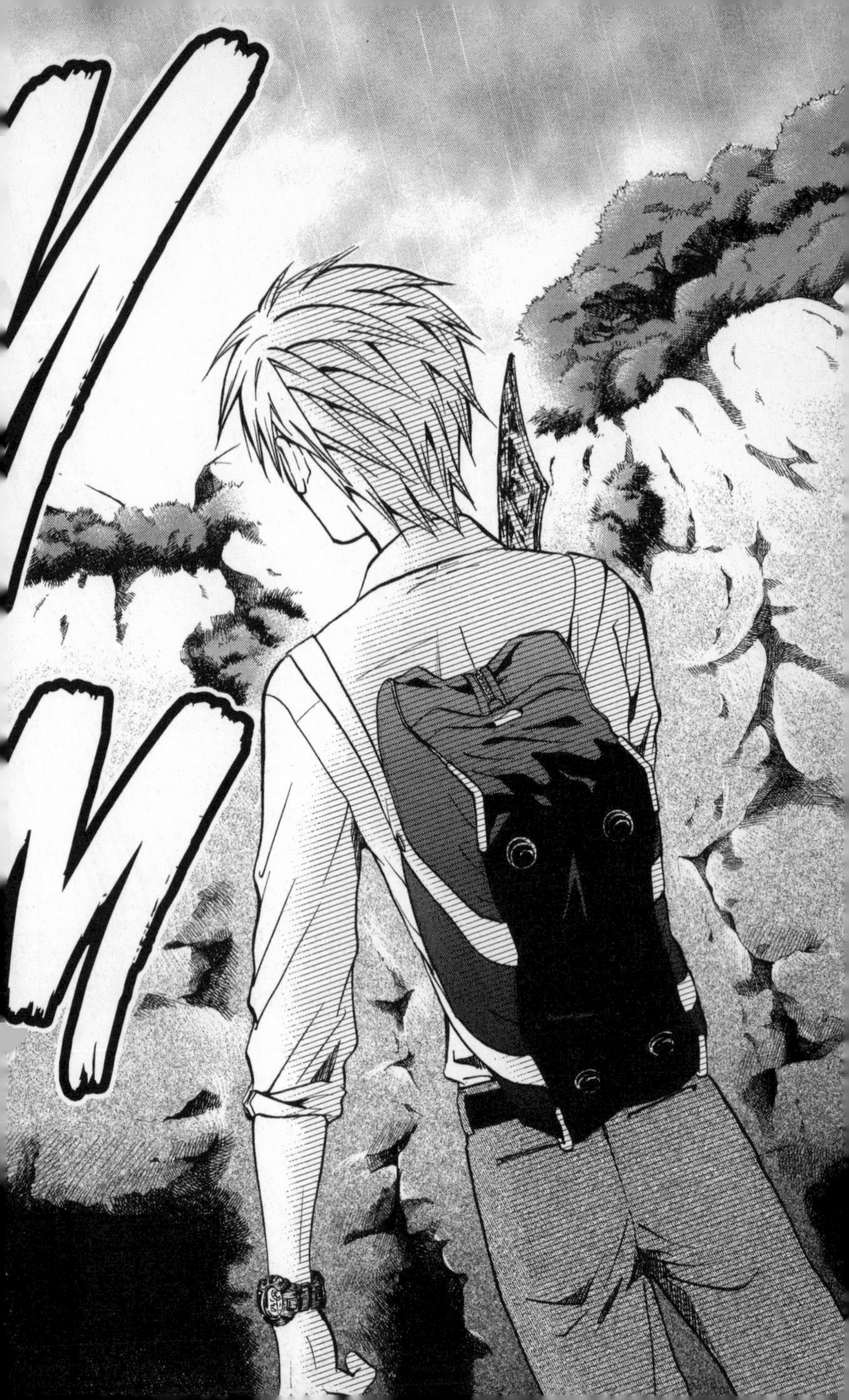

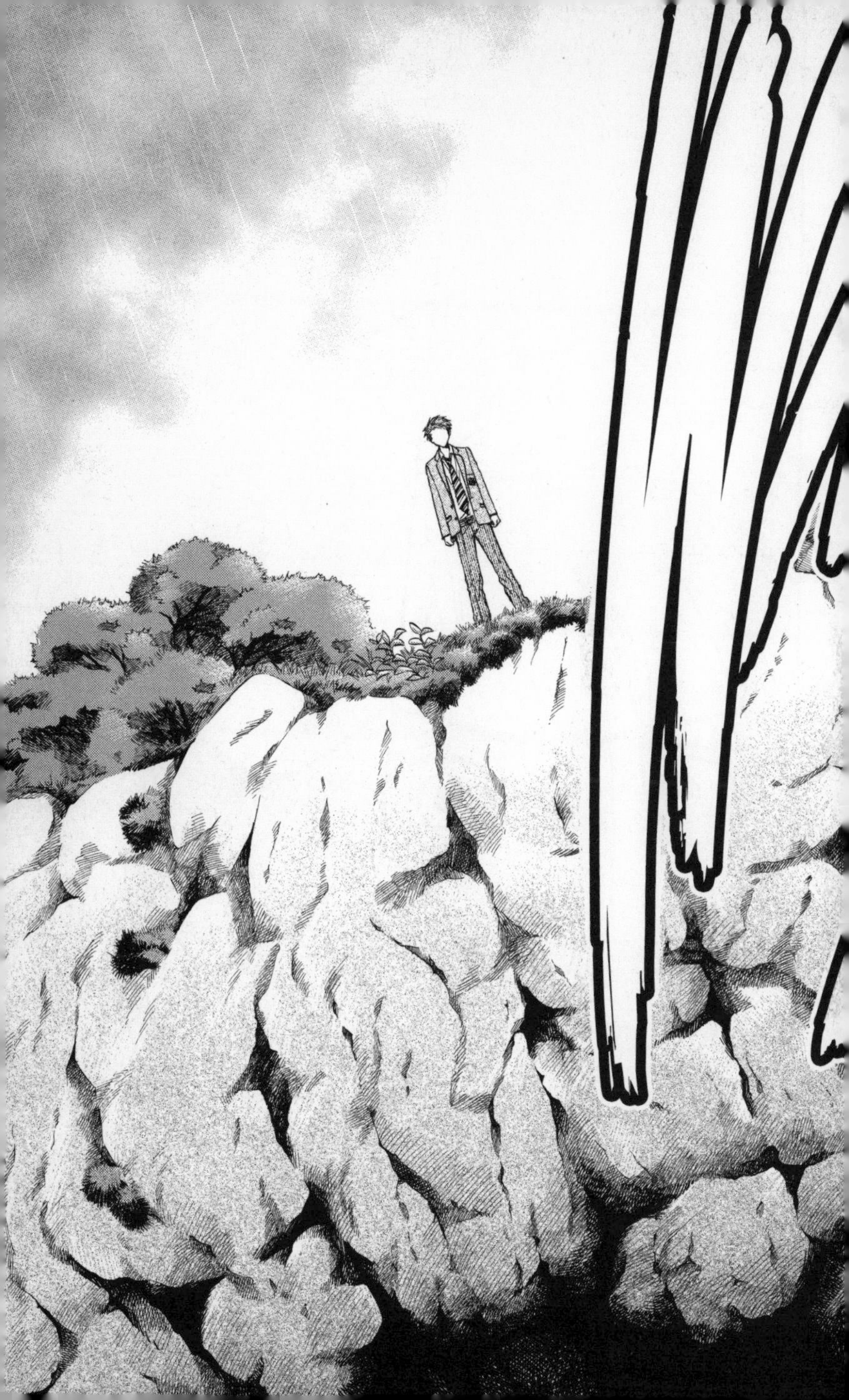

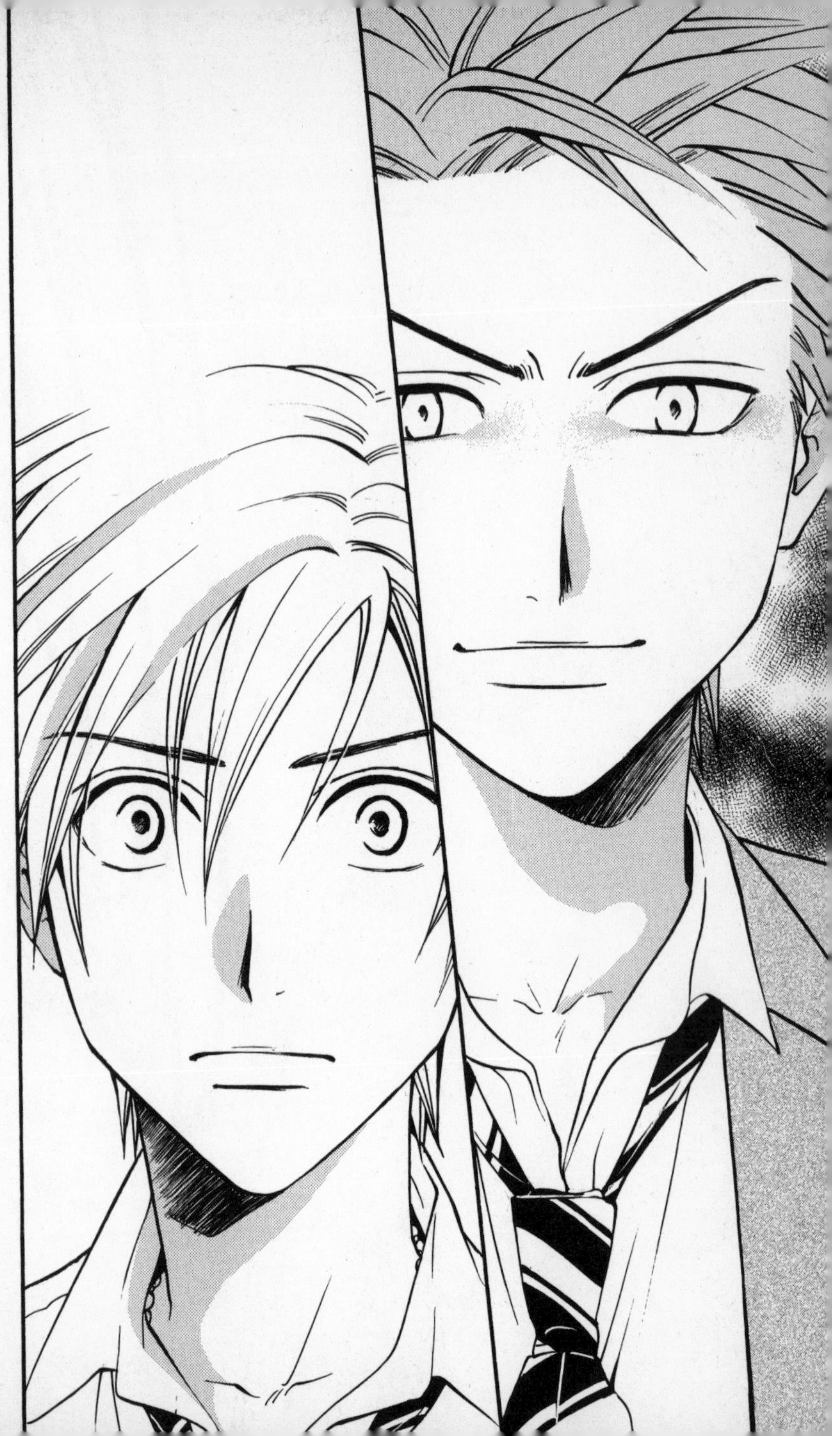

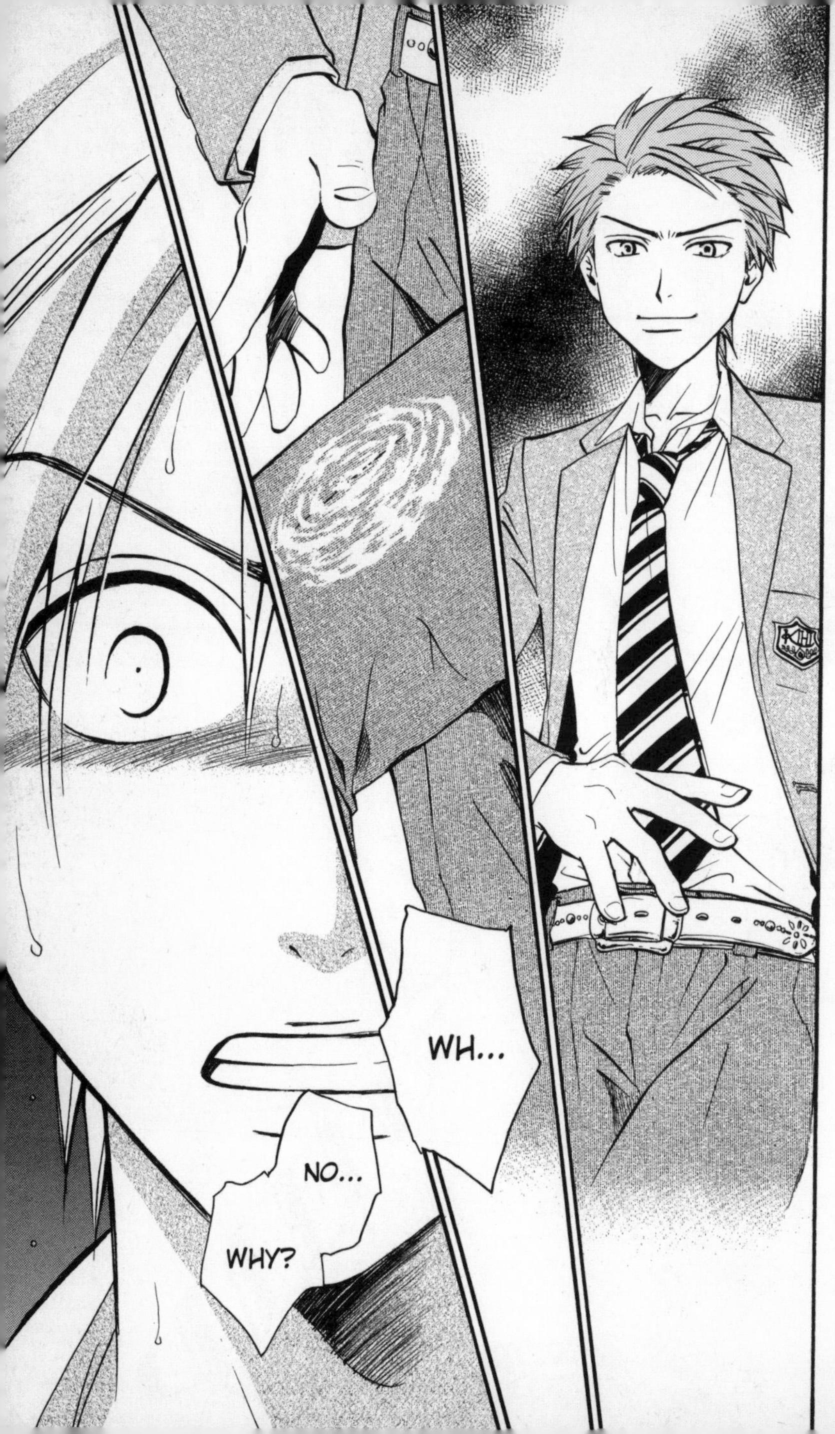
WH...
NO...
WHY?

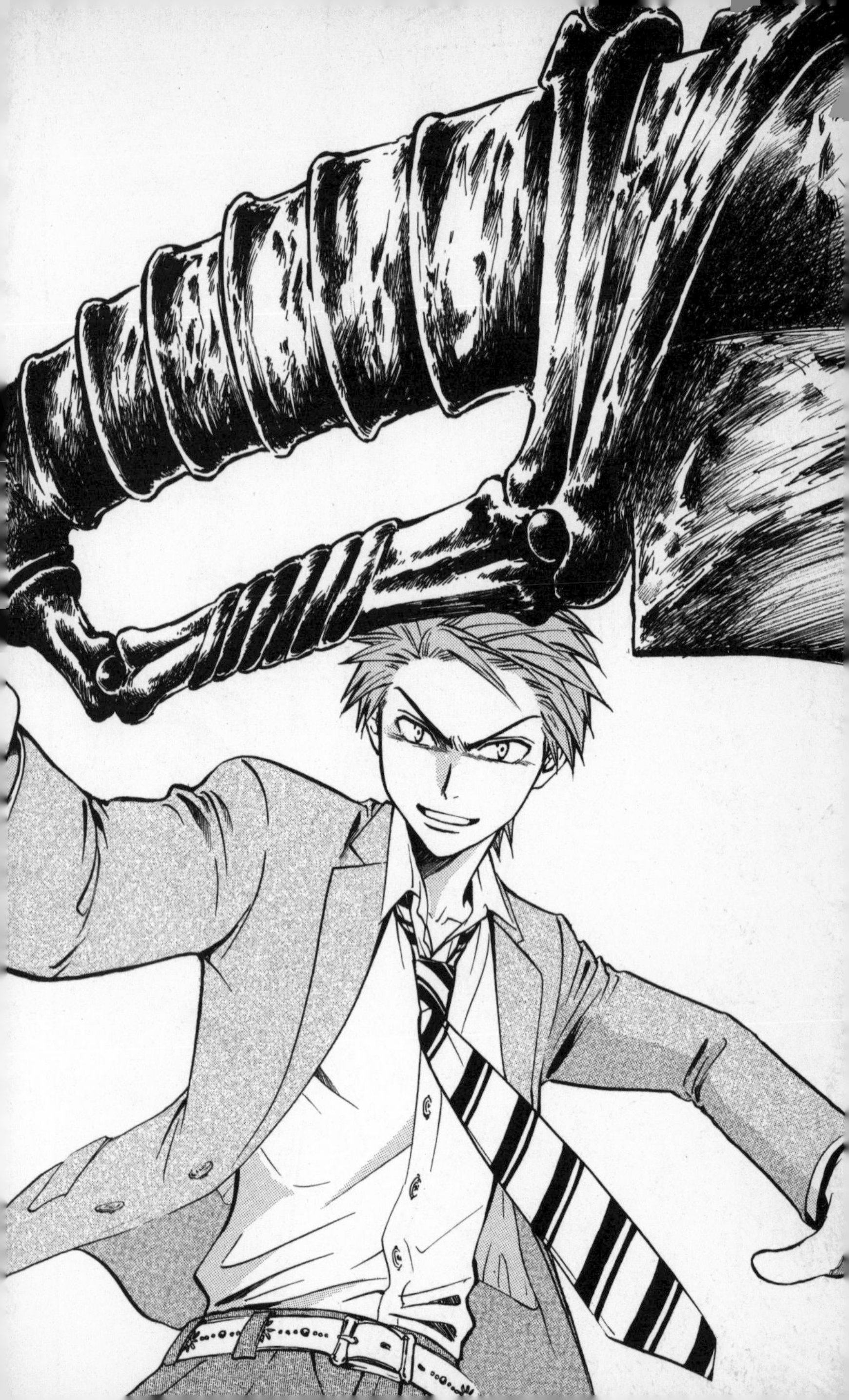

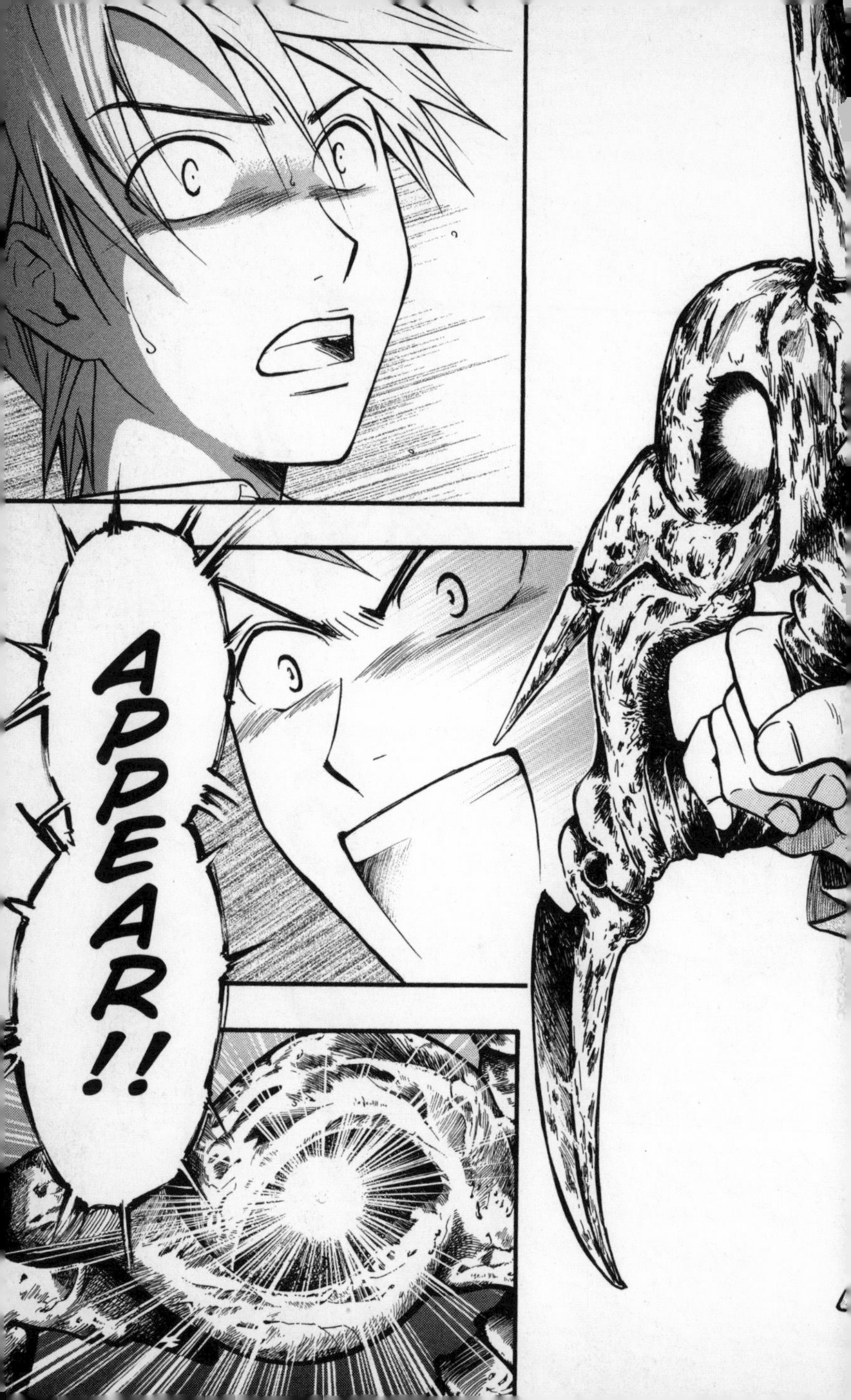
APPEAR!!

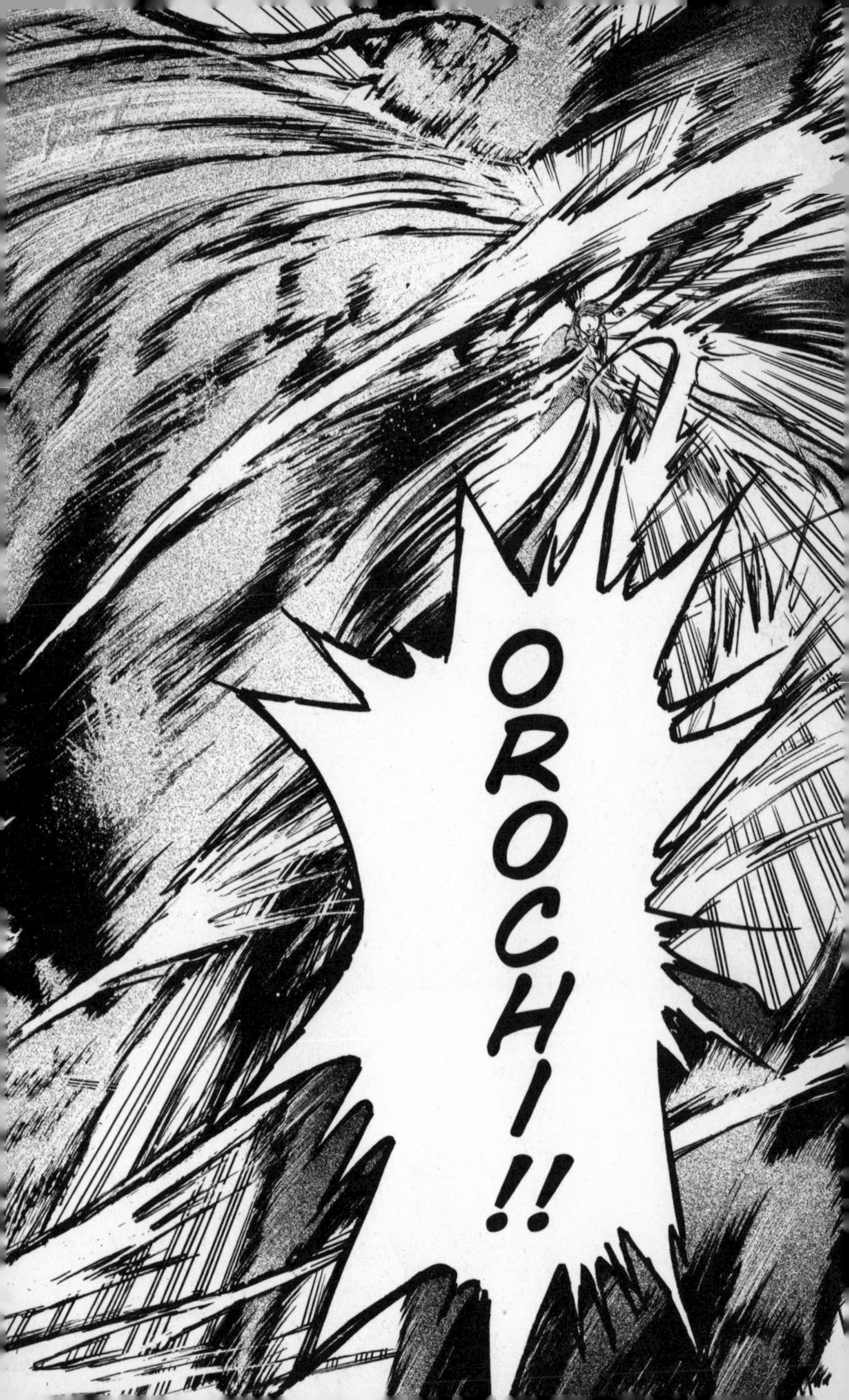
OROCHI!!

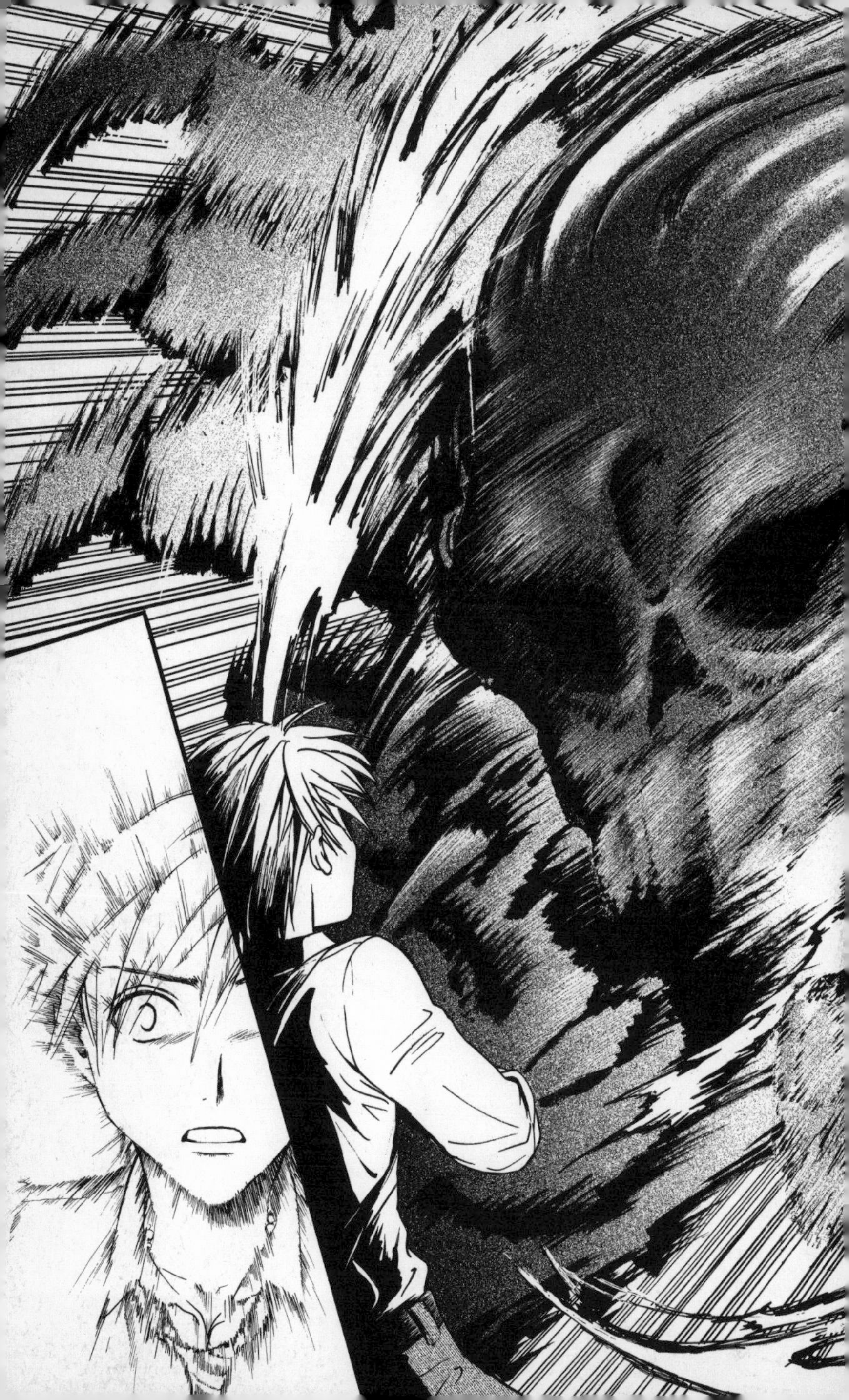

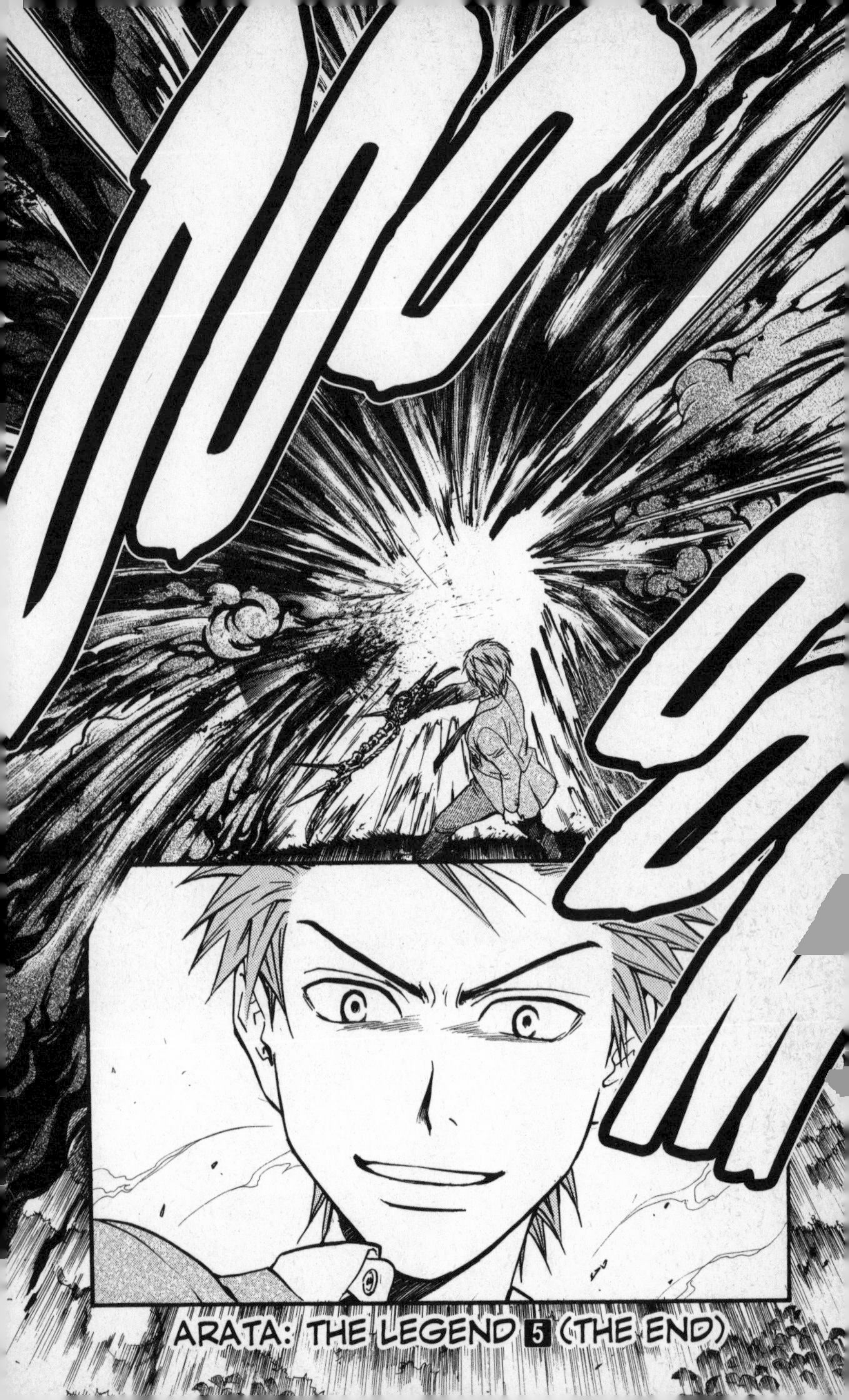
ARATA: THE LEGEND 5 (THE END)

Arata
THE LEGEND

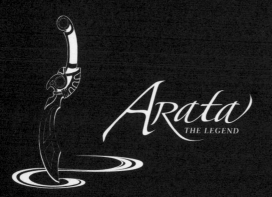

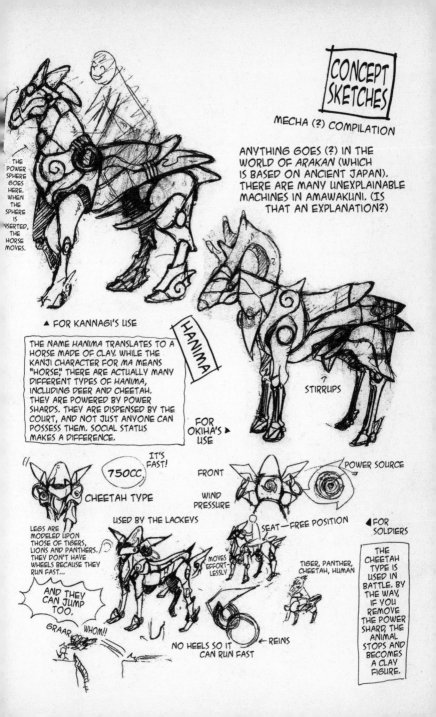

CONCEPT SKETCHES

MECHA (?) COMPILATION

ANYTHING GOES (?) IN THE WORLD OF *ARAKAN* (WHICH IS BASED ON ANCIENT JAPAN). THERE ARE MANY UNEXPLAINABLE MACHINES IN AMAWAKUNI. (IS THAT AN EXPLANATION?)

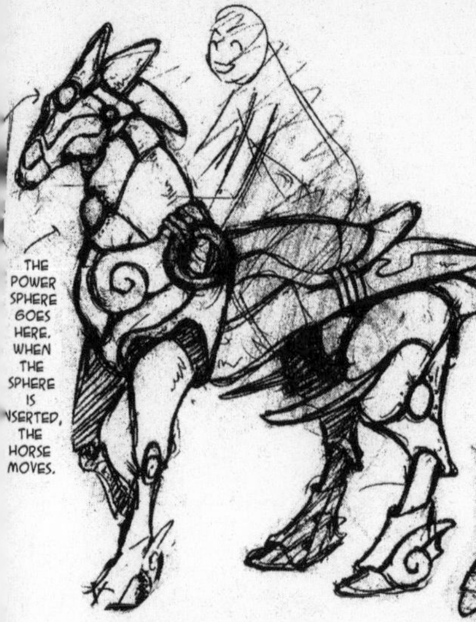
THE POWER SPHERE GOES HERE. WHEN THE SPHERE IS NSERTED, THE HORSE MOVES.

▲ FOR KANNAGI'S USE

HANIMA

THE NAME *HANIMA* TRANSLATES TO A HORSE MADE OF CLAY. WHILE THE KANJI CHARACTER FOR *MA* MEANS "HORSE," THERE ARE ACTUALLY MANY DIFFERENT TYPES OF *HANIMA*, INCLUDING DEER AND CHEETAH. THEY ARE POWERED BY POWER SHARDS. THEY ARE DISPENSED BY THE COURT, AND NOT JUST ANYONE CAN POSSESS THEM. SOCIAL STATUS MAKES A DIFFERENCE.

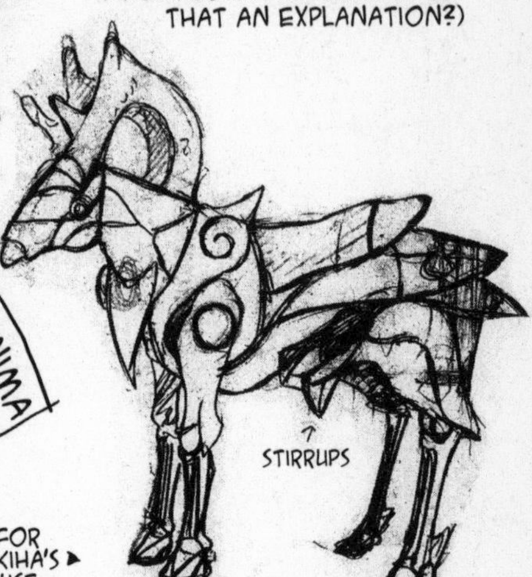
STIRRUPS

FOR OKIHA'S USE ▶

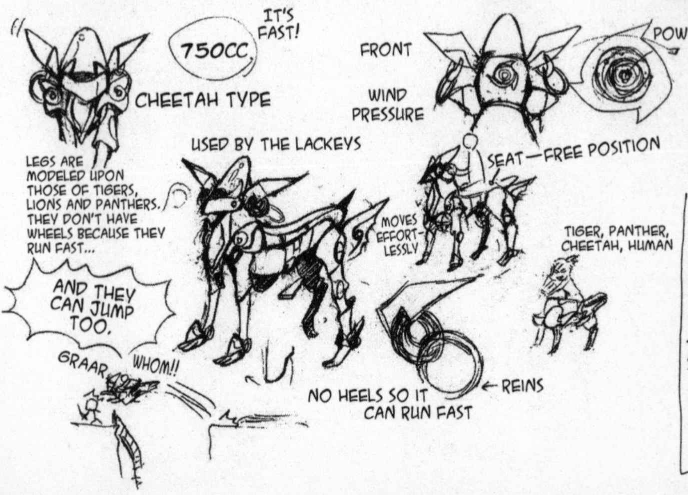
750CC
IT'S FAST!
CHEETAH TYPE
FRONT
WIND PRESSURE
POWER SOURCE
USED BY THE LACKEYS
SEAT—FREE POSITION
LEGS ARE MODELED UPON THOSE OF TIGERS, LIONS AND PANTHERS. THEY DON'T HAVE WHEELS BECAUSE THEY RUN FAST...
AND THEY CAN JUMP TOO.
MOVES EFFORTLESSLY
TIGER, PANTHER, CHEETAH, HUMAN
GRAAR
WHOM!!
NO HEELS SO IT CAN RUN FAST
REINS

◀ FOR SOLDIERS

THE CHEETAH TYPE IS USED IN BATTLE. BY THE WAY, IF YOU REMOVE THE POWER SHARD, THE ANIMAL STOPS AND BECOMES A CLAY FIGURE.

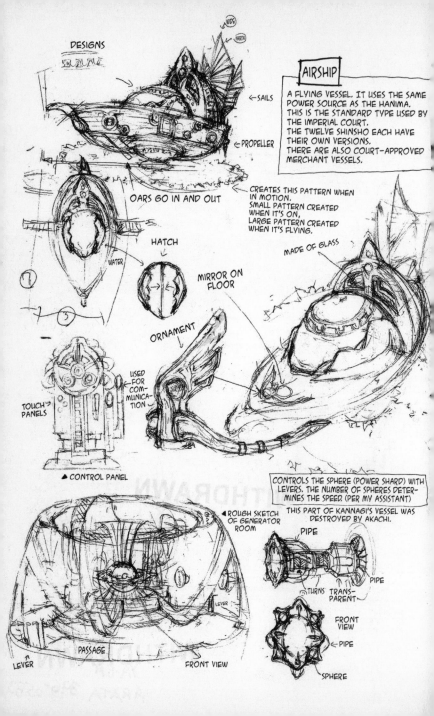

DESIGNS

← SAILS

(WIDE) (NARROW)

← PROPELLER

AIRSHIP

A FLYING VESSEL. IT USES THE SAME
POWER SOURCE AS THE HANIMA.
THIS IS THE STANDARD TYPE USED BY
THE IMPERIAL COURT.
THE TWELVE SHINSHO EACH HAVE
THEIR OWN VERSIONS.
THERE ARE ALSO COURT-APPROVED
MERCHANT VESSELS.

OARS GO IN AND OUT

CREATES THIS PATTERN WHEN
IN MOTION.
SMALL PATTERN CREATED
WHEN IT'S ON,
LARGE PATTERN CREATED
WHEN IT'S FLYING.

WATER

HATCH

MADE OF GLASS

MIRROR ON
FLOOR

ORNAMENT

USED
FOR COM-
MUNICA-
TION

TOUCH
PANELS

▲ CONTROL PANEL

CONTROLS THE SPHERE (POWER SHARD) WITH
LEVERS. THE NUMBER OF SPHERES DETER-
MINES THE SPEED. (PER MY ASSISTANT)

THIS PART OF KANNAGI'S VESSEL WAS
DESTROYED BY AKACHI.

◄ ROUGH SKETCH
OF GENERATOR
ROOM

PIPE

PIPE

LEVER

PASSAGE

LEVER

FRONT VIEW

► TURNS TRANS-
PARENT

FRONT
VIEW

← PIPE

SPHERE

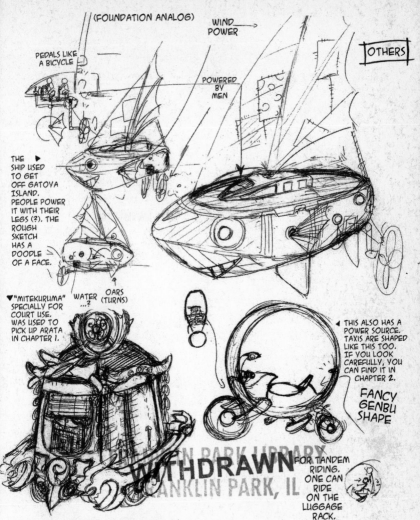

(FOUNDATION ANALOG)

WIND POWER

OTHERS

PEDALS LIKE A BICYCLE

POWERED BY MEN

THE ▶ SHIP USED TO GET OFF GATOYA ISLAND. PEOPLE POWER IT WITH THEIR LEGS (?). THE ROUGH SKETCH HAS A DOODLE OF A FACE.

WATER ...? OARS (TURNS)

▼ "MITEKURUMA" SPECIALLY FOR COURT USE. WAS USED TO PICK UP ARATA IN CHAPTER 1.

◀ THIS ALSO HAS A POWER SOURCE. TAXIS ARE SHAPED LIKE THIS TOO. IF YOU LOOK CAREFULLY, YOU CAN FIND IT IN CHAPTER 2.

FANCY GENBU SHAPE

FOR TANDEM RIDING. ONE CAN RIDE ON THE LUGGAGE RACK.

THERE ARE OTHERS, BUT DUE TO PAGE LIMITATIONS, THEY WERE CUT.

OKAY! IN VOLUME 5, KADOWAKI ENDS UP IN AMAWAKUNI! (THE STORY IN PRESENT-DAY IS STILL GOING ON THOUGH, SO WHAT'S GOING TO HAPPEN WITH MY COMIC STRIPS...?) WHAT WILL ARATA DO? WELL, WHATEVER. WHEN HE FACES HIS GREATEST FOE, HE SHOULD BE VERY PREPARED. A NEW FEMALE CHARACTER HAS APPEARED AND WILL CONTINUE TO HAVE MORE SCENES. SHE'S A TOTALLY DIFFERENT TYPE OF GIRL. OTHER ZOKUSHO WILL APPEAR TOO. (TENTATIVELY...)

THERE ARE TWO COUPLES—ARATA + KOTOHA AND ARATA + ORIBE. (WELL, NOT YET.) A LOT OF THINGS ARE COMING UP. VOLUME 6 IS COMING OUT IN MARCH, I BELIEVE. PLEASE CONTINUE TO SUPPORT THIS SERIES.

SLEEPY...ZZZ

FRANKLIN PARK LIBRARY
FRANKLIN PARK, IL
WITHDRAWN
WITHDRAWN
YA-GN
ARATA 396-0583